529 PLANS

What Every Planner Needs to Know

Nancy E. Shurtz | Alexander B. Fitch | Robert Tirrell

ABA
AMERICANBARASSOCIATION
Real Property, Trust and Estate Law Section

Cover design by Andrew Alcala

Printed in the United States of America.

25 24 23 22 21 5 4 3 2 1

A catalog record for this book is available from the Library of Congress.

To Our Families

Contents

Acknowledgments

We would like to thank Darcy Conners, Charlie Morris, Natalie Smith, and Matthew Tripp-Cox for their help with this book.

About the Authors

Nancy E. Shurtz, the Bernard A. Kilks Professor of Law at the University of Oregon School of Law, earned her B.A. from the University of Cincinnati, her J.D. from Ohio State University, and an LL.M. in Taxation from Georgetown Law. Prior to coming to Oregon, Professor Shurtz taught at the Wharton School of Business at the University of Pennsylvania and practiced law at the Washington D.C. firm of Ginsburg, Feldman and Bress. Professor Shurtz teaches and writes in the areas of taxation, estate planning, and sustainable business practice. She regularly addresses leading academic and policy consortiums, including the Critical Tax Conference, the Global Conference on Environmental Taxation, and the Law and Society Conference. Book publications include two leading tax hornbooks (Wolters Kluwer), *Sustainability and Business Law* (Carolina Academic Press), and *Education Planning: Taxes, Trusts & Techniques* (ABA Publishing).

Alexander B. Fitch, CRPC, AAMS, earned his B.S. from Oregon State and his M.B.A. from Seattle University. He currently works as an investment advisor representative. His areas of specialty are investment education, portfolio design, tax mitigation strategies, and retirement planning.

Robert Tirrell holds a bachelor's degree from Westfield State College. He is a 529 plan sales director at Principal Global Investors. He is responsible for positioning the tax-advantaged benefits of the Scholars Edge 529 Plan with financial professionals. Robert's public speaking and presentation skills help communicate Principal's value proposition on ways to save for education expenses at industry-sponsored virtual events, broker-dealer conferences, and directly to investors. His career is committed to excellence, partnering with financial professionals to help their clients strategize for college savings. Prior to joining Principal in 2019, Robert served as a 529 sales specialist at Voya.

Preface

In the late 1800s and early 1900s, much of the transfer of wealth came in the form of inheritance. Today, inter vivos expenditures for a good education are considered even more important than intergenerational transfers at death. Medical and technical developments continue to increase the probability of a lengthy life, creating greater wealth for parents and grandparents in later years. Skyrocketing tuition costs, coupled with the desired benefits of obtaining a good education (including K–12, undergraduate, and graduate degrees), have many American families scrambling to figure out how to finance these expenditures.

This book, focusing on 529 plans and comparing and contrasting them with other education techniques, will prove to be a great resource for a broad audience, ranging from the general practitioner to the estate tax specialist. Estate planners, tax lawyers, accountants, financial planners, trust officers, and financial aid administrators may also find the material contained herein invaluable. The purpose of this book, which is comprised of five parts and 19 chapters, is to (1) identify the need to develop strategies for financing K–12, college, graduate, or professional education, (2) detail the rules by which these goals may be accomplished, and (3) integrate education planning into one's comprehensive paradigm for financial, tax, retirement, and estate planning. While the text focuses on Section 529 plans, it also provides the planner with a thorough introduction to all the other education savings vehicles that are available. In addition, the text addresses strategies for financing education when savings prove inadequate. Important financial aid planning advice is also provided.

This book incorporates relevant material from the *Consolidated Appropriations Act of 2021*; the *Coronavirus Aid, Relief, and Economic Security Act of 2020*; the *Setting Every Community Up for Retirement Enhancement Act of 2019*; the *Tax Cuts and Jobs Act of 2017*; the *Stephen Beck Jr., Achieving a Better Life Experience (ABLE) Act of 2014*; the *Protecting Americans from Tax Hikes Act of 2015*; the *Bankruptcy Abuse Prevention and Consumer Protection Act of 2005*; the *Deficit Reduction Omnibus Reconciliation Act of 2005*; the *Higher Education Reconciliation Act of 2005*; the *Tax Increase Prevention and Reconciliation Act of 2005*; the *Pension Protection Act of 2006*; the *Tax Relief and Health Care Act of 2006*; the *Small Business and Work*

Opportunity Tax Act of 2007; the *College Cost Reduction and Access Act of 2007*; the *Higher Education Act of 2008*; *the Housing Assistance Tax Act of 2008*; the *Emergency Economic Stabilization Act of 2008*; and the *American Recovery and Reinvestment Act of 2009*.[1]

Italicized throughout the text of this book are terms that we define in the Glossary at the end of this book. Appendices contain various materials—acronyms, abbreviations, statutes, forms, and other resources—to assist the planner. Interspersed throughout the text are **PLANNING POINTERS**, which address some of the critical planning issues that arise in the education planning context.

1. For cites to these statutes, *see* "Acts" in the Glossary section at the end of this book.

"An investment in knowledge always pays the best interest."

~ Benjamin Franklin ~

PART I

WHY PLANNING PAYS

Most American families have come to the clear realization that the key to a bright future for their children and grandchildren is a quality K–12 experience plus a good college education. It is clear that a good education can be an excellent investment resulting in high lifetime earnings and job satisfaction. Unfortunately, how best to pay for this education often poses a challenge. Without savings, tax incentives, and/or financial aid, most Americans would be unable to take advantage of this opportunity. Even with recent developments to support private K–12 and college education, escalating education costs pose a serious barrier to many families' economic security—depleting retirement savings and reducing living standards.

With adequate planning, however, both education dreams and economic security can be accommodated. Consequently, expending some effort to create a good education plan makes sense. **Part I** of this book consists of five chapters. **Chapter One: Education Goals: Constructing a Plan** starts with the importance of a client questionnaire, understanding the goals of the client, and assessing whether these goals can be fulfilled. **Chapter Two: The Benefits and Costs of a Good Education** examines the benefits and costs of both a K–12 education (private and parochial) as well as college (undergraduate and graduate) education. **Chapter Three: It is Never Too Late to Save** emphasizes the importance of savings and how easy it can be to save large amounts of funds when saving begins early. **Chapter Four: The Best Ways to Save** provides a broad overview of the various savings strategies in existence for paying for K–12, college, or graduate education. **Chapter Five: When Savings Are Not Enough** discusses the pay-as-you go strategies and the after-college tax benefits when savings are not enough to finance the client's educational goals.

Now that you are done with her,
how about sending my kids to the Ivies?

Chapter 1

Education Goals: Constructing a Plan

In general, this book focuses on education planning in the context of planning for a beneficiary's K–12 or college education.[1] The *beneficiary* is usually the client's child or grandchild. However, in some instances the intended beneficiary is the client himself/herself. With the exception of purchasing a home, no single financial expenditure is likely to exceed (in importance and in size) the cost of a college education. *Education* for our purposes means not only college and graduate education but K–12, including private and parochial schools.

Planning Pointer

This book does not recommend any planning techniques that are considered abusive under the Advance Notice[2] of proposed regulations under Section 529. These proposed rules are discussed in **Chapter Eight: Federal Income Tax Planning with Section 529 Savings Plans** and **Chapter Nine: Estate Planning with Section 529 Savings Plans**.

The benefits of a good education are substantial, but the costs are often out of reach for the typical family. The benefits of a good education include better odds of achieving economic success, job satisfaction, job flexibility, the opportunity to discover new ideas, and the ability to meet new people. However, over the last decade, private K–12 as well as college educational costs have increased dramatically, outpacing increases in both the cost of living and median annual income of

---

1. Although the book covers some aspects of education planning for K–12 expenses, the major focus of this book is planning for college.

2. Advance Notice of Proposed Rulemaking (for regulation under I.R.C. § 529), 73 Fed. Reg. 3441 (Jan. 18, 2018).

the typical parent. Parents have found that a quality education can provide their children with an early start for a successful later life. Fortunately, parents (and grandparents) have numerous tax and other strategies available to them to help finance these rising education costs.

Education planning promises to become a staple in most families' long-term comprehensive financial strategy. Education planning is on the precipice of a movement reminiscent of that which has radically transformed the world of retirement planning in the past two decades. The combination of new financial aid developments and new tax laws makes choosing the best strategy and coordinating the rules particularly complex for the practitioner and client. The complexity of education planning coupled with its increasing importance affords legal professionals a unique opportunity to play a significant role in bettering their clients' lives and futures. Ransacking savings accounts or invading retirement plans for education purposes may not serve anybody's best interests. At a minimum, the advisor must understand that education planning is inextricably intertwined with retirement planning, estate planning, tax planning, financial planning, and financial aid issues.

A. Goals of Education Planning

The first thing that the practitioner needs to do is determine the goals of the client. The goals of education planning can include the following: (1) saving enough money so that the right K–12, college, or graduate school can be chosen when the time comes, (2) obtaining subsidies—in the form of financial aid, scholarships, grants, and loans—when savings prove to be inadequate, (3) effectively utilizing any tax advantages for education, (4) maximizing one's investments to ensure good returns, maximum control, asset protection, and minimal administrative hassles, and (5) having a flexible plan that can be changed easily.

In an ideal world, the client will have enough savings to pay for all costs of any K–12, college, or graduate school. Such a client will not need to worry about financial aid or loans. Such a client might consider tax-free scholarships and would want to ensure all savings investments obtain maximum returns with all accompanying tax advantages. The wealthy client might consider setting up an inter vivos incentive or other trust to provide incentives or pass on wealth with gift, estate, and generation skipping tax benefits.[3]

In the real world, however, most clients will probably not have enough savings to pay for all education costs. Consequently, grants, loans, pay-as-you-go tax techniques and after-college tax benefits become very important. These clients will still want any savings to have good returns, to have maximum control over investments, asset protection of funds, and minimal administrative hassles to utilize savings, as well as tax advantages. Although this client may not want to establish an inter vivos trust, proper estate planning will necessitate a testamentary trust that assures effective education planning in the unfortunate event of death.[4]

---

3. *See* Nancy E. Shurtz, Education Planning: Taxes, Trusts, and Techniques ch. 17 (ABA 2009).
4. *Id.*

Education plans must be flexible because the client's goals may evolve based on changed circumstances. For example, a taxpayer's education planning may change if: (1) the taxpayer has more children or grandchildren, (2) the taxpayer or the beneficiary becomes disabled or unemployed, (3) the taxpayer gets divorced, declares bankruptcy, retires early, or dies, (4) the taxpayer's child or grandchild decides to enroll in a different school, to delay college, or to not attend college at all, (5) the taxpayer's savings are depleted due to market fluctuations or other circumstances, or (6) the law changes. The COVID-19 virus and ensuing recession can illustrate just how quickly circumstances can change. Lost jobs, failed businesses, savings depleted, and long-distance learning have all changed education plans. For some, education planning may result in a realization that higher education is not the best plan for the intended beneficiary. Perhaps the resources that would have been used to fund education may better serve the beneficiary if used for another purpose.[5]

Education planning also means not compromising one's financial or retirement goals. When college goals conflict with other goals, such as financial security or retirement, some compromises may be necessary. In some situations, planning to share costs with the student may prove to be the best strategy for paying for college and safeguarding the family's other financial needs.

Chart 1-1 sets forth an example of a questionnaire that could be given to the client. Many of the chapters in this book will address these issues in more detail.

CHART 1-1 Client Questionnaire

Demographic information, such as name, address, number of children, wealth of grandparent(s), wealth of client, income of the client, etc.	
I.	What is the client's education goal for his/her children (or grandchildren)? 1. What type of K–12 education is the client expecting (boarding school, private school, public school)?[6] 2. What type of college does the client expect the child to attend? 3. Is the client expecting to pay for graduate or professional school?
II.	Has the client saved?[7] 1. How much is the current value of the savings? 1. What form has the savings taken? 2. What is the expected future value of this savings?[8] 3. Should Coverdells, savings bonds, or custodianships be converted to Section 529 plans?[9] 4. Is the client maximizing returns with asset protection and other benefits?

(continued)

5. With COVID-19, students have greater opportunities to negotiate the reduction of tuition costs. Many are deciding to attend college closer to home, choosing to take a gap year, or just forgoing college altogether.

6. *See* **Chapter Two: The Benefits and Costs of a Good Education**, A.1.

7. *See* **Chapter Four: The Best Ways to Save**.

8. *See* **Chapter Three: It Is Never Too Late to Save**.

9. *See* **Chapter Seventeen: Coordinating Section 529 Plans with Other Savings Techniques**, E.

III.	How much should the client be expected to have saved for K–12, college, or graduate school in the future? 1. What are the current costs of the desired education?[10] 2. What are the expected costs of the desired education?[11] 3. What is the time before the expected education expense? 4. What are the client's risk/return factors?[12]
IV.	Can the client pay for all or part of the education costs as these costs are incurred? 1. What are the client's annual earnings and savings? 2. Does the client expect any gifts from relatives?
V.	Will the client be entitled to use "pay-as-you-go" tax techniques?[13] 1. Will the client be entitled to the American Opportunity Credit? 2. Will the client be entitled to the Lifetime Learning Credit?
VI.	Is the client (or beneficiary) likely to qualify for scholarships, grants, loans, or other financial aid?[14] 1. Has the client investigated scholarship opportunities?[15] 2. Are subsidized or unsubsidized grants or loans likely?[16] a. What is the client's expected loan amount? b. What is the client's credit rating? c. What is the expected interest? d. What is the time frame for payment? e. Are there possible after-college loan deductions?[17] 3. If the client will apply for financial aid, what are strategies for qualifying for aid?[18] a. Titling assets in the parent's name. b. Consumption, conversion, etc.
VII.	How important are gift, estate and generation skipping tax considerations to the client?
VIII.	Does the client have any specific nontax wishes that should be considered? 1. Control a. Investment[19] b. Not wanting child to control the education fund at age 18. c. Incentives 2. Asset Protection[20] 3. Perpetuity 4. Disability[21] 5. Retirement Goals 6. Death
IX.	What is the exit strategy if the contemplated plan fails? 1. What circumstances could occur that could pose risks to the client's educational goals? 2. How does the plan change to meet these circumstances?

10. *See* **Chapter Two: The Benefits and Costs of a Good Education, Charts 2-3, 2-4,** and **2-5.**
11. *See* **Chapter Two: The Benefits and Costs of a Good Education.**
12. *See* **Chapter Fourteen: Choosing the Right Section 529 Savings Plan.**
13. *See* **Chapter Five: When Savings Are Not Enough.**
14. *See* **Chapter Nineteen: Coordinating Section 529 Plans with Financial Aid.**
15. *See* **Chapter Five: When Savings Are Not Enough.**
16. *See* **Chapter Five: When Savings Are Not Enough, Chart 5-4.**
17. *See* **Chapter Five: When Savings Are Not Enough.**
18. *See* **Chapter Nineteen: Coordinating Section 529 Plans with Financial Aid.**
19. *See* **Chapter Thirteen: Investment Planning with Section 529 Savings Plans.**
20. *See* **Chapter Twelve: Nontax Aspects of Section 529 Savings Plans.**
21. *See* **Chapter Eleven: Disability Planning with Section 529 Savings Plans.**

Planning Pointer

Planning to pay for K–12 or college education is best accomplished with a comprehensive financial plan that assures the client's ability to live and retire comfortably yet provides for adequate savings for anticipated college expenses. The advisor can provide a most valuable service by recommending to the client the importance of savings and by advising the client on what savings strategy is best, given tax and nontax factors and the client's particular circumstances.

B. Planning Based on Income Categories

Low-income families have the fewest education planning options available to them. These families are likely to have not saved at all, or not nearly enough, to pay for the rising costs of a college education. In contrast, *middle-income families* have the greatest variety of educational planning options. The *wealthy families* have the best ability to save for all levels of education, from K–12 boarding schools to expensive professional education.

1. Low-Income Families

Attending college can be extremely important to students from *low-income families.*[22] The fact may very well be that college is the only means by which a low-income child can escape poverty. The costs of college for them, however, may be daunting. All too often, the children in these families are relegated to community colleges and trade schools. Advisors, however, should make these clients aware of the liberal financial aid packages of many major elite colleges, if the student can qualify for admission.[23]

Taxpayers in low-income brackets have virtually no ability to save. However, if they do save, complex planning issues arise as to whether savings will reduce financial aid eligibility. In general, saving in the student's name will have a more adverse tax consequence than saving in the parent or grandparent's name.[24] However, both assets and income from assets can reduce financial aid.

This low-income group does not have a lot of assets. They probably rent their homes and most likely do not have adequate retirement savings. They are also not likely to receive gifts from relatives. In fact, they are probably struggling just to pay the cost of health care and other necessities of life.

---

22. Low-income families usually have adjusted gross income (AGI) of less than $50,000.
23. *See* **Chapter Five: When Savings Are Not Enough, Chart 5-6**.
24. *See* **Chapter Nineteen: Coordinating Section 529 Plans with Financial Aid**.

Low-income families are also not likely to have the ability to pay for immediate college expenses. In fact, they may not even be taxpayers. Thus, income tax, estate, and gift taxes are not going to be major considerations for this group. They may, however, qualify or partially qualify for educational credits, particularly the refundable American Opportunity Tax Credit (AOTC).[25]

The good news is that most low-income taxpayers will be eligible for financial aid in the form of grants and loans. Also, scholarships and student employment will be an essential part of their education plan. Furthermore, upon graduation and commencement of work in the marketplace, the low-income student may be able to take advantage of several tax benefits, such as the above-the-line loan interest tax deduction and loan forgiveness when working in the public interest.[26]

2. Middle-Income Families

Middle-income families[27] have a wide variety of education planning options available to them. This family can benefit from almost all the savings tax techniques—the 529 plan and Coverdell—but must be careful to save in a way that does not significantly reduce financial aid. This family may also be able to pay part of their child's education expenses currently, thus benefiting from the education credits. Thus, careful planning should enable this family to qualify for the various tax benefits as well as financial aid.

The middle-income family may have a home with significant equity, so they can take out a home equity loan to pay for any education costs. However, after the *Tax Cuts and Jobs Act of 2017*, a deduction for the interest on that loan will not be allowed until 2026. They may also have significant retirement savings that could be used for education purposes without penalty. However, care must be taken not to deplete this valuable resource that might be needed in later life. Lastly, they may have a life insurance policy that does not count for financial aid purposes which may be tapped for a possible loan.

Many middle-income families will qualify for need-based federally subsidized loans, either because the family has more than one child in college or their child is planning on attending an expensive school. Those middle-income families who may not qualify for need-based financial aid may be in the hardest position to finance future college costs if they have not saved. Unsubsidized loans and scholarships may, therefore, be the major means by which they pay for college. Numerous elite schools offer favorable aid packages that benefit middle-income families. And loan forgiveness after graduation is always a possibility.

---

25. *See* **Chapter Five: When Savings Are Not Enough**.
26. *See* **Chapter Five: When Savings Are Not Enough**.
27. Middle-income families usually have AGI of $50,000 to $150,000.

3. High-Income Families

The *high-income taxpayers* or *wealthy families*[28] have the best ability to save for college education. They can take advantage of the Section 529 plans to cover qualified higher education expenses, including up to $10,000 for K–12 tuition. They can combine these with traditional investments, like stocks and bonds, to cover nonqualified education expenses. They will definitely be interested in using custodianship accounts, trusts, and other entities to take advantage of overall income, gift, and estate tax benefits. They may be able to pay for college from current earnings, savings, or gifts from relatives. In addition, the children of the wealthy can qualify for scholarships based on merit, and the student may benefit from the student loan interest deduction as well as the federal loan forgiveness programs after graduation. On the other hand, students of high-income families will not be eligible for government need-based grants, subsidized loans, or pay-as-you-go tax code benefits. They can, as can their parents, take out unsubsidized loans (such as PLUS loans) in the event current earnings, savings, and scholarships do not adequately cover the costs of college.

C. Conclusion

The goals of the particular client with respect to education may vary, and thus the strategies for reaching those goals may vary as well. Low-income families may *not* be able to save and may be more dependent on financial aid. Middle-class families have the widest variety of options. The wealthy clients have the ability to save or pay as they go for any education goals they may want to pursue.

28. Higher-income families generally have AGI over $200,000.

Chapter 2

The Benefits and Costs of a Good Education

This chapter provides a general overview of the benefits and costs of both K–12 education and college. These benefits apply to a continually growing list of educational options, including those becoming more popular in our day and age such as homeschooling. With the Covid-19 pandemic closing schools across the U.S., more and more students are approaching their education differently. It is yet to be seen how businesses will adjust their hiring and recruiting efforts based on the Covid-19 pandemic and how those practices may impact students' educational aspirations. However, the benefits of receiving a good education at any level are quantifiable and consistent across the board. Those who prioritize and seek out education are much more likely to be successful and will be rewarded for doing so. With so many different options available, families can best decide what path makes the most sense for them and can create a personalized plan in their pursuit of education. While traditional public schools have appealing aspects to them, many benefits also exist for privatized schooling.

A. The Benefits of a Good Education

1. The Benefits of K–12 Education

Families have several options outside of the traditional public schooling system to best educate their children through their formative years. These include private schools (including parochial schools), boarding schools (private or parochial), and even home schools. These options all have advantages as well as disadvantages.

a. *Secular Private Schools*

Private schools provide an opportunity for families to align their school choice with their own values as private schools have the ability to develop and use their own curriculum, philosophy, and approach to education. Further, private schools are typically more dedicated to developing teacher-student relationships, and an emphasis is put on lower student-to-teacher ratios to better ensure personalized learning. Lastly, studies show that private schools provide a better academic experience than public schools. For example, a recent comparison of mathematics tests showed "private schools scored 18 points higher for eighth-graders and 8 points higher for fourth graders," and "[r]eading had the same results, with the private schools outscoring their public counterparts by 18 points in eighth grade and 15 points in fourth grade."[1] This remains a theme throughout the review of alternative options to public schooling for students, as nonpublic schooling options tend to generally provide higher test scores and graduation rates. Thus, these options often allow for the student to have opportunities to attend elite colleges and universities later in life.

b. Parochial Schools

Parochial schools are a viable option for families seeking alternative educational opportunities for the K–12 level. These schools are affiliated with religious organizations and have the unique ability to combine a common education curriculum with religious education. Here, families have the option to include personal core values in their children's daily education from a very young age. Parochial schools usually emphasize service and compassion, including volunteer hours and service opportunities built into the curriculum.

Like private schools, these schools tout higher graduation rates and test scores, including on both the ACT and SAT. However, here the costs are substantially lower than that of most private schools. This is because the tuition at parochial schools is typically subsidized by the sponsored religious group. These lower tuition costs allow for more students to attend these schools and receive the benefits of a privatized education while simultaneously promoting personal and core beliefs.

The parochial school option is becoming more and more limited as religious-based private schools continue to close in large numbers. For example, the Catholic Church has dominated America's private-school world for several decades.[2] However, over the last 50 years that dominance has faded.[3] The number of students who attend Catholic schools, nearly 1.7 million children in the 2019–2020 school years, is down from the high of 5.2 million in the early 1960s.[4] The National Catholic Education Association says that more than 150 Catholic schools were

1. *See* Hudson Lindenberger, *Private School vs. Public School: Facts, Benefits & Statistics* (updated Apr. 22, 2021), https://www.fatherly.com/love-money/private-school-vs-public-school-facts-benefits-statistics/.

2. *See* Alia Wong, *Private Schools Are Becoming More Elite*, The Atlantic (July 26, 2018), https://www.theatlantic.com/education/archive/2018/07/why-private-schools-are-becoming-more-elite/566144/.

3. *Catholic School Enrollment Sees Sharpest Drop in Nearly 50 Years*, Catholic News Agency (Feb. 8, 2021), https://www.catholicnewsagency.com/news/246412/catholic-school-enrollment-sees-sharpest-drop-in-nearly-50-years.

4. Giulia McDonnell Nieto del Rio, A Growing Number of Catholic Schools Are Closing Down Forever, N.Y. Times (Sept. 6, 2020), https://www.nytimes.com/2020/09/05/us/catholic-school-closings.html.

closed during the coronavirus pandemic due to "insurmountable financial" difficulties.[5] This shift in available options for those inclined to send their kids to religious private schools certainly impacts the enrollment rate across each state and may continue to do so into the future.

c. Boarding Schools

Although the idea of dropping a child off at school for months at a time may seem rather undesirable, many potential benefits can come from a boarding school education. With the opportunity to live on their own (typically beginning in middle or high school), children learn the importance of self-reliance, respect, and adapting to a different culture. These lessons are helpful for growth and development as the student transitions into college and adulthood. Additionally, fringe benefits often are offered, such as better sports facilities, art, music, and other programs compared to what public schools can often provide. Further, boarding schools enjoy smaller class sizes and more elective options for students. Boarding schools can also highlight unique opportunities based on their geographical location, giving students the ability to participate in events or activities they would not have had the chance to otherwise. Lastly, boarding schools can be safe havens for students to escape harmful or otherwise challenging living situations. Many families see boarding school as a way to remove a child from a particular environment and in turn provide a better space for them to grow and develop.

d. Home Schools

Outside of public and private schooling opportunities, homeschooling remains an option for families to consider when deciding how to best educate their children. A number of appealing factors apply to this type of education, such as the ability to determine the curriculum, adapting teaching methods to suit how a child best learns, and an overall flexible schedule.

Homeschooling offers parents the ability to freely provide religious or ethical instruction to their children. Such schooling can focus on the child's particular strengths and talents, including athletic, musical, or art abilities. The generally low costs associated with homeschooling, however, are typically offset by the amount of time required by the parents to ensure a successful in-home education. When the parent works outside the home, such schooling is almost impossible. In addition, disadvantages may arise when the student is not exposed to social interactions with others. COVID-19 has seen the establishment of "pandemic learning pods" comprised of students from several families who share the expense or burden of providing a challenging learning experience to their children. Here children get the socialization benefits of mingling with their peers while families minimize risk of infection. It is yet to be seen whether this trend may or may not continue.

---

5. *Id.*

2. The Benefits of a Community College and Other Training Programs

Countless studies show the benefits that come with a college degree, including higher average salaries and the opportunity to grow and develop as a person. While many studies tend to focus on the correlation between college degrees and higher-skilled jobs, equal data exists that suggests similar benefits result from attending community college or vocational and training programs. Good career opportunities do not have to necessarily be tied to advanced degrees and expensive graduate school programs. Many good jobs merely require an associate degree from a community college and do not expect applicants to have obtained a four-year bachelor's degree from a university.

According to the American Association of Community Colleges, community colleges conferred nearly 580,000 certificates in 2017–2018.[6] Often, these professional certificates can provide the student with profitable livelihoods in such fields as information technology, health, and the various licensing trades. With these professional certificates students can find readily available jobs within the community where family and friends are located; jobs usually geared to the needs of the local community.

The cost of attendance for community college is significantly lower than that of universities and state schools. Often the student will live at home and work part time. In fact, nearly 60 percent of students attending community colleges are doing so part time. This allows students to continue to work while obtaining an education at their own pace. Additionally, living at home often allows the student to save money on rent. These lower costs allow students to take on less debt, especially with the help of scholarships and grants. And community colleges also provide an easier transition into college for those who struggled in high school and may not be ready for the full-time investment in the pursuit of a college degree.

Community college is not a final destination for many students. Across the nation many two-year schools have agreements with public universities that allow qualified students to transfer their credits toward earning a bachelor's degree. According to National Student Clearinghouse Research Center data, 29 percent of community college students who started in the fall of 2011 transferred to a four-year institution within six years.[7]

3. The Benefits of College and Graduate Schools

Studies have shown that people with college educations are employed at greater rates and earn more than those with only a high school diploma. According to the

---

6. *AACC Fast Facts*, Am. Ass'n of Cmty. Colleges (2020), https://www.aacc.nche.edu/wp-content/uploads/2020/03/AACC_Fast_Facts_2020_Final.pdf.

7. *See* Travis Mitchell & Emma Kerr, *10 Reasons to Attend a Community College*, U.S. News (July 10, 2019), https://www.usnews.com/education/community-colleges/slideshows/10-reasons-to-attend-a-community-college?slide=10.

Bureau of Labor Statistics, people with a master's degree earn twice as much per year as those with only a high school diploma. (*See* **Chart 2-1**.) Over the course of a 40-year career, a four-year college graduate can earn 73 percent more (and a community college graduate 25 percent more) than the average high school graduate.[8] Over a lifetime, men with a bachelor's degree earn approximately $900,000 more in median lifetime earning than a high school graduate. (For women it is $630,000).[9] Men with graduate degrees earn $1.5 million more in median lifetime earnings. (Women $1.1 million more). Those who attend professional school, such as lawyers, doctors, and engineers, earn roughly $2,000,000 more over their lifetime than high school graduates.

CHART 2-1 Median Annual Income of Workers by Education Level[10]

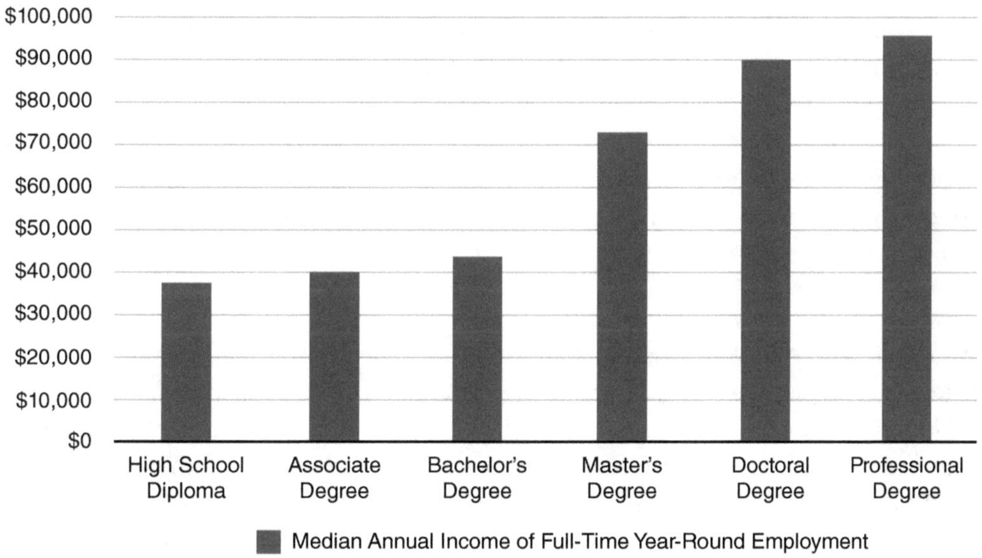

A college education is particularly important for women and minorities. Female college graduates earned an average of 124 percent more than women with only a high school diploma.[11] For an African American man, college results in a 112 percent higher wage than a similar high school graduate.[12] Also, each level of

8. Jennifer Ma, Matea Pender & Meredith Welch, *Education Pays: The Benefits of Higher Education for Individuals and Society*, CollegeBoard 9 (2019), https://research.collegeboard.org/trends/education-pays.

9. *Research, Statistics & Policy Analysis*, Soc. Sec. Admin. (Nov. 2015), https://www.ssa.gov/policy/docs/research-summaries/education-earnings.html.

10. Tim Stobierski, *Average Salary by Education Level: The Value of a College Degree*, Ne. Univ. (June 2, 2020), https://www.northeastern.edu/bachelors-completion/news/average-salary-by-education-level/; *The Average Salary by Education Level 2019–2020*, Smart Schools (Oct. 27, 2019), https://smartschoolsusa.org/blog/the-average-salary-by-education-level-2019-2020; *Median Household Income in the United States in 2019, by Educational Attainment of Householder*, Statista (Sept. 2020), https://www.statista.com/statistics/233301/median-household-income-in-the-united-states-by-education/.

11. *Id.*

12. Danielle Kurtzleben, *A Black Man with a College Education Is as Likely to Be Working as a White College Dropout*, Vox (June 26, 2014), https://www.vox.com/2014/6/26/5845468/a-black-man-with-a-college-degree-is-as-likely-to-be-working-as-a-white-college-dropout.

education has a greater payoff for black men than for white men. So, for example, getting a professional degree results in a 46 percent pay bump for a black man compared to 29 percent for a white man.[13] A college education may thus provide a means for women and minorities to overcome the earnings gap that continues to persist among these groups.

4. Some Reservations

A growing number of students are leaving or graduating from college without earning any more money than if they had only attended high school. Everyone has heard the stories of billionaires Bill Gates (the founder of Microsoft), Steve Jobs (the founder of Apple), and Elon Musk (the founder of SpaceX and Tesla), who all dropped out of college to start their businesses. If the parent compares the amount spent on college versus the amount needed to, for example, start up a business for the student, they may discover that it would have made better economic sense to forgo the college expenditures.

The rising use of debt to finance college education might also indicate that it does not always make economic sense to attend college. See **Example 2-1** below. Although this example uses high education debt (i.e., $300,000), it does highlight the risks of high debt in financing one's education.

EXAMPLE 2-1: Alex and Chris graduate from high school in Year 1. Alex immediately joins a plumber's union and makes $65,000 a year. Chris decides to fulfill her dream and become a dentist. She incurs $300,000 of education debt over an eight-year period. In Year 30, after Alex obtains several raises, he makes a total of $2,500,000 in after-tax disposable income after paying $500,000 in federal income tax. Chris initially makes $105,000, but because of her higher marginal tax rates and because she must use after-tax income to pay off her education debt, she makes a total of $2,220,000 in after-tax disposable income—after paying $700,000 in federal income taxes.[14]

13. *Id.*

14. See the example in Adam Hime, Note, *Getting Schooled by the Hybrid-Based Tax: Equity and Efficiency in the Federal Tax Treatment of Debt-Financed Post-Secondary Education Expenses*, 77 S. CAL. L. REV. 871, 875 (2004).

CHART 2-2 Alex and Chris's Income over Time

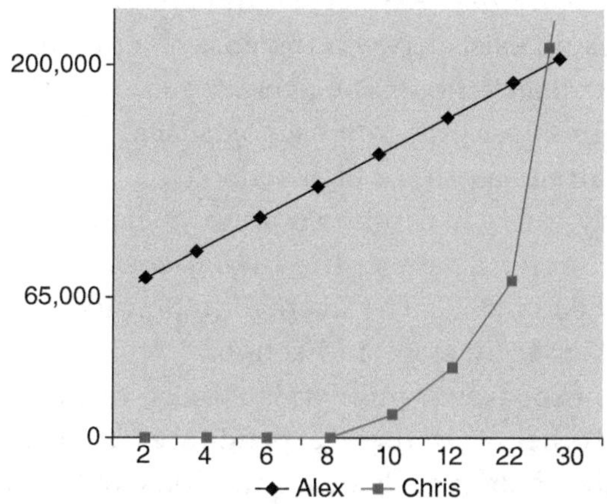

It is also important to note that this example accounts only for pure economics. Obviously, economic benefit is not the sole benefit of a college education. Noneconomic benefits of college also include job satisfaction, greater job flexibility, job security, and long-term career development. In addition, college offers exposure to new ideas and different kinds of people. In essence, college affords the student an opportunity for profound personal and intellectual growth and a chance to gain a broader perspective on the world.[15]

It is yet to be seen what the long-term effects of COVID-19 will have on higher education enrollments and costs going into the future. Perhaps COVID-19 and the shift to online learning will reduce tuition costs and make college more accessible, but it is much too early to tell. Certainly, changes in plans for students and families may affect their ability to afford college. Already, the IRS has announced changes to some rules. The *Coronavirus Aid, Relief, and Security Act of 2020* (CARES Act) was passed in March 2020[16] and delayed student loan payments and deferred repayment penalties for 60 days. More changes and exceptions are likely to follow as higher education adapts to the relatively new norms.

B. The Costs of a Good Education

1. The Costs of Private and Parochial K–12 Education

Private schools make up roughly 25 percent of all U.S. K–12 schools, and those student bodies collectively make up close to 10 percent of all students in K–12

15. Society also benefits from an educated citizenry with lower levels of unemployment, poverty, and crime and increased productivity, tax revenues, and civic participation.

16. Pub. L. No. 116–136 (H.R. 748). Title II, subtitle C, sections 2301 to 2308 contain most of the tax relief provisions.

grades.[17] According to a recent study, the national average for private school tuition is approximately $10,676 per year.[18] These numbers certainly differ from state to state, and differences do exist between the cost of a private elementary or middle school and a private high school. The average tuition nationwide for a private elementary school is $9,638 per year, while it costs significantly more—$14,522 per year—for a student to attend a private high school.[19]

As noted previously, parochial schools are a cheaper alternative to nonreligious private schools. So, for example, the tuition cost of a Catholic elementary school is just over $4,800 in 2020. The average tuition for private parochial high school is $16,040 but varies by state and school.[20] And of course, in addition to tuition costs, there are expenses for uniforms, books, technology, field trips, athletics, and other fees. To help with these expenditures, scholarship programs and other avenues for family aid are widely available. Some of this aid is based primarily on socioeconomic circumstances, while other aid is merit based.

Only a few hundred boarding schools exist in the United States.[21] Boarding schools will almost always require a considerable investment from parents. These schools are generally available only for middle school or high school students. The costs vary, but the yearly average for a five-day boarding school is $33,140, and the average for a seven-day boarding school is $37,590.[22] *See* **Chart 2-3.**

CHART 2-3 Average Annual Costs of Private K–12 School for 2020–2021 Academic Year[23]

	Catholic Elementary School	Private School	Private Boarding School
Tuition & Fees	$ 4,840	$ 12,350	$ 33,140–$ 37,590
Books & Supplies	$ 500	$ 500	$ 500
Technology, Uniforms, & other costs*	$ 3,200	$ 3,200	$ 3,200
TOTAL	$ 8,540	$ 16,050	$ 36,840–$ 41,290

*Includes transportation, entertainment, clothing, and miscellaneous costs and assumes student commutes from home for all three schools.

17. *See* CAPENET (COUNCIL FOR AM. PRIVATE EDUC.), https://www.capenet.org/facts.html (last visited Apr. 29, 2021).

18. *Average Private School Tuition Cost*, PRIVATE SCHOOL REV., https://www.privateschoolreview.com/tuition-stats/private-school-cost-by-state (last visited Apr. 29, 2021).

19. *Id.*

20. *Average Cost of Private School*, EDUCATIONDATA.ORG (Oct. 28, 2020), https://educationdata.org/average-cost-of-private-school.

21. *Id.* (list by state and institution).

22. *Id.*

23. *Id.*

2. The Costs of Home-Schooling

The costs of home-schooling will vary. If a stay-at-home parent is available and qualified to teach, then this alternative may be the cheapest as well as the best. On the other hand, if the parent has to quit his/her job to home-school or hire a qualified helper, then this alternative could be expensive. In fact, if one calculates the costs of the private education alternatives, one may determine that a low-paying market job (after taxes) will not cover these expenses.

Many parents may find it helpful to prioritize either an elementary or high school education. Thus, the parents may break up their child's education between a public and private school over the K–12 career. Other parents may forgo expensive private K–12 education altogether if college seems a more important priority; this option can be more appealing when the public schools in the area have a good reputation and a high graduation rate.

3. The Costs of Community College and Other Training Programs

Community colleges are continually the most affordable higher education option. Across the nation community college tuition remains very low and affordable. For 2021, the average cost was about $3,350 per year for in-state students.[24] Some states have recently enacted legislation to make two-year college educations free for residents. For example, in 2019 Governor Newsom signed legislation to provide free tuition for first-time students who were attending one of the 115 colleges or 78 educational centers in the California community college system.[25] This program is financially benefiting a sizeable number of students as about two million students, or approximately 25 percent of the nation's community college students, are attending California schools.[26]

Like California, several other states offer such benefits or are on the verge of doing so. Some states, like New York, are implementing requirements or thresholds as they became the first state through the Excelsior Scholarship to make tuition free for both in-state two-year and four-year colleges for undergraduates who meet certain requirements.[27] Currently, Oregon offers free community college to qualified high school graduates and those who completed a GED.[28] Tennessee is another state that offers high school students two years tuition free at Tennessee's

24. *Average Cost of Community College*, EducationData.org (Oct. 28, 2020), https://educationdata.org/average-cost-of-community-college. The average total cost to attend for in-state students is $10,300. For out-of-state students the tuition is $8,210.

25. Zack Friedman, *California Wants to Pay for Your College*, Forbes (Sept. 3, 2019), https://www.forbes.com/sites/zackfriedman/2019/09/03/california-free-college/#6a1cb16b6beb.

26. *Id.*

27. *Tuition-Free Degree Program: The Excelsior Scholarship*, N.Y. State, https://www.ny.gov/programs/tuition-free-degree-program-excelsior-scholarship (last visited Apr. 29, 2021).

28. Katie Lobosco, *Oregon Promised Free Tuition. Now It's Cutting Back*, CNN Money (Aug. 23, 2017), https://money.cnn.com/2017/08/22/pf/college/oregon-free-tuition-promise-scholarship/index.html.

public community colleges and technical schools.[29] These programs may indicate a trend to prioritize free community college education across the U.S.

4. The Costs of College and Graduate School

Over the past 30 years, the cost of college education has escalated on a nearly exponential basis. The total tuition increases have been more than 213 percent; these costs have drastically outstripped rising inflation, cost of living, and, most significantly, employment earnings and investments.[30] The average tuition at a four-year public institution jumped an astonishing 300 percent over this time period.[31] For students attending private four-year colleges, the increase was 129 percent.[32] (*See* **Chart 2-4**.)

CHART 2-4 College Tuition Costs over Time (from 2008 to 2020)[33]

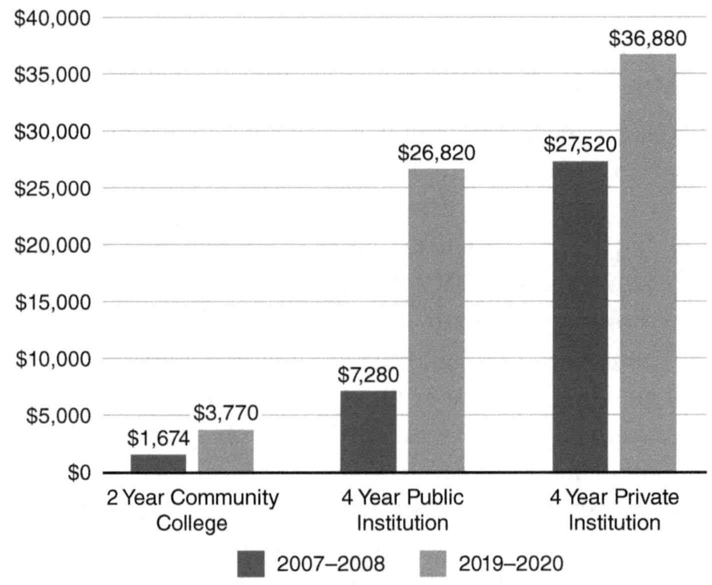

For the 2020–2021 school year, the average price of tuition for colleges in the United States dropped by 4–6 percent; despite this drop in tuition, higher education remains exorbitant. The average tuition and fees at a ranked private college was $37,650 for the 2020-2021 *academic year*; the average tuition and fees at a

29. Benjamin Wermund, *The Red State That Loves Free College*, POLITICO: THE AGENDA (Jan. 16, 2019), https://www.politico.com/agenda/story/2019/01/16/tennessee-free-college-000867/.

30. Emmie Martin, *Here's How Much More Expensive It Is for You to Go to College Than It Was for Your Parents*, CNBC: MAKE IT (Nov. 29, 2017), https://www.cnbc.com/2017/11/29/how-much-college-tuition-has-increased-from-1988-to-2018.html.

31. *Id.*

32. *Id.*

33. *See Trends in College Pricing 2019*, COLLEGEBOARD, https://research.collegeboard.org/pdf/trends-college-pricing-2019-full-report.pdf (for 2019 figures); Martin, *supra* note 30 (for 2018 figures).

ranked public out-of-state college was $27,020 a year and $10,560 for in-state college tuition and fees. This compares to the relatively cheaper average cost for tuition and fees of a two-year community college of $3,770. These numbers highlight the drop in average tuition—although even with this drop, the price of college is unattainable for many families.[34]

Of course, tuition and fees comprise only one portion of the cost of attending college. Books, supplies, room and board, meal plans, lab fees, transportation, and other costs are also increasing. For the 2020–2021 *academic year*, the average costs for room and board at a ranked private college was $13,120 and at a public state college was $11,620.[35] Books and supplies, transportation, and other expenses increased the total undergraduate costs dramatically.[36] (*See* **Chart 2-5**.) Couple these costs with the fact that only 38 percent of first-time freshmen entering four-year bachelor's degree programs actually complete their degrees within four years, and parents may be facing college expenses that easily rival a home mortgage.[37]

CHART 2-5 Average Annual Undergraduate College Costs for the 2020–2021 Academic Year[38]

	Two-Year Public Institution	Four-Year Public Institution	Four-Year Private Institution
Tuition & Fees	$ 3,770	$ 10,560	$ 37,650
Books & Supplies	$ 1,460	$ 1,240	$ 1,240
Room & Board	$ 9,080	$ 11,620	$ 13,120
Other Costs*	$ 4,240	$ 3,400	$ 2,870
TOTAL	$ 18,550	$ 26,820	$ 54,800

*Includes transportation, entertainment, clothing, and miscellaneous costs.

Unfortunately, over the last decade, increases in wage levels and median annual income have stagnated.[39] For example, median family income grew by only

34. Farran Powell & Emma Kerr, *See the Average College Tuition in 2020–2021*, U.S. News & World Report (Sept. 14, 2020), https://www.usnews.com/education/best-colleges/paying-for-college/articles/paying-for-college-infographic.

35. *Trends in College Pricing 2020: Highlights*, CollegeBoard, https://research.collegeboard.org/trends/college-pricing/highlights.

36. *Id.* The transportation expense was $1,840 for community college, $1,230 for public schools, and $1,060 for private schools. Other expenses were $2,400 for community college, $2,170 for public schools, and $1,810 for private schools.

37. *Fast Facts*, Nat'l Ctr. for Educ. Statistics, https://nces.ed.gov/fastfacts/display.asp?id=40 (last visited Apr. 29, 2021).

38. *Trends in College Pricing 2020: Highlights*, CollegeBoard, Tables CP-1 & 2, https://research.collegeboard.org/trends/college-pricing/highlights; *Trends in College Pricing and Student Aid 2020*, CollegeBoard, Table CP-1, https://research.collegeboard.org/pdf/trends-college-pricing-student-aid-2020.pdf.

39. Donald E. Heller, *Trends in the Affordability of Public Colleges and Universities: The Contradiction of Increasing Prices and Increasing Enrollment*, *in* The States and Public Higher Education Policy Affordability, Access and Accountability (Donald E. Heller ed., Johns Hopkins Univ. Press 2001).

3 percent during the same period that tuition and fees increased by 52 percent.[40] Thus, the amount of family income required to pay for college has increased dramatically. The impact on middle-income and lower-income families can be quite severe because the gap between high- and low-income families has significantly widened. For example, the share of income going to the 20 percent of families with the lowest incomes declined from 4.6 percent in 1989 to 3.9 percent in 2019, but the share of income going to the top 5 percent of families increased from 17.9 percent in 1989 to 21.9 percent in 2019.[41] Thus, higher-income families are making more money than ever, while lower-income families are making less. Statistics show that only 20 percent of families are able to pay the full cost of a child's college education. Many families are mortgaging their homes, delaying essential purchases, and raiding their retirement accounts to send their children to college.

The last decade has also shown that state and federal governments have reduced need-based grants,[42] making it even more difficult for the average family to afford increasing college expenses. As a consequence, a growing percentage of students are required to take out student loans. Nearly seven in ten high school seniors who graduated in 2019 took on debt.[43] In the last decade, the percentage of students taking out loans has increased from 46 percent to 70 percent.[44] As of March 2020, the average loan debt of a bachelor's degree recipient from a four-year college is now $28,800, making it difficult for the student to take public interest or other low-paying jobs.[45] The combination of large federal budget deficits and state budget cuts for education makes inevitable the likelihood that college costs will continue to rise in the foreseeable future. On the bright side, schools with large endowments are increasingly replacing student loans with grants and modifying financial aid formulae to cover middle class families.[46]

C. Conclusion

The benefits of pursuing a good education, whether K–12, community college, or university, will literally last a lifetime. A higher education may allow the child to

---

40. *Trends in College Pricing 2020: Highlights*, CollegeBoard, https://research.collegeboard.org/trends/college-pricing/highlights.

41. *Id.* at Tables CP-15A, 15-B.

42. *See* Michael Mitchell, Michael Leachman & Kathleen Masterson, *A Lost Decade in Higher Education Funding*, Ctr. on Budget & Policy Priorities (Aug. 23, 2017), https://www.cbpp.org/research/state-budget-and-tax/a-lost-decade-in-higher-education-funding.

43. Zack Friedman, *Student Loan Debt Statistics in 2019: $1.5 Trillion Crisis*, Forbes (Feb. 25, 2019), https://www.forbes.com/sites/zackfriedman/2019/02/25/student-loan-debt-statistics-2019/?sh=58e0fdeb133f.

44. Those in lower-income groups, the less well educated, and/or members of minority groups may be even less informed about college costs and how to pay for them. They may also be less likely to be willing to take out loans to pay for college. *See* Maggie Thompson, *Why Student Loan Debt Harms Low-Income Students the Most*, Talk Poverty (May 2, 2016), https://talkpoverty.org/2016/05/02/why-student-loan-debt-harms-low-income-students-the-most/.

45. *Trends in College Pricing and Student Aid 2020*, CollegeBoard 12, https://research.collegeboard.org/pdf/trends-college-pricing-student-aid-2020.pdf.

46. *See* **Chapter Five: When Savings Are Not Enough**, **Chart 5-6**.

pursue a career that genuinely interests and inspires them. With that satisfaction comes higher income, better employment benefits, and more advancement opportunities. Advisors can help to ensure that families are on an educational path that reflects their own morals, ideals, and overall goals. With the benefit of growing data and studies, no shortage of information exists that may be used to thoughtfully assess a child's education. It is vital for families to not only recognize that the various options are available, but to know that with the right planning for them, some of these options are possible.

Chapter 3

It Is Never Too Late to Save

The client will have many options to finance their educational goals, and the advisors' function is to fashion a comprehensive plan. The advisor should first determine the clients' educational objectives and their expected costs. The advisor will also need to determine the time frame before schooling commences. Only then can the advisor recommend a savings plan to accomplish their goals. When savings are inadequate, then pay-as-you-go techniques like loans may be available. The advisor should also determine whether the client will have current earnings, can count on relatives to help finance college costs, or expects the student to contribute to the costs through their own earnings. Only by determining the client's tax and nontax goals can the advisor come up with a comprehensive plan to accomplish these goals. *See* **Chart 3-1.**

CHART 3-1 Savings and Goal Questionnaire

1. What are the client's education goals?
2. What are the costs of the desired education goals?
3. How much time does the client have to save?
4. Can the client finance education costs without savings?
5. Will the client need savings or other resources to afford the educational expenditures?
6. Can the client count on relatives to help finance education expenditures?
7. How much of the costs of college will be supplied by the student? Through scholarships or through student work?
8. Does the parent or student anticipate taking out any loans?
9. Are pay-as-you-go tax techniques available that can help finance the educational expenditures?
10. Which tax factors are important to the client?
    a. Income (federal and state)
    b. Gift
    c. Estate
    d. Generation skipping
11. Which nontax factors are important to the client?
    a. Investment Returns
    b. Control
    c. Financial Aid
    d. Asset Protection
    e. Flexibility of Savings
    f. Other

A. The Importance of Savings

If the client has expensive educational plans such as boarding school, private college, and professional schools, it becomes imperative to calculate the needed funds for these goals. The client may not want to rely entirely on financial aid. If the financial targets cannot be met, perhaps the client will have to forgo one of these goals.

Not having enough savings may be a liability in the admissions process. A college may decide to admit only a certain percentage of needy students and fill the rest of the class with those who have the ability to pay the full college costs.[1] In addition, having adequate savings means the student need not consider and assess different financial aid packages, knowing that they can attend the school of their choice.

B. Calculating the Needed Savings

A plan for savings is therefore very important—and will depend on the total K–12, college, and graduate costs. Education costs, in turn, will depend on (1) the type of school the student plans to attend (public or private), (2) the inflation rate, and (3) the number of years before enrollment. If the goal is to save for K–12 expenditure, then savings must start early.

Using the following table (**Chart 3-2**), the taxpayer can estimate what the anticipated costs of college will be in the future and can then start planning accordingly.

CHART 3-2 Future Value of Present Savings

Time to Goal	(4%)	(5%)	(6%)	(7%)	(8%)
3 years	1.125	1.158	1.191	1.225	1.260
4 years	1.170	1.215	1.262	1.311	1.360
5 years	1.216	1.276	1.338	1.402	1.469
6 years	1.265	1.340	1.418	1.501	1.587
7 years	1.316	1.407	1.504	1.606	1.714
8 years	1.368	1.477	1.594	1.718	1.851
9 years	1.423	1.551	1.689	1.838	1.999
10 years	1.480	1.629	1.791	1.967	2.159
11 years	1.529	1.710	1.898	2.105	2.332
12 years	1.601	1.796	2.012	2.252	2.518
13 years	1.665	1.886	2.133	2.410	2.720
14 years	1.732	1.980	2.261	2.578	2.937
15 years	1.801	2.079	2.396	2.759	3.172
16 years	1.873	2.183	2.540	2.952	3.426
17 years	1.949	2.292	2.693	3.159	3.700
18 years	2.026	2.407	2.854	3.380	3.996

1. *See* Joseph Russo & Jim Blevin, How to Save for College 77 (Princeton Review 2004).

EXAMPLE 3-1: Your client, Caroline, wishes to have her son attend college. Her son is six years old. Assume she has 12 years to save for his college education and the current cost of the education institution she is considering is $40,000 a year. Assuming college expenses increase at a rate of 5 percent, she will need to save $71,840 ($40,000 × 1.796) to finance one year of her son's education. This assumes no financial aid, scholarships, or tax benefits.

The reality is that in order to come up with the funds required for the desired education, the family must have considerable excess earnings or savings. Even the middle-income family may spend all their earnings on necessities and thus have little disposable income to devote to educational purposes. Furthermore, taxes on earnings make it difficult to save. For example, if the taxpayer is in the 25 percent federal income tax bracket, a 5 percent state income tax bracket, and pays 7.6 percent social security and Medicare taxes, that leaves about 60 percent of earnings after taxes to take home for necessities and other everyday living expenses. Any savings the taxpayer is able to make will be taxable at ordinary income or capital gains rates (unless funds are in a nontaxable account, such as a 529, Coverdell, or tax-exempt securities). Consequently, it may be very difficult for the typical family to afford the escalating costs of education.

As was discussed in **Chapter Two: The Benefits and Costs of a Good Education**, it is important to attempt to calculate total college costs so that a plan for savings can be established. The following inflation factor chart can help estimate the necessary savings. *See* **Chart 3-3**.

EXAMPLE 3-2: If the current cost of one year at a four-year public college is $18,000 and the cost of education rises 5 percent each year, in 18 years that same expense will be over $45,540 ($18,000 × 2.53) per year (*See* **Chart 3-3**), resulting in a total four-year college cost of over $180,000.

Once costs are estimated, a plan for savings can be made. The closer the student is to attending the desired school, the more that needs to be saved. Investment performances and taxability of the savings fund are also important considerations. **Chapter Four: The Best Ways to Save** and **Chapter Thirteen: Investment Planning with Section 529 Savings Plans** will explore these issues.

CHART 3-3 Inflation Factors

Years to Start College	Inflation factors				
	5%	6%	7%	8%	9%
1	1.10	1.12	1.07	1.08	1.09
2	1.16	1.19	1.15	1.17	1.19
3	1.22	1.26	1.23	1.59	1.30
4	1.28	1.34	1.31	1.71	1.41
5	1.34	1.42	1.40	1.85	1.54
6	1.41	1.5	1.50	2.00	1.68
7	1.48	1.59	1.61	2.16	1.83
8	1.55	1.69	1.72	2.33	1.99
9	1.63	1.70	1.84	2.52	2.17
10	1.71	1.90	1.97	2.72	2.40
11	1.80	2.01	2.11	2.94	2.58
12	1.89	2.13	2.25	3.17	2.81
13	1.98	2.26	2.41	3.42	3.07
14	2.08	2.40	2.58	3.70	3.34
15	2.19	2.54	2.76	3.99	3.64
16	2.29	2.69	2.95	4.31	3.97
17	2.41	2.84	3.16	4.66	4.33
18	2.53	3.03	3.62	5.03	4.72

C. It Is Never Too Late to Save

By saving $25, $50, $100, or $500 a month, and by putting money in an investment account, large amounts of money can be saved for college. Much more will be accumulated if put in a tax-advantaged account, like a 529 plan. This offers tax deferral and elimination of tax on earning on the investment every year. The higher the interest rate on the earnings on the account, the more funds can be saved. (*See* **Chart 3-4**, which assumes an 8 percent return.)

CHART 3-4 Future Value of Savings with 8 Percent Return

Investment Each Month	One Year	Five Years	Ten Years	Fifteen Years
$ 25	$ 313	$ 1,835	$ 4,532	$ 8,494
$ 50	$ 626	$ 3,671	$ 9,064	$ 16,989
$ 100	$ 1,251	$ 7,341	$ 18,128	$ 33,978
$ 500	$ 6,257	$ 36,707	$ 90,642	$ 169,889

Planning Pointer

Saving on a tax-deferred basis makes the most economic sense, as this will maximize the taxpayer's ability to generate funds for education purposes.

EXAMPLE 3-3: Alice makes a one-time lump sum investment of $50,000. At annual returns of 8 percent and a combined federal and state tax rate of 35 percent, after 18 years a taxable account will grow to $124,524. A Section 529 nontaxable account, in comparison, will grow to $199,801—a difference of $75,277.

It must be remembered that significant savings could reduce the family's financial aid. While financial aid in the form of grants is more available to the low-income family, a growing amount of aid is in the form of loans or scholarships. Thus, for some taxpayers, it may not make sense to save for college.

D. Conclusion

The costs of college are significant and are higher than both the cost of living and wages. Yet, the economic and other benefits of college are significant. While financial aid, scholarships, and tax benefits are available to relieve some of the burden of increasing college costs, savings should be a part of every family's education plan. It is never too late to save, even for K–12 expenditures. The role of the advisor is to determine the clients' goals, calculate the expected costs, and come up with a comprehensive savings plan that works given the clients' objectives. *See* **Chart 3-5** for a summary of the necessary calculations.

CHART 3-5 Worksheet: Calculating Cost of Schooling and Necessary Savings*

A. Calculating Costs
1. Years until your child starts school ___________
2. Current annual cost of one year of school
   a. Boarding school (*See* **Chart 2-3**.)
   b. K–12 private school (*See* **Chart 2-3**.)
   c. Community college (*See* **Chart 2-5**.)
   d. Public college (*See* **Chart 2-5**.)
   e. Private college (*See* **Chart 2-5**.)
   f. Graduate or professional school
   g. Your anticipated total education costs ___________
3. College cost inflation factor ___________
   (*See* **Chart 3-3**.)
4. Future anticipated costs (#2 × #3) ___________
5. Future total cost of college (#4 × number of years in college) ___________

B. Calculating Savings
6. Select anticipated return given client risks and savings techniques
   (*See* **Chart 3-2**.) ___________
7. Calculate targeted annual amount to save (*See* **Example 3-2**.) ___________
8. Monthly amount needed to save (divide #7 by 12) ___________

*Source.www.finaid.org

Chapter 4

The Best Ways to Save

One of the best ways to finance K–12 or college education is through savings. Education savings strategies are numerous and often depend on the goals and unique facts of the client. However, we believe that the best overall strategy is the 529 plan, as everyone can take advantage of this technique regardless of income, and it offers both tax and nontax advantages. In some circumstances, the Section 529 *prepaid plan* might be better than the traditional 529 *college savings plans*. However, if the client is focused on K–12 education, the *Coverdell Education Savings Account (ESA)* must also be explored.

If financial aid will be a significant component of the client's plan, then assets such as savings bonds should be avoided, but insurance and retirement assets might have advantages.[1] Retirement assets might also be a good education savings technique when the client has an excess of those assets. For clients who have property and not cash, uniform transfers to minors, various trusts, and traditional investments should be explored. Some of these savings techniques provide tax advantages, others do not.[2] Some offer significant control over investments, others do not. The savings techniques may vary in terms of annual contribution amounts, income level for participation, account transferability, ease of set-up, and administration. The savings techniques or strategies that work best will vary depending on individual circumstances and goals of the client.[3]

A. The 529 Plan

In comparison to other education planning savings tools, Section 529 *college savings plans* or Section 529 *prepaid plans* are usually superior. The *savings plan* allows the taxpayer to put money into individual, state-run investment accounts designated for payment of *qualified higher education expenses*.[4] The *prepaid plan*

1. *See* **Chapter Nineteen: Coordinating Section 529 Plans with Financial Aid**.
2. *See* **Chapter Eighteen: Coordinating Section 529 Plans with Tax Benefits**.
3. *See* **Chapter Seventeen: Coordinating Section 529 Plans with Other Savings Techniques**.
4. *See* **Part II: Section 529 Savings Plans**.

allows taxpayers to pay for college tuition at today's rates. There are two types of prepaid plans—state-run plans and the relatively new *Private College 529 Plan* run by private education institutions.[5] We will discuss these prepaid plans in more detail in **Part III: Prepaid Tuition Plans**.

1. Prepaid Plans and Savings Plans Offer Similar Advantages

Both the Section 529 savings and the prepaid plans offer significant federal income, estate, and gift tax advantages. First, although the contributions are not tax deductible, no income restrictions apply, so even wealthy taxpayers may take advantage of this benefit. Second, the savings and accumulated earnings are exempt from federal income tax *if* the distributions are used for *qualified higher education expenses* (QHEE). QHEE can include tuition, room, board, a computer, and certain other college expenses. After the *TCJA* of 2017, up to $10,000 of K–12 tuition expenses for private or parochial schools will qualify as QHEE. After the *Setting Every Community Up for Retirement Enhancement (SECURE) Act of 2019*, the definition of QHEE has expanded to include amounts paid as principal or interest on any qualified education loan. Third, because contributions to a 529 plan are considered a *present interest*, contributions of up to $15,000 per beneficiary ($30,000 for a married couple using gift-splitting in 2021) are exempt from gift taxes. An accelerated gifting option allows the taxpayer to contribute five times the per-donee annual exclusion amount (up to $75,000 per beneficiary in 2021) and average the contribution over a five-year period to avoid gift taxes. Thus, married couples can contribute twice that amount (or up to $150,000 in 2021) per beneficiary through gift splitting. Furthermore, contributions in excess of these limits can be offset by using the taxpayer's *lifetime gift tax exemption*, which now is $10 million adjusted for inflation. (For 2021, this amount is now $11,700,000). Fourth, the assets in the plan are not considered part of the account owner's taxable estate, even though the account can be refunded or the beneficiary changed, except in the case of accelerated giving and death within five years. No generation-skipping tax applies unless the beneficiary is changed to a lower generation. Thus, both 529 savings and prepaid plans offer a saving technique that has minimal tax consequences.

In addition to the federal tax advantages, both types of plans can offer state tax advantages. Many states offer a full or partial state income tax deduction for contributions to the plan. Other states offer credits. Most states will offer tax-exempt qualified withdrawals.[6]

Both types of Section 529 plans also offer nontax advantages. First, they are easy to administer and set up. Second, the account owner controls access to funds. If the beneficiary does not go to college, the account owner can reclaim the money (with income taxes and a ten percent additional tax owed on earnings) or change the beneficiary to another family member. The beneficiary does not

---

5. *See* **Part III: Prepaid Tuition Plans.**
6. *See* **Chapter Ten: State Tax Planning with Section 529 Savings Plans.**

control or have access to the funds and is not entitled to the fund at the age of majority. Third, these plans have a low impact on financial aid eligibility under the federal methodology formula. Lastly, 529 savings plans can be coordinated with *ABLE accounts* and provide needed benefits to the other-abled who risk loss of governmental benefits with gift transfers.[7] All these above issues are discussed in greater detail in **Part II** and **Part IV** of this book.

2. The Advantages of the Savings Plans over the Prepaid Plans

The Section 529 savings plan has several advantages over the prepaid plans. First, Section 529 savings plans are widely available. Every state has at least one of these plans. *See* list in **Appendix C**. On the other hand, only 11 states have prepaid plans. Thus, advisors and financial planners across the nation will likely be well versed in the ins and outs of the Section 529 savings plans. Second, Section 529 plans have very high cumulative contribution limits, typically around $375,000 per beneficiary and as high as $529,000 per beneficiary.[8] They can be used for undergraduate and graduate tuition, as well as for room, board, and other education-related expenses. As we mentioned earlier, the *TCJA* of 2017 expanded the definition of QHEE to include K–12 tuition, and the *SECURE Act* of 2019 expanded the definition of QHEE to include payment on qualified education loans. On the other hand, most prepaid plans cover only undergraduate tuition, not room and board.

Third, Section 529 savings plans impose no restrictions on choice of college, other than that it must be an accredited post-secondary institution. State prepaid plans are meant to apply to public state schools, whereas the *Private College 529 Plan* plans cover some, but not all, private schools. Fourth, Section 529 savings plans offer flexible investment options, such as age-based or risk-based asset allocation strategies. Most of these plans are managed by experienced investment companies, such as TIAA-CREF, Vanguard, or Fidelity. Furthermore, the account owner can roll over funds to a different 529 plan or change investment strategies once a year if not satisfied with the initial plan. In addition, 529 plans can be coordinated with disability planning. In contrast, 529 prepaids are tied to tuition costs, and if the participant desires a refund from the prepaid plan (or rollover to a Section 529 savings plan), the refund might be severely limited, resulting in a loss of investment.

Many savings plans also include features that make it easy to set aside money regularly, such as payroll deduction and automatic transfers from a checking or savings account. In addition, the minimum investment amount is often much lower than that required by most mutual funds, making the savings plan more accessible and affordable for lower-income families. Unlike prepaid plans, there is no date by which funds must be used, unless state law provides otherwise.

---

7. *See* **Chapter Eleven: Disability Planning with Section 529 Savings Plans**.
8. *See* **Chapter Seven: Federal Rules and Regulations for Section 529 Savings Plans, Chart 7-2**.

3. The Advantages of the Prepaid Plans over the Savings Plan

The advantages of the prepaid plans over the Section 529 savings plans are several. First, the prepaid plans are guaranteed to keep up with increasing tuition costs even when market returns are low. Although the more aggressive investment options available in a savings plan offer a greater potential return, they are accompanied by a greater potential risk. Except for principal protection portfolios such as money market accounts and guaranteed investments (offered by a few states), the principal invested is at risk in a savings plan; if the program's manager makes bad investment decisions or the stock market declines, the account owner's money could be lost. Second, prepaid plans charge no advisor, investment, or service fees. On the other hand, in some savings plans expenses and sales charges can be high, eating into the overall return. Third, prepaid plans offer simplicity by limiting school choice. State prepaid plans are limited to in-state public schools. The *Private College 529 Plan* offers the additional benefit of portability among approximately 300 private schools.

Planning Pointer

Stock market prices may fluctuate and, in a recession, go down. Tuition rates, on the other hand, tend to steadily rise. Consequently, under certain market situations, a prepaid plan is an excellent education planning choice. In the alternative, the taxpayer could keep the college tuition funds in a "conservative" (bond, liquid, etc.) 529 savings plan, changing them to an equity fund later when the market makes an adjustment.

CHART 4-1 529 Savings & Prepaid—Similarities and Differences

Similarities	Differences
• Neither allows for federal income tax deductions. • Neither is taxable when used for qualified education expenses (QHEE). • Both qualify as present interest for federal gift tax purposes. • The value of the account is not in the estate of the donor/owner for federal estate tax purposes. • Both are easy to administer and set up. • Both can change beneficiary to another family member. • Both have low impact for financial aid purposes when owned by parent/student.	• Every state has a savings plan but only 11 states have a prepaid plan. • Most prepaid plans are limited to tuition and do not cover room and board and other expenses. • Prepaids offer limited school choices whereas savings plans can be used at any qualified institution. • Savings plans have greater risk than prepaid plans. • Prepaid plans guarantee tuition payment even when tuition rises.

B. When the Client's Goal Includes K–12 Education

Under the *TCJA* of 2017, up to $10,000 of tuition expenses for K–12 schooling can be QHEE under the 529 savings plans. However, many more types of K–12 expenses are covered with the *Coverdell Educational Savings Accounts (ESAs).* First, ESAs can be used for tuition expenses greater than $10,000, including room and board at private or parochial schools. As we mentioned earlier, the costs of boarding schools can exceed $30,000.[9] In addition, K–12 expenses that qualify under ESAs include computers, academic tutors, uniforms, transportation, and items not covered under Section 529 plans.[10] Thus, ESAs have a broader coverage of expenditures for K–12 planning purposes.

To qualify for the ESA benefits, contributions must be made in cash and are not deductible. However, like the 529 savings plan, earnings on these accounts can be tax deferred and withdrawn tax free if used for qualified education purposes. Coverdell ESAs are easy to set up and administer, allow broad control by the responsible party over investments, and provide for account transferability to a member of the family with the consent of the original beneficiary.

Unlike 529s, the ESA is restricted by income level—phasing out when adjusted gross income levels are between $95,000 and $110,000 for singles and head of households and between $190,000 and $220,000 for married couples filing jointly in 2021. The contribution limitation is $2,000 per year (which cannot be made after the beneficiary reaches 18 unless the beneficiary has special needs). In addition, mandatory distributions are required when the beneficiary turns 30, although the account can be rolled over to another family member with the consent of the beneficiary.

A contribution to an ESA is treated as an irrevocable gift and will pass to the beneficiary if not used for education purposes. Estate tax can be assessed to the account owner if he/she dies while the account is in existence. In addition, an *excess contribution* penalty may arise under Section 4973(f) even with inadvertent contributions over the $2,000 limit amount. Under recent legislation, the value of the account is not considered to be the student's asset for financial aid purposes, even though the student is considered the owner of this account.[11]

---

9. *See* **Chapter Two: The Benefits and Costs of a Good Education, Chart 2-3**.

10. IRS Pub. 970: Tax Benefits for Education 47 (2019) (Qualified Elementary and Secondary Education Expenses include special needs services for special need beneficiaries and even supplemental items and services, including extended day programs).

11. Deficit Reduction Omnibus Reconciliation Act of 2005, Pub. L. No. 109-171, § 8019(d)(5), 120 Stat. 9 (2006). *See* **Chapter Nineteen: Coordinating Section 529 Plans with Financial Aid**.

CHART 4-2 Coverdells—Advantages and Disadvantages

Coverdells' Advantages	Limitations and Disadvantages
• K–12 expenses allowed and have a broad application of what qualifies. • College expenses allowed. • Earnings can be tax deferred. • Tax-free upon withdrawal (if for education-related purposes). • Easy to set up. • Rollover or transferable to new beneficiary with beneficiary's consent. • Broad control of assets by the owner. • Low impact for financial aid purposes.	• Income limitations apply—unavailable for AGI greater than $95–110 K (single TP) and greater than $190–220 K (married TP) for 2021. • $2,000 annual contribution limit. • Cash contributions only. • Contributions are not tax deductible. • Risk of contribution penalty for excess contribution. • No contribution after beneficiary reaches age 18, with some exceptions. • Must distribute by age 30 or roll over to new beneficiary. • Irrevocable. • Risk of estate tax assessment on death of grantor.

C. When the Client Is Eligible for Financial Aid

For a client who is likely to qualify for financial aid, certain savings are better than others. Savings bonds are generally problematic, but insurance and retirement assets provide advantages. Financial aid considerations vary greatly for 529 plans depending on who owns the account. In general, assets are assessed differently than income. (*See* **Chart 4-3.**) For more details on these issues, *see* **Chapter Nineteen: Coordinating Section 529 Plans with Financial Aid.**

CHART 4-3 Expected Family Contributions

	Federal Methodology	Institutional Methodology
Grandparent's Assets	-0-	-0-
Parent's Assets	5.64%	3–5%
Parent's Income	22–47%	22–46%
Student's Assets	20%*	25%
Student's Income	50%	50%

*Recent legislation lowered this student asset rate from 35% to 20%.

1. Savings Bonds

Savings bonds provide some tax advantages to lower-income taxpayers when used for qualified education expenses.[12] Interest earned on qualified *series EE* or *series I* savings bonds can be excluded from federal income taxes if the proceeds from the bond are used for qualified education expenses. Regardless of purpose, the interest is not subject to state tax. The federal tax benefit is restricted by income level. The exclusion is phased out for 2021 when adjusted gross income levels are between $83,200 and $98,200 for single and head of household taxpayers and between $124,800–$154,800 for married taxpayers who are filing jointly.

The only allowed qualified education expense for the savings bond exclusion is tuition payments and academic fees. This exclusion is reduced by scholarships and grants, as well as by any expenses used for purposes of the education tax credits. The return on the investment is conservative, but bonds are a secure investment. These are considered an asset of the parent for financial aid purposes but when cashed reduce financial aid dollar for dollar. Thus, savings bonds are not advisable when financial aid is anticipated.

2. Insurance

Insurance is important in case the primary payor of the education expenses dies or becomes disabled and is unable to continue paying the expenses. In addition, the *cash surrender value* of insurance can be borrowed to pay for the costs of education, including those expenses (e.g., transportation, medical, clothes, entertainment, etc.) not covered by other education planning techniques. Furthermore, life insurance money is not considered an asset under either the federal or institutional formulae for financial aid purposes.

3. Retirement Assets

Retirement assets, like cash surrender value life insurance, are not considered assets under the federal financial aid formula. However, a tax-deductible contribution to a retirement fund during the base income year will be assessed as income. Any contribution made before the base year of the financial aid application will be shielded as an asset. In a year of a rollover—when a *Traditional IRA* is converted to a *Roth IRA*, income is increased by an amount reported on the return.

Increasing numbers of private schools under the institutional formula are asking about Roths and other retirement assets. These schools most likely are considering these as potential assets that could be tapped for college. Under the worst-case scenario, these would be assessed as the parent's asset contribution. If

12. I.R.C. § 135.

retirement assets are used to pay for college, however, 100 percent of the distribution—both income and principal—reduce financial aid dollar for dollar.

4. 529s and Coverdells

In general, 529s and Coverdells are considered assets of the parent (even when owned by the student) and are assessed at favorable rates, either 3–5 percent under the institutional method or up to 5.64 percent under the federal formula. Thus, these savings techniques have federal aid advantages over other savings mechanisms. For a detailed discussion of 529s and financial aid, see **Chapter Nineteen: Coordinating Section 529 Plans with Financial Aid.**

D. When the Client Has Ample Retirement Assets

The use of retirement plan assets may be a good education-planning technique for clients who have more than adequately saved for their retirement. With proper planning, it is possible to accomplish both education and retirement goals. *Traditional IRAs* and *Roth IRAs* offer the best planning opportunities here.

1. Traditional IRAs

Section 219 of the Internal Revenue Code sets forth the rules for the *Traditional IRA*. The rules allow taxpayers who are *not* "active participants" in an employer-provided retirement plan to make tax-deductible contributions to an account to the extent they have compensation.[13] Taxpayers who *are* active participants in an employer-provided plan can make deductible contributions only if their income does not exceed certain levels.[14] (*See* **Chart 4-6.**) The account grows tax free, and when withdrawals are made and the account owner is between the ages of 59½ and 70½, those withdrawals are taxed at ordinary rates, even for distributions for "qualified education expenses." A distribution for a "qualified education expense," however, will prevent the ten percent *penalty tax* if money is withdrawn before the account owner is 59½ years old. The minimum distribution rules apply, so a percentage of the money must be withdrawn from the account no later than the April 1 following the year in which the account owner turns 70½, or a 50 percent excise tax under Section 4974(a) will be imposed.

---

13. *See* Treas. Reg. § 1.219-2.
14. I.R.C. § 219(g).

CHART 4-4 The General Requirements of the Traditional IRA

- Those eligible to contribute are those not "active participants" in employer plan or who have limited income.
- Contributions are in cash.
- Contributions do not exceed set limits.
- The IRA must be administered by a trustee (a bank of other entity) approved by the IRS.
- The owner's interest is nonforfeitable.
- The assets are not commingled.
- The account is not invested in life insurance.
- The minimum distribution rules are followed.

a. Contribution Limits

Anyone can contribute to an IRA if he/she is not actively participating in another qualified retirement plan and has earned income at least equal to the amount of the contribution. The maximum annual contribution for 2021 is $6,000.[15] Those who have reached 50 years of age during the year may make additional annual "catch-up" contributions of $1,000.[16] This catch-up amount, unlike the annual contribution, is not adjusted for inflation. (*See* **Chart 4-5**.) If the taxpayer is married, these IRA amounts can be doubled to account for the taxpayer's spouse's retirement planning. All of these deductions are above the line, i.e., taken before calculating adjusted gross income.[17] No contributions can be made once the taxpayer reaches the age of 70½.[18]

CHART 4-5 Contribution Limits

Tax Years	Under 50 Years of Age	Over 50 Years of Age
2002–2004	$ 3,000	$ 3,500
2005–2007	$ 4,000	$ 5,000
2008	$ 5,000	$ 6,000
After 2008	$ 5,000 adjusted for inflation	Always $ 1,000 extra
2020	$ 6,000	$ 7,000
2021	$ 6,000	$ 7,000

Excess contributions to a Traditional IRA, just like excess contributions to a Coverdell, are subject to the excess contribution tax under Section 4973(f).

15. I.R.C. § 219(b)(5)(A).
16. I.R.C. § 219(b)(5)(B)(i)–(ii).
17. I.R.C. § 62(a)(6)–(7), (18).
18. I.R.C. § 219(1).

b. Income Phase-Outs

Certain adjusted gross income (AGI) limitations may apply that could reduce the amount that is tax deductible. The phase-out limits vary depending on whether or not the taxpayer is covered by a retirement plan. For the single taxpayer not covered by a retirement plan, there are no income restrictions. Also, no income restrictions apply if the taxpayer is married and neither spouse has a Section 401(k) retirement plan. If the taxpayer is covered by a retirement plan, then the phase-out for 2021 begins when modified adjusted gross income is between $66,000 and $76,000 for singles or head of households, $105,000 and $125,000 for married filing jointly, and $10,000 for a married couple filing separately. If the taxpayer is not covered by a retirement plan but their spouse has one, the AGI phase-out begins at $198,000 and is phased out at $206,000. As with other tax benefits, the AGI is modified and calculated without any deductible IRA.[19] Above those limits, there is no tax deduction.[20] Interestingly, unlike other education tax provisions, taxpayers who are married and filing separately are entitled to this benefit, but only if their modified AGI is less than $10,000.[21]

EXAMPLE 4-1: Assume that Alice, age 30, contributed $6,000 into her Traditional IRA (and assume she has a Section 401 retirement plan at work). If her modified AGI for 2021 is $71,000, her allowable IRA deduction is $3,000—calculated as follows: The difference between the upper limit of $76,000 and her modified AGI of $71,000 ($5,000) divided by $10,000, the range of income for the phase-out = 50 percent. Thus, Alice can claim a $3,000 deduction ($6,000 × 50%).

c. Distributions

A *ten percent penalty* is assessed for withdrawals or distributions made before the taxpayer reaches the age of 59½ unless the funds are used for "qualified education expenses" (QEE) of an "eligible student" at an "eligible education institution."[22]

19. IRS Pub. 590: Individual Retirement Arrangements (IRAs) 7 (2020).
20. I.R.C. § 219(g).
21. Phase-out begins at zero.
22. I.R.C. § 72(t)(2)(F). The other exceptions to the penalty include the following:

    (1) distributions made to a beneficiary (or to the estate) upon death;
    (2) payments attributable to the taxpayer becoming disabled as defined by section 72(m)(7);
    (3) payments made as "part of a series of substantially equal periodic payment (not less than annually)";
    (4) payments made on account of a tax levy under section 6331;
    (5) payments for certain medical expenses;
    (6) payments pursuant to a qualified domestic relations order as defined by section 414(p)(1);
    (7) payments for health insurance premiums of unemployed taxpayers;
    (8) payments for certain higher education expenses; and
    (9) payments for certain first-time home purchases.

"Qualifying education expenses" are defined exactly as they are under a Section 529 plan.[23] Thus, QEE includes tuition, fees, books, supplies, equipment, and room and board if the "qualified student" is enrolled at least *half-time* at a qualified educational institution. As with 529 plans, expenses for special needs children qualify. QEE also includes the newer expansions to the QHEE definition—K–12 tuition and loan repayments of up to $10,000. "Qualified student" and "qualified education institution" are also defined the same as under Section 529.[24] Unlike the 529 plan, which can include cousins, IRA education expenses are limited to the IRA owner, his/her spouse, children (including adopted and stepchildren), or grandchildren.

EXAMPLE 4-2: Alice, age 50, withdraws $30,000, which represents contributions of $22,000 and *accrued interest* of $8,000 from her Traditional IRA to pay for her son Ben's qualified education expenses. If Alice uses the full $22,000 plus the $8,000 interest (or all $30,000), to pay for these expenses, she will be taxed on the full amount at her marginal tax rate. No penalty will be imposed. On the other hand, if all funds are withdrawn but the qualified education expenses are only $20,000, the difference of $10,000 will be subject to the 10 percent penalty, which would amount to $1,000.

The big difference between the IRA and Section 529 plan is that the IRA contribution (although limited) is deductible and the distribution (even when used for qualified expenses) is all taxable. Thus, it may not make economic sense for a taxpayer to plan to use an IRA for education purposes. IRAs are taxed at ordinary rates and if the tax is assessed when the taxpayer is not retired, then the tax burden could be high if the taxpayer is currently earning a relatively high income. Consequently, it may be a hardship to pay taxes on the IRA distribution at the same time the taxpayer is paying for college. Any taxes will reduce the amount of money available to pay for education. Lastly, the client may be reducing his/her retirement when using these funds. If the client is young or has other adequate retirement, this may not be an issue, but for older adults this could be a problem.

d. Other Considerations

Traditional IRAs are easy to set up. They can be set up at almost any bank or investment firm. The fund can be invested in stocks, bonds, mutual funds, and so forth, often at favorable returns. The Traditional IRA can be in the name of the parent or a child; however, if the account is set up in a child's name, the child must have earned income.

---

23. I.R.C. § 72(t)(7)(A) (referencing the definition in § 529(e)(3)).
24. I.R.C. § 529(e)(3)(A).

EXAMPLE 4-3: In 2021 Alice's teenage son Ben makes $2,000 at a summer job and her daughter Mary makes $8,000. Ben can only contribute $2,000 to his Traditional IRA, and Mary can contribute only $6,000—the maximum limit for 2021.

Funds set up for the child will then be available when the child turns 18. This is true irrespective of the child's decision to attend college or not. In addition, the IRA could be considered the student's asset for financial aid purposes with a potential assessment of 20 percent or 25 percent in the expected family contribution. Therefore, it is advisable for the parent to own the IRA because, under the federal methodology for determining financial aid, retirement assets are not included in the parent's asset calculation, and under the institutional formula, they are only assessed at 3–5 percent. In addition, a parent, as owner, has greater control over the investments in the account as well as when the money should be withdrawn.

Planning Pointer

Using a Traditional IRA for college costs not only can compromise retirement goals but will also result in an income tax on the distribution. The distribution can also adversely affect financial aid. The only benefit is that there is no penalty on early withdrawal from the IRA if the withdrawal is used for qualified education expenses.

2. Roth IRAs

The *Roth IRA* was created by the *Taxpayer Relief Act of 1997* to allow taxpayers (even those covered by an employer-sponsored retirement plan) to make after-tax contributions to a retirement fund up to the amount they earn annually. Contributions to Roth IRAs are not tax deductible.[25] The contribution limit amounts are identical to that of the Traditional IRA, but the income phase-outs are slightly different. (*See* **Chart 4–6**.) The account's earnings will grow tax free, just like the Traditional IRA. However, unlike the Traditional IRA, the Roth IRA will generally not be taxed when withdrawn. Thus, Roth IRAs can be an effective education planning tool as long as the client's retirement goals do not suffer.

25. I.R.C. § 408A(c)(1).

a. Contribution Limits

The contribution limits for a Roth IRA are similar to the Traditional IRA. The annual amount is adjusted for inflation, but the "catch-up" for those over 50 is a constant $1,000.[26] Thus, for 2021, $6,000 can be contributed for taxpayers under 50; $7,000 can be contributed for taxpayers who have reached 50. However, the contribution maximum (i.e., limit) is reduced by any amounts the taxpayer contributes to a Traditional IRA.[27] Unlike the Traditional IRA, the taxpayer is not required to withdraw the funds in the Roth IRA account prior to the age of 70½, and contributions can be made even after the taxpayer turns 70½.[28] If the taxpayer makes an *excess contribution* to his/her Roth IRA, he/she will be subject to an excess contribution tax under Section 4973(f). This excess contribution tax is very similar to the excess contribution tax discussed with respect to the Traditional IRA and the Coverdell accounts.

b. Income Phase-Outs

An advantage of the Roth IRA is that the income limitations are more generous than those for the Traditional IRA.[29] Generally, in tax year 2021, the phase-out begins when adjusted gross income is between $125,000–$140,000 for singles or head of households, and $198,000–$208,000 for married filing jointly.[30] If the taxpayer is married and filing separately, that spouse's modified AGI must be less than $10,000, and if that taxpayer earns more than $10,000, then the taxpayer can contribute nothing to the Roth IRA.[31]

CHART 4-6 Phase-Out Amounts

Type of IRA	Tax Year	Single	Married
Traditional IRA	2021	$ 66,000–$ 76,000	$ 105,000–$ 125,000
Roth IRA	2021	$ 125,000–$ 140,000	$ 198,000–$ 208,000

c. Distributions

Roth IRAs are tax free *if* the account has been established for at least five years; remember, this is different than Traditional IRAs that are taxable upon withdrawal. Unless an exception applies, the Roth IRA must be open for a minimum period of five years before any tax-free distribution can be made.[32] Any sums converted from a Traditional IRA must also remain in the account five years to receive favored tax treatment. If a distribution occurs before this five-year period, the income portion

26. I.R.C. § 408A(c)(2).
27. *Id.*
28. I.R.C. § 408A(c)(4), (5).
29. I.R.C. § 408A(c)(3).
30. IRS Pub. 590: Individual Retirement Arrangements (IRAs) (2019).
31. *Id.* The doubling of the benefit allowed to a single or head-of-household taxpayer is not available to the married-filing-separately taxpayer.
32. I.R.C. § 408A(d)(2)(B).

will be taxed at ordinary rates and a ten percent *penalty tax* will be imposed on all of the distribution.[33] Even if the distribution is from a five-year-old account, the distribution must meet one of the exceptions for "qualified distributions" to avoid the ten percent penalty tax.[34]

EXAMPLE 4-4: Alice makes her first Roth IRA contribution on April 10, 2021. She can first receive a "qualified" distribution from this Roth IRA on January 1, 2026. Any distribution before that date will be subject to a 10 percent penalty tax.

The exceptions to the penalty are similar to (but slightly different from) those under the Section 529 plan. There is no ten percent *penalty tax* assessed if: (1) the taxpayer dies and the account goes to the estate or to the named beneficiary; (2) the taxpayer becomes disabled; (3) the taxpayer has attained the age of 59½; (4) the taxpayer uses the fund for "qualified education expenses," or (5) the taxpayer purchases a first-time residence and uses up to $10,000 for this purpose.[35] The first four exceptions are similar to those under Section 529, the last (or #5) is unique to the Roth IRAs.

Distributions prior to the taxpayer attaining the age of 59½ will be considered nonqualified and the earnings portion will be subject to tax, as well as a ten percent *penalty tax*.[36] However, if the funds from the otherwise nonqualified withdrawal are used for qualified higher education purposes (QHEE), the taxpayer will not be subject to the ten percent penalty tax. Qualified higher education is defined by reference to the definition embodied in Section 529(e)(3).[37] The taxpayer never pays a tax on the original contribution once he/she begins to withdraw the funds because the original contribution is a return of capital. On the other hand, any earnings/gain portion of the withdrawal will be taxed if withdrawn prior to the taxpayer turning 59½, *even if* it is used for QHEE.[38] After 59½, penalty-free withdrawals from both IRAs can be made for any purpose. Therefore, once the taxpayer has reached 59½, *everything* (all income and capital) can be withdrawn *tax-free* for *any purpose*.[39] Unlike a Traditional IRA, there are no mandatory minimum distributions from a Roth IRA during the taxpayer's lifetime—only after the taxpayer's death.

One aspect of the Roth IRA that is particularly important for education planning is that distributions are treated on a first-in first-out basis. According to the

---

33. I.R.C. §§ 408A(a), 72(t)(1).

34. I.R.C. § 408A(d)(2) lists the following four "qualified distributions": (1) made after individual attains 59½, (2) made when taxpayer dies, (3) made when taxpayer becomes disabled, or (4) made for a qualified special purpose.

35. *Id.*

36. I.R.C. § 72(t)(2)(E).

37. I.R.C. § 72(t)(7).

38. I.R.C. § 408A(d); Tax Increase Prevention and Reconciliation Act of 2006, Pub. L. No. 109-222, 120 Stat. 345 (May 17, 2006).

39. *See* I.R.C. § 408A(d)(2) (definition of qualified distribution).

regulations, distributions from a Roth IRA during any tax year are treated first as coming from regular contributions, then from conversions, and then from appreciation in the Roth IRA.[40] In other words, the distribution is first considered a return of capital to the extent that the contribution principal amounts remain in the account.[41] This ordering rule allows the taxpayer to withdraw tax-free principal from his/her Roth IRA for any purpose (if the account is more than five years old), even if he/she has not reached the age of 59½. Practically, this means that it is essential for the taxpayer to keep track of his/her basis in the Roth account.

EXAMPLE 4-5: Ben is about to attend college, and Alice, his mother, has a Roth IRA that she set up over five years ago. The account balance reflects a principal of $18,000 and interest of $3,000. She can withdraw the $18,000 for any purpose and not be taxed. She can keep the $3,000 interest in the account to earn more interest income.

d. Other Considerations

Assets in these Roth IRA plans are not considered in the federal financial aid formula used by most state schools. They may, however, be considered to be assets of the parent in the institutional formula used by private schools. Thus, if the student is attending a state school, the Roth IRA can be an effective tool to pay for qualified higher education expenses.

As stated previously, the taxpayer can make a rollover contribution to his/her Roth account. This rollover contribution from the taxpayer's Traditional IRA to a Roth IRA will be tax-free if the taxpayer meets the modified AGI limit.[42] Here, modified AGI is calculated by subtracting any income from the conversion of a Traditional IRA to a Roth IRA and adding the following deductions and exclusions: Traditional IRA deduction, student loan interest deduction, foreign earned income exclusion, foreign housing exclusion deduction, exclusion of qualified bond interest shown on Form 8815, exclusion of employer-paid adoption expenses shown on Form 8839 and qualified tuition and related expenses. Beginning in January 2008, amounts in 401(k) and similar accounts were allowed to be directly converted into a Roth IRA.

40. Treas. Reg. § 1.408A-6, Q & A (8).
41. I.R.C. § 408A(d)(4).
42. I.R.C. § 408A(3)(B).

Planning Pointer

Next to the Section 529 plan, the *Roth IRA* is one of the better ways to save for college for higher-income taxpayers who do not qualify for financial aid and who do not need the Roth IRA for their retirement. In particular, an older parent or grandparent is free to use qualified distributions from his/her Roth account to pay for the student's expenses that are not considered qualified education expenses (i.e., food, clothes, travel, entertainment expenses, etc.). Any taxpayer can withdraw tax-free principal for any purpose. Finally, the taxpayer has control over the investments in his Roth IRA and thus has the ability to invest in funds that are likely to appreciate.

CHART 4-7 Comparison of IRA Types with 529 Plans

Feature	Traditional IRA	Roth IRA	SEP/ Simple IRA	§ 401(k)	§ 529 Plans
Established by individual	Yes	Yes	No	No	Yes
Established by employer	No	No	Yes	Yes	Can be on behalf of employee
Maximum deductible contribution by individual	$ 6,000 in 2021 plus $ 1,000 catch-up	Same as Traditional	N/A	N/A	None
Taxable distribution	Earnings and deductible contributions	Earnings and not "qualified distribution"	In full	In full	No if QHEE
When assets can be withdrawn	Anytime but penalty tax may apply	Anytime but penalty tax may apply	Anytime but penalty may apply	Cannot withdraw until retire	Anytime but penalty tax may apply
When assets can be withdrawn w/o incurring 10% additional tax in general	Age 59½ rule	5-year rule and Age 59½ rule	Age 59½ rule	N/A	If for QHEE
Tax-free distributions if QHEE	No	Yes	No	No	Yes

Feature	Traditional IRA	Roth IRA	SEP/ Simple IRA	§ 401(k)	§ 529 Plans
Family restrictions on withdrawal for QHEE	IRA owner, spouse, children, grandchildren	IRA owner, spouse, children, grandchildren	N/A	N/A	Owner, spouse, lineal ancestors or descendants, siblings, nieces, nephews, in-laws, cousins, spouses of the above
Mandatory distribution at age 70½	Yes	No	Yes	No	No
Wide investment choices	Yes	Yes	Yes	Employer chooses	Limited by State Plan
Flexibility in uncertain times	Yes	Yes	No	No	Yes
Income (AGI) restrictions	(2021)	(2021)	None	None	None
Married filing joint	\$ 105,000–\$ 125,000	\$ 198,000–\$ 208,000			
Married filing separate	\$ 10,000	\$ 10,000			
Single/head of household	\$ 66,000–\$ 76,000	\$ 125,000–\$ 140,000			
May loans be taken	No	No	No	Yes, in hardship cases	No
Financial aid	No	No	No	N/A	Can be if owned by parent or student
Asset protection	Depends on state law	Depends on state law	Probably	Probably	Probably
Double benefits with other tax provisions	No	No	No	No	No

E. When the Client Has Property Other Than Cash and Wants to Finance Non-Qualified Education Expenses or Benefit Nonfamily Individuals

Often taxpayers do not have cash assets to contribute to a 529 savings plan. Many taxpayers hold most of their wealth in assets, such as the stock market, their homes, rentals, or businesses. In these circumstances, the taxpayer may be able to use savings techniques other than 529 plans to finance education expenses, such as custodianship accounts or trusts.[43] The most common asset is real estate, held in a principal residence, a vacation home, or a rental. In addition, the taxpayer may have traditional assets, such as stocks and bonds. Finally, the taxpayer may have a farm or other operating business.

Section 529 plans are restricted to qualified education expenses and to family members. Other savings mechanisms do not have the same restrictions as do 529 plans. Thus, these savings funds can go toward non-qualified education expenses, such as travel to and from school, clothing, cars, entertainment, etc. In addition, these savings mechanisms work when the beneficiary is a distant relative, a friend, or a partner. Section 529 plans, in contrast, are restricted to certain members of the family.

1. Real Estate and Investment Assets

Real estate can be an excellent way to save for a college education because of its potential to appreciate dramatically. The taxpayer's *principal residence* (and vacation house) can be used for a home equity loan or even sold when the children start college and the parents no longer need a large dwelling. When sold, an exclusion of the gain on a principal residence is $250,000 for single parents and $500,000 for married taxpayers.[44] In addition, rental properties and vacation properties can be sold, refinanced, purchased, or given to the beneficiary while they are in college. In the alternative, these assets can generate income that can be used for non-qualified educational expenses.

Traditional investments, such as stocks and bonds, usually do not have the advantages of investments in tax-favored accounts like 529s. An exception is tax-exempt investments, like municipal bonds. However, these bonds can be risky or yield a low return. Because of this disadvantage, traditional investments would need greater returns to be of equivalent value to the assets in a Section 529 savings account. However, they are great assets for funding custodianship accounts and trusts.

---

43. For more in-depth discussion of these, see Nancy E. Shurtz, Education Planning: Taxes, Trusts, and Techniques chs. 16 (Comparing Section 529s with UGMAs/UTMAs) & 17 (Comparing Section 5291 with Trusts) (ABA 2009).

44. I.R.C. § 121.

CHART 4-8 Traditional Investment Comparison Chart

	Tax-Exempt Securities	T-Bills	Corporate Bonds	Stocks	Mutual Funds	College Sure CD	Real Estate
Tax Advantages	Earnings are tax-free	Interest exempt when proceeds used for QHEE	Taxed at both state and federal levels	Taxed at both state and federal levels but at capital gains rates on dividends and upon sale	Taxed at both state and federal levels	Taxed at both state and federal levels	Rent is taxed at state and federal levels—gain is capital gain or excluded if principal residence
Risk	Very little	Very little	More than T-Bills or Tax Exempts	More than bonds	Less than stocks	Very little	Somewhat
Rate of Return on Growth	Quite low	Low but higher with longer maturities	May not keep up with college inflation	May keep up with college inflation	Moderate returns	Almost keeps up with college inflation	Can keep up with college inflation
Control	Medium	Depends on maturity date	Depends on maturity date	High	High	Low	Medium, depends on economy
Credit Protection	None	None	None	None	None	None	None
Financial Aid	Has an impact depending on who owns	Has an adverse impact when cashed in to pay for college	Has an impact depending on who owns	Has an impact depending on who owns	Has an impact depending on who owns	Has an impact depending on who owns	Has an impact depending on who owns

a. *Uniform Transfer to Minors*

Transfers to minors are yet another way a family can plan for college, but this might not be the most tax-effective method of saving. However, for the right family, this method can be very beneficial. The advantage of using custodianship accounts under the *Uniform Gifts to Minors Act* (UGMA) or the *Uniform Transfers to Minors Act* (UTMA)[45] is that the contributions can consist of property. In addition, no income or contribution restrictions apply when setting up these accounts. Furthermore, the fund can be used for any non-qualified expenses, such as clothes, a car, or a vacation. Lastly, broad investment latitude exists for such accounts and they are easy to administer.

A major problem with these accounts is that there is no tax deferral; income on the account is taxed annually. Under recent legislation, income cannot be shifted to the student until they are 24 years old.[46] Another disadvantage of such an account is that an estate tax is imposed on the custodian if the custodian (usually the parent) dies before the assets in the account are distributed. A third drawback is that the beneficiary will receive the account outright upon reaching 18, 21, or 25 years (depending on state law). Lastly, the account is likely to count against the child for financial aid purposes.

b. *Trusts*

Like the UTMA and UGMA accounts, a *trust* can be funded with property and used for any purpose set forth in the trust. Trusts are always important upon the death of the grantor if education goals have yet to be met. Trusts are also an excellent inter vivos income- and asset-splitting technique for wealthy taxpayers. In any case, the terms of the trust can be used to provide education incentives. The disadvantages of trusts are that they are costly to set up and administer and can also have onerous income tax consequences.

2. Business Property

Family businesses take all forms—from farms to industrial to rental properties. Often these businesses are operated in either the corporate form or noncorporate form, like the *family limited partnerships (FLP)* and the *limited liability companies (LLC)*.[47] FLPs and LLCs cannot be overlooked as potential education financing tools. The typical FLP consists of one or more general partners (usually the parents or grandparents) and one or more limited partners (usually the child or children). The partner(s) manages the assets in the FLP and makes investment

---

45. Uniform Transfers to Minors Act, § 2, 8C, U.L.A. 25 (2000); Uniform Gifts to Minors Act, § 2, 8A, U.L.A. 297 (2000).

46. I.R.C. § 1(g). A "kiddie tax" is imposed on the student at the high-income rates of the trust and estate.

47. *See* Shurtz, *supra* note 43, ch. 18 (Comparing Section 529s with Other Investments), at H. In addition to the LLC and FLP, taxpayers may also use the S corporation or a C corporation form for their business.

CHART 4-9 Comparison of Custodianships, Irrevocable Trusts, and Section 529 Plans

Feature	Custodianships	Irrevocable Trusts	§ 529 Savings Plans
Cash Contribution	No	No	Yes
Income Limit on Owner	No	No	No
Limit on Contribution Amount	No	No	Yes, reasonable education needs
Simple to Establish	Yes	No	Yes
Fiduciary Holds Title	No	Yes	No
Investments	More restricted under UGMA than UTMA	Most flexible	Flexible, depending on state plan
Age of Distribution	Usually age of majority	Anytime	None unless state plan provides
Multiple Beneficiaries	No, but could be earlier upon petition to court	Yes, but lapse of "5 & 5" power problems	No
Unequal Distributions	No	Yes	N/A
Only One Fiduciary	Yes	No	N/A
Fiduciary Entitled to Compensation	No	No	N/A
Fees and Costs	No legal drafting fee or court costs	Financial reporting & drafting document, administration expense	Yes, but vary depending on state and if advisor funds
Can Change Beneficiary	No	Can "spray and sprinkle"	No
Can Revoke the Transfer	No	No	Yes
Liability of Fiduciary	Prudent person rule	Prudence	N/A
Asset Protection	State law controls but usually protection unless donor is custodian	Yes if spendthrift clause	State law controls
Incapacity Planning	Yes	Yes	Special needs accommodated
Periodic Accounting	No, unless requested by interested party	Draft to avoid problem	Yes

(continued)

Feature	Custodianships	Irrevocable Trusts	§ 529 Savings Plans
Donor's Estate	Only if custodian	Not unless has interest under trust	No, unless dies within five years
Fiduciary Death	Includable in estate if fiduciary can affect beneficial enjoyment or use to discharge duty of support	No consequence unless trust holds taxable power or interest	N/A
Gift Tax	Can qualify for per-donee annual exclusion	Can qualify for per-donee annual exclusion	Can qualify for per-donee annual exclusion, and can front load up to five years of gifts in one year
GST Tax	Qualifies if annual exclusion	Qualifies if annual exclusion	Qualifies if annual exclusion
Income Tax	Subject to the "kiddie tax" if beneficiary under the age of 18, or 24 if beneficiary is a dependent student	Depends on terms of trust (taxed to grantor, beneficiary, or trust)	Not taxed if used for QHEE
Make Loans from Assets	Yes, if in best interest of beneficiary	Depends on the terms of the trust (taxed to grantor if loan carries no adequate interest)	No

choices. Similarly, the LLC can be managed by the parents, who can exert substantial control over distributions and investments.

Both of these entities are quite flexible, and provide income, estate, and gift tax advantages, as well as nontax advantages such as control and asset protection. They can be used for active businesses, for investment property (such as securities), and as borrowing tools. They can be amended and adapted to meet the changing needs of the family. Often, they will work better for the family for education purposes than the 529 savings plan. *See* **Chart 4-10**, summarizing and comparing the features of FLP/LLC interests with 529 plans.

CHART 4-10 Comparing FLP/LLCs with 529 Plans

	FLP/LLC Interest	**Section 529**
Contribution Restrictions	No contribution limits. No deduction for contribution (federal or state).	No contribution limits except reasonable education needs. State deduction possible.
Income Tax	Taxed to child but "kiddie tax" applies until full-time student is 24. Also, parents must be paid reasonable salary if service business.	Earnings are tax free when used for qualified expenses. States may allow contribution deduction or credit.
Gift Tax	Per-donee present interest plus marketability and control discounts (unless *Hackl* problem).	Per-donee plus five-year averaging rule.
Estate Tax	If structured as completed gift, then not in parent's estate.	Not included in parent's estate unless he/she dies within five-year averaging rule.
Control	Parent controls distributions and investments as general partner or manager but cannot make child use for education purposes or change beneficiary.	Donor can get fund back and can determine when fund is used, can change beneficiary but has more limited investment control (can change investment strategy once a year).
Asset Protection	Protection against parent's and child's creditors if LLC and limited partner (general partner not as protected).	Depends on state law. Can be protected under federal bankruptcy law.
Financial Aid	Assessed as asset of the owner and reported at fair market value. If considered a business asset, then discounted. Any income is passed through pro rata to owner—even if not distributed and this income is assessed to owner for financial aid purposes.	If parent owns (or if student owns under the federal formula) then assessed as parent's asset. If grandparent owns, then not assessed as asset. Distributions to student for QHEE do not constitute income or resource under federal formula.

F. Conclusion

Because of the significant advantages of the Section 529 plans over the other savings techniques, **Parts II, III**, and **IV** of this book will focus on those plans. **Part II** (Chapters 6 through 14) discusses in depth the requirements and advantages of the 529 savings plan. **Part III** (Chapters 15 and 16) examines the state and institutional prepaid plans, respectively. **Part IV** (Chapters 17 through 19) discusses coordination of 529 plans with other savings techniques, tax benefits, and financial aid. *See* **Chart 4-11** that compares and contrasts the 529 plans to other savings techniques.

CHART 4-11 Savings Incentive Programs (2021)

Program	Income Eligibility (AGI or Modified AGI)				Coverage	Expense Limit	Covered Expenses	Tax Impact
	Married		Single/Head of Household					
	Full	Phased Out	Full	Phased Out				
Qualified Tuition Programs § 529	N/A	N/A	N/A	N/A	Student	Up to 5 times annual exclusion using gift five-year averaging rule	Tuition (up to $ 10,000 for K–12), Fees, Books, Supplies, Required Equipment, Internet, Room, Board, Principal and Interest on $ 10,000 debt for beneficiary and siblings, and Special Needs	Defer tax until withdrawal; available with AOTC or LLC
Coverdell ESA § 530	$ 190,000	$ 220,000	$ 95,000	$ 110,000	Student	$ 2,000/year Contribution	Tuition, Fees, Books, Supplies, Room, Board (Elementary, Secondary, College, Private, Religious)	Defer tax until withdrawal; available with AOTC or LLC
Savings Bonds § 135	$ 124,800	$ 154,800	$ 83,200	$ 98,200	Student	None	Tuition and Fees	Exclude from Income
Traditional IRA § 219 for those who have a retirement plan	$ 105,000	$ 125,000	$ 66,000	$ 67,000	Student	$ 6,000, $ 7,000 if over 50	All	Taxable
Roth IRA § 408 A	$ 198,000	$ 208,000	$ 125,000	$ 140,000	Student	$ 6,000, $ 7,000 if over 50	All	Tax free if account has been established five years

Chapter 5

When Savings Are Not Enough

When the taxpayer has not saved enough for the costs of college, various pay-as-you-go benefits are available. These include tax credits and deductions, as well as loans, grants, scholarships, and student employment. All these benefits can reduce the cost of college—sometimes significantly. When the student has completed his/her education and entered the work force, the code can exclude the discharge of debt from income under certain *loan forgiveness* programs. In addition, a generous *above-the-line deduction* for student loan interest may be available. After the *SECURE Act of 2019*, Section 529 savings plans can be used to pay off a portion of principal or interest on qualified education loans. This chapter briefly discusses these techniques, highlighting their advantages and disadvantages.[1]

A. Pay-as-You-Go Techniques

If the taxpayer has not saved enough, several *pay-as-you-go* techniques may be available to pay (or help pay) for college expenses. Tax benefits include the *American Opportunity Tax Credit* (AOTC), the *Lifetime Learning Credit* (LLC), the trade- or business-related education deduction, and several employment-related exclusions. The above-the-line *tuition and fees deduction* was repealed for taxable years after 2020 but could be revived given its on-again off-again history. Even direct gifts (or inheritances) from relatives might be a possible source of revenue. In addition, financial aid, such as loans, grants, work-study, and scholarships, are all important education planning techniques.

1. For a more detailed analysis of these techniques, see Nancy E. Shurtz, Education Planning: Taxes, Trusts, Techniques (ABA 2009).

1. Tax Benefits

The tax code provides several tax benefits for education. First, current payment of tuition and related expenses can result in an educational credit under Section 25A. Second, the tax code provides a business-related education expense deduction under Section 162 if certain conditions are met. Third, several tax exclusions arise when education can be tied to employment. Fourth, the tax code provides an above-the-line deduction for tuition and fees under Section 222, at least through the end of 2020. Lastly, gifts and inheritances by relatives are excludable by the recipient from federal gross income and can be exempt from the federal estate and gift tax as well.

a. *The Credits*

The *Hope Scholarship Credit* applied to taxpayers prior to 2009. It was a nonrefundable credit equal to 100 percent of the first $1,000 of qualified education expenditures and 50 percent of the next $1,000 of expenditures for a total credit of $1,500, adjusted for inflation. The Hope Credit was only available for the first two years of college. It was a per-student benefit, indexed for inflation, and denied to a convicted drug felon. It covered "qualified tuition and related expenses," such as academic fees.

The *American Recovery and Reinvestment Act of 2009* modified the Hope Credit and renamed it the *American Opportunity Tax Credit* (AOTC). Although this credit has many similarities to the Hope Credit (it is a per-student credit for an eligible student at a qualified institution), it modified that credit by (1) making the credit available for the first four years of post-secondary education, (2) increasing the credit to 100 percent of the first $2,000 of qualified expenses plus 25 percent of the next $2,000 of expenses—for a total of $2,500, (3) expanding the definition of "qualified tuition and related" expenses to include "required course materials," (4) increasing the modified AGI limits (for 2021, the amounts are $80,000 if single/head of household and $160,000 if married with complete phase-outs at $90,000 and $180,000, respectively), (5) making the credit partially refundable, and (6) allowing the credit to offset the alternative minimum tax.

In addition to the AOTC, the code provides for the *Lifetime Learning Credit* (LLC). The qualified expenses only include tuition and fees required in order to enroll in the program or class, and the student need not be enrolled for a set period of time. This credit is nonrefundable and, as its name implies, can be used *any time* for up to 20 percent of $10,000 of expenditures for a maximum credit of $2,000. Unlike the AOTC, it is not denied to convicted drug felons and applies on a per-return, not a per-student basis. After the *Consolidated Appropriations Act of 2021*, the LLC will have the same modified AGI limits as under the AOTC.[2]

2. Before the *Consolidated Appropriations Act*, the LLC had a smaller AGI limit than the AOTC (between $59,000 and $69,000 if single or head of household and between $119,000 and $139,000 for joint returns in 2020).

CHART 5-1 Features of the Education Credits

Feature	AOTC	Lifetime Learning
Qualified Student	Student must attend at least ½ time and not a drug felon	Student need not attend school ½ time and OK if drug felon
Qualified Expenses	"Tuition and related fees" including "required course materials"	Same as AOTC
Qualified Institution	§ 481 HEA	Same as AOTC
Family covered	Taxpayer, spouse, dependent	Same as AOTC
Dollar Limit on Tax Benefit	100% of first $2,000 of qualified expenses and 25% of next $2,000 = $2,500	20% of the first $10,000 (not adjusted for inflation) = $2,000
2021 Phase-Out Limits for Single/Head of Household	$ 80,000–$ 90,000 of MAGI	$ 80,000–$ 90,000 of MAGI
2021 Phase-Out Limits for Married Filing Jointly	$ 160,000–$ 180,000 of MAGI	$ 160,000–$ 180,000 of MAGI
Year Requirement	First four years	Any time during life
Coordination	No double benefit	No double benefit
Return	Per student	Per return
Refundable	Yes	No

b. Education as a Trade or Business Expense

Education-related expenses can be ordinary and necessary business expenses under Section 162 and the associated regulations.[3] Such ordinary and necessary business expenses will qualify as *above-the-line deductions* if the expenses are incurred by the employer, partner, or by an employee, who is reimbursed by his/her employer. If the employee pays for the education-related expenses and is not reimbursed, the expenses are treated as a *miscellaneous itemized deduction* and, after the *TCJA* of 2017, are no longer deductible—at least not until 2026. If the employee pays for the education-related expenses and then is reimbursed by the employer, the employee can exclude the reimbursement from his/her taxable income pursuant to Section 132(d) and Section 132(a)(3)—the *working condition fringe benefit* provisions—if the employee could otherwise deduct the expense under Section 162.

To take a Section 162 deduction (or have a Section 132 exclusion), the taxpayer must meet one of two affirmative tests and must comply with two limitation or disallowance rules under Treas. Reg. §1.162-5. Under the first affirmative test, education-related expenses are deductible if they are incurred to maintain *or*

3. Treas. Reg. § 1.162-5. The current regulations were promulgated in 1967, replacing the earlier 1958 regulations. The old regulations relied on a primary purpose approach that relied on the taxpayer's subjective intent in contrast to the more objective test of the current regulations.

improve skills required by the individual in his/her employment or trade or business.[4] Under the second affirmative test, education-related expenses are deductible if they are incurred to meet the express employer requirement(s) or requirements imposed by applicable law or regulations.[5] In order to deduct education-related expenses, the taxpayer need meet *only one* of these tests—he/she does not have to meet both of them.

With respect to the limitation or disallowance rules, *both* must be met, or the education-related expenses will be denied. Under the first limitation rule, education expenses incurred to meet the minimum education qualifications for the job will not be deductible. Under the second limitation rule, education expenses that open the door to a new trade or business are not deductible. *See* **Chart 5-2** for a decision model matrix.

CHART 5-2:[6] Decision Model for Determining Business/Education Deductions

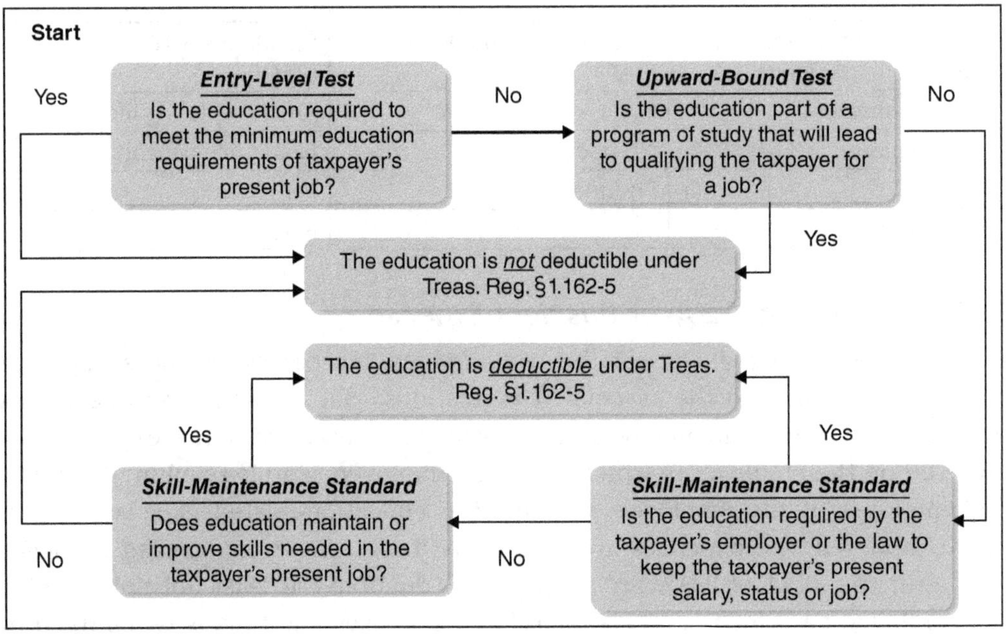

c. *Employment-Related Education Exclusions*

The tax code provides for three employment-related education exclusions. First, under Section 127, an employee can exclude up to $5,250 annually for employer-provided *education assistance*. Second, under Section 117(d), an employee of an educational institution can exclude tuition reduced or discounted by that institution (or a related institution). Third, under Section 132, an employer can pay for a

4. Treas. Reg. § 1.162-5(a)(1).
5. Treas. Reg. § 1.162-5(a)(2).
6. Adapted from IRS Pub. 970: Tax Benefits for Education 67 (2019) and Vincent G. Kalafat, *Rethinking Treasury Regulation § 1.162-5 and Slaying the Monster in the Education Tax Maze*, 80 Notre Dame L. Rev. 2001 (1985).

working condition fringe that involves certain business-related education expenses of the employees, and these can be excluded from the employee's income.

i. Employer-Provided Education Assistance

Up to $5,250 of qualified education-related expenses provided to an employee under an employer-provided *education assistance* program can be excluded from the employee's income.[7] In order to be excludible, such a program must be established by an employer pursuant to a written plan for the benefit of the employees.[8] The plan cannot favor highly compensated employees or principal stockholders owning more than 5 percent in the business.[9] The employer must have a nondiscriminating separate written plan, and reasonable notice of the availability and terms of the provision must be given to the eligible employees. Unlike the working condition fringe benefit discussed later, the employer cannot choose which employees are entitled to this benefit.

The exclusion for employer-provided education assistance is available even if the education is not job related. In addition, it is available for graduate-level courses.[10] "Eligible expenses" include tuition, fees, and similar expenditures as well as books, supplies, and equipment.[11] However, the term "eligible expense" does not include meals, lodging, or transportation.[12] The Treasury Regulations also make clear that tools or supplies provided by the employer will not be considered education assistance if the student is allowed to keep them after completing the course of study.[13] Courses involving sports, games, or hobbies are also not eligible for the exclusion unless there is a reasonable relationship between the course and the employer's business or the course is required as part of the student's degree program.[14] There is no minimum course load to qualify for this provision. All educational institutions qualify, and the student may still receive this exclusion even if they have a felony conviction.

The employees cannot be allowed to choose cash in lieu of the education-related benefit.[15] Thus, the education-related benefit plan cannot be part of a Section 125 cafeteria plan.[16] Only employees may claim the benefit. Eligible employees include those currently employed, on leave, retired, disabled, or laid off, as long as the benefits are provided because of the employment relationship.[17] If the

---

7. I.R.C. § 127(a)(2). *See also* IRS Pub. 970: Tax Benefits for Education 65 (2019).
8. I.R.C. § 127(b).
9. Treas. Reg. § 1.127-2(e) (stocks of children and parents are attributed to each other).
10. Treas. Reg. § 1.127-2(e)(4). Over the years the graduate/undergraduate requirements have gone back and forth, first allowing graduate school, then not allowing graduate school, and then (since 2002) allowing graduate school.
11. Treas. Reg. § 1.127(c)(1)(B).
12. Treas. Reg. § 1.127-2(c)(3)(ii).
13. Treas. Reg. § 1.127-2(c)(3)(i).
14. Treas. Reg. § 1.127-2(c)(3)(iii).
15. Treas. Reg. § 1.127-2(c)(2).
16. Treas. Reg. §§ 125(f), 127(b)(4).
17. Treas. Reg. § 1.127-2(d).

employer provides education assistance to the employee's spouse, domestic partner, or dependent children, the exclusion will not be allowed.

Any education benefits provided by the employer in excess of the $5,250 cap may be excluded as a *working condition fringe benefit* (WCFB)[18] if the employee could deduct the education expenses under Regulations § 1.162-5 (discussed in section b above). When the employee is ineligible to deduct these expenses, then the excess over $5,250 will be considered compensation to the employee and will be subject to income tax.

ii. Tuition Reduction at an Educational Institution

For employees of education institutions, Section 117(d) allows an exclusion for the *tuition reduction* to the employee, his/her spouse, and dependents, as long as the institution has a non-discriminating plan. The exclusion will fail, however, if the institution's plan discriminates in favor of highly compensated employees. Therefore, the benefit must be available on substantially the same basis for each member of a group of employees, and the employer must define the group under a reasonable classification.[19] Including employees such as maintenance workers and secretarial staff, as well as professors in the group, assures that the plan is nondiscriminatory.

EXAMPLE 5-1: Nogero provides tuition reduction for faculty members and their dependents. Secretaries, janitors, and other staff are excluded from the plan. The plan fails the antidiscrimination rules. Thus, faculty utilizing the plan cannot claim a Section 117(d) exclusion for the tuition reduction benefit. They must include the tuition reduction in their compensation income.

The tuition reduction benefit, as the name suggests, only applies to tuition; the tuition reduction benefit does not apply to books, supplies, room and board, or other education expenses. It also applies only to undergraduate education, unless the graduate student is engaged in research or teaching activities for the educational organization.[20] Often, schools have reciprocal agreements with similar institutions. Pursuant to these reciprocal agreements, tuition reduction benefits are extended to employees of member institutions, and these benefits also receive favorable treatment. Typically, reciprocal agreements will be seen between institutions of similar academic esteem or in similar geographical areas. For example, reciprocal agreements can be found between Ivy League schools, as well as between state schools in the same state system.

---

18. I.R.C. § 132.
19. *See* IRS Pub. 970: Tax Benefits for Education 8 (2019).
20. I.R.C. § 117(d)(5); FSA 2002-31016 (The IRS has held in a field service advice that graduate tuition reductions for an employee cannot qualify as a working condition fringe.).

For purposes of the *tuition reduction program,* Section 117(d) defines "employee" as including the "employee, the employee's spouse, and the employee's dependent children." Section 117(d) does not apply to domestic partners. In addition, the intent of Section 117(d) was to cover existing employees and their families, not students who become employees under scholarship, tuition waiver, or other education benefits provided by the education institution.

iii. Working Condition Fringe

Working condition fringe benefits (WCFB) paid by the employer are excludable by the employee under Section 132(a)(3) and 132(d) when such payments would have been deductible by the employee under Section 162(a). Therefore, if the employee qualifies under Treas. Reg. § 1.162-5 (discussed in section b above), the employee can exclude this benefit when paid directly by his/her employer. When the employer pays cash directly to the employee, the employee must use the payment for the intended purpose, and the employer must verify this purpose.[21]

The qualifying expenditures for purposes of the WCFB include all expenditures that would be allowed under the education regulations—tuition, fees, books, supplies, equipment, travel, lodging, and qualifying meals.[22] All of these education costs must be job related.[23] The definition of "qualified employee" who is eligible for this exclusion extends to a director of the employer, an independent contractor who performs services for the employer, and a partner who performs services for the partnership.[24]

Planning Pointer

Working condition fringe benefits (WCFBs) offer many advantages over the employer-provided education assistance program. First, there are no dollar limits on WCFB. Second, the WCFB can extend to more types of beneficiaries. Third, WCFBs cover more types of expenses. Fourth, no formal written plan is required. Finally, an employer can discriminate in favor of highly compensated employees or employer/owners. The major disadvantage of the WCFB is that the education must be deductible under the Section 162 regulations, which establish strict requirements. Another possible disadvantage is the WCFB must be job-related, whereas education assistance need not be related to job functions. *See* **Chart 5-3** for a comparison of employee education benefits.

---

21. Treas. Reg. § 1.132-5(a)(1)(v). If the employee does not provide adequate accounting, the payment is compensation. The substantiation requirement of Section 274(d) applies.

22. Treas. Reg. § 1.162-5(e). Under the *Consolidated Appropriations Act of 2021*, 100 percent of meals are allowed if eaten at restaurants, otherwise 50 percent of meals qualify. *See* I.R.C. § 274(n).

23. Rev. Rul. 76-352, 1976-2 C.B. 37, *as amplified by* Rev. Rul. 78-184, 1978-1 C.B. 304.

24. Treas. Reg. § 1.132-1(b)(2).

CHART 5-3 Comparison of Employee Education Benefits

	Education Assistance Program (§ 127)	Working Condition Fringe (§ 132(d))	Qualified Tuition Reduction (§ 117(d))	Ordinary Business Expense Deduction (§ 162)
Who Can Benefit	Employee	Employee, director of employer, an independent contractor who performs services for the employer, and partners performing services for partnership	Employee, spouse, dependent children	Any worker-employee, employer, sole proprietor/partner
Type of Qualifying Expense	Tuition, fees, books, supplies, equipment	Tuition, fees, books, supplies, equipment, transportation, qualifying meals, lodging, travel	Only tuition	Tuition, fees, books, supplies, equipment, transportation, qualifying meals, lodging, travel
Level of Education	Both undergraduate and graduate level courses	Both undergraduate and graduate but must qualify under § 162	Undergraduate, unless graduate engaged in research or teaching for the institution	Both undergraduate and graduate but must qualify under § 162
Job-related Requirement	No	Yes	No	Yes
Double Benefits	No	No	No	No
Dollar Limits	$ 5,250	None	None	None
Other Limitations	No floor limitation since exclusion	No floor limitation since exclusion	No floor limitation since exclusion	If unreimbursed employee, then miscellaneous itemized deduction and not allowed until 2026 (§ 67)

d. The Tuition and Fees Deduction

As of the writing of this book, the *tuition and fees deduction* has been repealed by the *Consolidated Appropriations Act of 2021*. However, because of its on-again off-again tax nature, we will discuss it briefly here. Section 222 was originally enacted by the *Economic Growth & Tax Relief Reconciliation Act (EGTRRA) of 2001* to allow for taxpayers with income levels slightly above the phase-out levels for the American Opportunity Credit and the Lifetime Learning Credit to receive an above-the-line tax deduction. However, the phase-out level was never indexed for inflation and therefore, in almost every circumstance, it will be better for the taxpayer to take the credits.

This *tuition and fees deduction*, slated to disappear under the EGTRRA after 2005, was extended to December 31, 2007, by the Tax Relief and Health Care Act of 2006, and to December 31, 2009, by the Emergency Economic Stabilization Act of 2008.[25] It was later extended by the American Taxpayer Relief Act of 2012 and expired on December 31, 2013. The Taxpayer Certainty and Disaster Tax Relief Act of 2019 extended this tax benefit through December 31, 2020. The *Consolidated Appropriations Act of 2021* repealed the provision for tax years 2021 and beyond. Given its history, it may be revived in the future, but the authors of this book think that it should not be reinstated as it complicates the rules and is never going to be better than the tax benefits of the credits.

Under Section 222, the student or parent taxpayer may take the deduction. Like the education credits, the deduction is allowed for the taxpayer's own education expenses or for expenses the taxpayer pays for his/her spouse or his/her dependent.[26] The taxpayer may deduct $4,000 of "qualified tuition and related expenses," as long as their adjusted gross income does not exceed certain amounts. For tax year 2020, single and head-of-household taxpayers who have a modified AGI of $65,000 or less ($130,000 for joint filers) may deduct up to $4,000. If the taxpayer's modified AGI is between $65,000 and $80,000 ($130,000 and $160,000 for joint filers), the maximum deduction is $2,000. Taxpayers with modified AGIs above $80,000 ($160,000 for joint filers) are not allowed to take the deduction.[27] The Section 222 deduction has not been indexed for inflation, perhaps a result of the fact that Section 222 seemed scheduled to expire (sunset) after December 31, 2009.[28] However, any taxpayer qualifying for this deduction is not eligible to take any of the education credits.[29]

Like the credits, the deduction is not allowed for individuals who are married and file separately.[30] It is also not allowed for a nonresident alien who did not elect to be treated as a resident alien for tax purposes. Also, a taxpayer-student cannot take the deduction if another person is entitled to claim the student as a dependent.[31] Unlike the credits, if the eligible student qualifies as a dependent, the parents can claim the deduction only if they also pay the qualified expenses.[32]

---

25. I.R.C. § 222(e).
26. I.R.C. § 222(a), (c)(3), (d)(1) (referring to I.R.C. § 25A(g)).
27. I.R.C. § 222(b)(2)(B).
28. *Id.*
29. I.R.C. § 222(c)(2)(A).
30. I.R.C. § 222(d)(4).
31. I.R.C. § 222(d)(4), (c)(3).
32. I.R.C. § 222(a); IRS Pub. 970: Tax Benefits for Education 39 (2019); I.R.C. § 222(d)(1).

Unlike other education benefit rules, if someone else pays the qualified expenses of a dependent student, such as the student or grandparent, no one is allowed the tuition and fees deduction.

e. *Gifts from Relatives*

One of the best ways to finance college education is through gifts, either from parents, grandparents, or other family members. Gifts are excludable from the recipient's gross income under Section 102 as long as the donor makes the transfer with a "detached and disinterested generosity."[33] Most direct gifts will also qualify for the Section 2503(b) *per-donee annual exclusion* for gift tax purposes. Additional gifts can be excluded under the *Section 2503(e) transfer*, which provides an unlimited exclusion for the donor when payments of tuition are made directly to the education institution. These gifts will also provide significant estate and generation-skipping opportunities to the donor. Furthermore, when tuition is paid for by gifts, the education credits may still be claimed by the donee or the donee's parents. For wealthy taxpayers, the Section 2503(e) payment of tuition can be combined with the Section 529 plan payment of room and board and the Section 2503(b) payments to cover other expenses.

The problem with counting on gifts from relatives to pay for college is that the transfers can be made only while the donor is living. However, it is also possible (although perhaps unfortunate) that an inheritance can pay for all the education expenses. Inheritances, like gifts, are excludable from the recipient's federal gross income.

Planning Pointer

A wealthy grandparent can make a *Section 2503(e) transfer* directly to the educational institution for tuition. Related expenses, books, supplies, and room and board can be covered either through a Section 529 plan and/or with the Section 2503(b) per-donee annual gift tax exclusion. The taxpayer should be careful in making gifts under Section 2503(b) so that the per-donee annual exclusion (which is $15,000 in 2021) is not exceeded with birthday gifts, holiday presents, and other transfers, in addition to non-tuition college expenses. When the exclusion is exceeded, a Form 709 gift tax return must be filed.

33. *See* Commissioner v. Duberstein, 363 U.S. 278 (1960).

2. Financial Aid

If the client saves the wrong way, he/she may be precluded from receiving financial aid. Similarly, if grandparents give the wrong way, financially disadvantaged (poor) grandchildren may be prevented from receiving financial aid. Sometimes simple planning steps can be taken to qualify the client for financial aid. An important role of the advisor is to ensure that optimum results occur; this means the client should be able to benefit from gifts from relatives and from free money, as well as other financial aid. Approximately 72 percent of students receive some form of financial aid as undergraduates.[34]

Planning Pointer

A good planner will test family income and assets under both the federal and institutional financial aid formulae. *See* **Chapter Nineteen: Coordinating Section 529 Plans with Financial Aid.** By applying today's college costs with the family's current income and assets, the planner will get a good sense as to whether the family will qualify for financial aid. Grants and scholarships are the best forms of financial aid because they do not have to be repaid. Also, the student may be eligible for work-study. Lastly, subsidized and unsubsidized loans are available.

a. Loans

Loans are making up a growing percentage of college financial aid and can have a significant impact on the student's future opportunities as well as on the parents' retirement and other financial plans. Over two-thirds of bachelor's degree recipients in the class of 2019 graduated with student loans, an average of around $30,000 per borrower.[35] Of the 14 percent of parents who took out loans for the children, the average loan was $37,200.[36] Loans can be a way that parents share the costs of college with their children; loans can allow both the student and the parents to bear the burden of college expenses together. They can be subsidized or unsubsidized and can be taken out by the student or the parent. Increasingly, loans are being replaced with grants for lower and middle-income families who attend well-endowed colleges. In some situations, loans can be forgiven and not taxed. Payment of loans can also help the student build a credit record.

---

34. Danielle Douglas-Gabriel, *Use of Financial Aid Continues to Grow, Though Fewer Students Are Borrowing for College*, WASH. POST (Jan. 30, 2018), https://www.washingtonpost.com/news/grade-point/wp/2018/01/30/use-of-financial-aid-continues-to-grow-though-fewer-students-are-borrowing-for-college/.

35. Mark Kantrowitz, *Average Student Loan Debt at Graduation*, SAVINGFORCOLLEGE.COM (July 23, 2020), https://www.savingforcollege.com/article/average-student-loan-debt-at-graduation?sfc_template=article_layout_v2.

36. *Id.*

The major loans available under the federal programs are the *direct subsidized*, the *direct unsubsidized loans*, and the *PLUS loans*. Over half of federal loans are subsidized, and these loans are available to undergraduate students in need. The unsubsidized loans are available to graduate and undergraduate students regardless of need. The PLUS loans are available to graduate and professional students and to parents. The borrower may be responsible for making interest payments on the loan while the student is enrolled in school. *See* **Chart 5-4.**

b. Grants and Work Study

Grants make up around 59 percent of financial aid. They can come from the federal government, the state government, the college, and private or nonprofit organizations. The Department of Education offers four types of federal grants: the *Pell Grant*, the *Federal Supplemental Educational Opportunity Grants* (ESEOG), the Iraq and Afghanistan Service Grants, and the Teacher Education Assistance for College and Higher Education (TEACH) Grants. *See* **Chart 5-4.**

Work study and federal tax benefits make up the remainder (or 8% in 2018–2019).[37] *Work study* provides part-time jobs for undergraduate and graduate students with financial need. The program allows the student to earn money to help pay for his/her education-related expenses. At some prestigious schools, work-study and grants make up most of the financial aid. Additionally, certain grants are available to high-income taxpayers.

c. Scholarships

Scholarships are given by numerous bodies—the schools, the state, tax-exempt organizations, and private organizations. Since many scholarships are based on merit, they can be available to high-income taxpayers. Thus, scholarships can be a planning tool utilized by all families. With the importance of the *U.S. News & World Report*, merit-based scholarships are increasing in number and size. Scholarships have the tax advantage of being exempt from tax as long as they are for tuition and related fees—not room, board, or work experience.

---

37. *See Trends in Student Aid 2019*, CollegeBoard, https://research.collegeboard.org/pdf/trends-student-aid-2019-full-report.pdf.

CHART 5-4 Summary of Federal Aid for Academic Year 2020–2021[38]

Federally Funded Student Aid	
Program	**Benefit**
Federal Pell Grant	Up to $ 6,495 per year. • Awarded to undergraduate students who show exceptional financial need, and who have not earned another higher-education degree. • The amount awarded depends on: (1) your Expected Family Contribution (EFC); (2) cost of attendance of the specific school; (3) whether the student will attend full-time or part-time; and (4) whether the plans are to attend for a full academic year or less. • Only has to be repaid under certain circumstances. • If certain requirements are met, an eligible student may receive up to 150% of their scheduled Pell Grant award for a single year. • If the student's parent died as a result of military service in Iraq, Afghanistan, or in the line of duty as a public safety officer, student may be eligible to receive a larger Pell Grant. • Students incarcerated in a federal or state institution are not eligible.
Federal Supplemental Education Opportunity Grant (FSEOG)	$ 100 to $ 4,000 per year. • Allocated by the institution based on the student's exceptional financial need and other resources. • Pell Grant recipients take priority. • Funds depend on availability at school. • Incarcerated students are eligible, but unlikely to receive based on priority guidelines.
Academic Competitiveness Grant (ACG)	1st year: Up to $ 750. 2nd year: Up to $ 1,300. • For Pell-eligible students enrolled at least half-time in their first or second year of study or in a certificate program of at least one year at a degree-granting school.
National Science and Mathematics Access to Retain Talent Grant (National SMART Grant)	Up to $ 4,000 a year. • For Pell-eligible students enrolled at least half-time in third or fourth year (or fifth year of a five-year program) majoring in certain subject areas with at least a 3.0 cumulative GPA.

(continued)

38. All dollar figures are from the 2021–2022 academic year as listed in Federal Student Grant Programs, https://studentaid.gov/sites/default/files/federal-grant-programs.pdf. *See also* https://studentaid.gov/.

Federally Funded Student Aid	
Program	**Benefit**
Iraq and Afghanistan Service Grant	Up to $ 6,495 a year. • To be eligible, must **not** be eligible for Pell Grant due to your EFC, but **must** meet the remaining Pell Grant requirements. • For students with a parent or guardian who died after the events of 9/11 as a result of military service in Iraq or Afghanistan. To qualify, a student must have been under the age of 24 at the time of his/her parent or guardian's death or enrolled in college or career school at least part time.
Teacher Education Assistance for College and Higher Education (TEACH) Grant	Up to $ 3,772 a year. • For undergraduate and graduate students who are taking or will be taking course work necessary to become an elementary or secondary teacher. • To be eligible, must meet basic eligibility requirements for the federal student aid programs, complete the Free Application for Federal Student Aid (FAFSA) form, maintain a certain GPA (generally 3.25), and receive TEACH Grant counseling. • Recipient **must** sign an Agreement to Serve saying that they will teach full-time in a designated teacher shortage area for four complete years (within eight years of completing academic program) at an elementary or secondary school serving children from low-income families in a high-need field.
Federal Direct Subsidized Loan	Up to $ 3,500 for dependent students for first year of undergraduate. Up to $ 3,500 for independent students for first year of undergraduate. • Available to undergraduate students with financial need. • School determines how much a student may borrow; amount cannot exceed a student's financial need. • US Department of Education pays interest on a Direct Subsidized Loan (1) while the student is enrolled at least half-time, and (2) for the first six months after the student leaves school, and (3) during a period of deferment. • Students incarcerated in a federal or state institution are not eligible.

Federally Funded Student Aid	
Program	**Benefit**
Federal Direct Unsubsidized Loan	Up to $ 2,000 for dependent students for first year of undergraduate. Up to $ 6,000 for independent students for first year of undergraduate. • Available to undergraduate and graduate students; **no** requirement of financial need. • School determines how much a student may borrow based on the cost of attendance and other financial aid the student received. • Student is responsible for paying the interest—if student does not pay interest while in school, during grace periods, or deferment periods, the interest will accrue and be capitalized. • Students incarcerated in a federal or state institution are not eligible.
Federal PLUS Loan	• Maximum amount is cost of attendance minus any other financial aid student receives—no minimum amount. • Loan to graduate and professional students and for parent of dependent undergraduates. • Always unsubsidized. • Borrower is responsible for all interest. Interest on loans fixed at 5.3% after July 1, 2020. • Students incarcerated in a federal or state institution are not eligible.
Federal Work-Study (FWS)	No annual minimum or maximum amounts. • Funds provided by government to institution for part-time student employment. • Student can be undergraduate or graduate, full-time or part-time. • Incarcerated students are eligible, but unlikely to receive based on priority guidelines.

B. The Impact of Financial Aid and Tax Benefits on the Costs of College

Students and families rarely pay the "sticker price" for college. Grants, scholarships, and tax benefits reduce the average price that students and families actually pay for college. Financial aid that comes in the form of grants and scholarships does not have to be paid back. But much of financial aid comes in the form of loans, much of which are unsubsidized. Even high-income taxpayers are eligible for loans and scholarships and can also benefit from many of the tax subsidies.

According to the college board, in 2019–2020, undergraduate students received an average of $14,940 per FTE (full-time equivalent) student in financial aid comprised of the following: $9,850 in grants, $4,090 in federal loans, $920 in education tax credits and deductions, and $80 in Federal Work-Study.[39] Graduate students received an average of $27,310 per FTE student in financial aid: $9,260 in grants, $17,470 in federal loans, $520 in tax benefits, and $60 in work-study.[40]

For the 2018–2019 *academic year,* over $93 billion in financial aid came in the form of loans. Almost $16.3 billion came from education tax benefits. Whereas, in contrast, *PELL grants* accounted for approximately $28.2 billion in financial aid. PELL grants are Federal grants offered to undergraduates from low-income households; PELL grants are the largest need-based grants. Work study accounted for slightly over $1 billion in aid. *See* **Chart 5-5.**

CHART 5-5 Estimated Undergraduate Student Aid by Source for Academic Year 2018–2019 (*Current Dollars* in Billions)[41]

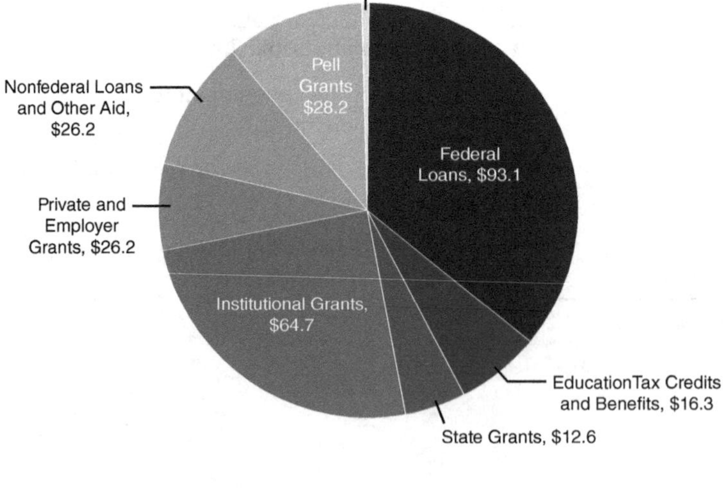

39. *See Trends in College Pricing and Student Aid 2020*, CollegeBoard, https://pnpi.org/college-board-trends-in-college-pricing-and-student-aid-2020/ (last visited May 12, 2021).

40. *Id.*

41. *See Trends in College Pricing and Student Aid 2020*, CollegeBoard, https://research.collegeboard.org/pdf/trends-college-pricing-student-aid-2020.pdf.

Ironically, many of the most expensive schools have the most generous financial aid programs. As **Chart 5-6** illustrates, some of the best schools (Princeton, Harvard, and Yale) with the best values, as indicated in the 2020 U.S. News Best Colleges ranking, offer some of the most generous financial aid packages. Some of these schools discount their tuition costs by over 60 percent and give aid to over 50 percent of students, including many middle-income taxpayers.[42]

CHART 5-6 Great Schools, Great Prices (2020–2021)[43]

Rank of School (State) (*Public)	Cost Before any Grants (tuition only, not including room and board)	% of Students Who Receive Need Based Grants	Average Cost After Grants
1. Harvard University (MA)	$ 54,002	52%	$ 14,898
2. Princeton University (NJ)	$ 53,890	62%	$ 16,014
3. Gallaudet University (DC)	$ 17,038	89%	$ 11,493
4. Yale University (CT)	$ 57,700	54%	$ 17,718
5. Massachusetts Institute of Technology (MA)	$ 53,818	62%	$ 20,350
6. Columbia University (NY)	$ 64,380	49%	$ 20,517
7. Stanford University (CA)	$ 56,169	50%	$ 21,070
8. Rice University (TX)	$ 51,107	42%	$ 19,102
9. Vanderbilt University (TN)	$ 54,158	49%	$ 20,906
10. Dartmouth College (NH)	$ 59,458	48%	$ 23,279
11. Brigham Young University—Provo (UT)	$ 5,970 (Latter-day Saint total) $ 11,940 (non–Latter-day saint total)[44]	39%	$ 13,524
12. California Institute of Technology (CA)	$ 56,862	50%	$ 24,705
13. Duke University (NC)	$ 60,488	44%	$ 23,874
14. University of North Carolina—Chapel Hill (NC)*	$ 9,021 (in-state) $ 36,200 (out-of-state)	36%	$ 19,508
15. Northwestern University (IL)	$ 58,701	45%	$ 25,970

(continued)

42. Richard Vedder, *A Story behind Tuition Breaks Tangled in Ivy-Covered Walls*, Register Guard (Jan. 27, 2008).

43. *Best Value Schools* (2020–2021 Edition), U.S. News & World Report, https://www.usnews.com/best-colleges/rankings/national-universities/best-value.

44. *See Cost of Attendance*, BYU Enrollment Servs., https://enrollment.byu.edu/financialaid/cost-of-attendance (last visited Apr. 29, 2021).

Rank of School (State) (*Public)	Cost Before any Grants (tuition only, not including room and board)	% of Students Who Receive Need Based Grants	Average Cost After Grants
16. John Hopkins University (MD)	$ 57,010	51%	$ 26,855
17. University of Pennsylvania (PA)	$ 60,042	45%	$ 26,783
18. Brown University (RI)	$ 60,696	42%	$ 25,476
19. University of Chicago (IL)	$ 59,298	40%	$ 27,806
20. Washington University in St. Louis (MO)	$ 57,386	41%	$ 26,185
21. Lehigh University (PA)	$ 55,260	41%	$ 23,720
22. University of Rochester (NY)	$ 58,208	55%	$ 28,629
23. Emory University (GA)	$ 53,868	46%	$ 28,945
24. Wake Forest University (NC)	$ 57,760	28%	$ 25,902
25. Cornell University (NY)	$ 59,316	46%	$ 31,312
26. University of Notre Dame (IN)	$ 57,699	46%	$ 31,811
27. Clark University (MA)	$ 48,602	63%	$ 27,761
28. Tufts University (MA)	$ 60,862	34%	$ 28,846
29. Georgetown University (DC)	$ 57,928	36%	$ 30,557
30. Carnegie Mellon University (PA)	$ 58,924	38%	$ 31,616

Savings can reduce the need for loans, which sometimes carry high interest rates that may not be deductible,[45] but saving for college will not necessarily disqualify the family from financial aid. Savings are considered assets, and assets of the parent are assessed at roughly 3 to 6 percent to determine the family's ability to pay for college. Therefore, savings in the parent's names will allow the parent to retain 94 to 97 percent of his/her assets if the student otherwise qualifies for financial aid. The student's assets are assessed at slightly higher amounts—20 percent under the federal methodology and 25 percent under the institutional methodology. Thus, savings in the student's name will have a more adverse impact on financial aid. However, some student savings, such as those in 529 plans and Coverdells, are favorably treated under the federal financial aid formula. Similarly, savings in the grandparents' name will have no effect on financial aid until used to pay for the student's cost of attendance. Then they may count as student income.

Income is generally assessed at much higher rates than assets. Student income is assessed at 50 percent under both the federal and institutional formulae. Parent's

45. *See* **Chapter Nineteen: Coordinating Section 529 Plans with Financial Aid.**

contribution of income for college varies from 22 percent to 47 percent depending on factors such as whether the parent has other kids in college, his/her age, and other factors. Under the federal formula, those with less than $50,000 of gross income who file the simplified tax form have zero contribution required. (*See* **Chart 5-7**.)

CHART 5-7 Expected Family Contributions

	Federal Methodology	Institutional Methodology
Grandparent's Assets	-0-	-0-
Parent's Assets	5.64%	3–5%
Parent's Income	22–47%	46%
Student's Assets	20%*	25%
Student's Income	50%	50%

*Recent legislation lowered this student asset rate from 35% to 20%.

C. Benefits after Graduation When the Student Has Debt

The tax code provides three tax benefits involving debt payment for student loans that usually occur after college graduation. First, Section 221 allows an above-the-line *student loan interest deduction* of up to $2,500 as long as the taxpayer has a modified AGI of less than a certain amount. Second, Section 108(f)(1) provides for an exclusion when debt is discharged or forgiven for taxpayers working in certain fields (such as public interest). Third, Section 529 allows the funds from the account to be used to pay off $10,000 of qualified student debt.

1. Student Loan Interest Deduction

To claim the above-the-line (ATL) student loan deduction of $2,500, the taxpayer must meet seven requirements.[46] First, the taxpayer must have a legal obligation to make the interest payments under the "qualified education loan."[47] Second, the payments must actually be of "interest."[48] Third, the interest must have accrued on loans incurred while attending an "eligible educational institution."[49] Fourth, the loan proceeds must have been used for "qualified higher education expenses."[50] Fifth, the taxpayer must not have more than a certain amount of adjusted gross income.[51] Sixth, the taxpayer may not be claimed as a dependent of another or be married, filing separately.[52] And lastly, certain reporting requirements must be met.

46. *See* Treas. Reg. § 1.221-1(b).
47. Treas. Reg. § 1.221-1(b)(1).
48. Courts have defined the term "interest" for income tax purposes as compensation paid for the use or forbearance of money. *See, e.g.*, Deputy v. Du Pont, 308 U.S. 488 (1940).
49. I.R.C. § 221(d)(2).
50. *Id.*
51. I.R.C. § 221(b)(2).
52. I.R.C. § 221(c), (e)(2); Treas. Reg. § 1.221-1(b)(2).

For purposes of Section 221, "interest" includes the following: (1) qualified stated interest as defined in Treas. Reg. § 1.1273-1(c) (i.e., interest that is unconditionally payable in cash or in property, or that will be constructively received under Section 451, at least annually at a single fixed rate) and (2) *original issue discount* including capitalized interest and certain loan origination fees.[53] Interest on revolving lines of credit, including credit card debt, is student loan interest if the borrower uses the line of credit (or credit card) only to pay qualified higher education expenses.[54] Interest on refinanced student loans, including consolidation loans, and collapsing loans, is qualified. *Original issue discount* is the excess of a loan's stated redemption price at maturity (all payments due under the loan other than qualified state interest payments) over its issue price (the amount originally lent). *Capitalized interest* is defined as any accrued and unpaid interest on a qualified education loan that, in accordance with the terms of the loan, is added by the lender to the outstanding principal balance of the loan. Loan *origination fees* paid by the borrower other than for property or services provided by the lender are included in the definition of original issue discount. To be a deductible loan origination fee, the fee must be for the use of money rather than for property or services (such as commitment fees or processing costs) provided by the lender.

An "eligible educational institution" is any college, university, vocational school, or other post-secondary educational institution described in Section 481 of the Higher Education Act of 1965 as in effect on 8/5/97 and certified by the U.S. Department of Education as eligible to participate in student aid programs administered by the Department. In addition, it includes an institution that conducts an internship or residency program leading to a degree or certificate awarded by an institution or a hospital or a health care facility that offers postgraduate training. If the higher education institution loses its eligibility status, the taxpayer may still take a deduction as long as it was qualified while he/she was enrolled.[55]

The student loan interest deduction is allowed for loans used for "qualified higher education expenses" (QHEE). These include tuition, fees assessed for the student's workload, room, board,[56] books, equipment, and other necessary expenses (such as transportation).[57] All expenses are covered to the extent they are included in the costs of attendance for federal student aid purposes. They also include amounts to attend graduate school. The double benefit rules apply to this tax deduction, so the taxpayer must coordinate this with other tax provisions.[58]

---

53. Treas. Reg. § 1.221-1(f).

54. *See* IRS Pub. 970: Tax Benefits for Education 31–36 (2019).

55. Treas. Reg. § 1.221-1.

56. The cost of room and board can be (1) the allowance for room and board that was included in the cost of attendance for federal financial aid purposes for a particular academic period, (2) the actual amount charged if the student is residing in university housing, or (3) for all other students, the amount reasonably incurred by such student for room and board. *See* 20 U.S.C. § 108711-(3).

57. Treas. Reg. § 1.221-1(e)(2).

58. *See* **Chapter Eighteen: Coordinating Section 529 Plans with Tax Benefits**.

The modified AGI limitations are indexed for inflation after 2001.[59] In 2021 this deduction is phased out for taxpayers who have modified AGI above $70,000 ($140,000 for married taxpayers filing jointly). The interest deduction is gradually phased out until it is no longer available for taxpayers once their modified AGI is above $85,000 ($170,000 for married taxpayers filing jointly).[60] The deduction is not allowed for those married filing separately.[61]

Generally, a taxpayer can claim the deduction if he/she is legally obligated to pay the interest on the qualified student loan and actually pays the interest on that loan. If someone makes a payment of interest on the taxpayer's behalf, the taxpayer will be treated as receiving the payment (for example, as compensation from an employer or gift from a relative) and as having paid the interest.[62]

Section 6050S sets forth reporting requirements with regard to qualified education loan interest. Lenders engaged in a trade or business and certain payees, including governmental units that receive payments of interest that aggregate $600 or more on one or more qualified education loans, must file Form 1098-E (by March 31 if electronic copy) and must furnish written information statements to taxpayers by January 31 to assist both in determining any interest deduction allowable for the tax year. Interest is defined to include state interest, loan origination fees (other than those for providing services), and capitalized interest.

2. Student Loan Forgiveness

Section 108(f) allows the taxpayer an exclusion for a discharge of indebtedness if the loan is a "student loan" and was "made by . . . the United States" in order "to assist the individual in attending" a college or university, and the individual works for a certain period of time in a "certain profession for any of a broad class of employers." Therefore, to qualify for the Section 108(f) *loan forgiveness* exclusion, several conditions must be met: (1) the taxpayer must work for the government, a tax-exempt organization, or an eligible educational institution; (2) the taxpayer must work at the particular employment for a defined period of time; and (3) the discharge of the taxpayer's student loan(s) must occur pursuant to a written plan. In addition, the loan must have been made by a qualified lender (i.e., a government lender) to assist the borrower in attending an eligible higher education institution.

One example of when Section 108(f) will apply is when a tax-exempt educational institution discharges student debt in exchange for services. Another typical example of a discharge that qualifies arises in the health context. If a nonprofit organization entices doctors and/or nurses to work in rural or urban areas and the nonprofit discharges part or all of the doctor or nurse's student loan debt, then no income will result from this forgiveness if the forgiveness otherwise qualifies

59. I.R.C. § 221(f).
60. Treas. Reg. § 1.221-1(d).
61. I.R.C. § 221(e)(2).
62. IRS Pub. 970: Tax Benefits for Education 34 (2019).

under Section 108. The underlying tax policy recognizes that these individuals will earn less money, often working in a less desirable geographical area than their counterparts in the private sector, and thus deserve a tax benefit for their work.

EXAMPLE 5-2: Ben has $20,000 in student loan debt. He is offered a job with the State of New York. New York's offer also includes a provision for the discharge of Ben's entire student loan debt. According to a written plan between Ben and his employer, Ben must work two years before the loan is discharged. All three of Section 108(f)'s requirements are met. Thus, Ben may exclude the entire amount of $20,000 of discharge of indebtedness income.

Because the double benefit limitation does not apply to Section 108, the taxpayer is not precluded from using other education tax benefits at the same time. For example, if the taxpayer had been making student loan payments and received this discharge, the taxpayer would not be required to recapture student loan interest deductions taken pursuant to Section 221.

In general, loan forgiveness will arise for the following workers: (1) child-care; (2) teachers; (3) Vista and Peace Corp volunteers; (4) those in the military; 5) those pursuing public interest law jobs; and (6) those in other related (including health) fields.[63]

3. Section 529 Payment of Loans

The *SECURE Act of 2019* expanded the definition of "qualified higher education expenses" to include the payment of principal or interest on any qualified education loan up to $10,000 for the *designated beneficiary* (DB) of the Section 529 plan or the DB's siblings. The $10,000 is a total limit, not a per-year limit.

EXAMPLE 5-3: Ben is the designated beneficiary of a Section 529 savings plan, and he borrowed $10,000 to pay for his undergraduate qualified expenses. Ben has three siblings who also borrowed the same amount. Up to $40,000 could be withdrawn from Ben's 529 plan to pay off all of these four qualifying loans.

This new rule could incentivize the taking out of Stafford-type subsidized loans, as those loans defer payment until after college and the student commences work. This would make sense as a strategy if the income earned on the 529 account exceeds the interest owed on the qualified student loan.

63. *Id.* at 38.

CHART 5-8 Tax Loan Benefits (2021)

Tax Benefit	Specific Benefit	Qualifying Expenses	Phase-out for Single or HOH	Phase-out for Joint	Eligible Taxpayers	Other Limitations
After-College Benefits	Student Loan Interest Deduction § 221	Tuition, fees, room, board for QHEE	$ 70,000–$ 85,000	$ 140,000–$ 170,000	The student with the loan	$ 2,500 per return
	Loan Forgiveness § 108(f)(1)	Loan for any education expenses	None	None	Health and education fields	Applies to certain employees
After or During College Benefits	§ 529 savings payment of up to $ 10,000 of qualified loan	Principal or interest on any qualified education loan	None	None	Designated beneficiary (DB) of the § 529 plan or DB's siblings	$ 10,000 total per beneficiary (not per year)

D. Conclusion

Planning for college education can be complicated, requiring an integrated approach. Not only are various savings techniques important but more than one savings device is often advisable. In addition, the tax system provides numerous benefits in the form of exclusions, deductions, and credits. All of these must be coordinated and integrated along with federal assistance—loans and grants—and scholarships. *See* **Part IV: Coordinating Section 529 Plans with Other Education Planning Techniques.** One thing is certain: today and in the future, failure to initiate financial planning early on will result in limited options for paying college-related expenses and increase the likelihood that students and their parents are left relying upon student loans to finance college.

PART II

SECTION 529 SAVINGS PLANS

Section 529 savings plans can be incredible savings devices for college education; additionally, and after the *Tax Cuts and Jobs Act of 2017*, 529 savings plans can be used up to $10,000 for K–12 tuition expenses, and after the *SECURE Act of 2019*, can be used to pay off $10,000 of student loans. Thus, 529 savings plans are versatile when it comes to education planning.

Why are Section 529 savings plans so versatile? The following are some of the most important reasons. First, Section 529 savings plans are available to taxpayers of all income levels. Second, substantial amounts of money can be invested in these plans, enabling the taxpayer to meet any education goal, from boarding school to graduate school. Third, earnings on the plan are not subject to income tax when used for qualified education expenses. Fourth, qualified education expenses are interpreted broadly to include not only tuition for college and K–12, but to also include expenses for room and board, books, computer, printer, internet, and much more. Fifth, the Section 529 savings plan can be used with other tax benefits such as the American Opportunity Tax Credit and the Lifetime Learning Credit. Sixth, Section 529 savings plans provide gift, estate, and generation-skipping tax advantages. Seventh, nontax benefits of these plans abound, including financial aid compatibility, owner control, perpetual existence, asset protection, and the opportunity to have a secure investment with good returns. Finally, for wealthier taxpayers, saving in these plans will not compromise other financial or retirement goals.

By enacting Section 529, Congress created a tax provision with multiple layers of complexity. Congress has modified, amended, or expanded Section 529 in ten different tax acts: the *Small Business Job Protection Act of 1996,* the *Taxpayer Relief Act of 1997,* the *Economic Growth and Tax Relief Reconciliation Act of 2001*, the *Tax Increase Prevention and Reconciliation Act of 2005*, the *Pension Protection Act of 2006*, the *Small Business and Work Opportunity Act of 2007*, the *American Recovery and Reinvestment Act of 2009*, the *Stephen Beck Jr., Achieving a Better Life Experience (ABLE) Act of 2014,* the *Tax Cuts and Jobs Act of 2017,* and the *Setting Every*

PSYCHIATRIST
Oh, doctor, I hope you can help him. He keeps on saying 529, 529, 529.

Community Up for Retirement Enhancement Act of 2019.[1] All of these statutes are discussed in **Chapter Six: History of Section 529 Savings Plans**. The *Coronavirus Aid, Relief, and Economic Security (CARES) Act of 2020*, the *Consolidated Appropriations Act of 2021*, and the *American Rescue Plan Act of 2021* did not directly deal with Section 529, but made several changes impacting 529 planning.[2]

Another layer of complexity is all the federal governmental rules that apply to these plans. Federal legislation sets forth detailed requirements as to the basic structure of these programs—including the income, gift, estate, and generation-skipping tax aspects. **Chapter Seven: Federal Rules and Regulations for Section 529 Savings Plans** addresses the federal requirements for the creation of a Section 529 savings plan. **Chapter Eight: Federal Income Tax Planning with Section 529 Savings Plans** explains the federal income tax rules. **Chapter Nine: Estate Planning with Section 529 Savings Plans** covers the federal gift tax, estate tax, generation-skipping tax, and trust planning aspects of Section 529 plans.

In addition to the federal tax rules, individual states have their own tax requirements. These state requirements increase the complexity of the Section 529 savings plan. Some state rules provide more benefits than the federal rules, while other state rules provide fewer benefits than the federal rules. Thus, it is imperative for an advisor to be aware of the difference between the federal and state rules and requirements, so they can adequately advise their client. **Chapter Ten: State Tax Planning with Section 529 Savings Plans** explores issues relating to the diverse nature of state taxation of these plans. **Chapter Eleven: Disability Planning with Section 529 Savings Plans** covers the interrelationship of ABLE accounts and 529 plans.

Nontax issues provide an additional layer of complexity to the consumer or tax advisor considering a Section 529 plan. One must consider such nontax issues as control, perpetuity, asset protection, and the impact of savings on a future student's financial aid package. These issues are addressed in **Chapter Twelve: Nontax Aspects of Section 529 Savings Plans**.

---

1. The Small Business Job Protection Act of 1996, 26 U.S.C.A. § 529, Pub. L. No. 104-188, tit. I, § 1806(a), 110 Stat. 1755 (1996); The Taxpayer Relief Act of 1997, 26 U.S.C.A. § 529, Pub. L. No. 105-34, tit. II, § 211(a), (b), (d), (e)(2)(A), & tit. XVI, § 1601(h)(1)(A)(B), 111 Stat. 788 (1997); The Economic Growth and Tax Relief Reconciliation Act of 2001, 26 U.S.C.A. § 529, Pub. L. No. 107-16, tit. IV, § 402(a)(1)–(4)(A), (C)–(D), (b)(1), (c)–(g), 115 Stat. 38 (2001); The Tax Increase Prevention and Reconciliation Act of 2005, 26 U.S.C.A. § 529, Pub. L. No. 109-222, 120 Stat. 345 (2006); The Pension Protection Act of 2006, 26 U.S.C.A. § 529, Pub. L. No. 109-280, 120 Stat. 780, H.R. Rep. No. 109-455, at 52 (2006); The Small Business and Work Opportunity Act of 2007, S. 349, 110th Cong. (2007); The American Recovery and Reinvestment Act of 2009, Pub. L. No. 111-5, H.R. 1, 111th Cong. (2009); The Stephen Beck Jr. Achieving a Better Life Experience Act of 2014, Pub. L. No. 113-295, 113th Cong. (2014); The Tax Cuts and Jobs Act of 2017, S. 2254, 115th Cong. (2017); The Setting Every Community Up for Retirement Enhancement (SECURE) Act of 2019, H.R. 1994, 116th Cong. (2019–2020).

2. These relevant provisions are discussed throughout the book. Coronavirus Aid, Relief, and Economic Security (CARES) Act of 2020, H.R. 748, 116th Cong. (2019–2020); The Consolidated Appropriations Act of 2021, Pub. L. No. 116-260, H.R. 133 (2021); The American Rescue Plan Act of 2021, H.R. 1319, 117th Cong. (2021).

Lastly, Section 529 savings plans vary from state to state and from plan to plan. Thus, the tax advisor additionally must consider the several investment options (with varying market performances) that may be available within a particular state plan. **Chapter Thirteen: Investment Planning with Section 529 Savings Plans** discusses the wide variety of choices the investor has in the various 529 plans. Finally, **Chapter Fourteen: Choosing the Right Section 529 Savings Plan** deals with other important considerations in deciding which is the best state 529 plan for the client.

Chapter 6

History of Section 529 Savings Plans

In 1986, the Michigan legislature created the *Michigan Education Trust* (MET) program under which residents of Michigan could pay a stipulated amount into a fund or trust to cover future tuition for a student attending any Michigan public college or university.[1] The Michigan legislature, intending to "make 'the means of education' available to its citizens," created the MET to allow Michigan residents to pre-purchase tuition plans for a beneficiary's future college education.[2] The state exempted all MET income from state income taxes and requested that the Internal Revenue Service (IRS) do the same at the federal level.[3]

In a private letter ruling regarding the MET, the IRS ruled that the purchaser of this prepaid tuition contract would not be taxed on the accrued income or value of the fund until it was actually distributed or refunded in the future.[4] The ruling also held that the purchaser had made a completed gift for gift tax purposes at the time of the purchase, but that the gift did not qualify for the gift tax exclusion for a tuition payment made directly to an education institution under Section 2503(e).[5] On the other hand, the IRS did rule that funds placed in the college fund qualify as a gift of a *present interest*, thus making the cash placed in the plan eligible for the per-donee annual exclusion under Section 2503(b). However, to the disappointment of Michigan, the IRS concluded that the trust itself was not an integral part of the state. Rather, the IRS characterized MET as an independently operating

1. Mich. Comp. Laws Ann. § 390.1421 *et seq.* (1986).

2. Michigan v. United States, 40 F.3d 817, 820 (6th Cir. 1994), *rev'g* 802 F. Supp. 120 (W.D. Mich. 1992).

3. *Id.* at 819, 821.

4. I.R.S. Priv. Ltr. Rul. 88-25-027 (June 24, 1988).

5. I.R.C. § 2503(e) provides that a "qualified transfer" (i.e., "any amount paid on behalf of an individual as tuition to [a qualified education organization] for the education or training of such individual") is not a taxable gift.

corporation. Thus, the MET itself was subject to federal income taxation as an association under Section 11(a) on the earnings from the invested fund.[6]

In 1990, the MET filed suit in the District Court for a refund on the tax the trust was required to pay on its investment income. Although the District Court held in favor of the IRS, in 1994 the Sixth Circuit reversed in *Michigan v. United States*.[7] The ultimate question on appeal was "whether the United States Internal Revenue Code impose[d] a tax on investment income realized by the Michigan Education Trust."[8] In reaching its decision in favor of Michigan, the Sixth Circuit considered Section 11(a), which mandates that a tax be imposed on the taxable income earned by all corporations.[9] Because the MET was set up as a "quasi corporation," it could technically be taxed under Section 11(a). However, the court noted that "this section has never been interpreted as imposing a tax on income earned directly by a state, a political subdivision of a state, or 'an integral part of a state.'"[10] The court concluded that the MET did constitute an integral part of the state despite the fact that the benefits of the program only accrued to those that utilized it.[11] The court found the IRS's benefit accrual argument unpersuasive with respect to characterizing the MET because the IRS's theory was equally applicable to other tax-exempt public entities, such as the Postal Service.[12] Thus, the court held "[t]he education trust *is* an integral part of the state, and its investment income is not currently subject to taxation under Section 11(a) of the Internal Revenue Code."[13]

Although this case was a victory for Michigan, it did not represent binding authority for all state plans. At that time, many states' college plans included similar features to those embodied in the Michigan plan. However, the features of some plans were different. Many of the original state plans were of the prepaid type, while later plans were more generally of the savings variety. (*See* **Chart 6-1** illustrating a timeline of when and which type of plans were adopted by the respective states.) In both types of plans, however, the basic state objective was the accommodation of increasing college costs. Both plans were intended as an incentive for its citizens to save for the education of their children.

---

6. I.R.S. Priv. Ltr. Rul. 88-25-027 (June 24, 1988).
7. Michigan v. United States, 40 F.3d 817 (6th Cir. 1994), *rev'g* 802 F. Supp. 120 (W.D. Mich. 1992).
8. *Id.* at 818.
9. *Id.* at 823.
10. *Id.*
11. *Id.*
12. *Id.* at 829.
13. *Id.* (emphasis added).

CHART 6-1 Timeline for Section 529 Plans[14]

Year	Prepaid Plan	Savings Plan
1986	Wyoming (end '95)	
1987	Florida	
1988	Michigan	
1989	Ohio	Ohio
1990	Alabama, Kentucky	Kentucky
1991	Alaska	Alaska
1992		
1993	Pennsylvania	
1994		
1995	Massachusetts U. Plan	
1996	Texas, Utah, Virginia	Utah
1997	Colorado, Indiana Louisiana, Mississippi, Tennessee, Wisconsin	Connecticut, Indiana, Louisiana, Wisconsin
1998	Connecticut, Delaware, Illinois, Iowa, Maryland, Montana, Nevada, New Hampshire, New Jersey, New York, North Carolina, Rhode Island, South Carolina, Washington, West Virginia	Delaware, Iowa, Montana, New Hampshire, New Jersey, New York, North Carolina, Rhode Island
1999	Arizona, Arkansas, California, Maine, Missouri, Vermont	Arizona, Arkansas, California, Colorado, Maine, Massachusetts, Missouri, Vermont, Virginia
2000	Kansas, New Mexico, Oklahoma, Wyoming	Illinois, Kansas, Michigan, New Mexico, Oklahoma, Tennessee, Wyoming
2001	Nebraska, Oregon, Idaho, Minnesota, North Dakota	Idaho, Maryland, Minnesota, Mississippi, Nebraska, Nevada, North Dakota, Oregon
2002	Georgia, Hawaii, South Dakota	Alabama, District of Columbia, Florida, Georgia, Hawaii, Pennsylvania, South Dakota, South Carolina, Texas, West Virginia
2003–2020		Washington

14. *See Research and Compare 529 Plans*, Saving for College, http://www.savingforcollege.com/529_plans/state_pages/states.php (last visited May 3, 2021).

By 1996, the growing number of states interested in providing savings incentives for education benefits resulted in efforts to garner federal government support of uniform rules and tax benefits for the plans. The U.S. Senate Committee on Finance took up the issue in June 1996.[15] Just two months later, the *Small Job Protection Act of 1996*[16] enacted Section 529 of the Internal Revenue Code. Section 529 was later modified by the *Taxpayer's Relief Act of 1997*,[17] the *Economic Growth and Tax Relief Reconciliation Act of 2001*,[18] *The Pension Protection Act of 2006*,[19] the *American Recovery and Reinvestment Act of 2009*,[20] the *Tax Cuts and Jobs Act of 2017*,[21] and the *Setting Every Community Up for Retirement Enhancement Act of 2019*.[22] Other acts, such as the *Small Business Work Opportunity Act of 2007*[23] and the *Achieving a Better Life Experience (ABLE) Act of 2014*,[24] along with the Section 529 proposed regulations made important changes impacting 529 planning.

A. The Small Business Job Protection Act of 1996

The Small Business Job Protection Act (SBJPA) of 1996 gave birth to Section 529, which provided tax-exempt status to certain "qualified state tuition programs" (QSTP) established and maintained by a state.[25] The *SBJPA* outlined the criteria states must meet in order to establish and maintain QSTPs, and clarified the tax treatment of distributions from them.[26] Any person, regardless of income level, could purchase tuition credits or certificates or make contributions to a savings account on behalf of a designated beneficiary to enable him/her to pay for "qualified higher education expenses" (QHEE).[27] While QHEE did not include room and board, it did encompass tuition, fees, books, supplies, and equipment required for the beneficiary's attendance at an eligible institution.[28]

Under the *SBJPA*, the tax on earnings attributable to prepayments or contributions was deferred until the earnings were distributed from the QSTP.[29] The taxable portion of any distribution during the year was to be computed under the annuity

---

15. S. Rep. No. 104-281, at 106 (1996), *reprinted in* 1996 U.S.C.C.A.N. 1474, 1580.

16. *See* Pub. L. No. 104-188, tit. I, § 1806(a), 110 Stat. 1755 (1996). *See generally* S. Rep. No. 104-281 (1996), *reprinted in* 1996 U.S.C.C.A.N. 1474; H.R. Rep. No. 104-737 (1996), *reprinted in* U.S.C.C.A.N. 1474.

17. *See* Pub. L. No. 105-34, 111 Stat. 788 (1997).

18. *See* Pub. L. No. 107-16, 115 Stat. 38 (2001).

19. *See* Pub. L. No. 109-280, 120 Stat. 780 (2006).

20. *See* Pub. L. No. 111-5, H.R. 1, 111th Cong. (2009).

21. S. 2254, 115th Cong. (2017).

22. H. Rep. No. 1994, 116th Cong. (2019–2020).

23. H. Rep. No. 109-455, at 52 (2006).

24. *See* Pub. L. No. 113-295, 113th Cong. (2014).

25. I.R.C. § 529, Pub. L. No. 104-188, tit. I, § 1806, 110 Stat. 1755 (1996).

26. *Id.*

27. *Id.* § 529(b)(1).

28. *Id.* § 529(e)(3).

29. *Id.* § 529(c)(3).

rules of Section 72.[30] The beneficiary, who was usually in a lower tax bracket than the account owner, paid taxes on the earnings at the time the withdrawals were used to pay his/her qualified expenses. If withdrawals were not used to pay for qualified expenses, then the taxes relating to the earnings would be imposed on the "distributee" (i.e., not necessarily the beneficiary—if the beneficiary did not actually receive the distribution).[31] In addition, the *SBJPA* required that there be "more than a de minimis" penalty on all nonqualified distributions—unless excused due to the death, disability, or receipt of scholarship by the designated beneficiary.[32] The proposed regulations indicated that a "more than de minimis" penalty was at least 10 percent of earnings.[33] (Most states had adopted a 10 percent penalty, but some states had higher or lower rates.)

Contributions to a qualified state tuition program (QSTP) were treated as incomplete gifts for federal gift tax purposes and thus did not qualify for the *per-donee annual exclusion* under Section 2503(b).[34] The federal gift tax consequences were determined at the time of the distribution from the program for the payment (or waiver) of the beneficiary's QHEE.[35] At that time, the distribution could qualify for the *Section 2503(e) transfer* exclusion from taxable gifts *if* the tuition payments were paid directly to the education institutions.[36] Also, such transfer would be exempt from generation-skipping taxes.[37] And, if the beneficiary died, nothing would be includable in his/her estate. On the other hand, if the contributor died, all amounts contributed to the plan, plus earnings, less distributions would be includable in his/her estate.[38] This was true regardless of whether the donor relinquished all ownership or control over the account.

The *SBJPA* specified that the contributions to the QSTP must be made in cash and that neither contributors nor beneficiaries could control the program's investments, directly or indirectly.[39] The state program required designation of a beneficiary and was required to maintain separate accounts for each designated beneficiary, and the beneficiary had to be specifically identified (unless the plan was set up by a charity).[40] The Act allowed for a change in the designated

30. *Id.* § 529(c)(3)(D).

31. If the earnings were taxed to the beneficiary student, he/she would be older than 18, so the "kiddie tax" would not apply. I.R.C. § 1(g).

32. I.R.C. § 529(c)(2), Pub. L. No. 104-188, tit. I, § 1806, 110 Stat. 1755 (1996).

33. Prop. Reg. § 1.529-2(e)(2)(ii).

34. This rule would make sense if the donor was the owner; however, if the donor was not the owner, then established principles would indicate a completed gift. In 2021, this exclusion is $15,000, up from $12,000 in 2008.

35. I.R.C. § 529(c)(3)(D)(4) (1996).

36. I.R.C. § 529(c)(5), Pub. L. No. 104-188, tit. I, § 1806, 110 Stat. 1755 (1996). At this time, room and board was not considered qualified; Section 2503(b) only applied to tuition. Again, if the donor was not the owner this would seem not to qualify under traditional Section 2503 principles.

37. I.R.C. § 2611(b)(1).

38. I.R.C. § 529(c)(4), Pub. L. No. 104-188, tit. I, § 1806, 110 Stat. 1755 (1996).

39. *Id.* § 529(b)(2), (5).

40. *Id.* § 529(b)(4).

beneficiary as long as the change was to a member of the same family.[41] The provision referenced Section 2032(A)(e)(2) for the definition of "family."[42] Furthermore, the state was required to report the earnings portion of the distributions from the plan to the federal government and collect a penalty for nonqualified withdrawals.[43]

B. The Taxpayer Relief Act of 1997

The Taxpayer Relief Act (TRA) of 1997 continued the 1996 rule that earnings from investments in a QSTP were deferred and taxed to the beneficiary upon distribution for QHEE (or to the distributee of a non-qualified distribution).[44] However, contrary to the earlier *SBJPA*, the *TRA* provided that a distribution to a beneficiary from a qualified state tuition program was *not* a taxable gift. Rather, contributions to the program were treated as a completed gift of a *present interest* eligible for the *annual per-donee gift exclusion* under Section 2503(b).[45] Distributions, however, were no longer considered eligible for the education exclusion from taxable gifts as a direct tuition payment to an institution under Section 2503(e).[46]

The *TRA* also provided for a five-year averaging election that allowed the donor to file a gift tax return in the year of contribution and make a gift of a *present interest* of up to five times the annual exclusion amount.[47] However, if the donor died before the five-year period, a portion of the contribution plus allocable earnings would be included in the gross estate of the donor for estate tax purposes. If the donor survived five years, then nothing would be includable in his/her estate. On the other hand, any amounts distributed from the plan on account of the beneficiary's death were includable in the beneficiary's estate—unless the account was rolled over to another qualified beneficiary in the same generation.[48] Despite the fact that the donor could revoke the transfer, the contribution was treated as a completed gift of a *present interest*, and the account was not includable in the owner's estate. Thus, the *TRA* rules were just the opposite of those under the *SBJPA*.

No generation-skipping transfer tax resulted when the contribution, when combined with any other contributions made by the donor to that same beneficiary, did not exceed the annual gift tax exclusion limit. A gift tax return needed to be filed with respect to any contribution in excess of the *annual per-donee gift*

41. *Id.* § 529(c)(3)(C)(ii).

42. Under Section 2032A(e)(2) "member of the family" means (A) an ancestor of such individual, (B) the spouse of such individual, (C) a lineal descendant of such individual, of such individual's spouse, or of a parent of such individual, or (D) the spouse of any lineal descendant in (C) above.

43. I.R.C. § 529(e), Pub. L. No. 104-188, tit. I, § 1806, 110 Stat. 1755 (1996).

44. I.R.C. § 529, Pub. L. No. 105-34, tit. II, § 211, 111 Stat. 788 (1997).

45. *Id.* At the time of the TRA amendments to Section 529, the amount considered as a completed gift for gift tax purposes was $10,000. That amount was indexed for inflation after 1998.

46. *Id.* § 529(c).

47. *Id.* § 529(c)(2)(B).

48. *Id.* § 529(c)(4)(c).

tax exclusion limit and the election for five-year averaging had to be made on that return. Any change in beneficiary or rollover of the account to a new beneficiary could result in a taxable gift and a generation-skipping transfer from the old beneficiary to the new beneficiary *if* the new beneficiary were assigned to a generation below that of the old beneficiary.[49]

The *TRA* also expanded Section 529 to allow qualifying expenses to include room and board in addition to tuition, fees, equipment, and supplies.[50] However, amounts treated as reasonable for room and board could not exceed the minimum amount included in the cost of attendance at the institution applicable to the student under Section 472 of the Higher Education Act. Under that Act at that time, the room and board could not exceed the following:

a) for a student living at home with parents or guardians, $1,500 per *academic year*,
b) for students living in housing owned and operated by the eligible institution, that institution's "normal" room and board charge; and
c) for all other students, $2,500.

The reference to a qualified student was modified in the *TRA*. No one convicted of a Federal or State felony for possession or distribution of a controlled substance was qualified. The Act also expanded the definition of "family" to include all those listed in (1)–(8) of the dependency provision, Section 152(a)–(e.g., sons, daughters, brothers, sisters, nephews and nieces, certain in-laws, etc.)—and any spouse of such a person.[51] The *TRA* also expanded the definition of "designated beneficiary" to clarify that the state or local government included an "agency or instrumentality of a state or local government."

In sum, the *TRA* established the 529 plan as an excellent income, gift, and estate tax savings device. Although income tax on investment earnings was not eliminated, it was deferred and shifted to the designated beneficiary, who usually was in a lower tax bracket than the contributor.

C. The Economic Growth and Tax Relief Reconciliation Act of 2001

The Economic Growth and Tax Relief Reconciliation Act (EGTRRA) of 2001[52] further expanded Section 529 programs by excluding from gross income all earnings from the fund when distributions were used for *qualified higher education expenses* (QHEE). These rules became effective in 2002. *EGTRRA* also permitted private

49. *See* I.R.C. § 2651.
50. I.R.C. § 529(e)(3)(B), Pub. L. No. 105-34, tit. II, § 211, 111 Stat. 788 (1997).
51. *Id.* § 529(e)(2). Interestingly, the TRA did not include the spouse of the taxpayer donor.
52. I.R.C. § 529(c)(3)(B), Pub. L. No. 107-16, tit. IV, § 402, 115 Stat. 38 (2001).

education institutions to set up prepaid plans.[53] Thus, the tax name changed from "qualified state tuition plans" to "qualified tuition programs" (QTPs).[54]

The *EGTRRA* no longer required states to collect a penalty for nonqualified withdrawals. Instead, a federal *penalty tax* of 10 percent was imposed directly on the recipient of any non-qualified withdrawal.[55] The exceptions under the *EGTRRA* were the same as those under the *SBJPA*—death or disability of the beneficiary or receipt of a scholarship by the beneficiary.[56] The *EGTRRA* further expanded the definition of qualified expenses by adding special needs services to the definition and increasing the dollar amount limitations on room and board.[57] For room and board qualified expenses, the rule remained the same for students living at home. For those residing in dorms, the actual room and board expenses charged could be used rather than the allowance in the Education Act. For students not living at home or in the dorms, the Higher Education Act (as of 2001) provided for reasonable amounts instead of the fixed amount of $2,500 in the previous Act.

The *EGTRRA* also expanded the definition of family to include first cousins of the beneficiary and provided for a rollover to a different program for the benefit of the same designated beneficiary once within any 12-month period.[58] Lastly, the *EGTRRA* provided coordination rules so that taxpayer could contribute to a Coverdell ESA and in addition obtain education credits—as long as the distribution was not used for the same expenses.[59] As the Section 529 plan covered room and board and the credits did not, coordination among the various provisions became possible under *EGTRRA*.[60]

D. The Pension Protection Act of 2006

Under EGTRRA, Section 529 was due to expire in 2010. With the passage of the *Pension Protection Act (PPA) of 2006*,[61] however, Section 529 has now become permanent. This means it is very unlikely that Section 529s will be repealed or significantly modified in the future.

53. *Id.* § 529(b)(1)(A).
54. *Id.*
55. *Id.* § 529.
56. These exceptions were also identical to those under Section 530 (the Coverdell Education Savings Account (ESA)).
57. I.R.C. § 529, Pub. L. No. 107-16, tit. IV, § 402, 115 Stat. 38 (2001).
58. *Id.*
59. *Id.*
60. *See* **Chapter Eighteen: Coordinating Section 529 Plans with Tax Benefits**.
61. *See* Pub. L. No. 109-280, 120 Stat. 780 (2006).

E. The Small Business and Work Opportunity Act of 2007

The *Small Business and Work Opportunity Act*[62] made major changes to the "kiddie tax" impacting custodianship accounts as well as the taxation of nonqualified distributions from 529 plans. These changes were later modified by subsequent acts.

F. The Section 529 Regulations of 2008

On August 24, 1998, the IRS issued proposed regulations for Section 529. On January 17, 2008, the IRS released an Advance Notice of proposed rulemaking for final regulations under Section 529. The Advance Notice indicated that most of the initial Section 529 regulations proposed in 1998 will be reproposed along with new rules primarily designed to prevent abuse in using 529 accounts. In addition, the new regulations indicated they might require new recordkeeping and reporting requirements for Section 529 programs. The proposed regulations and the Advance Notice will be discussed in later chapters of this book and appear in **Appendix E and F**.

G. The American Recovery and Reinvestment Act of 2009

The American Recovery and Reinvestment Act of 2009[63] expanded the definition of QHEE[64] to include expenses for "certain computer technology and equipment" used by the designated beneficiary while enrolled at an eligible educational institution. This new provision parallels the Coverdell provision,[65] which allows computer technology and equipment to qualify for qualified elementary and secondary education expenses. Internet access and related services are also covered. Expenses for computer software designed for sports, games, or hobbies are not covered "unless the software is predominately educational in nature."

---

62. H. Rep. No. 109-455, at 52 (2006).

63. The American Recovery and Reinvestment Act of 2009, https://www.congress.gov/bill/111th-congress/house-bill/1/text..

64. I.R.C. § 529(e)(3)(A).

65. I.R.C. § 530(b)(3)(A)(iii).

H. The Stephen Beck Jr., Achieving a Better Life Experience (ABLE) Act of 2014

The *Stephen Beck Jr., Achieving a Better Life Experience (ABLE) Act of 2014*,[66] was the most significant piece of legislation involving people with disabilities since the passage of the *Americans with Disabilities Act of 1990*.[67] The *ABLE Act* allows individuals with qualifying disabilities (or their families) to set up a tax-advantaged account to save for their daily and future expenses without affecting their eligibility for public benefits. These federal benefit programs include Supplemental Security Income, Medicaid, Supplemental Nutrition Assistance Program (SNAP), and United States Department of Housing and Urban Development (HUD) housing benefits. In addition, most states exempt ABLE assets from state and local means-tested benefit programs. These ABLE accounts have advantages over special needs trusts and, after the *TCJA* of 2017, can be coordinated with 529 savings plans. All of these changes will be discussed in great depth in **Chapter Eleven: Disability Planning with Section 529 Savings Plans.**

I. The Tax Cuts and Jobs Act of 2017

The Tax Cuts and Jobs Act (TCJA) of 2017[68] made two important modifications in the 529 plan. First, the act expanded the definition of QHEE to include payments of up to $10,000 in tuition expenses for parochial or private K–12 education. Second, *TCJA* allows for ABLE accounts to be rolled over into 529 plans.

In the broader education planning context, the *TCJA* made several other important changes. First, the above-the-line *tuition and fees deduction* under Section 222 was not renewed and thus terminated in 2017. (But it was later revised and extended through 2020 and then under the *Consolidated Appropriations Act of 2021* was repealed again).[69] Second, the *home equity* loan interest deduction under Section 163 was temporarily suspended. Third, ordinary and necessary educational expenses of an employee under Section 162 that are not reimbursed by the employer were also suspended. Lastly, the *kiddie tax* was modified so income of the child will be taxed at the high trust tax rates. All of these changes will be discussed in great depth in **Chapter Eight: Federal Income Tax Planning with Section 529 Savings Plans.**

---

66. Pub. L. No. 113-295, 128 Stat. 4056.
67. Pub. L. No. 101-336, 104 Stat. 326, 42 U.S.C. § 12101.
68. Pub. L. No. 115-97, 131 Stat. 2054.
69. *See* **Chapter Eight: Federal Income Tax Planning with Section 529 Savings Plans**, F.1.

J. The Setting Every Community Up for Retirement Enhancement (SECURE) Act of 2019

The *SECURE Act* of 2019 focused primarily on changes to retirement planning; however, several important changes to Section 529 were made. First, the *SECURE Act* allowed certain expenses associated with "registered apprenticeship programs" that are certified by the Secretary of Labor under the National Apprenticeship Act to meet the definition of QHEE.[70] These expenses include fees, books, supplies, and equipment. Second, QHEE was expanded to include "amounts paid as principal or interest on any qualified education loan.[71] As with the K–12 tuition payments, the limit is $10,000. However, this limit is a lifetime limit, not an annual one.[72] The *SECURE Act* also expanded this tax benefit to include not only the beneficiary of the Section 529 plan but any sibling.[73] Qualified education loan was defined exactly as under the above-the-line student loan interest deduction under Section 221(d).[74]

CHART 6-2 The Section 529 Features in Four Acts

Feature	SBJPA '96	TRA '97	EGTRRA '01 Changes	TCJA of 2017
Contribution in cash	Yes	Yes	Yes	No change
Taxability of earnings	Taxable to beneficiary at distribution	Taxable to beneficiary at distribution	Excluded if for QHEE	No change
Completed gift	At time of distribution	At time of contribution	At time of contribution	No change
Per-donee exclusion	No exclusion	Yes, at time of contribution	Yes, at time of contribution	No change
Five-year gift averaging	No	Yes	Yes	No change
Gift eligible for Section 2503(e) exclusion	Yes	No	No	No change
Estate tax of Contributor (if dies before distribution)	Yes	Only if dies within five-year gift averaging period	Only if dies within five-year gift averaging period	No change

(continued)

70. I.R.C. § 529(c)(8) (citing Section 1 of the National Apprenticeship Act at 29 U.S.C. § 50).
71. *Id.* § 529(c)(9).
72. *Id.* § 529(c)(9)(B).
73. *Id.* § 529(c)(9)(C)(ii).
74. *See* **Chapter Five: When Savings Are Not Enough**, C.

Feature	SBJPA '96	TRA '97	EGTRRA '01 Changes	TCJA of 2017
Estate tax of Beneficiary	Nothing	Yes, if amounts were distributed on account of the beneficiary's death	Yes, if amounts were distributed on account of the beneficiary's death	No change
Contributions exempt from GST	Yes	Yes	Yes	No change
Covered expenses	Tuition & related	Added room & board	Added special needs & adjusted room & board	Added tuition for K-12
Covered Relatives	Section 2032A	Section 152(1)–(8)	Section 152(1)–(8) plus first cousins	No change
Investment control	State	State	State but rollover easier	No change
Creation	Only state	Only state	State plus private institutions for prepaid	No change
Coordination with Coverdell ESA	Cannot contribute to both	Cannot contribute to both	Can contribute to both	No change
Coordination with education credits	Credits did not exist	No coordination	Yes, as long as distribution is not used for same expenses	No change
Rollover to another state plan	Not available	Not available	Available once within 12-month period	No change
Rollover from an ABLE account	Not available	Not available	Not Available	Now Available
Penalty	State-imposed more than a de minimis penalty (i.e., 10%)	State-imposed more than a de minimis penalty (i.e., 10%)	Federally imposed 10% penalty	No change

K. The Revolutionizing of 529 Plans

Prior to the *Small Business Job Protection Act of 1996*, the code provided for several education-related benefits: the scholarship exclusion provision (Section 117), employer-provided assistance (Section 127), the savings bond interest exclusion (Section 135), the exclusion from income of student loan forgiveness (Section 108), the business expense deduction (Section 162), and the home equity loan interest deduction (Section 163—but no longer allowed). In addition, prior to 1996 many tax laws negatively affected education planning, such as a penalty if retirement funds were used for education, student loan interest characterized as a nondeductible personal expense,[75] and the "kiddie tax" that taxed the investments of children under the age of 14 at the parents' rate, or more recently, the trust and estate tax rates.

The *SBJPA of 1996*, the *Taxpayer Relief Act (TRA) of 1997*, and the *Economic Growth and Tax Relief Reconciliation Act (EGTRRA) of 2001* constitute a stream of tax laws providing education initiatives passed by Congress over a five-year period. The *TRA* of 1997 introduced the Hope Scholarship and Lifetime Learning Credits, the Section 221 above-the-line deduction for student loan interest, the "education individual retirement account" (renamed the Coverdell Education Savings Account in *EGTRRA*), and the Roth IRA. The *TRA* of 1997 also extended the employer-provided education assistance provision (Section 127) and expanded the exclusion for cancellation of certain student loans to education organizations (Section 108(f)) for an additional three years. The *EGTRRA* introduced the Section 222 above-the-line deduction for education payments (since repealed).

The *American Recovery and Reinvestment Act of 2009* made the Hope Credit (renamed the American Opportunity Tax Credit) partially refundable. More recently, the *Tax Cuts and Jobs Act of 2017* expanded 529s for K–12 and for use in disability planning, and the *SECURE Act of 2019* now allows the 529 plan to be used to pay off a portion of qualified education debt.[76] All of these acts have revolutionized the Section 529 plan, making it the most important savings mechanism for education expenses.

L. Conclusion

The Section 529 plans, as they are now called, provide significant benefits for all taxpayers, particularly those that are able to save for the desired education expenses. Recent legislation has expanded the definition of QHEE to include up to $10,000 of K–12 tuition expenses and up to $10,000 of qualified student debt. In addition, 529s can now be coordinated with the ABLE account. Because the government and both political parties have shown commitment to education incentives in the past, and have in particular favored the Section 529 plans, these are not likely to be repealed in the near future. In fact, we might expect more changes that would make the Section 529 plans even more beneficial for taxpayers and students alike.

---

75. Prior to the Tax Reform Act of 1986, taxpayers could deduct personal interest, including interest on personal and student loans. I.R.C. § 163.

76. The *Consolidated Appropriations Act of 2021* did not impact 529s directly but equalized the adjusted gross income limits of the education credits.

Chapter 7

Federal Rules and Regulations for Section 529 Savings Plans

Although the rules for Section 529 savings plans are similar to Section 529 prepaid plans, this chapter and the following seven chapters will focus on the more popular Section 529 savings plans. **Part III** of this book will focus on the *prepaid tuition plans*. While legally construed by the federal government, the 529 savings plans are administered by each state under each state's respective set of rules. Thus, in addition to complying with applicable state rules,[1] the Section 529 savings plan must comply with the following federal guidelines:

(1) The "Creation of the State" Requirement,[2]
(2) "Contribution/Participation" Restrictions,
(3) The "No Investment Direction" Directive, and
(4) The "Not Pledged as Collateral" Rule.

Additional federal rules must also be followed to obtain tax advantages. First, the account must be used for *qualified higher education expenses* (QHEE). Second, the account must be used by an *eligible student*. Third, the fund must be used at an *eligible education institution*.

A. The "Creation of the State" Requirement

Section 529(b)(1) authorizes a state (or agency or instrumentality of a state) to "establish and maintain" *Qualified Tuition Programs* (QTPs), which were previously called *Qualified State Tuitions Plans* (QSTPs). The 1998 proposed regulations state

1. The state rules impacting Section 529 plans are discussed in **Chapter Ten: State Tax Planning with Section 529 Savings Plans** and **Chapter Twelve: Nontax Aspects of Section 529 Savings Plans**.

2. The *EGTRRA* amendment allowing private education institutions to set up Section 529 plans only allowed their participation in the creation of prepaid plans. I.R.C. § 529(b)(1).

that these programs are considered maintained by the state *if* the state sets all terms and conditions of the program. Such terms may include the following: who may contribute, when the contribution can be made, who may be a designated beneficiary, when and what benefits the program provides, how much can be contributed, what kind of investments are allowed, what penalties apply, whether the plan is open to nonresidents, asset protection considerations, and when the fund must terminate.[3] The state also must be "actively involved . . . in the administration of the program."[4] This includes supervision relating to the investments or a *plan manager*. Many states hire mutual fund companies, banks, and/or broker dealers to manage and market the plans. Examples of such companies include Merrill Lynch, TIAA/CREF, Putnam, Fidelity Investments, T. Rowe Price, Solomon Smith Barney, and Alliance Capital.[5] Other states manage the accounts through their state treasury.

At present, every state has a Section 529 savings plan,[6] although only a few have obtained private letter rulings on the qualifications of their programs.[7] Some states have multiple plans. For example, Alabama, Arkansas, Connecticut, District of Columbia, Iowa, Maine, Maryland, Michigan, Mississippi, New Hampshire, New Jersey, Ohio, Oklahoma, Oregon, South Carolina, Texas, Virginia, and Wisconsin have two programs. Alaska, Arizona, Illinois, Indiana, Kansas, Nevada, and West Virginia have three. Colorado and Nebraska have four. (See **Appendix C** for a list of these plans.) Each plan is unique and may allow different investment managers to operate different plans. Often these plans change and improve over the years. Although having so many options can lead to some confusion, it also provides competition and a wide variety of choice. For the advisor, it offers the opportunity to play a key role in deciding which particular plan is best for the client.

B. "Contribution (Participation)" Restrictions

Section 529 sets forth some definitional requirements, which relate to the contribution and participation aspects of the plan. First, there *must* be a *contribution donor*. Second, that donor may be different from the *account owner*. And third, a *designated beneficiary* is required. In addition, Section 529 specifically sets forth the requirements that contributions must be in cash,[8] that contributions should be for the "purpose" of providing education, that contributions should not be "in excess

---

3. Prop. Treas. Reg. § 1.529-2(b)(2), 63 Fed. Reg. 45,019 (Aug. 24, 1998). *See* **Chapter Fourteen: Choosing the Right Section 529 Savings Plan**.

4. Prop. Treas. Reg. § 1.529-2(b)(2)(ii), 63 Fed. Reg. 45,019 (Aug. 24, 1998).

5. Other examples include Oppenheimer Funds, Inc.; MFS Investment Management; Upromise Investments, Inc.; Pacific Life; The College Savings Bank; Securities Management & Research; Waddell & Reed; and Enterprise Capital Management, Inc.

6. *See* **Appendix C: Summary of State-by-State 529 Plans**. (Wyoming's plan is currently closed.)

7. I.R.S. Priv. Ltr. Rul. 20030030 (July 28, 2000) (Arizona); I.R.S. Priv. Ltr. Rul. 200214032 (Dec. 19, 2001) (Connecticut); I.R.S. Priv. Ltr. Rul. 200123065 (Mar. 12, 2001) (Indiana); I.R.S. Priv. Ltr. Rul. 200232025 (May 16, 2002) (Maine); I.R.S. Priv. Ltr. Rul. 200024055 (Mar. 21, 2000) (New Hampshire); I.R.S. Priv. Ltr. Rul. 200134032 (May 30, 2001) (New York).

8. I.R.C. § 529(b)(2).

of those necessary to provide for the qualified higher education expenses of the beneficiary,"[9] and that separate accounting for each beneficiary is required.[10]

1. Contributor/Donor

Under the federal rules, any "person" can be a *contributor* or *donor* to the Section 529 plan.[11] "Person" is defined as including an individual, trust, estate, partnership, association, company, or corporation.[12] A *contributor*[13] contributes money to the 529 fund and is the *donor*[14] unless the contributor is also the beneficiary (in which case there is no gift). Additionally, the *contributor* or *donor* is not required to have any relationship to the beneficiary.

2. Account Owner

The Section 529 Savings Plan *must* have an *owner* designated for the account. The owner is the one who has the ability to name and change the *beneficiary,* switch the investment plan, withdraw money, or make distributions from the account.[15] According to the proposed regulations, the account owner is a "person who under the terms [of the plan] is entitled to select or change the designated beneficiary of an account, to designate any person other than the designated beneficiary to whom funds may be paid from the account, or to receive distributions from the account if no such other person is designated."[16] The account owner is also the person who would certify that the beneficiary died, became disabled, or received a scholarship.[17] The account owner need not be the *contributor* or *donor*, and under federal law and in some states, the account owner can also be the *designated beneficiary.*

Usually, the donor will designate him/herself as the owner and a future student as the beneficiary. On the other hand, sometimes the donor is the grandparent and selects the parent as the owner. Care should be taken in designating the owner. For example, ownership in the hands of a grandparent may be a problem for financial aid purposes when distributions are made for education purposes.[18] Alternatively, ownership might be placed with a trust to ensure the account's perpetuity.[19]

---

9. *Id.* § 529(b)(6).
10. *Id.* § 529(b)(3).
11. *Id.* § 529(e)(1)(C).
12. *Id.* § 7701(a)(1).
13. *Id.* § 529(b)(4).
14. *Id.* § 529(c)(4)(C).
15. *Id.* § 529(e)(1). This is the designated beneficiary definition. It is implicit, but not explicit, in the statute that an owner is required.
16. Prop. Treas. Reg. § 1.529-1(c), 63 Fed. Reg. 45,019 (Aug. 24, 1998) (citing Section 7701(a)).
17. Prop. Treas. Reg. § 1.529-2(e)(4)(ii)(B)(2), 63 Fed. Reg. 45,019 (Aug. 24, 1998).
18. Under the federal methodology, ownership of the 529 account by the dependent student will constitute ownership by the parent and be assessed at a lower percentage than if considered the student's asset. When owned by the grandparent and a distribution is made, the distribution will be assessed as income of the student. *See* **Chapter Nineteen: Coordinating Section 529 Plans with Financial Aid**.
19. See discussion in **Chapter Nine: Estate Planning with Section 529 Savings Plans**.

Planning Pointer

Ownership planning should be contemplated at the outset of the creation of the Section 529 savings plan, as subsequent transfers of ownership may result in unintended tax consequences.[20]

Some state plans allow the original contributor to transfer ownership to another person while others do not. Some program materials use the word *participant* to refer to the account owner, while others equate *participant* to the contributor—who may not be the account owner. Some states restrict transfer of ownership to specific circumstances, such as divorce, incapacity, or death. The state may also not allow corporations, trusts, and other entities to be the account owner. In addition, the state may restrict who can be named as the successor account owner. Because this is an area of vast variety and uncertainty among the various state plans, the plan being considered should be closely scrutinized by the advisor to determine the applicable variations.[21]

a. *Community Property Issues*

Most Section 529 plans provide for only one account owner, and therefore community property issues may arise upon the death or divorce of that owner. Unlike Section 530, which governs Coverdell ESAs, Section 529 does not address community property issues. Thus, the general community property laws of the state would apply. Titling the asset in the name of one spouse should not defeat the community property nature of the property. Therefore, on divorce or death of the owner, the non–account-owner spouse would be entitled to revoke half of the plan or invest that half in another plan or change the beneficiary of that half.[22]

b. *Successor Owner*

In *all* cases, a provision for a successor owner should be made. Most states now address successor ownership when the account is opened. These states do so by requiring the naming of a successor or providing a provision in the original plan forms for a successor owner to be named.[23] Thus, if the donor is going to be the owner, ensuring successor ownership may be as simple as filling out the plan's forms.

Another alternative to guarantee a particular subsequent owner upon the death of the original owner is to name the successor in the owner's will. Barring

---

20. *Id.*

21. Note: most state plans are silent with respect to transferring ownership of the 529 plan during the original owner's lifetime.

22. For a discussion of prepaid plans and divorce, see **Chapter Fifteen: The State Prepaid Plan**, B.

23. *See How to Add a Successor Participant on Your 529 College Savings Plan*, Fidelity, https://www.fidelity.com/customer-service/how-to-add-529-successor-participant (last visited May 18, 2021).

limitations on account owners, a trust may be named as a successor owner. Should the plan owner pass away prior to naming a successor owner (either via the plan's original documentation or by will), most state plans provide a default owner or look to the inheritance laws of the state in which the decedent resided. In the case of incapacity, some states may permit the account owner to appoint a successor or agent under a power of attorney or to authorize a successor to be appointed under a power of attorney.

Planning Pointer

When the owner is concerned about whether the successor owner will change the beneficiary or seek a refund, the current owner may want to designate a custodianship account as successor owner to the 529 plan. Naming a custodianship as successor will assure that the successor owner exercises a fiduciary duty so that the funds go only to the designated beneficiary. Otherwise, the original owner would have no assurance that upon their death the beneficiary to the fund would not be changed.

EXAMPLE 7-1: Alice creates a Section 529 savings account for her son Ben and designates her sister as successor owner and custodian for Ben under a custodianship account. Normally an account owner of a Section 529 plan can revoke the plan or change the beneficiary. However, such a custodianship arrangement will assure that the funds will be used only for her son Ben's benefit.

c. *Employer as Owner*

An employer might also be the owner of a Section 529 plan. Employers may aid employees in the creation of Section 529 plans by offering them as a fringe benefit, by offering group enrollment, providing for payroll deductions, or even matching contributions.[24] Unlike most other fringe benefit rules,[25] no discrimination tests and few eligibility rules apply. One advantage of an employer-provided Section 529 plan is that the employer's research might result in the selection of a plan for the group based on the best tax and investment benefits for the employee. The disadvantage is that if the employer decides to make contributions to the plan on behalf of the employee or the employee's family, these contributions are likely to be considered taxable compensation to the employee.[26] It is not clear, however,

---

24. For example, the AAA Ohio Auto Club has established a program with the **Ohio Tuition Trust Authority** that allows employees to enroll in the state of Ohio 529 plan. This employer facilitates its full-time employees' savings by allowing 529 plan contributions to be accomplished through payroll deduction. *See* http://www.aaaohio.com/AAAOhio/AboutAAAOhio/FullTimeBenefits.aspx.

25. For example, see the requirements of the working condition fringe under I.R.C. § 132(d).

26. *See* Old Colony Trust Co. v. Comm'r, 279 U.S. 716 (1929).

whether the deemed compensation would be taxable at the date of the contribution or when distributions are made from the account.[27] Another issue might be whether a state tax deduction or credit for the contribution would be available to the employee if he/she is taxed. Arguably, if the employee were taxed at the time of the contribution, he/she would be the deemed donor for state tax deduction purposes.

d. Other Groups as Owner

Planning Pointer

The Advance Notice[28] of proposed rulemaking may require that an individual serve as the account owner, precluding account ownership by entities. This proposed rule seems to be contrary to Section 529(e)(1)(C), which clearly anticipates that governmental entities and charities would be account owners. The Advanced Notice hints that the proposed regulations may include special rules for contributions by entities that would look through to the individuals that control such entities.[29]

Even charities and other groups, such as the American Automobile Association, American Association of Retired Persons, Bar Associations, and Medical Societies, are beginning to understand the benefits of Section 529 plans. These various organizations are either providing advice to their members with respect to creating a 529 savings plan and/or providing a 529 group savings plan for their members.

3. Designated Beneficiary

In addition to an account owner, the Section 529 savings plan must have a *designated beneficiary*.[30] A *designated beneficiary* is defined as (1) "the individual designated at the commencement of participation in [the plan] as the beneficiary of amounts paid (or to be paid) to the program," (2) the individual who is the new beneficiary if a change in beneficiaries occurs pursuant to Section 529(c)(3)(C), and/or (3) the individual receiving a plan interest as a scholarship under a qualified program.[31] The only restriction in the proposed regulations is that the benefi-

---

27. If the employer transfers ownership to the employee, then compensation income should result on the date ownership is transferred. This compensation income should be equivalent to the fair market value of the account at the time.

28. *See* **Appendix F: Advance Notice of Proposed Regulations.**

29. *See* **Chapter Nine: Estate Planning with Section 529 Savings Plans.**

30. I.R.C. § 529(b)(1)(A)(i), (e)(1).

31. *Id.* § 529(e)(1).

ciary be an individual.[32] Thus, the account owner, his/her spouse, any relative or unrelated party can be the beneficiary. In addition, the rules do not require that a beneficiary even be notified as to the existence of the 529 plan.

Usually, an individual already born is designated as the beneficiary of the account, and that beneficiary is often the child or grandchild of the owner. However, the ultimate beneficiary need not be specified when the account is set up. Additionally, there is no requirement that the beneficiary have any traditional connection to the account owner, that is, the account owner is not limited to family when selecting a beneficiary. The account owner could set up an account for his/her long-lost childhood sweetheart's best friend's niece's daughter if he/she wished. However, changing the beneficiary to a family member unrelated to that beneficiary would result in tax consequences unless the new beneficiary is a member of the same family as the original beneficiary. (*See* **Chart 7-1**.)

CHART 7-1 Qualified Beneficiaries Upon Rollover to New Beneficiary

- A spouse of the original beneficiary
- A lineal descendent, such as child, grandchild, or great-grandchild, of the original beneficiary
- A stepchild, stepmother, or stepfather (but no step-grandchildren) of the original beneficiary
- A brother, sister, stepbrother, or stepsister of the original beneficiary
- A lineal ancestor, such as father, mother, or grandparent, of the original beneficiary
- A niece or nephew of the original beneficiary
- A mother or sister of the original beneficiary's mother or father
- A first cousin of the original beneficiary
- An in-law, either mother, father, sister, brother, son, or daughter, of the original beneficiary
- Husband or wife of anyone on this list

The code provides that tax-exempt organizations can set up scholarship programs for permissible beneficiaries of the future. Section 529(e)(1)(C) in part defines "*designated beneficiary*" as the individual receiving a distribution for qualified higher education expenses as part of a scholarship program maintained by a Section 501(c)(3) charity. This means that if a charity, whose purpose is to set up scholarships, establishes a Section 529 plan, any distribution to a person for qualified higher education or special needs expense will be permitted. By establishing such scholarship funds, charities are able to use the institutional expertise of the plan managers to help build their scholarship funds.

32. Prop. Treas. Reg. § 1.529-1(c), 63 Fed. Reg. 45,019 (Aug. 24, 1998).

4. Cash Requirement

The code provides that contributions to the plan must be made in cash.[33] The proposed regulations allow contributions to be made by check, money order, credit card, or similar method as long as they are permitted under the state program.[34] Some plans permit payroll deduction or electronic funds transfers, and some employers who provide the Section 529 plan as a fringe benefit require this. This "forced savings" aspect can encourage some who would not otherwise save to set cash aside for this program.

Appreciated securities, closely held business interests, and other investment assets do not generally qualify as cash. Therefore, these assets must first be sold and converted to cash before they can be transferred to a Section 529 plan. Even if the state program allows an account to be funded with these assets, the assets must be sold to meet the cash requirement. This transfer could constitute a gift to the beneficiary (if the previous form in which the assets were held did not already represent a gift to the beneficiary). Assuming the transfer from the prior nonliquid investment form to the Section 529 savings plan is treated as a gift, the beneficiary would then pay income tax upon the conversion and deemed liquidation of those assets. Under the new "*kiddie tax*" rule [section 1(h)], any income and gain will be taxed to the full-time student beneficiary under age 24—at the income tax rate applied to trust and estates. Any loss on the deemed sale of the noncash assets would also constitute the beneficiary's loss and could be limited by the loss limitation rules.[35]

Some states and custodianship laws might allow custodianship accounts under *Uniform Gifts to Minors Act* (UGMA)/*Uniform Transfers to Minors Act* (UTMA) or trust assets to be transferred to a Section 529 plan.[36] As is the case with other noncash assets, the UGMA/UTMA or trust assets are deemed sold. The taxes due on this deemed sale will be paid by the beneficiary (minor) because when the assets were held in the UGMA/UTMA account or trust, they were legally owned by the minor, despite the fact that a custodian or trustee had control of the account or trust until the minor reached the age of majority. As in the case of noncash assets, any income or gain will be taxed to the full-time dependent student under age 24 at the income rates applied to trusts and estates—and any loss could be limited by the loss limitation rules. After such a conversion, any earnings on the Section 529 fund are not taxed when used for qualified expenses.[37]

---

33. I.R.C. § 529(b)(2).
34. Prop. Treas. Reg. § 1.529-2(d), 63 Fed. Reg. 45,019 (Aug. 24, 1998).
35. I.R.C. §§ 165(c), 1211.
36. Uniform Gifts to Minors Act, 8C U.L.A. 25 (2000); Uniform Transfers to Minors Act, 8A U.L.A. 297 (2000).
37. For a discussion of these conversions, see **Chapter Seventeen: Coordinating Section 529 Plans with Other Savings Techniques**.

Planning Pointer

When a UGMA/UTMA account is funded, an irrevocable transfer of the asset to the beneficiary occurs. Thus, once the beneficiary reaches the age of majority, the donor cannot be assured that the funds will be used for higher education expenses because the beneficiary will have complete control over the account funds. When the 529 plan permits, transferring UGMA/UTMA assets into a Section 529 savings plan should be considered. Such a transfer may later deter the previous UGMA/UTMA beneficiary from taking the funds and using them for reckless and/or non-education purposes. Once contributed by the custodian to a Section 529 savings plan, the assets cannot be withdrawn for nonqualified expenses without incurring the imposition of an income tax and an additional ten percent *penalty tax*. The only drawback of such a strategy is the immediate imposition of a capital gains tax (at the income rate for trusts and estates when the "kiddie tax" applies) upon conversion of the custodianship assets to cash.

Obviously, one of the disadvantages of the Section 529 savings plan is this cash restriction. Since most people do not readily have available large sums of liquid assets to donate to these plans, any sale of capital assets will result in federal capital gains tax, a possible *net investment income tax* of 3.8 percent, as well as any applicable state tax. The cash requirement could be met by borrowing funds to invest in a Section 529 savings plan. However, after the *TCJA* of 2017, the taxpayer will no longer obtain a home equity interest deduction when borrowing from the principal residence to invest in a Section 529 plan—at least until 2026.[38] Despite these disadvantages, a Section 529 plan may still be the best option for the client as Section 529 savings plans typically provide significant tax and other advantages (for example, control, financial aid, and investment returns).

5. Limitation on Noneducation Purposes

The code requires that the contributions to a Section 529 savings plan be made "to provide for the qualified higher education expenses (QHEE)" of the designated beneficiary. (*See* Section E below). This means that the plan should not be set up as a retirement fund or a general investment fund but rather as an education fund. It is possible that an advisor might think of these 529 plans as retirement or investment funds because of (1) the benefit of tax deferral, (2) the fact that the funds might be protected from creditors, and (3) the return on the investment in these plans might be better than other investments. However, if the fund were so used, the earnings on the Section 529 fund would be taxed at ordinary rates, plus a 10 percent

38. I.R.C. § 163(h)(3)(C)(ii).

additional *penalty tax* would be imposed. Using a Section 529 plan as a retirement or investment plan vehicle, even if allowed under the code, would not make sense from a tax point of view as regular investment accounts are taxed at a maximum of 20 percent on capital gains and qualified dividends, as compared to 37 percent rate for ordinary income (the applicable rates in 2021).

6. Limitation on "Excess Contributions"

The code also requires that the state program establish procedures to prevent contributions beyond the *"reasonably expected qualified education expenses"* of the beneficiary. The proposed regulations provide a safe harbor—an amount determined by "actuarial estimates" to pay tuition, required fees, room and board for "five years of undergraduate school at the highest cost institution allowed by the program." However, it is not clear what the term "actuarial estimates" means. Although the date when a student begins college is relatively easy to determine, calculating the cost of qualified education expenses may be difficult because it is uncertain which school the beneficiary will attend and what those future costs may be. In addition, estimating earnings on the account may be uncertain given fluctuating market conditions.

Despite the "reasonable" need guideline, states vary greatly as to their limitations. Even states in close geographical proximity have widely differing contribution limits. (*See* **Chart 7-2**.) Some states base their limitation rules on total contributions, while others set the limit based upon the account's value. The limit for state school contribution plans tends to average around $375,000; however, some states set the limit as high as $529,000.

Many other programs do not follow the safe harbor rule and include graduate school costs and other qualified expenses in the computation of their contribution limits. Thus, "reasonable" can vary depending on whether the beneficiary will attend a state or private school or attend medical, law, or other graduate school. The IRS has issued private letter rulings allowing states to base their contribution limit on four years of undergraduate and three years of graduate school. According to the 1998 proposed regulations, "reasonable" limitation calculations are supposed to be done on a per-beneficiary basis, i.e., if there is more than one account for a particular beneficiary, the accounts are to be aggregated when determining if the contribution limit has been reached.

Interestingly, there is no enforcement mechanism in place to assure that this "reasonable" requirement is being met. The only thing a state can do is require a representation from the donor that multiple accounts do not exist. However, it is completely within the federal rules to set up multiple Section 529 savings plans, often in more than one state, as long as the contributions taken together do not exceed the "reasonable" need amount.

CHART 7-2 Reasonable Need Chart

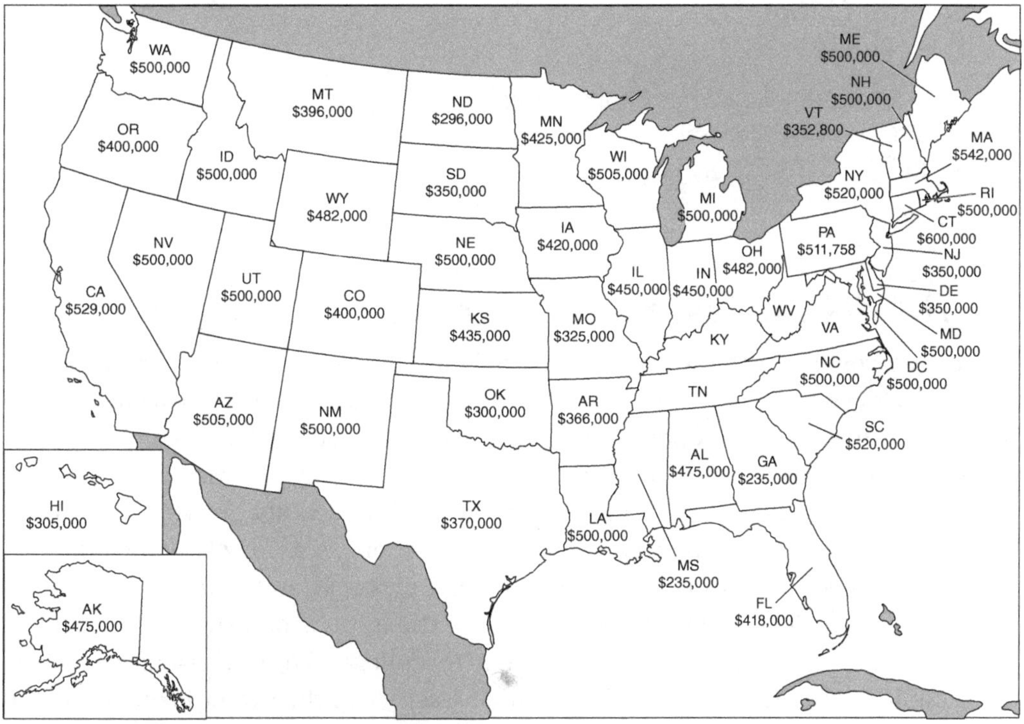

7. Separate Accounting Requirement

The code also requires that the separate account be established for each beneficiary.[39] Thus, multiple beneficiaries to one account are not allowed.[40] The reason for this requirement is that the state has the responsibility of reporting the earnings portion from the account for each tax period. Thus, if a nonqualified distribution is made, the government and parties involved can identify who the distributee is and his/her tax penalty liability. No restriction exists on the number of accounts one beneficiary may have, as long as the total funds of all accounts do not exceed the reasonably expected education costs.

In addition to periodically reporting the earnings portion from the account, the state will report (1) any contributions to the account, (2) any distributions from the account, and (3) any other matters as required by the Secretary.[41] After December 31, 2002, the state is not required to monitor whether the account goes to qualified expenditures. This is the individual taxpayer's responsibility. Nor is the state required to collect any additional tax associated with any nonqualified use.

39. I.R.C. § 529(b)(3).

40. Although there seems to be a contemplated exception for the beneficiaries of a QTP established by state or local government or by a nonprofit organization for the purpose of granting scholarships under Section 529(e)(1)(C).

41. I.R.C. § 529(d).

Planning Pointer

The taxpayer, not the state, is responsible for ensuring that the "reasonable need" limitation is not exceeded and that tax is paid on any nonqualified distribution from the Section 529 account.

C. The "No Investment Discretion" Directive

The code provides that the owner or beneficiary "may not directly or indirectly, direct the investment of any contributions to the program (or any earnings thereon)."[42] Whether the state chooses an investment *manager* or handles investments through their treasury, the state determines investment allocations by dictating portfolio design options (age based, balanced portfolio, equity growth, bonds) and sets minimum and maximum contribution limitations. The *age-based portfolio* is the most common type of fund, providing a mix of stocks and bonds based on the beneficiary's age. The younger the beneficiary, the more aggressive and riskier the investments. As the beneficiary gets closer to college age, the assets are put in more liquid forms. The age-based portfolio is best when the owner is unsure about whether the funds will be available when the beneficiary attends college. Many states offer riskier investment options, such as *Real Estate Investment Trusts* (REIT) funds and other *single-fund options*, such as small caps, global markets, etc.[43]

Because the states offer so many options, the owner (with the help of an advisor) can essentially affect the investments "indirectly."[44] This is true because the owner can decide initial investment strategy when the state offers various options, can decide whether to reallocate the account among available investment options once a year[45] or can decide to roll over the plan to a different plan once a year.[46] For example, the owner may choose all equities or a mixture of equities and fixed income. In addition, the owner can switch investments if the beneficiary is changed.

---

42. *Id.* § 529(b)(4).

43. The IRS's current policy is to allow the use of individual funds as qualified tuition programs. *See* Danielle A. Merrick, *529: States' Nightmare, Estate Planners' Dream*, 59 J. Mo. B. 316 (2003).

44. *See* **Chapter Thirteen: Investment Planning with Section 529 Savings Plans.**

45. I.R.S. Notice 2001-55, 2001-2 C.B. 299 (Sept. 24, 2001), states that "the Internal Revenue Service and the Treasury Department expect that the final regulations under Section 529 will provide that a program does not violate Section 529(b)(5) if it permits a change in the investment strategy selected for a section 529 account once per calendar year, and upon a change in the designated beneficiary of the account."

46. I.R.C. § 529(c)(3)(C)(i), (iii).

Planning Pointer

The owner of a Section 529 plan can choose a plan with an established management company, a plan with a particular investment strategy, or a plan with a particular investment category. In addition, the owner can change investment options once a year or rollover the plan to another state plan once a year. These choices have the practical consequence of allowing the owner to "indirectly" direct the investments. However, when the owner is risk averse and wants to ensure that funds will be available for the beneficiary, the *age-based portfolio* is best.

D. The "Not Pledged as Collateral" Rule

The code requires that the account owner not pledge the account as collateral or use the account as "security for a loan."[47] This requirement ensures that the funds will grow for college expenses. Generally, the account does not yet belong to the beneficiary, so the assets cannot be pledged by the beneficiary, nor can the beneficiary's creditors reach the assets.[48] However, the no-pledge requirement does not preclude the account owner's creditors from reaching the assets held in the Section 529 savings plan (or, in the case of a UGMA/UTMA transfer to a 529 account, the beneficiary's creditors). Any available asset protection, however, may arise either from state law or by the plan agreement itself.[49]

E. Used for "Qualified Higher Education Expenses"

Federal tax advantages arise under Section 529 when distributions from a Section 529 plan are used to pay the beneficiary's "*qualified higher education expenses*" (QHEE).[50] The definition of QHEE has changed over the years and includes tuition, fees, books, supplies, and equipment required for the enrollment or attendance of the designated beneficiary at an "eligible education institution."[51] Recently, QHEE has included expenses for K–12 tuition and payment of qualified student debt. Only "required" expenses are qualified. For those attending school at least *half-time*, qualified expenses also include *room and board* as long as those expenses are not greater than the allowance for room and board as determined by the *eligible*

---

47. *Id.* § 529(b)(5).

48. Except possibly in situations where UGMA/UTMA funds are transferred into a Section 529 plan. In that situation, the beneficiary's creditors may have a good claim to reach the now–529 plan funds because those funds originally belonged to the beneficiary when held in the UGMA/UTMA account. Obviously, once the funds are in the 529 account, the beneficiary could not pledge them without causing disqualification from Section 529 treatment.

49. See **Chapter Twelve: Nontax Aspects of Section 529 Savings Plans** for a discussion of this issue.

50. I.R.C. § 529(c).

51. *Id.* § 529(e)(3)(A). Described in Section 481 of the Higher Education Act of 1965 (20 U.S.C. § 1088).

education institution[52] or the actual invoice amount the student received from the eligible education institution for residing in housing.[53] If a student is living off campus, an allowance is permitted based on the cost of attendance for financial aid purposes as determined by the eligible education institution.[54] This limitation, which was modified by *EGTRRA* of 2001, may allow the school to determine this expense for purposes of what is qualified. For example, a student living with a parent is entitled to claim room and board as a qualified higher education expense but only if such expenses are actually paid to the parent.

After the *American Recovery and Reinvestment Act (ARRA) of 2009*, the definition of QHEE was expanded to include the purchase of computer or peripheral equipment (such as printers), computer software, and even the Internet access and related services.[55] All of this equipment, software, and services must be used primarily by the beneficiary during any of the years the beneficiary is enrolled at the eligible educational institution. No computer software designed for sports, games, or hobbies is allowed unless the software is predominantly educational in nature. Under *ARRA* these rules were to expire, but the *Protecting Americans from Tax Hikes (PATH) Act of 2015* permanently reinstated this definition.

Distributions from the Section 529 account can also be used for education expenses incurred when attending graduate or professional school. In addition, those funds can also cover expenses of "*special needs*" children—expenses incurred in connection with the child's enrollment or attendance at an eligible school.[56] No regulations exist yet discussing this issue, but logically the costs of special-education schools (no matter what level) for physically and mentally disabled beneficiaries would qualify. In other words, the scope of the definition of an eligible institution under Section 529 would be expanded beyond merely accredited colleges and universities; it could be expanded to include vocational training programs, vocational and tech schools, and so forth.

QHEE could cover "leisure" oriented courses, as long as the courses qualify for degree credits. One author has stated, "[a] school could offer a whale watching tour to taxpayers as long as they granted participants half-time credit toward a marine biology degree."[57] Another author has stated that a highly compensated individual, such as a partner in a major law firm, could open a Section 529 plan to provide for education, including living expenses, during a career change.[58] In Florida, there is a

52. Allowance for room and board at an eligible institution is defined in Section 472 of the Higher Education Act of 1965, Pub. L. No. 89-329, 79 Stat. 1219, 20 U.S.C. § 1001.

53. I.R.C. § 529(e)(3)(B). This code section applies to distributions after December 31, 2001.

54. *Id.* § 529(e)(3)(B)(ii)(I).

55. *Id.* §§ 529(e)(3)(A), 530(b)(3)(A). (Computer or peripheral equipment is defined in Section 168(i)(2)(B), and computer software is defined in Section 197(e)(3)(B).)

56. *Id.* § 529(e)(3)(A)(ii). *See* **Chapter Eleven: Disability Planning with Section 529 Savings Plans**.

57. Jacqueline E. King, Financing a College Education: How It Works, How It's Changing 140 (Am. Council on Educ.: Oryx Press Series on Higher Educ. 1999).

58. Helen W. Gunnarsson, *Law Pulse*, 90 Ill. B.J. 168, 174 (2002).

specialized school that offers "golf degrees"—primarily to attract owner beneficiaries of 529 plans. If the owner is the plan beneficiary, however, the state plan must be checked to make sure there are no restrictions limiting the owner from also being the beneficiary.

CHART 7-3 Qualified Education

- Undergraduate
- Graduate
- Professional
- Vocational Training
- Registered Apprenticeship Programs
- Special Needs

After the *Tax Cuts and Jobs Act of 2017*, the QHEE definition was expanded to include expenses for tuition in connection with enrollment or attendance "at an elementary or secondary public, private, or religious school."[59] The *TCJA* limited these tuition expenses to no more than $10,000 during any taxable year.[60] This amount should cover most tuition costs of many nonpublic schools, particularly the less expensive parochial schools. However, some private schools and many boarding schools may have larger tuition costs.[61] Thus, the need may arise to coordinate the Section 529 plan with the Coverdell, which would cover those higher tuition expenses, along with room and board, tutors, and other K–12 expenditures not covered by Section 529.[62] The *TCJA* also allowed 529s to be coordinated with the Section 529A ABLE accounts.[63]

After the *Setting Every Community Up for Retirement Enhancement (SECURE) Act of 2019*, the QHEE definition was further expanded. First, certain expenses associated with "registered apprenticeship programs" that are certified by the Secretary of Labor under the National Apprenticeship Act will be covered.[64] These include fees, books, supplies, and equipment. Second, QHEE was expanded to include amounts paid as principal or interest on any qualified education loan made to a designated beneficiary or sibling.[65] Those loans are defined exactly as they are for the above-the-line deduction under section 221(d) for student loan interest. As with the K–12 tuition payments, the limit is $10,000 of principal or interest.

59. I.R.C. § 529(c)(7).
60. *Id.* § 529(e)(3)(A).
61. *See* **Chapter Two: The Benefits and Costs of a Good Education**.
62. *See* **Chapter Eighteen: Coordinating Section 529 Plans with Tax Benefits**.
63. *See* **Chapter Eleven: Disability Planning with Section 529 Savings Plans**.
64. I.R.C. § 529(c)(8) (citing Section 1 of the National Apprenticeship Act at 29 U.S.C. § 50).
65. *Id.* § 529(c)(9).

However, this limit is a lifetime limit, not an annual one.[66] The *SECURE Act* also expanded this tax benefit to include not only the beneficiary of the Section 529 plan but any sibling.[67]

EXAMPLE 7-1: Suppose Ben has $10,000 of qualified student loans, as do his three siblings. Up to $40,000 could be withdrawn from Ben's 529 plan to pay off these loans, and this would be a deemed qualifying distribution (assuming this was recognized by the state where the plan is located).

This new provision not only expands the definition of QHEE but extends the planning time horizon. The taxpayer can thus keep funds in the 529 plan longer to ensure compounding of investments and then delay payment of the loans until after college. This strategy would work well when investments are high and loan interest is low. It also works well when the grandparent owns the 529 plan and the student qualifies for financial aid, since the 529 distribution can be saved for payment of that loan after college.[68] (*See* **Chart 7-4** for a summary of the definition of QHEE.)

CHART 7-4 Qualified Higher Education Expenses

- Tuition
- Room and board*
- Fees
- Books
- Supplies
- Equipment required for enrollment
- Certain computer technology/equipment
- Internet access and related services**
- Special need expenses
- K–12 tuition***
- Registered apprenticeship programs
- Qualified education loan repayments***

*Only if student is enrolled half-time and only if no greater than eligible education institution allowance.

**Computer software designed for sports, games, and hobbies not covered.

*** Up to $10,000.

66. *Id.* § 529(c)(9)(B).
67. *Id.* § 529(c)(9)(C)(ii).
68. *See* **Chapter Nineteen: Coordinating Section 529 Plans with Financial Aid.**

F. Used by "Eligible Student"

The law defines "*eligible student*" as an individual who is at least a *half-time* student in a degree or certificate undergraduate or graduate program.[69] A student is *half-time* if he/she is carrying at least one-half the normal full-time workload for the course of study the student is pursuing. In addition, an eligible student must not have been convicted of a federal or state felony consisting of the possession or distribution of a controlled substance.[70] (Murderers and rapists, on the other hand, could qualify). "Eligible student" also encompasses "special needs" students.

The "eligible student" must be the original "designated beneficiary" (or a member of the original beneficiary's "family" in a rollover situation). It is important to note that when making the determination of whether a new beneficiary is a member of the family (and thus whether the change in beneficiary will qualify for tax-free treatment), the point of reference is the prior beneficiary, *not* the owner.

EXAMPLE 7-2: Alice sets up a Section 529 account for her son, Ben, who is the son of an earlier marriage. If Alice dies and her current husband becomes the account owner, he cannot change the beneficiary to his children unless he had legally adopted Ben and thus his children were legally Ben's stepbrothers or stepsisters. Any person listed in **Chart 7-1** as it relates to Ben would be a permissible beneficiary. On the other hand, Alice's husband could have revoked the account with income tax payments and a *10 percent penalty.*

The following chart (**Chart 7-5**) sets forth who will qualify as "family" in relation to the original beneficiary when there is a rollover. Note that a person living in the taxpayer's abode who is not related by marriage or biology is not included. "Family" therefore excludes unmarried gay and lesbian couples or unmarried cohabitants.

EXAMPLE 7-3: Alice sets up a Section 529 account for her son, Ben. Ben is in a committed relationship with Charlie. Ben uses a portion of the Section 529 savings account to earn his undergraduate degree. Ben does not plan on attending graduate school, but his partner Charlie has been accepted to medical school. Alice cannot designate Charlie as the new beneficiary for the remainder of the Section 529 savings account without triggering income taxes as well as the *10 percent penalty.*

69. I.R.C. § 529(e).

70. This drug conviction requirement coincides with the financial aid requirements and with the requirements in I.R.C. § 25A.

CHART 7-5 Who Qualifies as "Family" of the Beneficiary

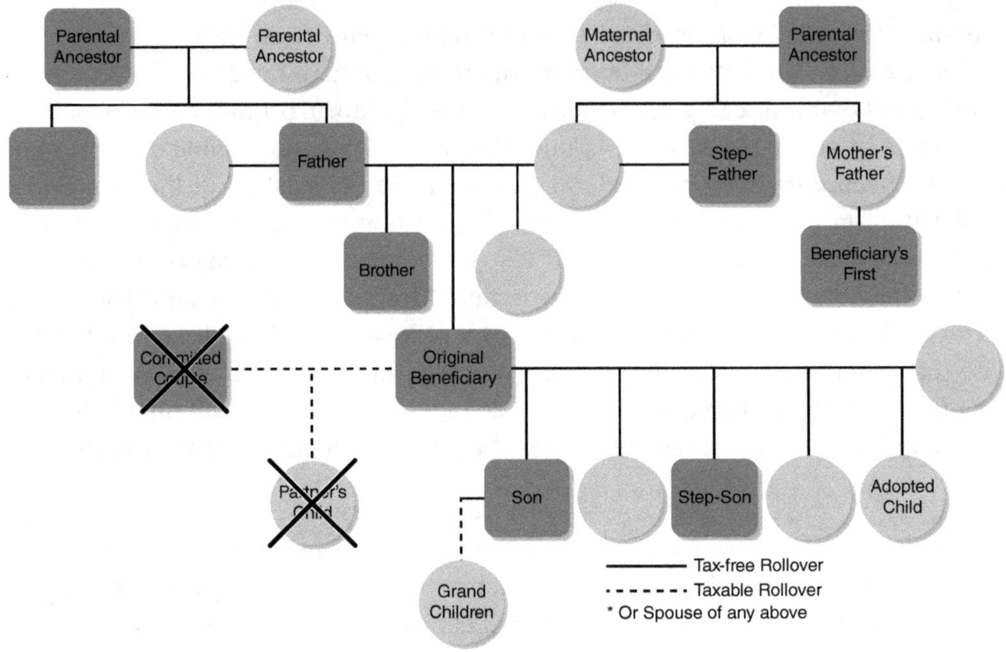

Planning Pointer

The ability of the owner to change the beneficiary to a wide variety of family members provides control and planning advantages. Parents, for example, can set up an account for a niece or nephew even before their own child is born. The parents can do this without notifying the niece or nephew and when their child is born (assuming the child is in the same generation as the niece or nephew) may change the beneficiary to the child without any tax consequences. The owner may also be able to control the behavior of the beneficiary before and during college. For example, if the owner does not like the behavior or grades of the beneficiary, he/she can simply change the beneficiary.

G. Used at "Eligible Education Institution"

The eligible student must be attending an "*eligible education institution*." An "eligible education institution" is defined as an institution that is described in Section 481 of the Higher Education Act of 1965 or as an institution that is eligible to participate in a program under Title IV of that Act.[71] Essentially, any accredited

71. Prop. Treas. Reg. § 1.529-1(c), 63 Fed. Reg. 45,019 (Aug. 24, 1998).

college or graduate school or post-secondary trade or vocational school in the United States that can participate in the federal student aid program will qualify. Foreign institutions may also qualify. K–12 educational institutions would also qualify. To verify that the school is accredited, one can contact the website of the school, ask the state manager sponsoring the plan, or go to two U.S. Department of Education websites: https://ope.ed.gov/dapip/#/home or https://studentaid.gov/understand-aid/types/international.

H. Qualified Payment Method

Section 529 does not require that tuition be paid directly to the education institution. Therefore, qualified distributions for QHEE payments could logically be made in four different ways. First, payment could be made directly to the eligible institution. Second, payment could be made to the designated beneficiary and to the eligible institution. Third, funds could be distributed to the designated beneficiary and the beneficiary will either supply documentation that the funds were used for qualified expenses at the institution or can certify in writing that the distribution will be spent within a "reasonable time" after the distribution for qualified expenses. Finally, for a special needs beneficiary, evidence of enrollment or attendance at an eligible institution should suffice.

Planning Pointer

Proceeds from the Section 529 account that are used for books, supplies, computers, education software, the Internet, and room and board will not preclude the availability of the gift tax exclusion under the Section 2503(e) for *tuition payment directly* to the education institution. For planning purposes, the Section 529 account should be used for books, supplies, room, board, and any tuition that is not paid with Section 2503(e) funds. Nonqualified expenses, such as those for clothes, computers, transportation, etc., can be covered by the Section 2503(b) *per-donee annual exclusion* ($15,000 in 2021).

I. Conclusion

The requirements of Section 529 are not complicated. The plan must be the "creation of the state," the contributions must be in cash, and the total value of the plan must not exceed what is reasonable for the expected higher education needs of the beneficiary. The account owner cannot direct investments or pledge the account. To qualify for tax deferral and favorable tax treatment upon distribution, the account funds must be used for "qualified higher education expenses" by an "eligible student" at an "eligible education institution." However, because Section 529 plans are the creation of the state, the state can impose its own rule variations, which could further restrict or extend these requirements.

Overall, the biggest disadvantage of the Section 529 plan is the cash requirement. A second disadvantage is the uncertainty of the application of several of the rules; most particularly, the reasonable need rule and the special needs requirements. Third, the investment options are defined by the state resulting in the owner having no direct control over these investments. Lastly, qualified distributions may be made only for QHEEs—not for all education-related expenses—and the calculation of QHEE can be complex.

CHART 7-6 Chart of Section 529 Requirements

Requirements	Federal Rules	State Law Variations
Contributor/donor	No relationship to beneficiary.	May require relationship between donor and beneficiary.
Owner	Any person. Owner need not be donor. Owner can be beneficiary.	Owner cannot be beneficiary. Owner can only be an individual.
Transfer of Ownership	Allowed but may result in gift tax.	May be restricted.
Beneficiary	Any Individual.	May limit to minors. May restrict adults.
Cash Contribution	Cash, including check, money order or credit card.	Electronic payroll; others same as federal. States may allow transfer of UGMA/UTMA accounts or other assets to the fund (but must be sold for cash).
Accumulation	For reasonably expected needs.	From $ 235,000–$ 529,000.
Multiple Accounts	Allowed.	State might not allow multiple accounts.
Pledged	Cannot be pledged.	Cannot be pledged.
Rollover	Once a year.	May result in tax consequences if move out of state.
Set Up	Individual, group, corporation.	May restrict for entities.
Payment Method	Need not be made directly to education institution.	May require direct payment.

Chapter 8

Federal Income Tax Planning with Section 529 Savings Plans

Section 529 savings plans offer excellent federal tax benefits to taxpayers at *all* income levels. Substantial amounts can be contributed to these accounts to meet the reasonably expected education needs of the beneficiary. Although contributions are not deductible on the federal return, the earnings grow tax-free and the appreciation, including earnings, are not taxed as long as the funds are distributed for qualified higher education expenses (QHEEs). In addition, the plan can be rolled over to a different plan or a different qualified beneficiary without tax consequences. Lastly, Section 529 plans can be coordinated with other tax benefits, such as the American Opportunity Tax Credit, the Lifetime Learning Credit, and financial aid. This chapter will discuss the tax consequences of contributions, distributions, and rollovers.

This chapter will also discuss the recent changes made by the *Tax Cuts and Jobs Act of 2017* and other legislation. The last chapter discussed the *TCJA* expansion of the definition of *qualified higher education expenses* (QHEE) to include tuition of up to $10,000 paid for K–12 education. It also discussed the *SECURE Act* of 2019 expansion of QHEE to cover up to $10,000 of qualified student loan payments for the designated beneficiary and siblings. This chapter will address six other important tax changes that have had a direct or indirect impact on 529 federal income tax planning. First, the *above-the-line tuition and fees deduction* under Section 222 will expire on December 31, 2020, unless revived. Second, losses in the 529 account realized when the investment in the account is closed are now a *miscellaneous itemized deduction* and will no longer be allowed. Third, if the parent borrows to invest in a Section 529 plan using home equity, they will no longer be entitled to that *itemized deduction* for interest paid on that loan. Fourth, ordinary and necessary educational expenses of an employee under Section 162 will no longer be allowed as a deduction if the employee is not reimbursed for these by the employer. Fifth, the "kiddie tax" rules have changed so that the child is taxed at trust and estate tax rates when taxable accounts are established. Lastly, the *dependency exemption* was eliminated and replaced by a meager *dependent credit.* Except for the *tuition and fees deduction*, all these tax changes will sunset at the end of 2025.

A. Contributions and Earnings

Although no federal income tax deduction is allowed for a contribution to a Section 529 savings plan,[1] the contribution can be made by anyone, no matter what his/her income level. The earnings and growth are not taxed upon accumulation or upon withdrawals *if* distributions from the Section 529 savings plan are used for QHEE.[2] The taxpayer can contribute to the account up to five times the *per-donee exclusion amount* (or double for *split gift* elections of married couples)—avoiding adverse gift tax consequences when averaged over five years.[3] The only restriction on the amount that can be contributed is that which is reasonable for the particular beneficiary's education needs.[4] Although some states may have contribution restrictions, there is no federal prohibition against having more than one account per beneficiary.

EXAMPLE 8-1: In 2021, Bill and Mary (husband and wife) elect to split a gift of $150,000 to establish a Section 529 account for their daughter. Bill and Mary will not have a federal income tax deduction for this contribution,[5] nor will they incur a gift tax on the transfer.

The tax deferral from these accounts can be significant and is greatest when large amounts of money are invested over longer periods of time. For example, if the taxpayer invested $15,000 per year for 18 years in an account earning 5 percent, $457,467 could be accumulated for QHEE. Likewise, if the taxpayer invests $75,000 every five years for 18 years in an account earning 10 percent, almost $1,000,000 could be available for qualified expenses. (*See* **Chart 8-1** and **Chart 8-2**.)

1. Some states allow a deduction for all or part of the contribution, and this can be an important factor in picking a plan. *See* **Chapter Ten: State Tax Planning with Section 529 Savings Plans**.

2. I.R.S. § 529(c)(3)(b)(ii). *See* **Chapter Seven: Federal Rules and Regulations for Section 529 Savings Plans**, E, Chart 7-3.

3. *See* **Chapter Nine: Estate Planning with Section 529 Savings Plans**.

4. See **Chapter Seven: Federal Rules and Regulations for Section 529 Savings Plans**, B.6, for a discussion of reasonably expected education needs.

5. They may, however, have a state income tax deduction for part of this contribution. *See* **Chapter Ten: State Tax Planning with Section 529 Savings Plans**.

CHART 8-1 Investment Growth Assuming 5% Rate for Annual Per-Donee Exclusion Gift

	Contribution	Start of Year	Growth (5%)	End of Year
Year 1	$ 15,000	$ 15,000	$ 750	$ 15,750
Year 2	$ 15,000	$ 30,750	$ 1,537.50	$ 32,287.50
Year 3	$ 15,000	$ 47,287.50	$ 2,264.44	$ 49,551.94
Year 4	$ 15,000	$ 64,551.94	$ 3,227.60	$ 67,779.54
Year 5	$ 15,000	$ 82,779.54	$ 4,138.98	$ 86,918.52
Year 6	$ 15,000	$ 101,918.52	$ 5,095.93	$ 107,014.44
Year 7	$ 15,000	$ 122,014.44	$ 6,100.72	$ 128,115.16
Year 8	$ 15,000	$ 143,115.16	$ 7,155.76	$ 159,270.91
Year 9	$ 15,000	$ 174,270.91	$ 8,713.55	$ 182,984.46
Year 10	$ 15,000	$ 197,984.46	$ 9,899.22	$ 207,883.68
Year 11	$ 15,000	$ 222,883.68	$ 11,144.18	$ 234,027.86
Year 12	$ 15,000	$ 249,027.86	$ 12,451.39	$ 261,479.25
Year 13	$ 15,000	$ 276,479.25	$ 13,823.96	$ 290,303.21
Year 14	$ 15,000	$ 305,303.21	$ 15,265.16	$ 320,568.37
Year 15	$ 15,000	$ 335,568.37	$ 16,778.42	$ 352,286.79
Year 16	$ 15,000	$ 367,286.79	$ 18,364.34	$ 385,651.13
Year 17	$ 15,000	$ 400,651.13	$ 20,032.56	$ 420,682.68
Year 18	$ 15,000	$ 435,682.68	$ 21,784.13	$ 457,466.81
Earnings Ratio = 5%				

CHART 8-2 Investment Growth Assuming 10% Rate for $75,000 Gift Every Five Years

	Contribution	Start of Year	Growth (10%)	End of Year
Year 1	$ 75,000	$ 75,000	$ 7,500	$ 82,500
Year 2	-0-	$ 82,500	$ 8,250	$ 90,750
Year 3	-0-	$ 90,750	$ 9,075	$ 99,825
Year 4	-0-	$ 99,825	$ 9,982.50	$ 109,807.50
Year 5	-0-	$ 109,807.50	$ 10,980.75	$ 120,788.25
Year 6	$ 75,000	$ 195,788.25	$ 19,578.83	$ 215,367.08
Year 7	-0-	$ 215,367.08	$ 21,536.71	$ 236,903.79
Year 8	-0-	$ 236,903.79	$ 23,690.38	$ 260,594.17
Year 9	-0-	$ 260,594.17	$ 26,059.42	$ 286,653.59
Year 10	-0-	$ 286,653.59	$ 28,665.36	$ 315,318.95
Year 11	$ 75,000	$ 390,318.95	$ 39,031.90	$ 429,350.85
Year 12	-0-	$ 429,350.85	$ 42,935.09	$ 472,285.94
Year 13	-0-	$ 472,285.94	$ 47,228.59	$ 519,514.53
Year 14	-0-	$ 519,514.53	$ 51,951.45	$ 571,465.98

(continued)

	Contribution	Start of Year	Growth (10%)	End of Year
Year 15	-0-	$ 571,465.98	$ 57,146.60	$ 628,612.58
Year 16	$ 75,000	$ 703,612.58	$ 70,361.26	$ 773,973.84
Year 17		$ 773,973.84	$ 77,397.38	$ 851,371.22
Year 18		$ 851,371.22	$ 85,137.12	$ 936,508.34
Earnings Ratio = 10%				

Planning Pointer

The tax disadvantages of a Section 529 plan are that (1) the plan converts possible capital gains into ordinary income if funds are not used for qualified purposes, (2) a 10 percent additional *penalty tax* is imposed on earnings of nonqualified distributions, and (3) the plan may result in higher investment and management fees than traditional investments. Nevertheless, there is a huge economic advantage to using these funds for education purposes because income taxes are not paid on any deferred earnings from the fund if used for QHEE.

B. Qualified Distributions or Withdrawals

The cash contributed to a Section 529 savings plan will *never* be subject to income tax even if used for a nonqualified purpose. Upon distribution or withdrawal, the cash contribution merely represents a return on investment or of capital. The earnings from a Section 529 investment will also never be taxed if distributed for QHEE.[6]

EXAMPLE 8-2: Alice opens a Section 529 savings account for the benefit of her son, Ben. In 2009, she contributed $65,000 cash to the plan. In 2021 she withdraws $30,000 for QHEE for Ben. Nothing is taxed.

Caution should be taken so the client matches the education expense during the year with the amounts from the Section 529 plan. A qualified distribution from a Section 529 account must occur in the same year as the QHEE to which the distribution relates. For taxpayers utilizing the cash method of accounting, this means that the proceeds from the 529 account can be used to pay the QHEE in the term those expenses are due. The 529 proceeds cannot be used to reimburse for any prior calendar year expenditures.[7]

6. I.R.C. § 529(c).
7. A similar problem can exist for the education credits.

Planning Pointer

The qualified distribution must correspond to the amount of QHEE incurred in the same calendar year as the distribution or by March 31 of the following year. Therefore, limited withdrawals in advance of expenditures will be permitted, but reimbursements for prior calendar year expenditures will not be permitted.

For distributions made from a Section 529 plan after December 31, 2002, the plan administrator does not have to verify that the distributions were used for qualified education expenses. Nor is the administrator required to collect the additional tax associated with nonqualified use of the Section 529 funds.[8] This rule alleviates much of the hassle of administering these plans. The program administrator's *only* duty is to issue a 1099-Q to the owner of the Section 529 savings plan in the year of distribution. The 1099-Q will disclose the total distribution from the program during the year and the *earnings ratio*—the earnings portion of the account divided by the total value of the account.[9] Form 1099-G (or 1099-Q) is to be sent to the *recipient* of the distributions.[10]

C. Nonqualified Distributions or Withdrawals

Distributions from the Section 529 plan will be taxed if the distributions are nonqualified. Examples of nonqualified uses are if the proceeds are used by an ineligible student, or for a nonqualified expenditure, or at a nonqualified institution. Other nonqualified distributions or withdrawals can include the owner withdrawing the funds for an emergency or other personal need, changing the plan before the one-year waiting period expires, or rolling the account over to a non–family member. Under these circumstances, all or a portion of the earnings on the nonqualified distribution will be taxed.

CHART 8-3 Nonqualified Distributions

- Used by ineligible student
- Used at nonqualified institution
- Used for nonqualified purpose
- Used for other than tuition, room, and board, etc.
- Withdrawn by donor
- Rolled over to nonqualified beneficiary
- Plan changed before the one-year waiting period

8. I.R.S. Notice 2001-81, 2001-02 C.B. 617 (Dec. 26, 2001).

9. I.R.S. Notice 2001-81, 2001-02 C.B. 617 (Dec. 26, 2001), prescribes procedures so that the plan administration reports basis and earnings portions each year.

10. *Id.*

When distributions are not qualified, the annuity rules under Section 72 are used to determine the excluded principal or contribution amount.[11] The distributions are generally treated as consisting of two components, either (1) earnings, which are taxed, or (2) principal or contributions, which are generally not taxed.[12] The earnings portion is taxed as ordinary income, even if attributable to capital gains. The portion representing earnings from the nonqualified distribution is also subject to a 10 percent additional *penalty tax*.

The portion of the distribution that consists of nontaxable principal equals the exclusion ratio (Section 529 plan contributions/present value of the Section 529 account) times the amount withdrawn for a nonqualified use. This amount is then subtracted from the total amount withdrawn.[13] This amount (determined after the subtraction) represents the interest earned on the portion of the account distributed, i.e., the amount that is taxable at ordinary rates.[14]

The following example shows how an allocation must be made when both qualified and nonqualified uses are made.

EXAMPLE 8-3: Alice opens a Section 529 savings account for the benefit of her son, Ben. In Years 1 through 5, she deposited $15,000 into the account for a total contribution of $75,000. At the close of Year 5, the account was valued at $86,981 (*See* **Chart 8-1**). The exclusion ratio is .86 ($75,000 / $86,981). The inclusion amount is .14 (1.0 – 0.86). Ben withdrew a total amount of $10,000. He spent $4,000 of the distribution on QHEE and $6,000 on a car. The portion of the distribution that represents interest earned is $1,400 (14% × $10,000). Of the $1,400 interest earned, $560.00 will be excludible from Ben's income because this part of the interest earned is attributable to the part of the distribution used for QHEE ($4,000/$10,000 × $1,400 = $560.00). Ben will include $840 of the $10,000 distribution in his gross income ($6,000/$10,000 × $1,400 = $840.00). In addition, Ben must pay a 10 percent penalty tax, i.e., $84.00 ($840.00 × .10).[15]

The QHEE may be reduced because the student receives the following: (1) scholarships (Section 117), (2) veterans education assistance, (3) *PELL grants*, (4) employer-provided assistance (Sections 117(d), 132(d) and 127), and (5) any

11. I.R.C. § 529(c)(3)(A).

12. *See id.* § 72(e)(2)(B), (e)(9). Also see discussion in Section C and Example 10-3 in **Chapter Ten: State Tax Planning with Section 529 Savings Plans**, illustrating when contributions that have been deductible under state law will be taxed if withdrawn for nonqualified purposes.

13. Prop. Treas. Reg. § 1.529-3(b), 63 Fed. Reg. 45,019 (Aug. 24, 1998).

14. *See* Taxpayer Relief Act of 1997, H.R. Rep. No. 105-220, at 357, *available at* https://www.congress.gov/congressional-report/105th-congress/house-report/220/1.

15. Another way to calculate the amount of the nonqualified distribution that is taxed is to multiply the *earnings ratio* (shown on Box 2 of Form 1099-Q and illustrated in Charts 8-1 and 8-2) by a fraction, the numerator of which is the nonqualified education expenses paid during the year and the denominator of which is the total amount distributed.

other nontaxable payment (other than gifts and inheritances) received as education assistance.[16] In these circumstances any earnings on the portion of the Section 529 distribution attributable to this reduction will be subject to tax. However, no additional *penalty tax* will be imposed. (*See* section D below.)

EXAMPLE 8-4: Same as **Example 8-3** except the qualified higher education expenses were $10,000 and Ben received a $6,000 scholarship. Thus, Ben's adjusted qualified expenses are $4,000. Otherwise, the answer is the same as **Example 8-3** (Ben will include $840 in gross income) except there is no additional tax.

Prior to 2003, the earnings portion of the account was determined as of the close of the calendar year by adding back the amount of all distributions made during the year.[17] However, starting in 2003, the earnings portion is generally determined as of the date of distribution.[18] Some states may report a nonqualified distribution as a distribution to the account owner, although some states permit an account owner to direct a nonqualified distribution to the beneficiary. If the state plan imposes its own separate penalty on the nonqualified distribution, the amount of that penalty should be subtracted from the earnings attributable to the account. Thus, the taxpayer should only owe tax on the earnings less the penalty.

1. Shifting the Tax Burden and the "Kiddie Tax"

The Tax Increase Prevention and Reconciliation Act (TIPRA) of 2005[19] expanded the "*kiddie tax*" from children under age 14 to those under age 18, starting in 2006. Under the "kiddie tax" rules at the time, the child was taxed at the parent's top marginal tax rate. *The Small Business and Work Opportunity Act (SBWOA) of 2007*[20] extended the "kiddie tax" further to include full-time dependent students up to the age of 24, starting in 2008. Both rules apply only if the child's earned income does not exceed one-half of his/her support.

Before *TIPRA*, the strategy was to purchase low or deferred income-generating investments, such as stocks or U.S. *Series EE/I bonds*, for a child under 14, often placing these in custodianship accounts. When the child attained age 14 or more, the assets were usually sold or redeemed because the "kiddie tax" no longer applied. With the extension of the "kiddie tax" to those under age 18 and students under age 24, this income-shifting strategy has completely eroded. Now with the *TCJA* of 2017, the unearned income of the qualifying child will be taxed at the highest tax rates, those imposed on trusts and estates.

16. I.R.C. § 529(c)(3)(B).
17. *Id.* § 529(c)(3)(D); Prop. Treas. Reg. § 1.529-1(c), 63 Fed. Reg. 45,019 (Aug. 24, 1998).
18. I.R.S. Notice 2001-81, 2001-02 C.B. 617 (Dec. 26, 2001).
19. 26 U.S.C.A. § 529 (2005).
20. H.R. Rep. No. 109-455, at 52 (2006).

Shifting of the ordinary income tax and the tax on the earnings to a lower bracket taxpayer is still possible when (1) the recipient of the nonqualified distribution is the beneficiary, (2) state law permits such a distribution to the beneficiary, and (3) when the beneficiary is at least 24 years of age and no longer subject to the "kiddie tax."[21] Under these circumstances, any nonqualified distribution up to the standard deduction amount of the kid will not be subject to taxation.

EXAMPLE 8-5: Same as **Example 8-3** above. If Ben were 25 years old and had taxable income of less than the standard deduction amount, he would not actually pay any tax on the $840. He would, however, still need to pay the penalty of $84.

When the nonqualified distribution is to a student under the age of 24, the tax is imposed at the marginal rates of a trust and estate. If, on the other hand, the donor/owner is taxed, because they withdrew the funds from the account, for example, the earnings on the nonqualified distribution will be taxed to them. After the *TCJA*, those ordinary income tax rates go up to 37 percent. After the *TCJA*, the tax rates under the "kiddie tax" will almost always be greater than the tax rates of an individual or married donor or owner with comparable income.[22]

2. Taxation of Distribution to Account Owner If Third Party Donations

The account owner may also be taxed on any funds withdrawn from the 529 account. Under the Advance Notice of proposed rulemaking, the Treasury expects to develop rules that will tax as income, rather than a return of capital, amounts withdrawn by an account owner that correspond to the contribution made by a person other than the account owner. The purpose of this rule is to discourage gifts to the account when an account owner transfers a Section 529 account to a new owner.

EXAMPLE 8-6: Mary and John, Alice's parents, set up a 529 for Alice's son, Ben, contributing $150,000 in Year 1 to the 529 account. In Year 2 they transfer the account ownership to Alice, and she withdraws all the funds from the account. According to the Advance Notice, the total distribution ($150,000 plus the earnings) will be taxed to Alice.

21. I.R.C. § 1(h). The "kiddie tax" would apply if the beneficiary is a dependent student and is younger than 24 years of age. The income of the dependent student would be taxed at the tax rates for trusts and estates.

22. *See id.* § 1. (Separate rate tables apply to a single individual, a head of household, a married couple filing jointly, a married person filing separately, and then the higher tax rates applicable to trusts and estates.)

3. Multiple Accounts

When the owner has accounts for the same beneficiary in several states, an issue arises as to whether the accounts must be aggregated to determine the earnings portion of an unqualified distribution. IRS Notice 2001-81[23] provides that such accounts need not be aggregated. Thus, separate accounts or different account owners may provide planning opportunities. For example, if the donor established a fixed income account in one plan and an equity account in another plan, a non-qualified distribution could be taken from the account with the lower earnings ratio. The same advantage could occur if the husband and wife (or others) set up two accounts for the same beneficiary.

D. Additional Tax (or Penalty) on Nonqualified Distributions

As the preceding examples illustrate, a nonqualified distribution may or may not result in a penalty tax. The 2001 *EGTRRA* replaced the "more than de minimis" penalty rule with a mandatory 10 percent federal "*additional tax*" on the earnings portion of any nonqualified distribution.[24] This is the same penalty that is applied to nonqualified Coverdell ESA distributions and to nonqualified distributions from IRAs before age 59½. The purpose of the additional tax (or *penalty tax* or *10 percent penalty*) is to discourage distributions for noneducation purposes.

However, there are several exceptions to the 10 percent penalty. The first is when the distribution is made subsequent to the designated beneficiary receiving a tax-free scholarship or tax-free assistance[25] *if* the distribution does not exceed the amount of the scholarship or assistance.[26]

EXAMPLE 8-7: Alice opens a Section 525 savings account for the benefit of her son, Ben. In Years 1 through 10, she deposits $15,000 per year into the account. In Year Ten, when Ben enters college, the fund is worth $207,883.68 (*see* **Chart 8-1**) and has earned interest of $9,899.22. The exclusion ratio is $150,000/$207,883.68 or 72 percent. Ben receives a scholarship of $20,000 for his freshman year education expenses. Alice directs that $20,000 of the Section 529 plan go to Ben to use as he pleases. There will be no penalty. However, Ben will pay tax on the earnings portion of the distribution (28 percent × $9,899.22 = $2,776.78). This will be treated as ordinary income to Ben. If Alice had directed $20,000 for herself, she would be taxed—possibly at higher ordinary income rates. If not spent, this amount would eventually be includable in her estate.

23. I.R.S. Notice 2001-81, 2001-02 C.B. 617 (Dec. 26, 2006).
24. I.R.C. § 529(c)(6).
25. Veteran's benefits, PELL Grants, or employer-provided education assistance.
26. I.R.C. §§ 529(c)(6), 530(d)(4)(B)(iii).

The second exception is when the beneficiary becomes disabled.[27] "*Disability*" is defined as a mental or physical disability. Again, the penalty would not be imposed, but a portion of the earnings would be taxable to the distributee. Arguably, the fund could be converted to a "special needs" fund. However, regulations have not yet been issued discussing this possibility.

The third and final exception is when the beneficiary dies.[28] In this case, the proceeds of the Section 529 plan should go to the beneficiary's estate to avoid the penalty. The value of the account will be included in the beneficiary's estate. This is true irrespective of the fact that during his/her lifetime the beneficiary had no control over the Section 529 assets and the fact that the beneficiary's consent was not a requirement for establishing the Section 529 account. In fact, the beneficiary may not even know of the existence of the account, but the account will still be included in the beneficiary's estate. Additionally, note that when the Section 529 asset account is transferred to the beneficiary's estate, the estate has no liquid assets to pay the tax due. However, because of the "reasonable expected qualified education expense" limit requirement discussed earlier,[29] and because of the large unified credit equivalent amount under the estate tax, this might not pose much of a problem. The earnings portion will be taxed and must be reported in the beneficiary's last return. However, the penalty will be avoided.

EXAMPLE 8-8: Alice has set up a Section 529 savings plan for her son, Ben. When contributions to the plan equal $66,000 and the value equals $156,000, Ben dies. If the proceeds of the plan go to Ben's estate, no penalty is imposed—although the earnings ($90,000) are still subject to income tax.

If the proceeds do not go to the beneficiary's estate, they could be rolled over to another qualified beneficiary or could be refunded to the owner. Designating another qualified beneficiary will avoid any tax and is the best strategy. When this is impossible, the fund will be returned to the owner, and the owner will pay a tax on the earnings plus the 10 percent penalty. Return of the funds to the owner will not only have immediate negative tax consequences, it could also frustrate the estate plan of the owner since the Section 529 funds will now be includable in the owner's estate (if not spent or given away or covered by the unified credit equivalent amount).

The federal penalty does not apply to a distribution that is subject to income tax because the education expense for which it was used was claimed either under the American Opportunity Credit or the Lifetime Learning Credit.[30] For a nonqualified distribution, the taxpayer must fill out Form 5329.

27. *Id.* §§ 529(c)(6), 530(d)(4)(B)(ii).
28. *Id.* §§ 529(c)(6), 530(d)(4)(B)(i).
29. *See* **Chapter Seven: Federal Rules and Regulations for Section 529 Savings Plans**, B.6.
30. The Job Creation and Worker Assistance Act of 2002, Pub. L. No. 107-147, 116 Stat. 21 (2002).

E. Rollovers: Changing the Plan or Beneficiary

The proceeds in a Section 529 savings plan can be distributed or *"rolled over"* to a different plan without federal tax consequences in two situations. First, the owner can change the plan but not the beneficiary.[31] Second, the owner can change the beneficiary.[32]

1. Changing the Plan

If the owner decides to *roll over* from one plan to a different plan with the same designated beneficiary, the owner has 60 days to set up the new plan before there are tax consequences.[33] The Code allows this type of rollover only one time in any 12-month period.[34] This restriction applies on a per-beneficiary basis and is intended to discourage creation of multiple accounts for the same beneficiary. This type of rollover is also intended to allow the owner of a Section 529 plan to have some investment control and move assets from one investment manager to another investment manager.[35] This will occur when either the owner wants to change to a different state plan or change investments or plans within the state.[36]

If two accounts are combined, then the investment in the first account is added to the investment in the second account.

EXAMPLE 8-9: A Section 529 account with an investment of $100,000 and a value of $120,000 is rolled over into an account with an investment of $90,000 and a value of $80,000. The new account now has an investment of $190,000 and a balance value of $200,000 with an earnings ratio of $10,000/$200,000 or 5 percent.

2. Changing the Beneficiary

If the owner decides to change the beneficiary on an existing plan, no time restrictions apply.[37] The only restriction is the new beneficiary *must* be a family member of the beneficiary for whom the plan was originally established.[38] (*See* **Chart 7-1.**) The old plan must provide the new plan with a statement of earnings; otherwise,

---

31. I.R.C. § 529(c)(3)(C)(i)(I).
32. *Id.* § 529(c)(3)(C)(i)(II), (c)(3)(C)(ii).
33. *Id.* § 529(c)(3)(C)(i)(I).
34. *Id.* § 529(c)(3)(C)(iii).
35. *See* **Chapter Thirteen: Investment Planning with Section 529 Savings Plans.**
36. Note: some states will tax a rollover to another state's plan. Some states will do so only if the rollover occurs within a set number of years from the year in which the account was created. *See* **Chapter Ten: State Tax Planning with Section 529 Savings Plans.**
37. I.R.C. § 529(c)(3)(C)(ii).
38. *Id.* § 529(c)(3)(C)(i)(II).

the entire rollover amount will be considered earnings.[39] For transactions involving 529 plans after December 31, 2001, the earnings will be determined as of the date of distribution.[40]

No adverse tax consequences occur if the new beneficiary is a family member and is the same generation (or an older generation).[41] If the new beneficiary is a family member but in a younger generation, the rollover may trigger a gift and a *generation-skipping* (GST) tax. However, if the new beneficiary is not a family member of the beneficiary, the *rollover distribution* is disqualified. Thus, the earnings will be taxed, and an additional tax will be imposed. See **Chapter Nine: Estate Planning with Section 529 Savings Plans** for a discussion of these issues.

3. Adverse Consequences from Rollover

If the Section 529 plan is "rolled over" to a different plan and does not meet one of the two qualifying circumstances (qualified rollover and qualified beneficiary), the rollover is considered a taxable distribution. In this case the "distributee" will be taxed on the earnings and incur a 10 percent penalty or additional tax. Presumably, the taxpayer is the account owner.

EXAMPLE 8-10: Assume that an account has a contributed investment of $100,000 and value of $120,000 (with $20,000 attributable to earnings). If this account is rolled over to a new plan in less than the one-year period of the last rollover, *or* the beneficiary is not a member of the family, the full $20,000 of earnings will be taxed to the owner— the owner is the person making the nonqualified rollover.

Planning Pointer

Funds from a Coverdell ESA or a qualified U.S. savings bond can be rolled into a 529 savings plan.[42] When this occurs, everything is considered earnings until *"appropriate documentation"* of the basis and earnings portion of such contributions is received by the new 529 account.[43] In the case of a rollover contribution

39. The earnings in a 529 plan have adverse tax effects only if distributions are made for nonqualified expenses. I.R.S. Notice 2001-81, 2001-02 C.B. 617 (Dec. 26, 2001).

40. *Id.*

41. *Id.* The Working Families Tax Relief Act of 2004 Section 406(a) changed Section 529(c)(5)(B) to clarify that there is no gift or GST tax when there is a rollover or change of beneficiary and the new beneficiary is assigned to the same generation or a higher generation and is a member of the family of the old beneficiary.

42. *See* **Chapter Seventeen: Coordinating Section 529 Plans with Other Savings Techniques**.

43. I.R.S. Notice 2001-81, 2061-2 C.B. 617 (Dec. 26, 2001).

from a Coverdell, "appropriate documentation" means an account statement issued by the financial institution that acted as trustee or custodian of the Coverdell that shows basis and earnings in the account. In the case of a rollover from the redemption of a qualified U.S. savings bond, an account statement or Form 1099-INT issued by the financial institution that redeemed the bonds showing interest from the redemption of the bonds will qualify as "appropriate documentation."

F. Recent Changes Impacting Education Planning with 529s

In addition to the kiddie tax changes discussed in C1 above, the *TCJA* of 2017 made several other important changes to the tax code that impact tax planning for 529 savings plans. Essentially, recent tax changes have modified or disallowed the following four types of deductions: (1) the above-the-line *tuition and fees deduction*, (2) the deduction for losses in the account, (3) the education expenses that are ordinary and necessary business expenses but are *not* reimbursed by the employer, and (4) the home-equity interest deduction. Numbers 2 and 3 above became denied *miscellaneous itemized deductions* under the *TCJA*. The other major change made by the *TCJA* was the elimination of the dependency exemption and the replacement with a dependent credit. This change has significant importance in determining who should be the taxpayer, the student, or the parent.

1. Tuition and Fees Deduction

The tuition deduction has historically been an on-again off-again tax benefit.[44] The *TCJA* of 2017 let this deduction under Section 222 expire. But then the Bipartisan Budget Act of 2018 (BBA) retroactively renewed it for the 2017 year, and then it expired again. Finally, the Taxpayer Certainty and Disaster Relief Act of 2019 reinstated the deduction retroactively to 2018 so it can be claimed through the end of 2020. Then, the *Consolidated Appropriations Act of 2021* repealed it. Unlike the other tax changes discussed in this section, the tuition and fees deduction does not return in 2026. However, given its history, it might be renewed. But, for the time being, the tuition and fees deduction no longer applies.

---

44. *See* Nancy E. Shurtz, Education Planning: Taxes, Trusts, and Techniques ch. 22 (The Tuition Deduction) (ABA 2009) (arguing that the deduction in all circumstances will produce less desirable tax results than the tax credits). *See also* **Chapter Five: When Savings Are Not Enough,** A.1.d.

2. Losses in the Account

Another interesting tax issue arises when there are losses in the Section 529 account. According to the IRS these losses are allowed only when "all amounts from that account have been distributed" and only when "the total distributions are less than [the] unrecovered basis."[45] The account owner must, therefore, fully liquidate the account. If losses are recognized, however, they are not an above-the-line deduction from the sale or exchange of a capital asset because no capital asset is involved.[46] Also, since no securities are involved, the *"wash-sale"* loss limitation rule under Section 1091 will not apply. Instead, any losses would be treated as a *miscellaneous itemized deduction* (MID)[47] and under the *TCJA* of 2017, would not be allowed as a deduction under Section 67. This limitation, like all the 2017 tax changes, sunsets at the end of 2025.[48]

If the taxpayer receives a final distribution from one account that results in a loss, and in the same year a distribution from another account that results in taxable earnings, the earnings from the profitable account can reduce the loss from the other account.

EXAMPLE 8-11:[49] In a year in which Ben has $6,000 of qualified expenses, Ben has a final distribution from one account of $1,000 where his contribution basis was $3,000. In the same year, Ben has a distribution of $9,000 from another 529 account whose contribution basis is $1,500. Thus, Ben's total distribution is $10,000, and the total basis in these distributions is $4,500. So, the difference ($5,500) is subject to tax on the portion not considered qualified 4,000/10,000 or 40 percent × $5,500 or $2,200.

Planning Pointer

The Advanced Notice confirmed that investment losses in Section 529 plans may be deducted only as a "miscellaneous deduction," which prior to the *TCJA* of 2017 were subject to the 2 percent of adjusted gross income limitation. However, with the *TCJA* of 2017, this deduction is no longer allowed, at least through 2025.

45. IRS Pub. 970: Tax Benefits for Education 59 (2019).
46. I.R.C. §§ 165, 1211, 62(5).
47. *Id.* §§ 67, 212.
48. Section 68 was also eliminated by the *TCJA* of 2017. Under that section, the MID deduction under I.R.C. § 67 in excess of 2 percent (prior to *TCJA*) was further limited by the lesser of (1) 80 percent of certain itemized deductions (not medical, casualty, or net investment interest) or (2) 3 percent of the taxpayer's AGI over "the applicable amount."
49. Adapted from example in IRS Pub. 970: Tax Benefits for Education 59 (2019).

3. Education That Is an Ordinary and Necessary Business Expense

An employee can exclude as a work-related fringe benefit any reimbursements made by the employer for education expenses (including transportation, lodging, and a portion of meals).[50] These education expenses must either maintain or improve the employee's skills or meet the employer's job requirements; however, these expenses cannot qualify the employee for a new trade or business or meet the minimum requirements of the job. Under the *TCJA* of 2017, an employee who incurs this type of education expense and is *not* reimbursed by his/her employer will not be able to take a deduction for those expenses. Just like the losses on the 529 account, these expenses are now Section 67 *miscellaneous itemized deductions* (MIDs) and are no longer allowed.[51]

4. Home Equity Loan Interest

Before the *TCJA* of 2017, the *home equity loan* or *line of credit* was a wonderful source of funding education for those who held wealth in their principal residence or vacation home. The loan could be used for any expense, not just those that are QHHE. The interest on the home equity loan was an itemized deduction but was limited to the amount of $100,000. These loans, of course, can still be used to fund education expenses, but the interest on these loans will no longer receive a tax deduction, at least not until the beginning of 2026.

5. Dependency

College students are often unmarried individuals who receive support from their parents. Because of this dependency status, the parent may be able to receive several tax benefits. First, the parent may claim the head of household status, which provides a form of income splitting between a single parent and the dependent. Second, even if the parent cannot claim head of household status because he/she is married, the parent may receive a *dependent tax credit.* But when the student is married or independent, the student, not the parent, will be the taxpayer. In this circumstance, both the student and the parent pay taxes based on their status—single, married filing jointly, married filing separately, or head of household.

a. *Head of Household Status*

The head of household status only applies to single taxpayers because married couples can split their income through the joint filing status. The head of household status can lead to lower federal tax rates than single taxpayers or married couples filing separately. In addition, heads of households receive a larger federal

50. I.R.C. § 374(n). (The 50 percent limit was changed by the *Consolidated Appropriations Act of 2021* to 100 percent of meals eaten in restaurants.)

51. *See* **Chapter Five: When Savings Are Not Enough**, A.1.b.

standard deduction than either of those other categories. For example, in 2021, the standard deduction is $12,550 for singles, $18,800 for heads of household, and $25,100 for married couples filing jointly (half that if they file separately).

To qualify as head of household, the taxpayer must pay for more than half the "maintenance costs of the home" for a "qualifying person." Home maintenance includes rent, repairs, utilities, property insurance, mortgage interest, and property tax, but also includes food consumed at the home. For a college student, payment of room and board would be considered "maintenance" for purposes of this status. Temporary absences for special circumstances—such as a student living away from home—count as time lived in the taxpayer's home.

For a student to be a "qualifying person," they must meet three tests: (1) a *relationship test*, (2) a *support test*, and (3) a *gross income test*. For the *relationship test*, the eligible person must be either a "qualifying child" or a "qualifying relative."[52] Students will usually be considered qualifying children. The relationship test of Section 152 requires the "qualifying" child" to be the taxpayer's son, daughter, stepson, stepdaughter, brother, sister, stepbrother, stepsister, half-brother, half-sister, or a descendant of such individual (*e.g.*, a grandchild, nephew or niece).[53] A qualifying child also includes an adopted or eligible foster child. If the child is married and files a joint return, however, he/she cannot be claimed as a dependent.[54]

The *support test* generally requires the person claiming the head of household status to provide over half the support of the "qualifying child." The support test might not be met, however, if the Section 529 proceeds are used for over half the support expenditures of the student. Support includes room, board, clothing, and other necessities. Since the 529 savings plan can be used to cover room and board, the parent may not qualify under the support test. While scholarships and loans taken out by the student are not considered parental support,[55] loans taken out by the parent (such as PLUS loans) and used for necessities do count as parental support. If the parent pays the tuition directly to the institution, this will also count as support. Under state law, a college education might not be treated as an obligation of the parent; but if it is, then tuition and books would also be considered part of support.

52. *See* Working Families Tax Relief Act of 2004, Pub. L. No. 108-311, 118 Stat. 1166 (2004).

53. I.R.C. § 152(f)(3) allows a dependency for an unrelated person living in the taxpayer's abode in a relationship that is not "contrary to local law."

54. I.R.C. § 152(c)(3)(A).

55. I.R.C. § 152(f)(5) provides that scholarships at qualified education organizations will not be taken into account in determining parental support.

EXAMPLE 8-12: Alice, a single parent, has a son, Ben, who is 23 years old. Ben is pursuing a philosophy degree at a well-known undergraduate institution. Ben uses the funds from the Section 529 savings plan to pay for room and board—consisting of over half of his support. Under these circumstances, Alice will not be entitled to head of household status as she does not provide over half the support for Ben.

The third test of a qualifying person is the *gross income test*. This test is met if the student either makes less than the exemption amount or is under the age of 24. Since most undergraduate students are under the age of 24, they qualify, if the other tests of dependency are met.[56] Some graduate students may also be under the age of 24. Even if the student is over 24, they can still meet this gross income test if they are considered having less than the dependency exemption.[57]

a. Dependent Credit

The *TCJA* eliminated the dependency exemption and adopted a new provision: the *dependent tax credit*. In general, credits are better than exemptions for poorer taxpayers; vice-versa, exemptions are better than credits for higher taxpayers. However, under the new provision, the taxpayer will receive only a meager $500 nonrefundable dependent credit. In addition, the new credit is only allowed if the dependency requirements discussed above are met. But in addition to the relationship test, the support test, and the gross income test, the dependent must also be a *citizen* or national and can no longer be an alien resident of the U.S. or a resident of a country contiguous to the U.S., i.e., that of Canada or Mexico.[58]

Even when the taxpayer can claim the dependent tax credit under the rules listed above, the exemption is phased out for taxpayers in the top brackets.[59] The credit amount is lowered by $50 for each $1,000 (or fraction thereof) of MAGI over the taxpayer's "threshold amount." This amount is $400,000 for married couples filing jointly and $200,000 for other taxpayers.[60] Thus, from a planning point of view, at the present time it may be more advantageous if the student is not claimed as a dependent for dependent credit purposes. In this case, the student has his/her own standard deduction as he/she will be the taxpayer. Of course, the head of household status could be quite valuable to the single parent as no phase-out rules apply to this status.

---

56. Higher Education Amendments of 1992, Pub. L. No. 102-325, § 480(d)(4), 106 Stat. 448, 607 (1992) (codified as amended at 20 U.S.C. § 1087d4 (Supp. IV 1992)).

57. The dependency exemption was eliminated by the *TCJA* of 2017, but the IRS has held that for gross income purposes the exemption amount for 2020 is $4,300. *See* IRS Pub. 501: Dependents, Standard Deduction, and Filing Information 4 (2020).

58. I.R.C. § 24(h)(4)(B).

59. *Id.* § 151(d)(3).

60. This threshold is not adjusted for inflation. *Id.* § 24(b)(1).

Planning Pointer

The tax advisor should determine whether it is best for the parent to claim a dependent credit or have the student file his/her own taxes with the liberal standard deduction. For a single parent, the head of household splitting benefits will in many cases make the dependent credit planning issue moot. Planning can occur around the support test, which is controlled in part by the distributions from a 529 plan. State law should be checked to determine if tuition and books are part of the parental support requirement, as this can make a difference in meeting the support test requirements.

G. Coordination with Other Education Benefits

A taxpayer can claim a tax-free distribution from a 529 plan, and in the same year have a tax-free distribution from a Coverdell ESA, *and* in addition use either the *American Opportunity Credit* (AOTC) or the *Lifetime Learning Credit.*[61] The only restriction is that the distribution from the Section 529 plan is not used to pay expenses for which either a credit is claimed or the Coverdell distribution is used. Since the Section 529 (and the Coverdell) cover room and board but the credits do not, the total higher education expenses can be allocated to maximize the greatest tax benefit.

EXAMPLE 8-13: Assume that Ben is a full-time student with the following expenses: \$15,000 tuition; \$7,000 room and board; \$2,000 books, equipment, and supplies. Ben may claim the Lifetime Learning Credit using up \$10,000 of the tuition, claim a \$5,000 Coverdell distribution for the remaining tuition and still use \$9,000 from the 529 plan to pay for room, board, books, equipment, and supplies.

If a distribution from a Section 529 plan and the Coverdell pays for the same higher education expenses, the expenses must be allocated between the distributions in each account and a tax paid based on the respective *earnings ratios* of each account. On the other hand, if any of the distribution from the Section 529 plan is used to pay expenses used for either the AOTC or Lifetime Learning Credit, then an allocation can be made based on the best overall tax results.

A comparison between the tax savings realized from taking an excludable withdrawal from the Section 529 plan must be compared with the tax benefits realized from claiming the credit. If the student does not owe taxes, it will be better to use

61. *See* **Chapter Eighteen: Coordinating Section 529 Plans with Tax Benefits**.

the proceeds of the Section 529 plan for the qualified expenditures.[62] All of these coordination rules are discussed in **Chapter Eighteen: Coordinating Section 529 Plans with Tax Benefits.**

H. Conclusion

The federal income tax treatment of a Section 529 savings plan is extremely favorable to the taxpayer. Although the contributions are not deductible, the earnings from the fund are tax free when the proceeds are used for QHHE. Only when the distributions are nonqualified are they taxed and an additional tax or penalty imposed. Even if taxed, they are often taxed at the beneficiary's lower tax rates.

When planning, the advisor must be aware of several potential tax changes made by the *TCJA* of 2017. First, any losses in the account will be a denied miscellaneous itemized deduction, as will be any unreimbursed employee educational business expenses. Second, if the parent borrows to invest in a Section 529 plan using home equity, they will no longer be entitled to that deduction on the interest on that loan. Third, the "kiddie tax" rules have changed so that the child is taxed at trust and estate tax rates. Lastly, a parent could lose the head of household status and other tax benefits by establishing and using a 529 plan. All these tax changes will sunset at the end of 2025, except for the tuition and fees deduction, which expired at the end of December 31, 2020.

62. I.R.C. § 529(c)(1).

Chapter 9

Estate Planning with Section 529 Savings Plans

In addition to income tax benefits, Section 529 savings plans offer significant gift, generation-skipping, and estate tax advantages. The donor can accelerate the per-donee annual exclusion by contributing five times that amount to the 529 plan—with no adverse gift tax consequences. Married couples can contribute twice that amount if they split the gift. In addition, the portion excludable from gift tax is also excludable from generation-skipping tax (GST) consequences—even if the beneficiary is a grandchild.[1] Furthermore, the donor or owner is not subject to estate tax consequences on the fund value, even though the owner can change the beneficiary of the plan, switch state investment strategies or plans, or reclaim the fund for his/her personal benefit. This chapter discusses the gift, estate, and GST benefits as well as two other issues: planning for the incapacity of the owner and trust ownership of Section 529 savings plans.

A. Gift Tax

As with the income tax rules, the normal gift tax rules are modified under Section 529. First, contributions to a Section 529 savings account are *deemed completed gifts*. This is true even though the donor/account owner (1) can "undo" the gift by taking the funds back, (2) can change the beneficiary, and (3) can modify the investment plan. An effective retraction by the account owner will have income tax consequences on any earnings from the fund as well as trigger the 10 percent additional tax penalty.[2] Under the 2008 Advance Notice of proposed rulemaking, a

---

1. *See* Prop. Treas. Reg. § 1.529-5(a), 65 Fed. Reg. 45,019 (Aug. 24, 1998). *Generation-skipping* tax will be triggered, however, when a Section 529 savings plan is "rolled over" and the new beneficiary is in a generation lower than the current beneficiary.

2. *See* **Chapter Eight: Federal Income Tax Planning with Section 529 Savings Plans**, C.

retraction of funds by an account owner when those funds have been donated by another could trigger an income tax on 100 percent of the distribution.[3]

A second modification of the normal gift rules occurs because the owner's contribution to the Section 529 savings plan will be eligible under Section 2503(b) for exclusion as an annual gift of a *present interest* (up to the annual exclusion amount)—even though the account will be distributed in the future. Furthermore, when the gift exceeds the *per-donee annual exclusion amount*, the taxpayer-donor can elect to accelerate the gift tax exclusion for up to five years. For 2021, the annual exclusion is $15,000. Thus, a total of $75,000 for a single individual and $150,000 for a married couple (who elect to *split the gifts* on their respective returns) can be transferred to a Section 529 plan. The taxpayer can repeat this election with no gift tax consequences in subsequent five-year periods.

Planning Pointer

It is pertinent to note that the taxpayer cannot reap a double gift-tax benefit by invoking both Section 529 and Section 2503(e) for the *same expenses*. However, the taxpayer can obtain the maximum per-donee exclusion for contributions to the 529 plan while gifting an additional amount for the direct tuition payments to a qualified education institution under Section 2503(e).[4] However, Section 529 covers more than tuition. Therefore, there is nothing[5] to prevent a donor from obtaining the Section 2503(e) exclusion when the donor makes a direct gift to the education institution for payment of tuition not covered by the Section 529 plan in the year in which the beneficiary attends college. The Section 529 plan can then pay for books, supplies, room, board, and other qualified expenses (*see* **Chart 7-4**). A gift of the tuition will also not preclude the taxpayer parent or student from taking the education credits.[6]

EXAMPLE 9-1: In 2021, Alice can transfer $75,000 to a Section 529 account for her granddaughter, Katie, without incurring any gift tax. Alice may also pay Katie's noncovered[7] tuition directly to Katie's college. Alice can use the Section 529 account to pay for Katie's books, supplies, room, and board. Both transfers will then be tax free for purposes of the gift tax. The tuition gift by the grandparent will also not preclude Katie or her parents from taking the American Opportunity Tax Credit or Lifetime Learning Credit.[8]

---

3. *See* Example 8-6 in **Chapter Eight: Federal Income Tax Planning with Section 529 Savings Plans**.
4. I.R.C. § 529(c)(2)(A)(ii).
5. Such a transfer would be treated as a "resource" for financial aid purposes and reduce financial aid dollar for dollar. Thus, such a transfer is not recommended when the student could qualify for financial aid. *See* **Chapter Nineteen: Coordinating Section 529 Plans with Financial Aid**.
6. For a more detailed discussion of education credits, see **Chapter Five: When Savings Are Not Enough**, A.1.a., and **Chapter Eighteen: Coordinating Section 529 Plans with Tax Benefits**.
7. That is, tuition that is not already paid for by the Section 529 plan.
8. *See* **Chapter Eighteen: Coordinating Section 529 Plans with Tax Benefits**.

The gift tax exclusion is indexed for inflation, and for 2021, it is at $15,000. Any cost-of-living adjustment (i.e., increase to the annual exclusion amount) will allow the taxpayer to make additional contributions to the Section 529 savings plan.[9]

EXAMPLE 9-2: In 2021, Alice transfers $75,000 to a Section 529 account for her granddaughter. Suppose that in 2023 the exemption amount is increased to $16,000. Alice will be allowed to add $1,000 to her Section 529 plan for Year 3 and the two remaining years under the five-year rule. Therefore, Alice may add $3,000 to the plan in Year 3.

1. The Deemed Completed Gift

Section 529 provides that any "contribution to a qualified tuition program on behalf of any designated beneficiary (i) shall be treated as a completed gift to such beneficiary."[10] The statute indicates that the designated beneficiary is the donee,[11] and that "in no event shall a distribution from a qualified tuition program be treated as a taxable gift."[12] A completed gift therefore arises at the time of the transfer of funds to the plan, even though the owner of the fund can revert the beneficial title to the property to him/herself. Under regular gift principles, a completed gift does not result when the donor can change the beneficiary or when the donor can demand a refund.[13] The 2008 Advance Notice of proposed rulemaking is suggesting the Treasury will impose, in new regulations, a tax upon distribution to a person other than the contributor for nonqualified purposes.

Planning Pointer

The new regulations might limit the circumstances under which an account owner may withdraw funds from a Section 529 account, change the designated beneficiary, or transfer account ownership.

2. Gift upon Change in Account Ownership

If a completed gift occurs at the outset under Section 529, then an issue arises as to whether there could be a gift if the owner establishes another person as the account owner or if the owner is changed during the term of the fund. Any new

9. Prop. Treas. Reg. § 1.529-5(b)(2)(iv), 63 Fed. Reg. 45,019 (Aug. 24, 1998). H.R. 2568, introduced in 2005, would increase the annual exclusion amount to $50,000 and the lifetime exclusion to $10 million, plus retain the cost-of-living adjustment.

10. I.R.C. § 529(c)(2)(A).

11. *Id.* § 529(c)(2)(A)(1).

12. *Id.* § 529(c)(5)(A).

13. Treas. Reg. § 25-2511-2(a).

owner would have the power to withdraw the fund, thus receiving something of value. On the other hand, since the statute states the initial transfer is a completed gift to the beneficiary, arguably no gift will result when the account changes ownership. Allowing such a change in ownership, however, could circumvent the income and gift tax rules of Section 529.

EXAMPLE 9-3: Alice is the owner and her granddaughter, Katie, is the designated beneficiary. Alice would like to make a distribution from the 529 plan to her new boyfriend. Since her boyfriend is not a family member, changing the beneficiary would trigger income tax and a penalty and possibly a gift tax to the boyfriend. If, on the other hand, Alice changed the account *owner* to her boyfriend, she can accomplish the same results without gift tax. Her boyfriend can now withdraw the account balance.

The 2008 Advance Notice makes it clear that this abuse shall be curtailed by either (1) imposing an income tax whenever a person other than the contributor withdraws funds from the account for nonqualified purposes or (2) imposing a new gift tax when any change in account ownership is made. The new regulations could impose both an income and a gift tax.

EXAMPLE 9-4: Same as **Example 9-3**. Upon changing the account ownership to her boyfriend, Alice would have a gift tax on the value of the investment plus earnings. Furthermore, an income tax could be due on the whole distribution (including Alice's original capital investment) upon the withdrawal of the funds by the boyfriend for nonqualified purposes.

It must be noted that many 529 plans permit the account owner to designate a successor in the event of "disability."[14] Therefore, such a change in account ownership is a permitted *inter vivos transfer* and should not result in any tax. Nothing in the statute or proposed regulations precludes such a change. Under the federal financial aid rules, ownership of the plan by the grandparent will not be assessed as owned by either the student or the parent. However, any distribution from the plan will constitute income to the student and be assessed at 50 percent.[15] Under the Advance Notice, such a transfer could result in gift tax or income tax if the new owner withdraws the funds.[16] Thus, a more favorable financial aid result will occur

14. See Section D later in this chapter.

15. If the owner parent could transfer the Section 529 account to the grandparent, then the asset would not be counted in either the federal or institutional formula. A 529 plan owned by the student is assessed under the federal formula as if owned by the parent. **See Chapter Nineteen: Coordinating Section 529 Plans with Financial Aid.**

16. No adverse estate tax consequences would result for the successor owner at death because I.R.C. § 529(c)(4)(A) provides that the account is not included in the estate of the account owner.

if the ownership is transferred to the parent or the student, or the 529 funds are used after college to pay off up to $10,000 of student debt.[17]

When the account ownership changes, the new account owner has the right to terminate the account. If a gift occurred at this point, it would be from the designated beneficiary to the new account owner. However, the beneficiary's interest has not changed, so no gift should result.

3. No Gift When Contributor and Beneficiary Are the Same

No prohibition exists against setting up a Section 529 plan for oneself. Because an individual cannot make a gift to him/herself, such a transfer will not trigger a gift tax. However, upon a subsequent change in designated beneficiary, a gift *should* occur. Although such a contributor may want to claim that a change in designated beneficiary to a member of the contributor's family who is in the same or higher generation avoids the gift tax under the special transfer tax rules of Section 529,[18] the Advance Notice indicates that the proposed regulations will consider such a transfer abusive.[19]

4. A Present Interest for a Future Distribution

Since the designated beneficiary will not use, possess, or enjoy the property in the 529 account until a future date, the interest is a future interest.[20] However, under Section 529 the transfer of property to the Section 529 plan is treated as a gift "which is not a future interest in property."[21] Thus, the gift qualifies as a *present interest*. This exception, therefore, ensures that the contribution is sheltered from the generation-skipping tax. Although there is precedent for disregarding the future interest for gifts to minors, this precedent only applies when the identity of the donee is limited to one individual and the distribution of the interest is mandated at age 21.[22] Thus, the *present interest* designation is unusual.

5. The Five-Year Election

Section 529 permits the donor to contribute five times the annual exclusion amount—with no adverse gift tax consequences. In 2021, $75,000 ($150,000 if married and a *split gift*) can be contributed to the 529 in one year. If the five-year election is made, the length of the spread period is not optional. Therefore, the contributor cannot spread the gift over fewer than five years.[23] On the other hand,

---

17. *See* **Chapter Nineteen: Coordinating Section 529 Plans with Financial Aid.**
18. I.R.C. § 529(c)(5)(B).
19. Guidance on Qualified Tuition Programs under Section 529, 73 Fed. Reg. 3441 (Jan. 18, 2008). *See* **Appendix F**.
20. Treas. Reg. § 25.2503-3(a).
21. I.R.C. § 529(c)(2)(A)(i).
22. *See id.* § 2503(c).
23. *Id.* § 529(c)(2)(B).

if the full annual exclusion is not used each year, additional gifts can be made up to that amount.

EXAMPLE 9-5: In 2021, Alice makes a contribution of $40,000 to the Section 529 plan and makes the five-year election. Alice is deemed to have made a gift of $8,000 each year ($40,000 divided by the five years). Alice can still make an additional $7,000 ($15,000 annual exclusion amount less $8,000) contribution to the Section 529 plan in each of these five years or give a $7,000 gift to the beneficiary outside the Section 529 plan in each of these five years. If, however, Alice fails to give the additional $7,000 in Year 1, she cannot allocate the original gift other than pro rata over five years.

It is unclear whether a second election can be made when the gifts for any one year do not exceed the annual exclusion amount. It appears that as long as the total amount is no greater than five times the annual exclusion, a second election should be permissible.[24]

EXAMPLE 9-6: Same as **Example 9-5** except in Year 3, Alice makes another contribution of $15,000, the annual exclusion amount, to the 529 account. The donor should be allowed to make the five-year averaging, which would allow a gift of $5,000 for Years 3 through Year 5 ($15,000 divided by three). Alice still has some unused exclusion amount—$2,000 for each of those years (assuming the exclusion amount remains at $15,000). Thus, in Year 4, Alice should be able to make a gift to the 529 plan in the amount of $4,000—the remaining available five-year amount for those two years.

The five-year election is filed on Form 709, the gift tax return. Schedule A, Question B on that form has a box to check when electing to treat transfers as made ratably over five years. An explanation must be attached to the gift tax return stating the amount of the contribution for each beneficiary, the amount for which the election is being made, and the name of the individual for whom the contribution was made. (*See* **Chart 9-1**.) The instructions to Form 709 state, "[t]he election must be made for the calendar year in which the contribution is made." Form 709 needs to be filed only once every five years. The 2008 Advance Notice makes these rules clear when spreading the gift over the five-year period.

---

24. An example in the 1998 proposed regulations may suggest otherwise. See Prop. Treas. Reg. § 1.529-5(b)(2), 63 Fed. Reg. 45,019 (Aug. 24, 1998).

CHART 9-1 Sample Attachment to Form 709

On ________, 2021, the Donor made a contribution of $75,000 in cash to a qualified tuition program (name of plan) for the benefit of the Donor's grandchild (name of beneficiary). The Donor elects to treat the gift of $75,000 as made over a five-year period.

Planning Pointer

The five-year election is a great way to gift substantial funds to a grandchild. However, once the full exclusion amount for the year is given, no further annual exclusion gifts can be made for that year without reducing the taxpayer's lifetime gift tax exemption. Therefore, for wealthy taxpayers, the direct tuition payment under Section 2503(e), in combination with a Section 529 plan and other gifts, may be the best education strategy.

6. Excess over Annual Exemption or Five-Year Amount

Any amount contributed to the Section 529 savings account in excess of the exemption amount (either annual or five-year if elected) will have gift tax consequences. For gift tax purposes, the taxpayer must file Form 709, and the excess contribution will be reported as a taxable gift and reduce the taxpayer's *lifetime gift tax exemption.*[25]

EXAMPLE 9-7: In 2000, Alice contributes $40,000 to a Section 529 plan for her son, Ben. Alice is unmarried. She elects on Form 709 to make this gift to Ben under the five-year rule. A pro rata portion, or $8,000, will be the gift per year for the next five years. In 2021, Alice makes another contribution of $15,000 to the 529 account. Total gifts for 2021 are the original $8,000 plus $15,000 or $23,000—of which only $15,000 will qualify for the per-donee annual exclusion. The remaining $8,000 will not. Therefore, Alice must use part of her lifetime gift tax exemption to avoid the imposition of a gift tax on this amount.

25. See **Chart 9-4** for these exemption amounts. The lifetime gift tax exemption is currently $1 million (adjusted for inflation), allowing the taxpayer to make a total of $1 million of taxable gifts over his lifetime ($11,700,000 in 2021) before owing any federal gift tax. This amount is in addition to the unlimited number of $15,000 per-donee annual gifts a taxpayer can make to different recipients each year.

If the gift exceeds five times the annual exclusion, the 1998 proposed regulations[26] as well as the instructions to Form 709 indicate that the entire excess must be reported as a taxable gift in the first year (not apportioned over the five-year period). Once the taxpayer has reached the limit of his/her lifetime gift tax exemption, gift taxes will be due.[27]

EXAMPLE 9-8: In 2021, Alice transfers $75,000 into a Section 529 savings plan for her son Ben. In addition, she made a prior gift to him of $100,000 during the calendar year. This additional $100,000 reduces Alice's lifetime gift tax exemption. Alice must file a gift tax return on Form 709 for her contribution to the 529 plan but will pay no gift tax because the $75,000 gift does not exceed five times her $15,000 annual exclusion.

7. Split Gifts

When a *split gift* is made, the IRS treats the split gift election as being made before the five-year averaging.[28] Thus, if the married couple decides to split the gift, each will independently decide on whether to make the five-year election. Each must file a gift tax return making this election. If the parties divorce in a later year, the portions of the gift attributable to the earlier years are still considered split.

EXAMPLE 9-9: In Year 1, Husband and Wife decide to make a $150,000 contribution to a Section 529 Plan for the benefit of their daughter. If they elect to split their gift, in Year 1, each will make a five-year election and file Form 709. If they divorce in Year 2, the portion of the gift attributable to Years 3 through 5 is still split.

If, on the other hand, one spouse elects the five-year averaging, and the other does not, the portion of the gift attributable to the nonelecting spouse in any future year would itself not be considered split. This becomes relevant if a spouse divorces and remarries during the five-year period. The nonelecting spouse could then make *split gifts* with the new spouse.

8. Gift by Beneficiary (or Account Owner)

One negative gift tax consequence could result if there is a rollover or change in a designated beneficiary and the original beneficiary is assigned to a higher generation than the new beneficiary. Such a rollover or change will cause the original

---

26. Prop. Treas. Reg. § 1.529-5(b)(2), 63 Fed. Reg. 45,019 (Aug. 24, 1998). *See* **Appendix E.**

27. Upon the death of the donor within the five-year gift period, an estate tax may be imposed. It is unlikely, however, that the gift tax paid due to the excess contribution from earlier years will be "grossed up" in the donor's estate.

28. *See* Instruction to Form 709.

beneficiary to make a taxable gift to the new beneficiary. However, the original beneficiary could elect to treat the gift under the five-year averaging rule.[29] Assuming the Section 529 savings account holds more than $75,000 and the annual gift exclusion has not been increased, the original beneficiary may well have to use part of his/her lifetime gift tax exemption to avoid any gift tax consequences.

Causing a gift tax consequence to a beneficiary—who might not even know they are a beneficiary—seems very inequitable. The 2008 Advance Notice indicates that under the new proposed regulations, liability for payment of gift tax due upon an account owner's designation of a new beneficiary of a lower generation will be shifted from the prior beneficiary to the account owner. This will be achieved by treating the transaction as distribution of the account to the account owner and the opening of a new account, and the making of a new gift by the account owner for the new beneficiary. It is possible that such a gift transfer will also result in *generation-skipping* tax (GST) consequences.

EXAMPLE 9-10: Alice made an initial gift of $75,000 to a Section 529 plan for her daughter, Marie, and a gift of $75,000 to a Section 529 plan for her son, Ben. Every five years she made additional $75,000 gifts. Ben goes to college, uses his 529 plan, marries, and has a child. Marie does not go to college, marries against her mother's wishes, and moves to Europe. Twenty-five years after Marie's account was funded (when its value is over $1 million), Alice rolls over Marie's account to Ben's child. As a result, Alice would use up Marie's lifetime gift tax exemption and create a gift liability for Marie.

EXAMPLE 9-11: Same as **Example 9-10,** under suggested proposed regulations there will be a gift from the owner to the granddaughter and assessed to the owner. Such a transfer should also be subject to GST because this constitutes a "direct skip."

Although at the time of the rollover, the beneficiary might not have significant wealth, that same beneficiary in later years could have wealth and at that time will have used part or all of his/her unified credit amount.

Planning Pointer

Under the 2008 Advance Notice, a change of the original beneficiary to a lower generation beneficiary will trigger a gift tax to the owner (and possibly a generation-skipping tax).

29. H.R. Rep. No. 105-220 (1997) (Conf. Rep.), *reprinted in* 1997-4 C.B. 1835.

CHART 9-2: 529s and Established Gift Principles

Established Gift Principles	§ 529 Principles
Gift is incomplete if donor reserves the power to name new beneficiaries	Completed gift
Gift is incomplete if donor can revoke	Completed gift
Gift is incomplete if donor can change the beneficiary	Completed gift
Gift is complete if donor transferred account ownership	No gift with account owner change
No present interest if enjoyment, use, or possession commences in future	Present Interest
Only modest amounts (currently $ 15,000) sheltered by the annual exclusion	Contributions of $ 75,000 (or $ 150,000 if split gift) are sheltered up front

9. Gift When Owner Is Beneficiary

There is nothing in Section 529 or the regulations that prevent the owner of an account from establishing themselves as the beneficiary. Obviously, no gift tax is due in the situation because the contributor donor is the beneficiary, and one cannot make taxable gifts to oneself. However, if the owner changes the beneficiary, then such change, under the 2008 Advance Notice of proposed regulations, will result in a distribution to the owner contributor and a gift by the contributor to the new beneficiary. This rule closes the loophole arising from the fact there is no gift to oneself and no gift upon changing the beneficiary to another member of the beneficiary's family who is the same or higher generation as the contributor.

B. Generation-Skipping Tax (GST)

Contributions to a Section 529 plan that qualify for the annual exclusion are not considered *generation-skipping* transfers.[30] Therefore, such a gift would have an inclusion ratio of zero.[31] If the transfer qualifies for the annual exclusion, no *generation-skipping tax* (GST) will be imposed even where a grandparent contributes directly to a Section 529 savings plan held for the benefit of his/her grandchild (a "direct-skip" transfer).

To the extent a gift does not qualify for the gift tax annual exclusion, either because the gift exceeds the exclusion amount or prior gifts during the year used the available annual exclusion amount, the gift would not qualify for the GST annual exclusion. Similarly, contributions to a "skip person" in excess of the annual exclusion will be subject to the GST.[32] Currently, the exemption amount to the GST is the same as for the estate and gift tax.[33] *(See* **Chart 9-4.)** Thus, to the

30. I.R.C. § 529(c)(5)(B).
31. *Id.* § 2642.
32. *Id.* §§ 2612(c), 2613(a).
33. *Id.* §§ 2632(c), 2010(c).

extent of the exemption amount allocated, no GST will be due on the remaining excess contribution.

Another GST issue arises when the donor dies within the first five-year election period and a part of the contribution is brought back into the donor's estate. If the portion of the account included in the donor's estate is deemed to be a "transfer" for GST purposes, it would be a "direct skip" if the designated beneficiary were a skip person. If, however, the designated beneficiary is later changed to a nonskip person or the account assets are returned to a nonskip person, there appears to be no provision for a refund of the GST.

If a GST transfer is triggered, the decedent's estate should be able to allocate the GST exemption. If there is no remaining exemption, the estate plan should not direct that the GST tax be paid from the 529 assets because that would trigger a nonqualified distribution.

EXAMPLE 9-12: In 2021 Alice contributes $75,000 to a Section 529 plan for her grandchild and elects the five-year averaging rule. Alice dies in 2023 with two years remaining on the five years. Alice's estate must include $30,000 (2 years × $15,000 annual exclusion) in her estate, and this would constitute a direct skip subject to GST.

The statute provides that a GST could be imposed where a Section 529 designated beneficiary rollover occurs and the new beneficiary is a generation below the original beneficiary.[34] This is consistent with a view that the GST transferor is the original donor, because the GST generally only applies if a person is assigned to a generation that is two or more generations below the transferor.[35] The one lower generation rule seems to assume that the original beneficiary will always be one generation below the donor. When the new beneficiary is one generation below the original beneficiary, then the rollover is treated as a gift made by the original beneficiary to the new beneficiary. As mentioned earlier, the original beneficiary can use the annual gift exclusion as well as the five-year averaging rule.[36] Therefore, if the gift transfer is exempt by reason of the annual gift exclusion, it will be exempt for GST purposes.

EXAMPLE 9-13: When the per-donee gift tax exclusion was $12,000, Alice made a gift of $60,000 to a Section 529 savings account designating Marie, her daughter, as beneficiary. Twenty years later, when the account has grown in value to $170,000, Alice removes her daughter's name and designates her granddaughter

---

34. *Id.* § 529(c)(5)(B).
35. *Id.* § 2613(a)(1).
36. H.R. Rep. No. 105-220 (1997) (Conf. Rep.), *reprinted in* 1997-4 C.B. 1835.

as the new beneficiary. The naming of the granddaughter is treated as a gift from the daughter to the granddaughter of the entire amount in the account under current rules. The deemed taxable transfer will equal $110,000 [$170,000 – $60,000 = $110,000]. Because of the annual exclusions, $60,000 will be excluded for purpose of the gift tax GST.

This result might not be a problem if the original beneficiary has no other outstanding gifts or GST transfers. On the other hand, in some circumstances, this would be inequitable since the beneficiary had no control over the rollover.

Interestingly, the 1998 proposed regulations confuse the issue by stating the GST will apply only "if the new beneficiary is assigned to a generation which is two or more levels lower than the generation assignment of the old beneficiary."[37] The proposed regulations focus on the original beneficiary as the transferor, not the original donor. Therefore, if the original beneficiary were a grandchild, a rollover to a great-great-grandchild of the donor (but the grandchild of the grandchild) would remain exempt from the GST.

Planning Pointer

Regardless of whether the code rule or proposed regulations rule applies, for planning purposes it would make sense to name the youngest beneficiary possible in the original transfer. Of course, shifting among the same generation is permissible without any gift tax or GST.[38]

C. Estate Tax

Section 529 provides a broad exemption from estate tax, stating that "[n]o amount shall be includable in the gross estate of any individual for purposes of [the estate tax] by reason of an interest in a qualified tuition program."[39] Two exceptions apply to this rule. One deals with the recapture of gifts when the donor does not survive the five-year election period (this is often referred to as the claw-back provision). The other is when the account is distributed on account of the death of the beneficiary.

37. Prop. Treas. Reg. § 1.529-5(b)(3)(ii), 63 Fed. Reg. 45,019, 45,032 (Aug. 24, 1998).

38. See Danielle A. Menick, *529: State's Nightmare, Estate Planner's Dream*, 59 J. Mo. B. 316, 320 (2003), for potential abuses.

39. I.R.C. § 529(c)(4)(A).

1. Death of Account Owner

Under traditional estate tax rules, Section 2038(a)(1) would impose an estate tax on interests in which the donor has retained the power to "alter, amend, revoke, or terminate." Since the account owner of a Section 529 plan has the power to revoke as well as the power to change the designated beneficiary, the value of the account would normally be included in the owner's estate. In addition, under traditional estate tax rules, Section 2036(a)(2) would impose an estate tax on retained powers "to designate the persons who shall possess or enjoy the property or the income therefrom," and Section 2036(a)(1) would impose a tax if the transfer satisfied a legal obligation of support of the decedent. Again, under these rules the owner of a 529 plan would be subject to estate tax. In addition, if the donor is not the same person as the owner, but the owner has the power to distribute the account to him/herself, the owner should be considered to possess a general power of appointment under Section 2041, and the assets would be includable in his/her gross estate.

However, under Section 529, the plan assets are *not* included in the account owner's estate. One narrow exception is when the account owner has made the Section 529(c)(4)(c) election (i.e., elects to contribute $75,000 in 2021, for example, and prorate that amount over a five-year period) but dies prior to the expiration of the five-year period. In this situation, a prorated portion of the gift will be added to the owner's estate to calculate any estate tax liability. In other words, in the year of the donor's death, the portion of the contribution allocated to the years after the donor's death is brought back into the donor's estate. If, on the other hand, the donor survives into the fifth year, no estate tax will apply.[40]

EXAMPLE 9-14: In 2021, Alice gave her four grandchildren $75,000 (5 × $15,000 annual exclusion amount) each (for a total of $300,000) and made the five-year election. Alice died in 2023. Thus, two years remain in the five-year period. Alice's estate must include $120,000 (4 grandchildren × 2 years × $15,000) for purposes of calculating the estate's tax liability. The remaining $180,000 contribution plus earnings would not be included in Alice's estate.

Note that in this example, any earnings on the account are not taxed. Consequently, the full fair market value of the account on the donor's death is irrelevant. This inclusion rule is inconsistent with traditional estate tax principles. Under Section 2031, the full fair market value of property (not just the original contribution) is brought back into the decedent's gross estate. Also, if the account declines in value, the amount includable would still be based on the contributions.

40. *Id.* § 529(c)(4)(B).

CHART 9-3 529s and Established Estate Tax Rules

Established Estate Tax Principles	§ 529 Principles
Donor taxed on retained power to revoke [§ 2038(a)(1)]	No estate tax
Donor taxed on power to change the designated beneficiary [§ 2036(a)(2)]	No estate tax
Donor taxed on transfer satisfying legal obligation [§ 2036(a)(2)]	No estate tax
Nondonor owner who has power to distribute property to oneself has a taxable general power of appointment [§ 2041]	No estate tax
Donor taxed on full fair market value of property brought back into estate	Donor taxed on gift contribution if makes a five-year election and dies before five years
No estate tax if beneficiary has no right to control the account or change the beneficiary	Beneficiary taxed if dies and account is received by beneficiary's estate

a. Marital Deduction Issue

A *marital deduction* issue may arise when the donor's estate is taxable on a portion of the original contribution if the successor owner is the surviving spouse. Arguably, the surviving spouse could revoke the Section 529 account, and thus the account would not be a terminable interest. Otherwise, the value of the assets in the Section 529 plan brought back in the estate under the five-year rule would not qualify for the Section 2056 marital deduction. As a precautionary matter, an estate planner should include a provision in a will or trust that the marital deduction gift cannot be funded with assets that do not qualify for the marital deduction.

b. Additional Nontax Issues

Beyond estate and gift tax issues, additional problems may arise if, upon the death of the owner, no successor owner is named or the successor is dead or incapacitated. When successor ownership of the Section 529 savings plan has not been contemplated (during life or by will) or fails, the probate laws of the state that the now-deceased owner resided in will control. If intestacy statutes govern the ownership of the Section 529 savings plan, unfortunate results may occur. The Section 529 savings account could be held by multiple owners with adverse interests. Most importantly, the decedent's intent may be thwarted.

EXAMPLE 9-15: Alice, a widow, creates a Section 529 savings account for her granddaughter Katie. Katie has lived in the same town as Alice her entire life. Furthermore, Katie has been a very devoted granddaughter, often mowing Alice's lawn and doing Alice's grocery shopping. Alice has another grandchild, Bobby. Bobby lives out of the area, rarely sees Alice (in fact he has never brought his children to meet her) and has already attended college. Alice fails to name a successor during her lifetime or in her will. The state Alice resided in follows the modern *per stirpes* form of distribution when there is no surviving spouse.[41] Alice is survived by two grandchildren and three great-grandchildren. Under the state's intestacy statute, the Section 529 plan would pass to Katie and Bobby to be held in joint ownership. Further complications arise because the state's Section 529 plan does not allow the owner to be the beneficiary of the plan. Family strife ensues after Bobby subsequently changes the beneficiary designation from Katie to his three children. During probate, Katie's equitable arguments fail. Katie cannot sue Alice's attorney for malpractice because this state strictly enforces the privity of contract doctrine. Alice rolls over in her grave.

In addition, unintended results can arise if ownership of a Section 529 account falls into the wrong hands. The new owner may revoke the account or designate a new beneficiary.

EXAMPLE 9-16: Account owner Alice has named Ben as the beneficiary on the 529 account. Alice dies, and by will the account ownership goes to her husband (who is not the father of Ben). The husband closes the account, gets the money back or changes the account so his son, George, who is unrelated to Ben, becomes the current beneficiary.

Most state Section 529 plans either require or allow a successor owner to be designated when the plan is opened and the owner files the initial forms. Additionally, many plans provide forms such that subsequent changes to the identity of the successor owner can be made. To avoid unintended and/or adverse results, it is *imperative* to contemplate successor ownership and regularly maintain this aspect of the Section 529 savings plan.

2. Death of Beneficiary

The second statutory exception to the inclusion in estate tax of Section 529 fund assets is when the designated beneficiary dies and the assets are received by the estate of the beneficiary.[42] The 2008 Advance Notice clarifies that if the designated beneficiary dies, the value of the account will be included in the beneficiary's estate *only if* the account owner causes the entire account to be distributed to such estate within six months of the death. It is unclear under the Notice what the

41. *See, e.g.*, O.R.S. § 112.045.

42. I.R.C. § 529(c)(4)(B). The statute itself calls for includability only in the case of "amounts distributed on account of the death of the beneficiary."

estate tax consequences will be on a distribution of less than the entire account to the beneficiary's estate, or the distribution of the account to the beneficiary's estate more than six months after the beneficiary's death. Given most account limits and the likely case that the beneficiary is not independently wealthy, inclusion in the estate rarely would cause an immediate estate tax problem. The unified credit exemption amount of the beneficiary (for 2021, $11,700,000 when adjusted for inflation) will most likely cover the value in the account. In rare circumstances, however, it might be unfair to tax the beneficiary given that the now deceased beneficiary never had control or ownership of the assets. Of course, the beneficiary's estate could have considerable assets, and once the account was distributed to the deceased beneficiary's estate, the power of the owner to designate a subsequent beneficiary would no longer exist.

Planning Pointer

From a planning perspective, the contribution to a Section 529 savings plan may revert to the donor and thus be included in the donor's estate. For example, if the account owner receives a distribution of the plan assets by reason of the death of the designated beneficiary (and no new beneficiary is, or can be, designated), those funds could be includable in the donor's estate. If, on the other hand, the donor timely designates the beneficiary's estate as the recipient of the funds, no such reversion will occur.

CHART 9-4 Comparison of Exemption Amounts under Estate, Gift, and GST Tax

	2001	2004–2005	2006–2008	2009	2017–2021
Estate Unified Credit Amount	$ 1.0 million	$ 1.5 million	$ 2.0 million	$ 3.5 million	$ 10 million (adjusted for inflation) $ 11.7 in **2021**
Lifetime Gift Tax Exemption	Same as estate	$ 1.0 million	$ 1.0 million	$ 1.0 million	$ 10 million (adjusted for inflation) $ 11.7 in **2021**
Lifetime GST Exemption	$ 1.0 million	$ 1.5 million	$ 2.0 million	$ 3.5 million	$ 11.7 in **2021** (same as for gift and estate tax)

D. Planning for Incapacity of the Owner

If the account owner becomes incompetent, transfer of ownership to someone else may result in adverse tax consequences.[43] The planner may address this situation by drafting an attorney-in-fact or power of attorney with specific authorization to change the designated beneficiary, transfer contributor rights, roll over to another plan, and/or otherwise make decisions that are within the discretion of the contributor. The state 529 plan may also allow designation of an attorney-in-fact or power of attorney. Most broadly defined powers of the attorney-in-fact or power of attorney will include powers to enter into contracts and make investment decisions. However, the power to make gifts of the contributor's assets is more unusual.[44] Even if the power of attorney expressly allows a gift, a question arises as to the extent of the gift (5 & 5 power[45] or gift tax annual exclusion) and whether the class of potential recipients is limited. If there is no power of attorney or if none is allowed by the state plan, the federal requirements expect there to be an owner. If ownership is changed, the tax consequences are uncertain.[46]

E. Planning with Trusts

Under many state plans, a Section 529 savings plan can be created by a trust. In other words, if the state plan permits, a trust could be the original contributor and owner of the Section 529 plan. Additionally, under these state plans, the original owner of a Section 529 savings plan could contribute his/her existing Section 529 plan to a trust. Furthermore, in states that allow trust ownership, a trust could be designated as the successor owner in the event that the original owner dies prior to distribution of the account.

There are numerous reasons for using trust ownership in Section 529 planning. First, the trust allows continuity of control over the Section 529 assets. Continuity of control is important in situations where the contemplated beneficiaries are grandchildren or even great-grandchildren. Second, unlike a Section 529 plan, a trust can have multiple beneficiaries. Third, holding the Section 529 plan in trust form might ensure better investment planning. This is true because the trust would have broad investment powers and, as is customary for a trust, would follow the *prudent investor rule*. Therefore, the trustee would ensure that the funds invested in a Section 529 plan are placed in a plan with good returns and low fees. Moreover, if the originally selected plan was poorly chosen, the trustee would be

43. See Section A(2) earlier.

44. Estate of Casey v. Comm'r, 948 F.2d 895 (4th Cir. 1991).

45. A common clause in many trusts that allows the trust's beneficiary to make an authorized withdrawal of the greater of $5,000 or 5 percent of the trust's fair market value.

46. For details on planning with ABLE accounts, see **Chapter Eleven: Disability Planning with Section 529 Savings Plans**.

responsible for rolling the funds to a better Section 529 savings plan. The trustee would also monitor the plan and make appropriate changes when necessary.

Fourth, the trustee is bound by a fiduciary duty to ensure that the funds will be used for the purposes set forth in the trust agreement and that the funds are used impartially. Fifth, any nonqualified distribution would not result in the trust funds being included in the donor's estate (although they could still be included in the beneficiary's estate under the trust agreement). Finally, the trust could contain a spendthrift clause that would protect the trust assets from the beneficiary's creditors and/or from dissipation by the beneficiary. This last consideration is especially important when the state plan or state law does not provide adequate protection for the Section 529 savings plan assets.

On the other hand, there could be some disadvantages to designating the trust as the owner. First, if the trust is considered the owner, it will not get the per-donee annual exclusion. Thus, when the trust is the original contributor to the Section 529 savings plan, gift tax and/or GST liability may arise. Additionally, if the donor/owner contributes to the trust, as opposed to directly to the Section 529 plan, the contribution will not qualify for the election embodied in Section 529(c)(2)(B); in other words, the owner will not be able to make the election that allows the owner to contribute five times the annual exclusion amount and then spread that contribution over a five-year period. Second, trusts are generally subject to higher income tax rates than are individuals. In other words, given the same nonqualified distribution, the trust will pay more taxes than would the individual donor/owner. If the trust is a grantor trust, however, this negative aspect is resolved. Third, any trust with existing investments must sell them to make cash contributions to a Section 529 plan. Finally, Medicaid issues are more certain and more restrictive when a trust is involved. When the donor transfers funds for the Section 529 plan or the Section 529 plan itself to the trust and this transfer falls within certain "look-back" rules, the law might treat the Section 529 account as part of the donor's assets for Medicaid calculation purposes.[47]

Possible problems may also arise where the trust is named as the successor owner of the Section 529 plan in the event that the original owner dies. Few or no problems should arise when the Section 529 savings plan becomes part of a bypass trust, if the beneficiary of both the Section 529 savings plan and the bypass trust are the same, and the trust documents are drafted so that the trust assets can be used for the beneficiary's maintenance, health, and/or education.

However, problems will almost certainly arise when the ownership of the Section 529 savings plan passes to a marital trust, for example a power of appointment trust or a QTIP trust. With marital trusts (other than estate trusts), the law (especially tax law) requires distribution of any income on the trust principal to the surviving spouse. Thus, the trustee will be legally required to close the Section 529

47. Medicaid may not be an issue for a wealthy individual. *See* **Chapter Twelve: Nontax Aspects of Section 529 Savings Plans**, C.3.

account for the benefit of the surviving spouse. This would be true even where, for example, the Section 529 savings plan was established for the couple's children and the surviving spouse wanted the children to have the benefit of the 529 account when they reached college age. Under these circumstances, the 10 percent additional *penalty tax* would be triggered by the nonqualified distribution to the surviving spouse. In the alternative, if the Section 529 plan was still owned by a QTIP trust at the time the surviving spouse passed away, the full value of the plan would be included in the surviving spouse's estate.

Planning Pointer

Use of existing trusts to hold Section 529 assets precludes the five-year gift election and may cause gift and GST problems. Naming the trust as the successor owner can create plan management and administration issues.

F. Conclusion

For higher-income or wealthy taxpayers, Section 529 savings plans offer significant gift, generation-skipping, and estate tax benefits. Many of the Section 529 rules are just the opposite of established gift and estate tax principles and thus offer significant advantages. The donor can transfer free of gift tax five times the annual exclusion. And even though the donor/owner can terminate the account and change the beneficiary or investment options, the transfer is a completed gift of a *present interest* and nothing will be brought back into the donor's estate unless he/she dies within the five-year averaging period, or in the unusual circumstance where the beneficiary dies and the fund returns to the owner. In some situations, trust ownership of the plan may provide additional benefits and thus be appropriate. However, adverse tax and nontax consequences may result from such ownership.

Chapter 10

State Tax Planning with Section 529 Savings Plans

State tax law provides additional tax benefits for those choosing a Section 529 plan. These state tax benefits often surpass those provided by federal tax law. For example, contributions to a Section 529 savings plan may be partially or totally deductible against state income taxes. On the other hand, state law may pose some barriers. Not all states conform to the federal law, as some will not allow 529 distributions to pay for K–12 tuition or for repayment of student loans to qualify for qualified expenses. In addition, state law may pose a greater barrier than that posed by federal law when the owner wishes to roll the Section 529 savings plan to another state's plan or withdraw the funds. State law may impose recapture of state income tax benefits and/or penalties that do not exist at the federal level.

Whether a contribution is deductible or eligible for a credit for state income tax purposes depends on the law of the state in which the donor/contributor resides. The law where the plan is established determines the taxation of accumulations and penalties upon withdrawal or rollover to another state's plan. The laws of the distributee's state of residence control the taxability of any distributions. The law where the donor or owner resides or is domiciled will determine the state gift and estate tax consequences of the plan. Thus, the advisor should carefully research the laws of the appropriate state (or states).

CHART 10-1 Possible State Tax Advantages

- An income tax deduction for contributions.
- An income tax credit for contributions.
- A deferral of income tax on undistributed earnings.
- An exemption from income tax on the earnings when distributed if used for qualified purposes.
- An exemption for account owners from state death taxes.

A. State Tax Deductions or Credits

In determining any state tax deduction or credit for contributions to a Section 529 plan, the law of the state in which the donor/contributor resides will control. Twenty-eight states and the District of Columbia offer annual upfront tax deductions to residents for all or a portion of the contribution the resident makes to a state Section 529 plan. Five states—Indiana, Minnesota, Oregon, Utah, and Vermont—offer some form of credit. Some states even allow an unlimited deduction—for example, Colorado, New Mexico, South Carolina, and West Virginia. Other states allow a significant deduction. For example, Pennsylvania allows up to $15,000 ($30,000 for married filing jointly). Illinois, Mississippi, Nebraska, and Oklahoma allow an annual deduction up to a maximum of $10,000 ($20,000 for married filing jointly). An allowance of $2,000 to $3,000 per year, however, is more typical. Some states allow a carryover of any unused deduction in one year to a future year (Louisiana, Ohio, and Virginia). Some deductions are per beneficiary (Minnesota, Oklahoma, Ohio, and Pennsylvania), while most are in the aggregate for the year. Most provide double the amount for married couples than for other taxpayers, but several states are marriage neutral (Indiana, Iowa, Nebraska, Oregon, and Virginia). (*See* **Chart 10-2**.) As illustrated, states treat tax deductions of contribution differently, so it is essential for an advisor to research and know state law.

It is common for the sponsoring state to provide tax benefits only to its residents for contributions made to its own state plan. This practice, called the *parity issue*, has been challenged by the Securities Industry Association (SIA).[1] The SIA wants the states to provide the same tax benefits for in- and out-of-state plans. In response, Pennsylvania became the first state to offer its residents a state income tax deduction for gifts to any Section 529 plan. Arizona, Arkansas, Kansas, Minnesota, Missouri, and Montana have recently passed legislation with similar effects.[2] Thus, seven states offer tax parity for contributions to any 529 plan.

In nine states (Iowa, Massachusetts, Missouri, Montana, Nebraska, New York, Rhode Island, Utah, Virginia, plus the District of Columbia), only the 529 account owner (or spouse) may claim a state income tax benefit.[3] In other states, the deduction may be available only for certain donors, such as parents or guardians of the beneficiary (e.g., Georgia). State law also may not permit a deduction or credit if a contribution is made to an account of which the account owner is also the beneficiary. In some states, deductions or credits are not permitted for

1. *See Investing for the Future: 529 State Tuition Savings Plans* (Statement of Marc E. Lackritz, President, Sec. Indus. Ass'n, before the H. Fin. Servs. Comm.) 5, https://archives-financialservices.house.gov/media/pdf/060204ml.pdf.

2. *See* Matthew Toner, *How Much Is Your State's 529 Plan Tax Deduction Really Worth?*, Saving for College (Mar. 3, 2021), https://www.savingforcollege.com/article/how-much-is-your-state-s-529-plan-tax-deduction-really-worth.

3. Kathryn Flynn, *529 Plan Gifts May Be Deductible on State Income Tax Returns*, Saving for College (Oct. 20, 2020), https://www.savingforcollege.com/article/529-plan-gifts-may-be-deductible-from-state-income-tax. Average tuition and fees at a ranked private college were $37,650 for the 2020–2021 academic year; the average tuition and fees at a ranked public out-of-state college was $27,020 a year and $10,560 for in-state.

rollovers from another state's program. On the other hand, some states permit rollovers from another state's program. Often states restrict their tax benefits to initial contributions.

Whether a state allows a tax deduction or credit for contributions to a Section 529 plan is perhaps the *most important factor* in choosing a plan—at least up to the amount of the tax benefit. Some states allow no deduction or credit even though they have an income tax system (California, Delaware, Hawaii, Kentucky, Maine, New Jersey, and North Carolina.). Other states do not provide for any tax benefit as there is no income tax in the state (Alaska, Florida, Nevada, New Hampshire, South Dakota, Tennessee, Texas, Washington, and Wyoming). Even when the state offers the benefit of a deduction or a credit, the taxpayer must decide whether the state plan has enough other benefits to warrant investment in that state's plan.[4] When fees are high and/or investment performance is low, other states' plans should be investigated.[5]

For most taxpayers, no requirement exists for holding funds in the plan for a specified amount of time to claim the state income tax benefit. Taxpayers can contribute up to December 31 (and in many states until April 15th) and still qualify for the deduction or credit. However, Montana and Wisconsin do impose time limits, and Michigan and Minnesota base state income tax benefits on annual contributions net of distributions.

CHART 10-2 State Tax Deductions or Credits

State	Deduction for Contribution Or CREDITS	Citation
Alabama	YES $ 5,000/year/ $ 10,000/year/married filing jointly	ALA. CODE § 16-33C
Alaska	N/A (no state income tax)	ALASKA STAT. § 14.40.802
Arizona	YES $ 4,000/year/ $ 8,000/year/married filing jointly (to any 529 plan)	ARIZ. REV. STAT. § 15-1875
Arkansas	YES $ 5,000/year/ $ 10,000/year/married filing jointly (to any 529 plan)	ARK. CODE ANN. § 6-84-111
California	NO	CAL. REV. & TAX. CODE § 17140
Colorado	YES unlimited	COLO. REV. STAT. § 23-3.1-309
Connecticut	YES $ 5,000/year/ $ 10,000/year/married filing jointly	CONN. GEN. STAT. § 3-22
Delaware	NO	DEL. CODE tit. 14, § 3485
Florida	N/A (no state income tax)	FLA. STAT. § 1009.981

(continued)

4. See **Chapter Twelve: Nontax Aspects of Section 529 Savings Plans** for discussion of nontax benefits that may entice a potential donor to contribute without the benefit of a state income tax deduction.

5. *See* **Chapter Fourteen: Choosing the Right Section 529 Savings Plan**.

State	Deduction for Contribution Or CREDITS	Citation
Georgia	YES $ 4,000/year/ $ 8,000/year/ married filing jointly	GA. CODE ANN. § 20-3-636
Hawaii	NO	HAW. REV. STAT. § 256-4
Idaho	YES $ 6,000/year/ $ 12,000/year/ married filing jointly	IDAHO CODE § 33-5404
Illinois	YES $ 10,000/year/ $ 20,000/year/ married filing jointly	110 ILL. COMP. STAT. 947/75
Indiana	CREDIT of 20% on contributions up to $ 5,000/year	IND. CODE § 21-9-10-2
Iowa	YES $ 3,439/year/ $ 6,878/married filing jointly (for 2020)	IOWA CODE § 120.9
Kansas	YES $ 3,000/year/ $ 6,000/year married filing jointly (to any 529 plan)	KAN. STAT. § 75
Kentucky	NO	KY. REV. STAT. § 164A.370
Louisiana	YES $ 2,400/year/ $ 4,800 for married filing jointly (rollover of any unused deduction to future years)	LA. REV. STAT. ANN. § 17:3095
Maine	NO	ME. REV. STAT. ANN. § 11479
Maryland	YES $ 2,500/year/ $ 5,000/year/ married filing jointly	MD. CODE ANN., EDUC. § 18-1912
Massachusetts	YES $ 1,000/year/ $ 2,000/ married filing jointly	MASS. GEN. LAWS ANN. ch. 15C
Michigan	YES $ 5,000/year/ $ 10,000/ married filing jointly	MICH. COMP. LAWS SERV. § 390.1486
Minnesota	YES $ 1,500/year/beneficiary $ 3,000/year/beneficiary for married filing jointly (to any 529 plan) or take a tax CREDIT of 50% of contribution reduced by withdrawals, up to $ 500 (to any 529 plan)	MINN. STAT. ANN. § 136G
Mississippi	YES $ 10,000/year/ $ 20,000 for married filing jointly	MISS. CODE ANN. § 37-155-113
Missouri	YES $ 8,000/year/ $ 16,000 for married filing jointly (to any 529 plan)	MO. REV. STAT. § 166.435

State	Deduction for Contribution Or CREDITS	Citation
Montana	YES $ 3,000/year/ $ 6,000 for married filing joint (to any 529 plan)	MONT. CODE § 15-62
Nebraska	YES up to $ 10,000 maximum/ $ 5,000 married filing separately	NEB. REV. STAT. § 85-1801
Nevada	N/A (no state income tax)	NEV. REV. STAT. § 353B.310
New Hampshire	N/A (no state income tax)	N.H. REV. STAT. § 195-M:10
New Jersey	NO	N.J. STAT. § 18A:71B-41
New Mexico	YES unlimited	N.M. ADMIN. CODE tit. 5, § 7.30
New York	YES $ 5,000/year/ $ 10,000 for married filing jointly	MCKINNEY'S EDUCATION LAW 695
North Carolina	NO	N.C. GEN. STAT. § 116-209.25
North Dakota	YES $ 5,000/year/ $ 10,000 for married filing jointly	N.D. ADMIN. CODE § 12.5-02-01-04 N.D. CENT. CODE § 6-09-38
Ohio	YES $ 4,000/year/beneficiary with unlimited rollover	OHIO REV. CODE § 3334
Oklahoma	YES $ 10,000/year/ $ 20,000/married filing jointly	OKLA. STAT. ANN. tit. 68, § 2358
Oregon	CREDIT on contributions of $ 150 single/ $ 300 married filing jointly	OR. REV. STAT. § 316.680
Pennsylvania	YES $ 15,000/year/beneficiary $ 30,000/year/beneficiary for married filing jointly (to any 529 plan)	24 PA. CONS. STAT. § 6901.301
Rhode Island	YES $ 500/year/ $ 1,000 if married filing jointly	R.I. GEN. LAWS § 16-57-6.3
South Carolina	YES unlimited	S.C. CODE ANN. § 59-2-20
South Dakota	N/A (no state income tax)	S.D. CODIFIED LAWS § 13-63-1
Tennessee	N/A (no state income tax)	TENN. CODE. ANN. § 49-7-822
Texas	N/A (no state income tax)	
Utah	CREDIT of 5% up to $ 102 if single/ $ 204 if married filing jointly (in 2020)	UTAH CODE ANN. § 53B-110

(continued)

State	Deduction for Contribution Or CREDITS	Citation
Vermont	CREDIT 10% of up to $ 250 if single/$ 500 if married filing jointly	VT. STAT. ANN. tit. 16, § 2879c
Virginia	YES $ 4,000/year/per account, unused is rolled over	VA. CODE ANN. § 23-38.83
Washington	N/A (no state income tax)	WASH. REV. CODE § 28B.95
West Virginia	YES, unlimited	W. VA. CODE § 18-30-2
Wisconsin	YES $ 3,340/year/beneficiary ($ 1,670 married filing separately)	WIS. STAT. § 14.64
Wyoming	N/A (no state income tax)	WYO. STAT. § 21-16-815
District of Columbia	YES $ 4,000/year/ $ 8,000 for married filing jointly	D.C. CODE § 47-4509

Planning Pointer

For the higher income taxpayer, it may make sense to invest in a state Section 529 plan up to the state income tax deduction—as long as the contribution does not exceed federal gift tax amounts. The taxpayer could additionally invest funds in excess of the state tax deduction in an out-of-state plan with lower fees and better investment performance. Again, for federal gift tax advantages, this total amount should not be greater than $75,000 ($150,000 for a married couple electing to split the gift) in 2021.

B. Accumulations

The law where the plan is established will determine the taxation of any accumulations on the account. Under most state laws, money that accumulates in the account is not subject to state income tax. Some states, however, will tax earnings on out-of-state plans. A few states tax both the in-state and out-of-state earnings of Section 529 plans.

Example 10-1: Alice has contributed $75,000 to an out-of-state 529 plan. The earnings on that plan are $4,000 this year and are not subject to federal income tax. Nevertheless, some states will tax this $4,000 under state law.

States with no income taxes may have a tax on dividends, interest, or other investment income. Tennessee, for example, taxes interest on notes, bonds, or dividends on stock (including distributions from mutual funds) and thus could tax income that is generated on an out-of-state 529 plan.[6] Florida also has a tax on investment income. Because a Section 529 savings plans will qualify as investment income, the earnings from these accounts may be taxed by some states. The advisor must check relevant state laws in counseling his/her clients.

C. Withdrawals or Distributions

In determining state taxation of withdrawals or distributions, the state laws of the state in which the beneficiary/distributee resides controls. Most states follow federal law and do not tax distributions or withdrawals when used for qualified purposes. (*See* **Chart 10-3**.) Other states exempt only resident beneficiaries. Thus, in eleven states—Alabama, Arizona, Arkansas, Colorado, Indiana, Iowa, Massachusetts, Mississippi, New Jersey, North Carolina, and District of Columbia—withdrawals from out-of-state programs are subject to state income tax when used by a resident beneficiary. In five of these 11 states, no state deduction is given for contributions to the in-state plan.[7] Consequently, in those states there is no direct incentive to invest in the state plan, yet a disincentive to invest in another state's plan.

Planning Pointer

A tax at the state level upon withdrawal—even for qualified education purposes—can offset the tax-deferred benefits of the 529 plan. Thus, it is important for the advisor to check relevant state law when choosing which plan is best for the client.

EXAMPLE 10-2: Alice, who resides in Massachusetts, where the income tax rate is a flat 5.6 percent, sets up a Section 529 plan in Massachusetts. There is no income tax deduction for any contribution to a Section 529 plan. Therefore, there is no state tax advantage to investing in her home state's plan.[8]

6. *See* Tenn. Dep't of Revenue Notice 03-09 (Apr. 1, 2003).

7. Alabama, Arizona, Massachusetts, New Jersey, and North Carolina.

8. This example would be true for the following states as well: California, Hawaii, and Idaho. Also note there is no state income tax advantage for saving in states without an income tax: Alaska, Florida, Nevada, Tennessee, Texas, South Dakota, Washington, and Wyoming.

CHART 10-3 State Taxation of Withdrawals from 529 Savings Plan for Qualified Higher Education Expenses

	Tax Free Withdrawal?	Citation
Alabama	YES—exempt only residents	ALA. CODE § 16-33C
Alaska	No state income tax	ALASKA STAT. § 14.40.802a(10)
Arizona	YES—exempt only residents	ARIZ. REV. STAT. § 15-1875
Arkansas	YES—exempt only residents	ARK. CODE ANN. § 6-84-111
California	NO—even residents with state sponsored plan pay tax	CAL. REV. & TAX. CODE § 17140
Colorado	YES—exempt only residents	COLO. REV. STAT. § 23-3.1-306
Connecticut	YES—follow federal law—tax-free withdrawal	CONN. GEN. STAT. § 3-22
Delaware	YES—follow federal law—tax-free withdrawal	DEL. CODE tit. 14, § 3491
Florida	No state income tax	FLA. STAT. § 1009.981
Georgia	YES—follow federal law—tax-free withdrawal	GA. CODE ANN. § 20-3-634
Hawaii	NO—even residents with state sponsored plan pay tax	HAW. REV. STAT. § 256-4
Idaho	NO—even residents with state sponsored plan pay tax	IDAHO CODE § 33-5404
Illinois	YES—follow federal law—tax-free withdrawal	110 ILL. COMP. STAT. 947/75
Indiana	YES—exempt only residents	IND. CODE § 21-9
Iowa	YES—exempt only residents	IOWA CODE § 120.9
Kansas	YES—follow federal law—tax-free withdrawal	KAN. STAT. § 75
Kentucky	YES	KY. REV. STAT. § 164A.370
Louisiana	YES—follow federal law—tax-free withdrawal	LA. REV. STAT. ANN. § 17:3095
Maine	YES—follow federal law—tax-free withdrawal	ME. REV. STAT. ANN. § 11479
Maryland	YES—follow federal law—tax-free withdrawal	MD. CODE ANN., EDUC. § 18-1912
Massachusetts	YES—exempt only residents	MASS. GEN. LAWS ANN. ch. 15c, § 16
Michigan	YES—follow federal law—tax-free withdrawal	MICH. COMP. LAWS SERV. § 390.1477
Minnesota	YES—follow federal law—tax-free withdrawal	MINN. STAT. ANN. § 136G.13
Mississippi	YES—exempt only residents	MISS. CODE ANN. § 37-155-17
Missouri	YES—follow federal law—tax-free withdrawal	MO. REV. STAT. § 166.430

	Tax Free Withdrawal?	Citation
Montana	YES—follow federal law—tax-free withdrawal	MONT. CODE § 15-62
Nebraska	YES—follow federal law—tax-free withdrawal	NEB. STAT. § 85-1812
Nevada	No state income tax	NEV. REV. STAT. § 353B.310
New Hampshire	YES—exempt only residents	N.H. REV. STAT. § 195-M:8
New Jersey	YES—exempt only residents	N.J. STAT. § 18A:71B-41
New Mexico	YES—follow federal law—tax-free withdrawal	N.M. ADMIN. CODE tit. 5, § 7.30
New York	YES—follow federal law—tax-free withdrawal	MCKINNEY'S EDUCATION LAW 695-e
North Carolina	YES—exempt only residents	N.C. GEN. STAT. § 116-209.25
North Dakota	YES—follow federal law—tax-free withdrawal	N.D. ADMIN. CODE § 12.5-02-01-04 N.D. CENT. CODE § 6-09-38
Ohio	YES—follow federal law—tax-free withdrawal	OHIO REV. CODE § 3334
Oklahoma	YES—follow federal law—tax-free withdrawal	OKLA. STAT. ANN. tit. 70, § 3970.7
Oregon	YES—follow federal law—tax-free withdrawal	OR. REV. STAT. § 348.870
Rhode Island	YES—follow federal law—tax-free withdrawal	R.I. GEN. LAWS § 16-57-6.1
Tennessee	YES—follow federal law—tax-free withdrawal	TENN. CODE. ANN. § 49-7-822
Utah	YES—follow federal law—tax-free withdrawal	UTAH CODE ANN. § 53B-8a-112
Vermont	YES—follow federal law—tax-free withdrawal	VT. STAT. ANN. tit. 16, § 2879a
Virginia	YES—follow federal law—tax-free withdrawal	VA. CODE ANN. § 23-38.81
Washington	No state income tax	WASH. REV. CODE § 28B.95.110
Wisconsin	YES—follow federal law—tax-free withdrawal	WIS. STAT. § 14.64
Wyoming	No state income tax	WYO. STAT. § 21-16-815
District of Columbia	YES—exempt only residents	D.C. CODE § 47-4509

Some states (e.g., Colorado and Washington, D.C.) recapture the deductible contribution if a nonqualified withdrawal is made. Other states (e.g., California and Kentucky) impose their own penalty upon a nonqualified distribution. Not all states conform to new federal tax law. With the expansion of the definition of QHEE under the *TCJA* of 2017 (up to $10,000 per year tuition at eligible K–12 schools) and under the *SECURE Act* of 2019 (payment of up to $10,000 for loan repayments), many states consider these unqualified distributions. So, for example, thirteen states consider payment from the 529 plan for K–12 tuition as nonqualified and thus subject to income tax.[9] Nine of those states allow an income tax deduction for 529 plan contributions (Vermont offers a credit) which is subject to recapture if funds are withdrawn to pay for K–12 tuition. (*See* **Chart 10-4**.)

CHART 10-4 State Tax Distributions Issues

State	Taxation of nonqualified distributions	Are K–12 distributions exempt from state tax?	Are outbound rollovers subject to recapture?
Alabama (AL)	Nonqualified withdrawals plus 10% of the amount of the nonqualified withdrawal is included in AL income tax; AL does not exempt distributions from non-AL 529 plans.		Yes
Arizona		No	
Arkansas			Yes
California (CA)	2.5% CA penalty tax on nonqualified distributions.	No	
Colorado		No	Yes
Connecticut		No	
Georgia (GA)	Earnings from nonqualified distribution must be reported on the account owner's (not the beneficiary's) GA income tax return.		
Hawaii		No	
Idaho			Yes
Illinois		No	Yes
Indiana			Yes

9. Kathryn Flynn, *States That Do Not Conform with Federal 529 Plan Tax Laws*, Saving for College (Feb. 27, 2019), https://www.savingforcollege.com/article/states-that-do-not-conform-with-federal-529-plan-tax-laws.

State	Taxation of nonqualified distributions	Are K–12 distributions exempt from state tax?	Are outbound rollovers subject to recapture?
Iowa		Must be an IA K–12 school or accredited under IA Code Section 256.11.	
Louisiana		Only through K–12.	
Michigan		No	
Minnesota		No	
Montana (MT)	Distributions taken within 3 years of opening 529 account taxed at the highest marginal MT tax rate.	No	Yes
Nebraska		No	Yes
New Mexico		No	Yes
New York		No	Yes
Oklahoma			Yes, outbound rollovers made within 12 months of the date of contribution are subject to recapture.
Oregon		No	
Rhode Island			Yes, outbound rollovers are subject to recapture in the 2 taxable years following the year of an income tax benefit claimed.
Utah		Not allowed.	Yes
Vermont		No	Yes
Virginia			Yes
Wisconsin (WI)	Distributions taken within 365 days of contribution must be added back to WI taxable income if previously deducted.		

D. Tracking Basis When State Law Allows a Deduction

A taxpayer must know his/her Section 72 exclusion amount or basis in the Section 529 plan to determine what portion of the distribution might be taxed upon a nonqualified or other taxable withdrawal. Under the federal rules, the contribution to the plan is easily calculated because there is no deduction. But in a state that allows a total or partial deduction for the contribution, that portion should not be included in the calculation of the Section 72 formula. Consequently, on a nonqualified distribution, all of the original contribution will be taxed if it were deductible under state law.

EXAMPLE 10-3: Alice has contributed $2,000 each year to a Section 529 plan. Under state law, she has been allowed to deduct this amount every year for 15 years. The fund has increased to a value of $50,000, of which $20,000 represents earnings. When her son goes to college, she distributes $45,000 to him for qualified purposes (leaving $5,000). If the plan is terminated and returned to Alice, she will have to include 100 percent of the $5,000 in her taxes (in addition to paying a penalty). Since the original contribution was deductible under state law, none of the $5,000 should be tax exempt now.

E. Rollovers

The law where the plan is established determines the tax consequences when there is a rollover from one state to another. Some state programs do not permit rollovers at all or require the funds to remain in the account for a specific period of time. Some states (New York, for example) consider a rollover to another state's plan a nonqualified withdrawal subject to tax. Some states recapture the tax benefit of any deduction when the plan is rolled over to another state's plan (Nebraska, New York, South Carolina, and Virginia). Others recapture the benefit only if it was rolled over within a certain time period. For example, Washington, D.C. recaptures the income tax deduction if a rollover is made within two years. If the client wants flexibility and control in moving the plan to another state, the advisor must be aware of states with rollover restrictions and penalties.

For plans that do not allow ownership changes, the balance from the taxpayer's 529 plan could be rolled over into a different 529 for the benefit of the same student or a member of the beneficiary's family. It is also possible to do this manually by taking a distribution from the original account and contributing it to another account within 60 days. It may be necessary to locate both accounts in the same state, however, for tax purposes.

CHART 10-5 State Savings Plans Unavailable to Nonresidents[10]

State Plan	Unavailable to Nonresident
Connecticut Higher Education Trust (CHET) Advisor Plan	Account owner must have CT mailing address or be a CT resident on active duty in the U.S. armed forces.
Florida 529 Savings Plan	Must be FL resident at time of program enrollment.
Louisiana—Student Tuition Assistance and Revenue Trust Program (START) Savings Program	Account owner or beneficiary must be a LA resident.
New Jersey NJBEST College Savings Plan	The contributor or the beneficiary must be a NJ resident at the time of enrollment.
Pennsylvania 529 Guaranteed Savings Plan	The account owner or beneficiary must be a PA resident at the time of the program enrollment.
South Carolina Future Scholar 529 College Savings Plan (Direct-Sold)	The account owner or beneficiary must be a resident of SC or an employee of SC at the time of program enrollment.
South Dakota CollegeAccess 529 (Direct-Sold)	The account owner or designated beneficiary must be a SD resident at the time of program enrollment.
Texas Tuition Promise Fund	The beneficiary must be TX resident or have a parent who is a TX resident and is the named purchaser at the time of enrollment.
New Jersey—Better Education Savings Trust	The contributor must be a NJ resident at the time of enrollment.
Washington Guaranteed Tuition (GET)	Account owner or beneficiary must be WA resident at the time of program enrollment.
West Virginia Direct College Savings	Account owner must have WV mailing address or be a WV resident on active duty in the U.S. armed forces (if advisor-sold).

F. Gift and Inheritance Tax Issues

The law where the donor or owner resides or is domiciled will determine state estate and gift tax issues. State law may be different than federal law. For example, a contribution to the Section 529 plan may not qualify as a completed gift. Furthermore, even if the state considers the transfer a completed gift, some states may not consider this a *present interest* and impose a gift tax. A state may also not allow the donor to contribute the equivalent of five years of *per-donee annual gift tax exclusions* ($75,000 = 5 × the federal gift tax annual exclusion amount in

10. *State Residency Requirements*, Saving for College, https://www.savingforcollege.com/compare_529_plans/?plan_question_ids[]=47&page=compare_plan_questions (last visited May 6, 2021).

2021 of $15,000). This five-year averaging election rule may not apply for state tax purposes. In Tennessee, for example, the donor must limit the contribution to the annual exclusion amount.[11]

In some states the value in the Section 529 account will be included in the account owner's estate for state death tax purposes—this is the case in Tennessee.[12] It is also possible that a nonresident account owner might be taxed on such an account, requiring an ancillary state death tax return to be filed. For example, the North Carolina disclosure document states that a nonresident account owner may be required to include the value of this account in a North Carolina estate tax filing.[13] When there are no significant tax benefits or tax detriments to a particular state plan, nontax considerations play an important role in the decision-making process.[14]

Planning Pointer

The advisor must carefully research: (1) the law of the state where the donor resides to determine contribution benefits and restrictions, (2) the law where the plan is established to determine recapture rules on rollovers, and (3) the law of the state where the distributee resides to determine taxability of withdrawals from the plan. The advisor must also check to determine whether the state law comports to federal law as to distributions for K–12 tuition and student loan indebtedness.

G. Conclusion

Although Section 529 savings plans are a creation of federal law, state tax law also plays an important role in selecting a plan. Unfortunately, many states have their own rules as to the taxation of these plans. This fact adds further complexity to the donor or advisor's analysis of the relevant tax issues. When selecting a Section 529 plan, the advisor and/or donor should pay special attention to assessing the existence of a state income tax deduction or credit for all or part of the contribution and assessing whether accumulations, withdrawals, rollovers, or other forms of removal from the contemplated state plan will result in negative tax consequences.

11. Tenn. Dep't of Revenue Notice 03-09 (Apr. 1, 2003).
12. *Id.*
13. N.C. Gen. Stat. § 116-209.25.
14. For further discussion of the nontax benefits of a Section 529 savings plan, see **Chapter Twelve: Nontax Aspects of Section 529 Savings Plans**.

Chapter 11

Disability Planning with Section 529 Savings Plans

The *Stephen Beck, Jr., Achieving a Better Life Experience (ABLE) Act of 2014*[1] created Section 529A in the code, which allows states to create tax-advantaged savings programs for eligible individuals with disabilities. The purpose of Section 529A is to enable blind and disabled people to maintain health, independence, and quality of life by having the ability to save money for certain disability expenses *without* disqualification from federal or state benefit programs. Section 529A is intended to supplement, not supplant, benefits otherwise available to the disabled individual, whether these benefits come from private sources, employment, public programs, or otherwise. Congress recognized that families raising children with a disability have a special financial burden throughout that child's lifetime.

The 529 *ABLE account* was designed to emulate many of the provisions of a traditional 529 savings account. With an ABLE account, the disabled person has the ability to shelter balances held within the account with no tax consequences when distributed for qualified disability expenses. Although legally construed by the federal government, these plans are administered by each state under each state's respective set of rules.[2] Thus, in addition to complying with the federal guidelines, the ABLE accounts must also comply with the applicable state rules. As of August 1, 2021, *all* states had such programs or had partnered with other states to provide these plans.[3]

1. Tax Increase Prevention Act of 2014, Pub. L. No. 113-295, 128 Stat. 4010 (2014) (the *ABLE Act* was part of this act).
2. I.R.C. § 529A(b)(1).
3. *Id.* § 529A(e)(7).

A. History and Directives

Section 529A directed the United States Department of Treasury to draft needed regulations,[4] and after an initial first draft was released on June 19, 2015, and subsequent comments were made, proposed regulations were promulgated. Proposed Treasury Regulations §§ 1.529A-0 through 1.529A-7 outlined how to (1) enforce the one beneficiary per account rule; (2) disseminate information and procedures to open an account; (3) further define "qualified disability expenses"; (4) coordinate the accounts with the Social Security Administration; (5) prevent "fraud and abuse" regarding claimed disability expenses; (6) coordinate the account with estate, gift, and generation-skipping tax; and (7) roll over or transfer assets from one account to another.

On December 18, 2015, the *Protecting Americans from Tax Hikes (PATH) Act*[5] was passed; *PATH* amended the original *ABLE Act* by removing the restriction that ABLE applicants must open an account only in the state where they reside. In December 2016, the Social Security Administration (SSA) issued a Program Operations Manual System (POMS) for ABLE.[6] POMS are the primary source of information used by the SSA to process claims for Social Security benefits. On January 6, 2017, the U.S. Department of Agriculture (USDA) issued announcements that ABLE balances are exempt from certain benefit calculations.[7] On September 7, 2017, the Centers for Medicare & Medicaid Services (CMS) released a similar guidance source for state Medicaid programs.[8] On December 7, 2015, the IRS issued Notice 2015-81,[9] which issued three modifications to the proposed regulations: (1) ABLE plans need not distinguish between qualified disability expenses or other expenses, such as housing expenses, but each designated beneficiary will be required to keep track of these distributions on their own returns; (2) no requirement is necessary to collect the taxpayer's identification number for each contribution to an account, but each program must merely request such number when contributions exceed limits; and (3) certification of disability can be from the disabled individual, parent, or legal guardian. Then, on October 10, 2019, new proposed regulations adopting the modifications in the Notice were issued.[10]

The *Tax Cuts and Jobs Act of 2017* further modified the *ABLE Act* in four respects. First, *TCJA* increased the amount of the contributions that are allowed

4. *Id.* § 529A(g).

5. Consolidated Appropriations Act of 2016, Pub. L. No. 114-113, 129 Stat. 2242 (2016) (codified as amended at I.R.C. § 529A(a), (b), (d)).

6. *Program Operations Manual System (POMS), SI 01130.740 Achieving a Better Life Experience (ABLE) Accounts*, Soc. Sec. Admin. (2016).

7. USDA Food and Nutrition Service, 82 Fed. Reg. 2010, 7 C.F.R. pt. 273, 2018 (Jan. 6, 2017).

8. Brian Neale, *Dear Colleague Letter: Implications of the ABLE Act for State Medicaid Programs*, Ctrs. for Medicare & Medicaid Servs., U.S. Dep't of Health & Human Servs. 1 (Sept. 7, 2017).

9. IRS Notice 2015-81, 2015-49 I.R.B. 784.

10. Notice 2018-62, 2018-34 I.R.B. 316 (Aug. 2018), announces the intent of the Treasury Department and the IRS to issue proposed regulations to address the *TCJA* of 2017 modifications; *see Contribution Limits Applicable to ABLE Accounts*, Fed. Reg. (Oct. 9, 2019), https://www.federalregister.gov/documents/2019/10/10/2019-21477/contribution-limits-applicable-to-able-accounts.

to be made to an ABLE account and added special rules for the increased contribution limit. Second, *TCJA* allowed an ABLE account's designated beneficiary to claim the saver's credit contributions to the account.[11] Third, the *TCJA* required that a responsible party maintain adequate records to ensure compliance with the law. Finally, *TCJA* allowed rollovers in limited amounts from a 529 qualified tuition program account of the designated beneficiary to the ABLE account of the designated beneficiary or his/her family member. Then, on November 19, 2020, final regulations to Section 529A were promulgated.[12] These six documents—the *TCJA*, the final regulations, the ABLE POMS, the USDA initiative, the GMS guidance, and the Notice—remain as the official bureaucratic pronouncements from the federal government on how ABLE accounts should operate.[13]

B. Establishing an ABLE Account

Not all people with disabilities are eligible to open an ABLE account. Under the *ABLE Act*, only two categories of people may do so. First, the recipients of Social Security Income (SSI) and Social Security Disability Insurance (SSDI) are eligible because they have already been determined to be "disabled." For other individuals that do not receive SSI and SSDI, a certification from a licensed physician *must* attest that the individual meets the Social Security Act's disability definition, as follows:

> "The individual has a medically determinable physical or mental impairment, which results in marked and severe functional limitations, and which can be expected to result in death or which has lasted or can be expected to last for a continuous period of not less than 12 months, or is blind . . ."

The regulations elaborate that these certifications must (1) state the person's diagnosis, (2) detail the limitations on the person's daily living activities, and (3) certify that the disability began before the person turned 26. To be clear, ABLE account holders can be older than age 26, but they must have first experienced their disability before their 26th birthday.[14] Unfortunately, many individuals with traumatic brain injury or mental illness may not be able to show their disability started prior to age 26 and will be precluded from establishing an ABLE account.

An eligible individual or designated beneficiary can establish the account and is always the owner.[15] The designated beneficiary may also be an eligible individual who has succeeded the former designated beneficiary in that capacity. If the

11. A credit of 50 percent, 20 percent, or 10 percent of their annual contributions to the ABLE account—up to $2,000.

12. 85 Fed. Reg. 224, 74,010 (Nov. 19, 2020).

13. In addition, the IRS issued Notice 2015-81, 2015-049 I.R.B. 784 (Dec. 7, 2015), which describes how the Treasury Department and the IRS intend to revise the proposed regulations.

14. Several bills have been introduced into Congress to raise this age to 46, but none of them has passed.

15. I.R.C. § 529A(e)(3).

individual ceases to be eligible, the account will continue and will not be deemed to be distributed. The most likely situation here is when the impairment goes into remission. When this occurs, then beginning the first day of the next year, no contributions may be made to the account. Contributions can resume, however, after the impairment recurs. If actual distribution occurs during this period, then tax will be imposed under section 72 annuity rules.

EXAMPLE 11-1: In 2021, Alice is an eligible individual with $2,400 in her ABLE account: $2,000 is from contributions and $400 from earnings. During 2020, Alice's disability goes into remission. In 2021, a distribution of $2,400 is made to Alice from the account. The earnings portion (or $400) is included in Alice's gross income in 2021.

$$\frac{\text{The year's total distributions for qualified disability expense}}{\text{The year's total distributions}} \times \text{Earnings portion of the year's distributions} = \text{Amount non-taxable for the year}$$

1. When the Beneficiary Is Unable to Establish the Account

Situations may arise where the eligible individual is not able to establish the account on their own behalf due to incapacity; or, in other cases, an individual might simply prefer for another person to establish or to serve as the person with signature authority over the account. In the circumstance of incapacity, the ABLE account may be established on behalf of the eligible individual under a power of attorney or, if none, by a parent or legal guardian.[16] The final regulations, however, make it clear that even if the eligible individual has legal capacity, they may also want to delegate these responsibilities to another person, and that is fine. Thus, the final regulations provide a cheaper and less cumbersome alternative to a court-appointed guardian for the individual who has no agent under a power of attorney or no parent to exercise the signature authority on the account. The regulations provide an expanded hierarchy of persons who may establish the account and serve as representative. The regulations establish the following hierarchical order: (1) the individual selected by the eligible individual or the eligible individual's agent under a power of attorney, (2) a conservator or legal guardian, (3) a spouse, (4) a parent, (5) a sibling, (6) a grandparent, or (7) a representative payee (whether an individual or organization) appointed by the SSA.

The eligible individual with legal capacity can also remove and replace the representative of the account and name a successor signatory. Also, in the case of incapacity of the eligible individual, a person with signature authority may name a

16. Prop. Treas. Reg. § 1.529A-2(c)(1), 63 Fed. Reg. 45,019 (Aug. 24, 1998).

successor signatory as long as this is consistent with the order set forth in the regulations. Such a representative, however, will never have any ownership or beneficial interest in the account, although they serve the important role of manager. Such a manager must ensure that an eligible individual continues to be eligible.

Planning Pointer

Under final regulations, even an eligible individual with legal capacity can delegate the responsibility to manage the ABLE account to another. Here is the hierarchical order:

- the individual selected by the eligible individual or the eligible individual's agent under a power of attorney,
- a conservator or legal guardian or conservator,
- a spouse,
- a parent,
- a sibling,
- a grandparent,
- a representative payee appointed by SAA.

2. Control Issues

The individual with the qualifying disability will have sole control of the ABLE account. There is no trustee. Therefore, ABLE accounts work best when that individual does not need a court-appointed guardian and is capable of handling his/her account. If a court-appointed guardian or conservator is needed, a court will need to approve the creation of the account and distributions from the account. A surety bond might also need to be purchased.

3. The One-Account Rule[17]

An ABLE account is only available to *U.S. citizens* and legal residents. A qualified ABLE account does not have to be established in the state of residency of the eligible individual. It can be established in any state. However, a state may limit the program to State residents. States are the only entity that may establish and maintain an ABLE program. Each state will have slightly different rules and procedures for opening and operating the account, so the advisor must be aware of those rules. However, federal law allows *only one account* to be established for the designated beneficiary. But remember, the one account need not be established in the state of residency of the beneficiary.

---

17. *See Contribution Limits Applicable to ABLE Accounts*, Fed. Reg. (Oct. 9, 2019), https://www.federalregister.gov/documents/2019/10/10/2019-21477/contribution-limits-applicable-to-able-accounts.

Once an ABLE account is opened for the designated beneficiary, no further ABLE accounts can be opened by or for that person.[18] To ensure this requirement, the applicant must verify under penalty of perjury that there are no other existing accounts. Thus, if divorced parents or multiple family members wish to establish funds for a person with a disability, only the first account will qualify. Should a second ABLE account be opened, the account will not be treated as an ABLE account. Thus, the second account will be countable for SSI and Medicaid purposes and will not have tax advantages. Furthermore, the balance in the second account must be returned in accordance with rules that apply to excess contributions. The only exception to the one account rule occurs when a designated beneficiary or authorized representative transfers an existing ABLE account from one state program to another program offered in a different state (discussed in the rollover section below). Thus, it is essential that the advisor ensures there are no existing ABLE accounts for the beneficiary when establishing one.

C. Contribution Restrictions

The ABLE account may be funded by the beneficiary or a third party. In other words, anyone can contribute to an ABLE account, including related parties (such as family members, friends, employers) or unrelated third parties (like nonprofit organizations). As with traditional 529 accounts, ABLE accounts require a contribution of "cash" to the account. The proposed regulations permit "check, money order, credit card, electronic transfer, or other similar method."[19] State as well as federal restrictions may apply to these contributions. A state limit, a minimum and maximum federal limit, and a special federal contribution limit for employed beneficiaries also apply.

1. The State Contribution Limits

A qualified ABLE program must provide adequate safeguards to ensure that the total contributions to the account do not exceed the State's limit for aggregate contributions. The contribution to the ABLE account may not exceed "the limit established by the State under section 529(b)(6)," preventing contributions which are more than necessary, including "contributions under any prior qualified ABLE program of any state, agency or instrumentality thereof."[20] This rule is intended to limit the account from being a tax-free vehicle for excess assets. If the balance in the account ever exceeds that amount, then the account will become a resource for Medicaid eligibility purposes, will not receive favorable income-tax-free treatment and will be subject to a 6 percent federal tax penalty.[21]

---

18. I.R.C. § 529A(b)(1)(B), (c)(4).
19. Prop. Treas. Reg. § 1.529A-2(g), 63 Fed. Reg. 45,019 (Aug. 24, 1998).
20. I.R.C. § 529(b)(6); Prop. Treas. Reg. § 1.529A-2(g)(3), 63 Fed. Reg. 45,019 (Aug. 24, 1998).
21. Prop. Treas. Reg. § 1.529A-3(a), 63 Fed. Reg. 45,019 (Aug. 24, 1998).

2. The Federal Contribution Limits

In addition to state laws, federal law provides for two other limits based both on annual and aggregate dollar amounts. The maximum *annual* amount that can be contributed to an ABLE account is equal to the amount of the federal *gift tax per-donee annual exclusion*.[22] In 2021, this amount is $15,000. The aggregate *total* amount of the account cannot exceed $100,000. If the account exceeds this amount, even for one day, the individual losses SSI and Medicaid benefits.

Lastly, under the *TCJA* of 2017, certain beneficiaries who work (either as an employee or self-employed) can make additional contributions to their ABLE account. Any additional contribution is the lesser of these amounts: (1) the designated beneficiary's compensation for the tax year, or (2) the poverty line amount for a one-person household, determined by using the poverty guideline applicable in the state of the designated beneficiary's residence.[23]

An excess contribution over the annual amount must be returned, and if any interest has accrued on this amount, it must be returned as well to the designated beneficiary. It will be the sole responsibility of the designated beneficiary (or person acting on their behalf) to identify and request this return. Similarly, should the account reach the maximum aggregate savings limit permitted under state law, the excess (and any income attributable to that contribution) must be returned to the contributor. Contributions must be returned on or before the due date (including extensions) of the designated beneficiary's federal income tax return for the taxable year in which the excess contribution was made. If the contribution is not received within this period, a 6 percent excise tax will be levied on the designated beneficiary. This tax goes on Form 5329, Part VIII.

D. Distributions for Qualified Disability Expenses

Each distribution from a qualified ABLE account will consist of part return of capital or investment and part earnings or interest. However, no amount of this distribution will be taxable if the payment is for a "qualified disability expense" from the ABLE account. These distributions must be for the benefit of the designated beneficiary, and only that beneficiary or an authorized representative can make such a request. The *ABLE Act* defines "qualified disability expenses" as "expenses related to the eligible individual's blindness or disability which are made for the benefit of an eligible individual who is the designated beneficiary." It then goes on to list a range of categories of potential uses for funds set aside in ABLE accounts, including:

---

22. I.R.C. § 529A(b)(2)(B).

23. IRS Guidelines Regulations make clear that these poverty guidelines refer to those that are updated periodically in the Federal Register by the U.S. Department of Health and Human Services under the authority of 42 U.S.C. § 9902(2). However, separate guidelines exist for (1) the contiguous 48 states and Washington D.C., (2) Alaska, and (3) Hawaii.

> "Education, housing, transportation, employment training and support, assistive technology and personal support services, health, prevention and wellness, financial management and administrative services, legal fees, expenses for oversight and monitoring, funeral and burial expenses, and other expenses, which are approved by the Secretary under regulations and consistent with the purposes of this section."

The regulations reiterated that the term qualified disability expenses should be "broadly construed" to include any benefit related to the designated beneficiary "in maintaining or improving his/her health, independence, or quality of life." There is no requirement that the benefit be medically necessary or that it benefit only the designated individual. Thus, this could include bus fare or travel expenses (even for a companion), financial management services, or even a smartphone. The proposed regulations specify that a smart phone could qualify as a covered expense, provided that it serves as an "effective and safe communication or navigation aid for a child with autism."[24]

Planning Pointer

There is no need to get approval to withdraw funds and pay for a qualified disability expense. However, to protect against future inquiries from the IRS, it might make sense for the beneficiary (or authorized representative) to maintain detailed records of expenses paid for by ABLE account assets, as well as how these expenses relate to their disabilities, to ensure that they are qualified. Misuse of ABLE account funds could result in tax penalties and possible loss of public benefits. Thus, detailed records are required in case the expenditures are ever questioned by the IRS.[25]

E. Coordination with Federal and State Benefit Programs

An ABLE account is essential for disabled individuals who want to save assets but still qualify for and receive federal and state benefits. One of the most important features of an ABLE account is to shelter income and assets from federal, and sometimes state, benefit programs. Qualification for these programs usually include income, assets, and resources to determine government assistance. The ABLE statute provides means-testing exemptions for certain governmental programs, but

24. Prop. Treas. Reg. § 1.529A-2(g), 63 Fed. Reg. 45,019 (Aug. 24, 1998).
25. *TCJA* of 2017 and regulations interpreting those rules.

this exemption is not absolute. Care must be taken not to have a nonqualified withdrawal, as this might negatively impact benefit eligibility or amounts.

The ABLE statute specifically addresses Supplemental Security Income (SSI) benefits. These benefits, administered by the Social Security Administration (SSA), provide funds to disabled adults and children who have limited income and assets or resources. In order to receive SSI, an individual is typically required to have no more than $2,000 in resources or if married no more than $3,000.[26] The SSA will count as a resource distribution for a housing expense under certain circumstances.[27] For all other expenses, this is not the case. ABLE account balances are not counted as a resource until those balances exceed $100,000. Once over that amount, the SSI benefits will be suspended, but not terminated, until the balance drops below that amount.

The ABLE statute also addresses Medicaid health benefits. Medicaid provides health insurance for individuals with a disability who have limited income and assets. This program is administered and funded by the Center for Medicare & Medicaid Services (CMS) in partnership with each state. Unlike SSI, ABLE balances have no impact on Medicaid eligibility. However, an ABLE account must "pay back" or reimburse the state when the beneficiary dies for all medical services that the state paid through their Medicaid program. This reimbursement is required even when the funds were contributed by others.

While the SSI, Medicaid, and distribution for housing expenses are specifically mentioned in the ABLE statute, other federal and even state means-testing requirements can be disregarded in certain circumstances. For example, the Food and Nutrition Service of the USDA considers balances held in the ABLE program to be excludable for the Supplemental Nutrition Assistance Program. This means that an individual can still qualify for food stamps, even if they have an ABLE account. Unfortunately, the United States Department of Housing and Urban Development has not followed suit with similar guidance as to determining housing benefits.

F. Tax Advantages

Like the 529 savings plan, the 529A ABLE account provides federal income, federal estate, gift, and *generation-skipping tax* (GST) advantages, as well as state income tax benefits. In general, these accounts are not subject to these taxes.

1. Federal Income Tax Advantages

Distributions from an ABLE account must cover qualified disability expenses for a qualifying individual. When that occurs, the account will not be subject to federal

26. *Supplemental Security Income (SSI)*, Soc. Sec. Admin. 6 (2020).

27. *Id.* They will specifically do this if the distribution of the housing expense is retained into the month following the month of receipt.

income tax. Earnings on funds invested in an ABLE account are also not subject to federal income tax if the funds are used for qualified expenses of the qualified beneficiary. Additional exclusions from gross income include rollovers and certain changes in beneficiaries to members of the family.

Any nonqualified distribution will result in federal income taxation of the earning portion, and a *10 percent penalty tax* will be imposed on that distribution. In addition, a 6 percent penalty can be imposed on any excess contributions to an ABLE account.

Under the *TCJA* of 2017, a certain percentage of the contribution to the qualified ABLE account can be deducted via a Saver's Credit. The percentages vary depending on the contributor's income and can be as high as $2,000 for a single taxpayer or $4,000 if the person is married and filing joint taxes. The percentages are 10 percent, 20 percent, or 50 percent. For 2021, single individuals with *adjusted gross incomes* of less than $19,750, head of household taxpayers with less than $29,625, and married couples filing jointly with less than $39,500 receive a 50 percent credit amount of their contributions. So, for example, if a single person making $15,000 in adjusted gross income contributes $2,000 toward an ABLE account, he/she can receive a $1,000 (50% × $2,000) credit on his/her tax return by claiming the Saver's Credit. This figure drops to 20 percent if the individual person's adjusted gross income is between $19,751 and $21,500, or for head of household taxpayers, between $29,626 and $32,250, or if married filing jointly between $39,501 and $43,000. The credit goes to 10 percent if the single person earns between $21,501 and $33,000, or if head of household between $32,251 and $49,500, or if married filing jointly between $43,001 and $66,000. The credit is not available to people making an income above these amounts.

Anyone contributing to an ABLE account could potentially be eligible for the credit, although it is not available to people under age 18 or full-time students, as well as people who are listed as dependents on another person's tax return. The Saver's Credit can be claimed by filling out IRS Form 8880 Credit for Qualified Retirement Savings Contributions.

2. Federal Gift and GST Advantages

In addition to income tax advantages, ABLE accounts receive favorable gift tax treatment. Any contribution to the qualified ABLE account shall be considered a completed gift not subject to gift or *generation-skipping* tax. In addition, each contribution is considered a *present interest*. Any contribution, however, must not exceed the per-donee annual exclusion amount (which in 2021 is $15,000). A distribution from an ABLE account is also not a taxable gift. As in the income tax area, rollovers, or program-to-program changes to members of the family will not be subject to gift and GST taxes.

3. Federal Estate Tax Advantages

Certain payments made after the beneficiary's death are not included in the beneficiary's gross estate for estate tax purposes, nor are they penalized. In general, the ABLE account can be used to pay all of the beneficiary's qualified expenses and all outstanding payments due for these expenses. However, the balance transfer to the estate cannot occur if state law prohibits this because a valid claim under Medicaid exists.[28] However, any such amounts paid under the Medicaid claim can be a deductible estate tax payment. A *10 percent penalty* will be imposed on any nonqualified distribution at death.

4. State Tax Advantages

Just like contributions to the regular 529 plans, a state may allow a deduction or a credit of a contribution to an ABLE account. Such a deduction usually applies to the state taxpayer's investment in the state plan. As with the 529 plan, recapture rules might apply.[29]

G. Rollovers

Under the *TCJA* of 2017, rollovers may be made without penalty from a Section 529 tuition account to an ABLE account *if* the beneficiary of the ABLE account is the designated beneficiary of the tuition account *or* is an eligible family member under 529 rules.[30] Under that Act, any distribution made after December 22, 2017, and before January 1, 2026, is not subject to income tax *if*, within 60 days of the distribution, it is transferred to an ABLE account of that designated beneficiary or qualified family member. The amount of any rollover to an ABLE account is limited to the amount that, when added to all other contributions made to the ABLE account for the taxable year, does not exceed the annual gift tax exclusion amount.[31]

In addition to the 529 rollover, once a year a rollover can occur from one ABLE account to another ABLE account, either indirectly or directly. An indirect rollover is a withdrawal of all funds from an account in one ABLE program, followed within sixty days of that withdrawal by a contribution of those funds into an account managed by a different ABLE program or to a person who is an eligible individual

28. Most states allow Medicaid to "claw back" any income or assets of the recipient of Medicaid.

29. *See* **Chapter Ten: State Tax Planning with Section 529 Savings Plans**.

30. *See* **Chart 7-1** in **Chapter Seven: Federal Rules and Regulations for Section 529 Savings Plans**.

31. I.R.C. § 529(c)(3)(C)(i). This limited rollover is described in more detail in Notice 2018-58, 2018-33 I.R.B. 305 (Aug. 13, 2018). Notice 2018-62, 2018-34 I.R.B. 316 (Aug. 20, 2018), announces the intent of the Treasury Department and the IRS to issue proposed regulations to implement these changes and describes the anticipated rules to implement the statutory changes. These proposed regulations incorporate, without substantive change, the anticipated rules described in that Notice.

member of family. A direct rollover, often referred to as a Program-to-Program Transfer, means the direct transfer of the entire balance from one ABLE account into another ABLE account of the same beneficiary. In the case of a direct rollover, the transferor ABLE account is closed upon completion of the transfer. Again, the ABLE account can be transferred to another eligible individual who is a qualified member of the family. As long as the rollover is made within 60 days of the date of withdrawal, and no rollover has been made to an ABLE account for that same designated beneficiary within the prior 12 months, the direct rollover has no tax consequences.

Failing to close the old ABLE account within the 60-day time period results in the account receiving the funds not being a qualified account. Thus, distributions from that nonqualified account will not be exempt from means testing and will be subject to adverse tax consequences. Noncompliance with the 60-day rule could also result in the imposition of federal taxes on the whole distribution, as well as penalties. For example, a state receiving a rollover will treat the entire amount as earnings unless they receive documentation of the earnings portion.

EXAMPLE 11-2: A designated beneficiary executes a rollover and transfers his $15,000 ABLE account balance from State X's program to State Y's program. He fails to provide State Y with a breakdown of how much of the $15,000 is interest and how much is principal. If the designated beneficiary soon thereafter makes a nonqualified withdrawal, the entire $15,000 will be subject to income tax. In addition, the beneficiary will pay a 10 percent penalty or $150 extra.

Finally, a change of an ABLE account's designated beneficiary is not treated as a distribution and is not includable in the designated beneficiary's gross income *if* the successor designated beneficiary is an eligible individual for that calendar year *and* is a member of the family of the former designated beneficiary.

H. Planning Options

ABLE accounts provide lots of flexibility to make the quality of life of a disabled person better. The ABLE account can be used as a receptacle for certain funds, including those from a 529 savings plan. In addition, ABLE accounts can be coordinated with a *special needs trust* (SNT).

1. Receptacle for Certain Funds

One practical planning option for an ABLE account is as a repository for child support, alimony, or even earned wages. Using an ABLE account for sources of income such as these can shield them from being counted as a resource of the child for government benefit programs. As mentioned earlier, an ABLE account is very flexible, and any payments deposited into the account can easily be used to pay for many of the expenses that the designated beneficiary may have. Similarly, any bank account or custodian account (under many state laws) will become the resource of the child when they turn 18. Again, the ABLE account can be used as a receptacle for money from the custodianship or bank account.

Planning Pointer

An ABLE account may be a good planning device in the following circumstances:

- the individual is capable of managing his/her own financial account and does not have a court-appointed guardian,
- the individual receives an inheritance of less than the per-donee annual exclusion amount,
- the individual receives a litigation settlement of less than the per-donee annual exclusion amount, or
- the individual has unspent SSI, Social Security Disability back payments, or earnings that will result in the individual's resources exceeding the allowable amount for SSI and Medicaid and wishes to "save" that amount (which may not exceed the per-donee annual exclusion per year).

2. Better Than a Special Needs Trust

An ABLE account can be better than a *special needs trust* (SNT) in several respects. First, it is often expensive and time consuming to set up a SNT. In comparison, setting up an ABLE account is much simpler. If the disabled child or beneficiary is expecting to receive a small settlement or tort award, or even an inheritance or gift, they can transfer *the per-donee annual exclusion* amount into the account and then purchase an annuity for the remaining amount. Second, a SNT often must use a designated trustee to manage the trust, and each and every expenditure would need to be approved. In contrast, an ABLE account can be managed and controlled by the beneficiary or a delegated responsible party. An ABLE account gives the beneficiary access to money that he/she alone can decide how to spend or save. This autonomy also allows the beneficiary to make important saving decisions, like whether to save for a home, a car, or even a wedding. This control can also provide a boost in self-esteem to the disabled person. Such control will also prevent a penalty that might arise if the ABLE account is used to pay for certain expenses that might trigger SSI's "in-kind support and maintenance" (ISM) if a third party, including a SNT, made the same expenditure. When it comes to its ISM rules, the Social Security Administration considers money in an ABLE account as if it were the SSI beneficiary's money, so there is no penalty when the recipient of a government benefit uses his/her own funds from an ABLE account to pay for his/her own housing expenses.

The most important difference between a SNT and an ABLE account is that there are no age restrictions when establishing a SNT. In comparison, for an ABLE account to be created, the individual must have first experienced their disability before the age of 26. Thus, if the individual first experienced their disability after age 26, a SNT would still be a viable option for them. However, a SNT that is funded using assets belonging to the beneficiary *must* be established before an individual that meets Social Security's disability criteria reaches the age of 65. No pay-back rules apply to a SNT.

A SNT may be more suitable for a beneficiary who cannot effectively manage the funds or who has no person that can assume delegated responsibility for the account, as there is a trustee. Another major difference is that an individual can have many SNTs, and more importantly, there are no limits to how much money the trusts may hold. However, the SNT does not necessarily have the tax advantages of the ABLE account. All income is taxed to the beneficiary in a SNT. Nevertheless, no tax will be owed if the standard deduction lowers the tax bracket to zero.

Lastly, there are no limitations on disbursements from a SNT. This means a SNT can pay for entertainment, recreation, furnishings, and many types of services that may not be permitted from an ABLE account. Of course, an ABLE account can be used in conjunction with a SNT to craft a strategy that best fits the disabled individual's needs now and in the future.

Planning Pointer

Since the rules governing SNTs and ABLE accounts are quite different, individuals with disabilities should consider their specific circumstances before establishing one or even both. To find out how an ABLE account might benefit a child in conjunction with a SNT, a special needs planner, elder lawyer, or estate planning specialist should be contacted.

I. Conclusion

The ABLE account under Section 529A has been used since it was first instituted in 2014. Several modifications to the original act have been made by government guidance, proposed and final regulations, and by statute. The *Tax Cuts and Jobs Act of 2017* has specifically allowed a regular 529 savings account in limited amounts to be rolled over to an ABLE account. With proper planning, the ABLE account can not only avoid federal and state taxation but help the with the important purpose of making the disabled person's life better. Lastly, the ABLE account can be coordinated with the special needs trust.

Chapter 12

Nontax Aspects of Section 529 Savings Plans

In addition to the tax benefits of a Section 529 savings plan, there are a number of nontax advantages as well. First, the owner of a Section 529 savings plan retains significant control, including the right to revoke the fund. Second, unlike most tax-advantaged gifts, a minor will not gain control of the Section 529 fund at the age of 18. Third, some states allow Section 529 plans to last forever. Fourth, under federal bankruptcy law, as well as in many states, Section 529 plans are not subject to creditors' claims. Fifth, Section 529 plan assets may not count as assets of the beneficiary for financial aid purposes. Lastly, the taxpayer can set up this plan with minimal expense and with the assurance of a secure investment and good returns.

A. Control

Control is perhaps one of the most important considerations in deciding what education savings technique to adopt. The owner of an asset wants to be able to determine how the asset is used, how to invest the asset, and who should receive the income from the asset. When this control is unreasonably restricted, then the savings technique may not be that desirable.

1. The Owner's Control

The owner of a Section 529 savings plan has significant control over the assets. In particular, the owner has control over when the assets are used and who uses them. The only requirement is that the assets be used for *qualified higher education expenses* (QHEE). Although the owner has no direct control over the Section 529 investments, the owner can control the initial investment strategy, change the plan once a year, or roll over the account to another account. The owner may also change the beneficiary at any time, although to change the beneficiary without tax consequences, the new beneficiary must be a member of the old beneficiary's "family."[1] There is no requirement that the beneficiary even know that an account has been set up in his/her name. Lastly, in the event of an emergency, the owner can get the funds back. This recovery will cause adverse tax consequences (i.e., an income tax plus a 10 percent additional penalty tax), but at least the owner can be assured that the funds will be available if an unexpected need arises.

CHART 12-1 Owner/ Donor Controls

- Control over when assets used for QHEE
- Control over who uses assets for QHEE
- Control over initial investment strategy
- Can change investment strategy once a year
- Can roll over the account to another account once a year
- Can change the beneficiary at any time as long as to another member of the family
- Can get the funds back anytime

Planning Pointer

As the law does not prevent the owner from changing the beneficiary for any reason, the owner can directly influence the beneficiary's choice of university, choice of degree or major, and the location of the school. If the owner is unhappy with the beneficiary's academic performance in school or the beneficiary's behaviors (drugs or speeding tickets, for example), the owner can simply change the beneficiary. Furthermore, if the funds of the Section 529 savings plan are not needed or are not used for college, the account can be transferred to a different beneficiary. The ultimate control is that the account can be returned to the owner at any time.[2]

2. The Beneficiary's Control

Even though the transfer into a 529 plan is considered a completed gift to the beneficiary, the beneficiary has virtually no control or rights over the Section 529 plan. The beneficiary does not even have the right to know that he/she is a beneficiary! In most of the popular gift alternatives to a Section 529 plan, the beneficiary exercises much greater control than in a 529 plan. For example, in a custodianship

1. *See* **Chart 7-1** in **Chapter Seven: Federal Rules and Regulations for Section 529 Savings Plans.** When the beneficiary changes to a younger generation, however, a GST may be imposed on the current beneficiary. See discussion in **Chapter Nine: Estate Planning with Section 529 Savings Plans**, B.

2. Of course, such withdrawal may cause income tax on earnings and a penalty fee. *See* **Chapter Eight: Federal Income Tax Planning with Section 529 Savings Plans.**

account the beneficiary may have ownership control and complete dispositive authority at age 18. Even in a Section 530 Coverdell ESA, the consent of the beneficiary must be obtained before a new beneficiary can be designated. Only in a trust can the beneficiary be as constricted as in a 529 plan. It seems hardly fair, however, that under Section 529 the beneficiary is taxed under the *generation-skipping* tax when the owner changes the beneficiary to a younger generation. The 2008 Advance Notice predicts new regulations that will change this result.[3]

B. Perpetuity

In many states, the donor can set up a 529 plan and save for a child, or even for a grandchild, that is not yet born. Whether a Section 529 savings plan can exist for this purpose depends upon the terms of the plan and the state's adherence to the *rule against perpetuity.* Federal law requires a "designated beneficiary," however, a plan can be set up for each existing child, grandchild, great-grandchild, nieces, nephews, and cousins, and then changed with the birth of a child or grandchild. Moreover, if the child or grandchild does not use the funds, the account can be rolled over to benefit grandchildren or great-grandchildren that are "family members" of the old beneficiary. This *rollover* feature of the Section 529 plan essentially allows the establishment of an account that is reminiscent of a dynasty-type trust. If a child ends up not going to college, dies, becomes ill, wants to start a family, buy a house, or start a business, the fund can be transferred to other children, grandchildren, or great-grandchildren and be used for their educational expenses. These plans can even be rolled over for the benefit of an extended family member (such as a first cousin).[4]

Although Section 529 prevents contributions beyond those "reasonably expected" to provide for higher education,[5] there is no limitation as to the number of accounts that can be established. Many states have quite liberal limits (e.g., California allows $529,000 and South Carolina allows $520,000 per designated beneficiary). Thus, depending on state law, large accumulations of wealth can be set aside for future generations.[6]

Planning Pointer

The Section 529 plan could be set up for the benefit of the donor, the donor's spouse, or another relative (such as a niece or nephew who need never know about the plan) in anticipation of rolling the account over to a new beneficiary

3. *See* **Example 9-13** in **Chapter Nine: Estate Planning with Section 529 Savings Plans**; **Appendix F**.
4. This individual may never even know of the fund but could be subject to GST tax.
5. I.R.C. § 529(b)(6).
6. *See* **Chart 7-2** in **Chapter Seven: Federal Rules and Regulations for Section 529 Savings Plans**.

when that family member comes along.[7] This presents an especially savvy young couple with the opportunity to maximize their savings potential by saving prior to the birth of their potential child or children. Furthermore, their contribution to a 529 savings plan can be accomplished with no gift, estate, or generation-skipping tax consequences—assuming their child is the ultimate beneficiary and is in the same generation as the present beneficiary.

EXAMPLE 12-1: In 2021, Alice makes a gift of $75,000 into a Section 529 plan and names her niece, Mary (age 6), as beneficiary. When Alice's child, Ben, is born three years later, Alice changes the beneficiary to her son.

C. Asset Protection

Section 529 does not specifically offer protection from creditors. However, generally, the assets in a Section 529 plan cannot be attacked by the creditors of the beneficiary. As a practical matter, this is true because the owner can change the beneficiary designation at any time. However, the *owner's* creditors may be able to reach the plan assets. The ability of the owner's creditors to reach the Section 529 savings plan assets depends on the particular state plan, state law, or—if the owner goes bankrupt—federal law. The *Bankruptcy Abuse Prevention and Consumer Property Act of 2005*[8] provides protection for funds placed in a 529 account a year before the bankruptcy petition. However, absent bankruptcy or state laws protecting the account, the owner's creditors may be able to attach the assets. This is true irrespective of the fact that federal rules do not allow the owner to pledge the plan's assets.

An additional consideration is whether the assets in the Section 529 plan will be considered assets for purposes of determining whether the owner will be eligible for state-run financial assistance programs, such as Medicaid. The advisor must check applicable state law if this is a possible concern.

1. State Law and Plan Protection

Some states protect Section 529 funds from both the account owner's and the beneficiary's creditors.[9] In Virginia, no Section 529 savings account "shall be assigned for the benefit of creditors, used as security or collateral for any loan, or otherwise be subject to alienation, sale, transfer, assignment, pledge, encumbrance or

7. Some states restrict the donor/owner from also being a beneficiary. Thus, this is a point of state law that the advisor must check. In addition, a GST may result if the new beneficiary skips a generation.

8. The Bankruptcy Abuse Prevention and Consumer Protection Act of 2005, Pub. L. No. 104-188, 119 Stat. 23, § 2265, 11 U.S.C. § 541 (2005).

9. *See* ALASKA STAT. § 14.40.802(h)(i).

charge."[10] A few other states, like Florida, Texas, and Tennessee, potentially offer protection to any plan established under the laws of any state.[11]

In most states, however, creditor protection is provided only for an account established within the state.[12] Under New Jersey law, funds are protected from the creditors of the account donor and the beneficiary, but not the account owner. New York[13] offers more beneficial protection to the owner than New Jersey. In New York, the entire account is exempt from creditors of the account owner if the designated beneficiary is a minor; otherwise, the exemption is limited to $100,000.

On the other hand, some states provide no such protections. In fact, in Nevada, the Attorney General has even issued an opinion that confirms that these assets can be reached by creditors in the absence of state statutory (or trust) restrictions.[14]

Even when the state does not impose statutory asset protection for the Section 529 plan, the program itself may contain a *spendthrift clause* (or a prohibition protecting the interest from being reached by creditors, which may be enforceable under state law). A majority of 529 plans now have such spendthrift provisions.[15] When the plan contains such a spendthrift provision, the funds should be sufficiently protected under state law.

A question arises regarding applicable state law in a conflict of laws situation.[16] Is it the law where the owner is domiciled, where the plan was created, or where the beneficiary resides? If the owner has debts, it makes sense that the state law where the owner is domiciled might be controlling. On the other hand, it may be more rational for the law of the state in which the Section 529 plan was created to control. Those making the latter argument would bolster the argument by pointing to the presence of a contract between the Section 529 sponsoring state and the owner. An additional consideration is the fact that the beneficiary's state of domicile has an interest in any possible legal disputes because these funds are essentially held in trust for the beneficiary and may reduce the beneficiary's need for state assistance when attending college.

---

10. *See* VA. CODE ANN. § 23-38.81. *See also* Jeffrey L. Kwall, *Can Creditors Invade Qualified College Savings Plans?*, 14 J. FIN. PLANNING 125 (Mar. 2001).

11. Cole Schotz, *Section 529 Plans—Protection from Creditors*, JDSUPRA (June 6, 2012), https://www.jdsupra.com/legalnews/section-529-plans-protection-from-cred-74849/.

12. *Id.*

13. N.Y. C.P.L.R. § 5205(j).

14. *See* 99 Op. Att'y Gen. 10 (Nov. 1999).

15. Kwall, *supra* note 10, lists the following 11 states that provide protection: Alaska, Colorado, Kentucky, Louisiana, Maine, Nebraska, Ohio, Pennsylvania, Tennessee, Virginia, and Wisconsin. However, according to an editorial on saving by Joe Hurley, *Monthly Top Tips No. 18*, SAVING FOR COLLEGE (Apr. 29, 2005), https://www.savingforcollege.com/top-tip/guru.php?guru_id=18, a majority of 529 plans have spendthrift provisions.

16. 68A AM. JUR. 2D *Secured Transactions* § 8 (2003).

2. Federal Law

If the state provides spendthrift protection or if the program has a similar provision, the plan should not become part of the bankruptcy estate if the owner files for bankruptcy. Bankruptcy Code 11 U.S.C. Section 541(c)(2) provides that "[a] restriction on the transfer of a beneficial interest of the debtor in a trust that is enforceable under applicable nonbankruptcy law is enforceable in a case under [the bankruptcy code]." Section 225 of the Bankruptcy Code provides that "Section 529 plan accounts of an owner who files bankruptcy will not be included in the bankruptcy estate if the funds were contributed to the Section 529 plan for the benefit of a child or grandchild not less [sic] than 720 days prior to the filing for bankruptcy." The law was changed after at least one case, *In re Darby*,[17] held that prepaid tuition plans were included in the bankruptcy estate.

It is in the interests of the federal government to protect education funds, not only because fewer government grant and loan funds will be used if students have their own savings, but also because an educated workforce promotes a better economy and a more enlightened citizenry. Additionally, there is precedent as well as procedure for protecting similar accounts in the retirement area. The *Employee Retirement Income Act of 1974*[18] requires that assets in employer-sponsored plans be protected from creditors. In addition, Individual Retirement Accounts (IRAs) are protected from creditors in many states.[19] Like Section 529 plans, IRAs grant tax deferment and provide important economic government interests.

3. Medicaid

Whether the Section 529 plan will be included in an individual's asset assessment for Medicaid qualification purposes also depends on state law. Resolution of this issue is still murky. In general, states that currently still consider assets when testing for Medicaid eligibility treat 529 accounts as "countable" assets.[20] All 529 plans permit the owner to get back the fund assets. Since it is possible that the account owner may incur medical and nursing home expenses, then the argument is that they will need to use the Section 529 assets to cover these expenses. If this is a concern for a grandparent donor with minimal assets, the beneficiary's parent can be designated as the owner. This may solve the issues revolving around Medicaid qualification; however, there is still a possibility that the "look back" rule under Medicaid rules will envelop the 529 plan assets.

---

17. 212 B.R. 382 (Bankr. M.D. Ala. 1997).

18. 26 U.S.C.A. § 401 (West Supp. 2003); 29 U.S.C. § 1056 (West Supp. 2003).

19. *1999 Institute State Survey of IRA Protection in Bankruptcy*, Inv. Co. Inst. (Mar. 24, 2000); see table available at https://www.actec.org/assets/1/6/50_STATE_INHERITED_IRA_CHART.pdf.

20. *Do 529 Plans Count against Medicaid Benefits?*, Saving for College, https://www.savingforcollege.com/grandparents/answer/do-529-plans-count-against-medicaid-benefits (last visited May 7, 2021).

Planning Pointer

Whether Section 529 savings funds are reachable by creditors in conflict of law situations and for Medicaid qualification purposes is unclear. The advisor should be aware of these uncertainties when establishing the 529 plan and advise his/her clients accordingly.

D. Financial Aid

The *Deficit Reduction Omnibus Reconciliation Act of 2005*[21] modified the federal financial aid rules for Section 529 plans. The value of the plan funds is not counted as an asset for financial aid purposes *if* the plan is *owned by the student*. Instead, it is assessed as if *owned by the parent*. Thus, if owned by the student or parent, a small percentage (up to 5.64%) may be considered the parent's asset for education purposes. Under the institutional formula, these assets will be counted if either owned by the student (assessed at 25%) or the parent (assessed up to 5%). It is unclear whether distributions from these plans will be counted in the income portion of the financial aid calculations when used for the student's benefit.[22] Under both the federal and institutional formulae, this student income would be assessed at 50 percent.[23] Under the federal formula, the parent income is assessed up to 47 percent, whereas under the institutional formula, the parent income is assessed up to 46 percent. Under both formulae, the value of the Section 529 plan is not included as an asset if it is owned by a grandparent or anyone other than the parent or student. However, a distribution from the 529 plan owned by the grandparent will constitute income to the student and be assessed at 50 percent. *See* **Chart 12-2** for the effect of 529 ownership on financial aid.

---

21. Pub. L. No. 109-171, 120 Stat. 4, § 8019(d)(5) (2006).
22. Some state schools, such as the University of Oregon, are counting this distribution as income.
23. *See* **Chapter Nineteen: Coordinating Section 529 Plans with Financial Aid**.

CHART 12-2 Effect of 529 Ownership on Financial Aid

	Years Before 2005–2006		Years 2005–2006		Years Beginning 2006–2007	
	Federal	**Institutional**	**Federal**	**Institutional**	**Federal**	**Institutional**
Student-Owned	35%	25%	20%	25%	Assessed as Parent's; up to 5.64%	25%
Parent-Owned	Up to 5.64%	Up to 5%	Up to 5.64%	Up to 5%	Up to 5.64%	Up to 5%
Grandparent (or other nonparent relative)	0%	0%	0%	0%	0%	0%

E. Easy to Set Up

Section 529 plans are easy and inexpensive to establish. There are three easy ways to set up these plans. First, an application can be obtained by phone or from the website (*see* **Appendix C**) and mailed to the 529 Plan administrative entity of choice. Second, some plans allow online enrollments. Lastly, an application can be submitted through a broker, who may charge a fee for doing this, but who can help in the selection of the plan and the choices of investments in the plan.

F. Good Investment

Whether or not the Section 529 savings plan is a good investment depends on the various fees, the different investment options offered by the plan, and the performance of the fund. These considerations will be discussed in the next chapter along with the other state plan limitations and restrictions.

G. Conclusion

Although tax factors are important in selecting a Section 529 savings plan, non-tax factors are important as well. Section 529 plans are easy to set up, can offer good returns at minimal costs, and offer significant control to the owner. If the goal of the client is to set up a perpetual dynasty trust, for example, only a few states may allow the Section 529 assets to be included in the trust. The risk of losing the assets to creditors or under Medicaid rules might be an important consideration for some. For middle-income taxpayers, creating a plan that does not adversely impact the student's financial aid eligibility will be crucial. Thus, proper planning with respect to the owner designation can make the 529 savings plan a viable option even for students who will be eligible for financial aid.

Chapter 13

Investment Planning with Section 529 Savings Plans

The educational planner has a wide variety of investment choices within the Section 529 savings plan. These choices can be risky investments, like REITs, or less risky and more conservative investments, like bonds. The investor can choose from a wide variety of options, from age-based to *advisor sold*. Investors may also want a different strategy for K–12 education than for college or graduate school. This chapter will explore the various considerations in choosing these investments.

A. Investment Performance and Options

Picking the correct investment option or options is affected by a combination of the risk, rate of return, and diversification, as well as the time when the funds will be spent on K–12 or college education. *See* **Chart 13-2**. Preferences will depend on the taxpayer's *tolerance for risk* and many plans have investment choices based on the degree of risk: growth, balanced, aggressive growth, secure funds. Some plans offer risk-based options within the age-based options. For example, both Putnam Investment and Fidelity Investments have different age-based investment choices as well as several static portfolios that are not age-based. Some programs offer a principal protection option that assures a return of original investment even if the market goes down. Others guarantee that the investments keep up with increased college costs. Only a few are FDIC insured and these tend to have conservative investment options.

Planning Pointer

Mutual funds geared to college savings plans show surprisingly large variations in their investment mixes of stocks, bonds, and cash. Investors who consider themselves "moderate" or "conservative" for their Vanguard-managed 29 college savings plans will own *no* stock at all the last couple of years before college. In contrast, those investors managed by T. Rowe Price will still have 20 percent in equities even after the student commences college.[1] Because of these variations it is imperative that an informed advisor be consulted before investing in these plans.

The length of time the plan has been in existence, the investment manager, and the fund's performance over time are key factors in choosing a plan. Just as in other investment programs, some managers do a better job than others. Although the contributor to a Section 529 savings plan has no ability to pick and choose individual stocks and bonds in the fund, by picking the right plan (or plans), the right investment option within the plan, and the right fund manager, the contributor can save considerable time and also make an excellent investment.

Some states have plans that offer a wide variety of investment choices, while most other states' plans are more limited. Usually, the investments combine stocks and bonds with an age-based formula, i.e., more high-risk investments for younger beneficiaries, and more conservative investment for older beneficiaries who are closer to college age. Sometimes the taxpayer may choose several investment options: a fixed income (bonds and savings accounts), equities (company stock), a blended account (a mixture of the above), or a pre-mixed age-based portfolio.

Obviously, with so many choices the consumer could make the wrong choice. For example, if the taxpayer puts all of his/her money in a single mutual fund or bond fund, the market performance may be disappointing and inadequate to cover college costs. If the beneficiary is close to college age and needs a large amount of money to pay for college expenses, a more aggressive fund may be advisable—assuming the taxpayer is not risk averse.

1. Age-Based

Most plans offer an *age-based* portfolio that begins with a more aggressive strategy when the beneficiary is young but ends up with a more conservative strategy when the beneficiary reaches college age. Although this is a good approach, some plans contain well-diversified equity securities, while others might be too aggressive or

1. *See* Karen Blumenthal, *Assessing Risk: The Questions to Ask Yourself,* Wall St. J., Dec. 31, 2008, at D1.

too conservative for the client's desired risk level. For K–12 the parent may want more aggressive investments because the time frame may be shorter than, for example, professional school.

2. Equity or Growth Portfolios

If a more aggressive strategy is desired, equity funds might be the preferred investment choice. Many of the plans offer a variety of the following: growth funds, value funds, small-cap funds, mid-cap funds, large-cap funds, global funds, international funds, and emerging market funds. In general, smaller companies, global or international funds, and emerging market bonds (even aged investments and undiversified investments) have greater risk and a higher return.

3. Secure Income

If more conservative investments are desired, then investments that are secure but have little growth potential are available. Often, these investments pay a fixed rate of return. The rate of return may vary, however, among guaranteed investment certificates, bonds, certificates of deposit, or treasury notes. For example, long-term treasury notes are higher risk than short-term notes and therefore have slightly higher return. Both, however, are very secure—guaranteed by the U.S. Treasury. Treasury notes are more secure than corporate bonds, and thus the return will be slightly less. Other investments, such as mutual funds, can also provide a secure investment.

4. Index Funds

If a good middle ground between secure income and more risky investments is preferred, indexed funds could be the best choice. These funds generally have lower fees and expenses than actively managed funds. These funds can be quite diverse and, when the fees are low, are often one of the best investment options.

5. Other Investments

In recent years, some 529 savings plans have offered other investment options. Several offer investments in REITs—real estate investment trusts. These are riskier than equity funds, but the returns can be high. *See* **Chart 13-1** for a comparison of the features of traditional investment options.

6. Broker/Advisor Sold

When the taxpayer feels more comfortable not making the investment decision, they can select a broker-sold fund. Some plans, such as the *Virginia College America* plan, offer almost two dozen funds from American Funds.

CHART 13-1 Traditional Investment Comparison Chart

	Tax-Exempt Securities	T-Bills	Corporate Bonds	Stocks	Mutual Funds	Real Estate
Tax advantages irrelevant when in a 529 plan as all will be tax free if distributed for qualified expenses	Earnings are tax-free	Interest exempt when proceeds used for QHEE	Taxed at both state and federal levels	Taxed at both state and federal levels but at capital gains rates on dividends and upon sale	Taxed at both state and federal level	Rent is taxed at state and federal levels—gain is capital gain or excluded if principal residence
Risk	Very little	Very little	More than T-Bills or Tax Exempts	More than bonds	Less than stocks	Somewhat
Rate of Return on Growth	Quite low	Low but higher with longer maturities	May not keep up with college inflation	May keep up with college inflation	Moderate returns	Can keep up with college inflation
Control is irrelevant with a 529 but not with a Coverdell	Medium	Depends on maturity date	Depends on maturity date	High	High	Medium, depends on economy

CHART 13-2 Investment Options and Features

Investment Type	Risk	Rate of Return	Diversification
Age-based portfolios	Varies	Varies	Well diversified
Growth portfolios	Could be high	Could be high	Can be diversified
Small and mid-cap equity portfolios	Moderate	Could be high	Can be diversified
Active investments	Could be high	Could be high	Can be diversified
Global and International	Could be high	Could be high	Can be diversified
Index Funds	Low	Could be high	Can be diversified
Passive investments	Could be high	Could be high	Not much diversification
Secure Income	Low	Low	No
Guaranteed investment certificates	Low	Low	No
Long-term corporate bonds	Low	Fixed	No
Money market accounts	Medium	Medium	No
Certificates of Deposit	Low	Fixed	Yes
Treasury Notes	Low	Fixed	No
REITS	High	High	No
Mutual Funds	Low	Varies	Can be diversified
Advisor-fold	Low	Varies, but fees can be high	Can be diversified

Planning Pointer

Assessing the different plan choices and the variety of investment options available in many plans can be complicated and may depend on the clients' goals, risks, timetables, and other considerations. Consequently, the client should consult an advisor in making these decisions.

7. Rollovers

If the client does not like the investment options of a particular plan, he/she may transfer the Section 529 assets to another state's plan without federal tax penalty once a year. In addition, the owner can change the plan any time the named beneficiary is changed. However, state law might impose a state tax upon withdrawal from another state's 529 plan or recapture the contribution if rolled over to another state. Most states that grant a tax deduction or credit for contributions impose a recapture tax on contributions when the plan is rolled over to another state's plan.[2]

EXAMPLE 13-1: Alice has a son, Ben, who is only three years old. In Year 1, she contributes $75,000 to her state 529 plan (the maximum allowed at the time) and allocates her savings in the first five years as follows: 80 percent equity, 10 percent money market, and 10 percent fixed income. In Year 6, when Ben is eight years old, she contributes another $75,000 to the 529 plan and invests her account as follows: 60 percent equity, 20 percent money market, and 20 percent fixed. In Year 11, when Ben is 13, she transfers the plan to another state, invests another $75,000 in the account, and allocates 33.3 percent equity, 33.3 percent money market, and 33 percent fixed. Depending on state law, in Year 11 Alice may have to pay state tax on any deductible contribution made to her state plan in Year 1 and Year 6.

B. Some of the Best 529 Plans

If the taxpayer lives in a state, like Arizona, Arkansas, Minnesota, Missouri, Montana, or Pennsylvania, where state tax benefits are allowed no matter where the 529 is established, then the taxpayer can focus on low fees, investment, mix investment, and investment performance to pick the best overall plan. For states that allow a deduction or credit only for contributions to their own plan and that tax

2. For more information *see* **Chapter Ten: State Tax Planning with Section 529 Savings Plans**.

benefit is restricted, the taxpayer can invest in out-of-state plans once the tax benefit has been reached.[3]

Several rating services, like Morningstar,[4] savingforcollege.com,[5] Kiplinger,[6] CNN, and Money Magazine, are available to determine what plan is best for the client. The rating systems generally look at the fees, the investment options, and their quality. *See* **Chapter Fourteen: Choosing the Right Section 529 Plan** for more details.

C. Fund Scandals and Market Uncertainties

Investigations into reports of improper trading practices at several mutual fund companies have given investors in college savings plans a new cause for concern.[7] Oregon,[8] Ohio, Rhode Island, and Wisconsin are among the states who have experienced problems with their 529 plan investment management companies.[9] In one state (Oregon) the fund manager resigned, and in Utah, the fund administrator was fired for malfeasance.[10]

Unfortunately, in some instances the fund scandals do not originate solely in the investment company. Furthermore, investors in Section 529 plans are not protected by federal securities laws.[11] Because of the stock crash of 2008 and the uncertain future of the market, investors often put their money in more conservative investments, such as *Treasury securities* or *T-bills*. In this uncertain time, it is imperative that caution be used when investing in 529 plans.

D. Conclusion

As with any investment strategy, the client has a wide variety of options available to them. Often these choices will depend on how risk averse the client is or their knowledge of investments and investment strategy. The conservative client may just opt for the age-based 529 plan or seek the assistance of a broker/advisor.

---

3. *Id.*
4. *See* www.morningstar.com.
5. *See* www.savingforcollege.com.
6. *See* Thomas M. Anderson, *Best 529 College-Savings Plans*, Kiplinger (Jan. 5, 2012), https://www.kiplinger.com/article/college/t014-c000-s001-best-529-college-savings-plans.html.
7. John Kimelman, *Fund Scandal Puts College Savings Plans on Alert*, N.Y. Times, Nov. 24, 2003.
8. Oregon fired its program manager, Strong Capital Management, in November 2003. *See* Letter from Randall Edwards, State Treasurer & Oregon 529 College Savings Network Board Chair, to Oregon College Savings Plan participants (Nov. 18, 2003).
9. *See* Kimelman, *supra* note 7.
10. *Id.*
11. *An Introduction to 529 Plans*, U.S. Sec. & Exch. Comm'n (May 29, 2018), https://www.sec.gov/reportspubs/investor-publications/investorpubsintro529htm.html.

Chapter 14

Choosing the Right Section 529 Savings Plan

Establishing a 529 plan is easy. Choosing the right plan, on the other hand, is more difficult. Fifty states and the District of Columbia all offer at least one version of the 529 savings plan. (*See* **Appendix C** for a list.) The prior chapter dealt with the investment choices within the plan. This chapter explores in greater depth the factors that may be important in *choosing* a 529 plan (or plans). The factors to consider include the following: (1) residency restrictions, (2) state tax considerations, (3) investment fees, (4) account ownership, (5) beneficiary limitations, (6) contribution and withdrawal restrictions, (7) participation in retail rebate savings programs, (8) customer service, and (9) investment performance.

In choosing a plan, both state law and the account agreement are relevant. Prior to the enactment of the *EGTRRA* in 2001, the plan had to include certain federal restrictions, limitations, and penalties, etc. These restrictions were lifted somewhat in the *EGTRRA*. The first step in choosing a plan is to see if state law or the agreement has been broadened or still contains pre-*EGTRRA* restrictions.[1] Furthermore, not all state plans allow for K–12 tuition distributions or payment on qualified student loans, so this limitation should be kept in mind.[2]

Planning Pointer

Two excellent websites that list the details of each state plan are www.savingforcollege.com and www.collegesavings.org. (*See* **Appendix C** for a list of all 529 plans with details of each plan.)

---

1. Kerry O'Boyle, *The Best and Worst 529 Savings Plans*, MORNINGSTAR (Feb. 25, 2005). (For example, distributions from Alabama's 529 plan still do not conform to federal tax treatment and therefore the earnings from the account may be subject to tax.)

2. *See* **Chart 10-4** in **Chapter Ten: State Tax Planning with Section 529 Savings Plans**.

A. Residency Restrictions

As mentioned earlier, some Section 529 savings plans are available only to those who reside in the state in which the plan is administered.[3] If residency is required, several issues arise: (1) does residency apply to the owner or to the beneficiary (or both), (2) how long must one be in the state to be a resident, (3) the effect if either the owner or the beneficiary moves out of state, and (4) what happens if the owner changes the beneficiary to a nonresident.

Residency might be a problem if the account owner becomes disabled or dies and a nonresident succeeds to the ownership of the plan. If the account owner becomes incapacitated, the plan may permit an attorney-in-fact to take action with respect to the plan. If the account owner dies and no successor account owner is designated, the beneficiary may become the account owner—even if a will or other testamentary instrument provided otherwise. Some of these issues may be addressed in the plan itself. Other plans may not be clear on this point and state law must be examined.

Most states do not require the owner or the beneficiary to be a resident of the state. Since more states do not have a residency restriction, most taxpayers will decide whether to invest in the state's plan given tax considerations, investment option fees, and plan performance. **Chart 14-1** sets forth a decision model for choosing the right 529 savings plan.

CHART 14-1 Decision Model for Choosing a 529 Savings Plan

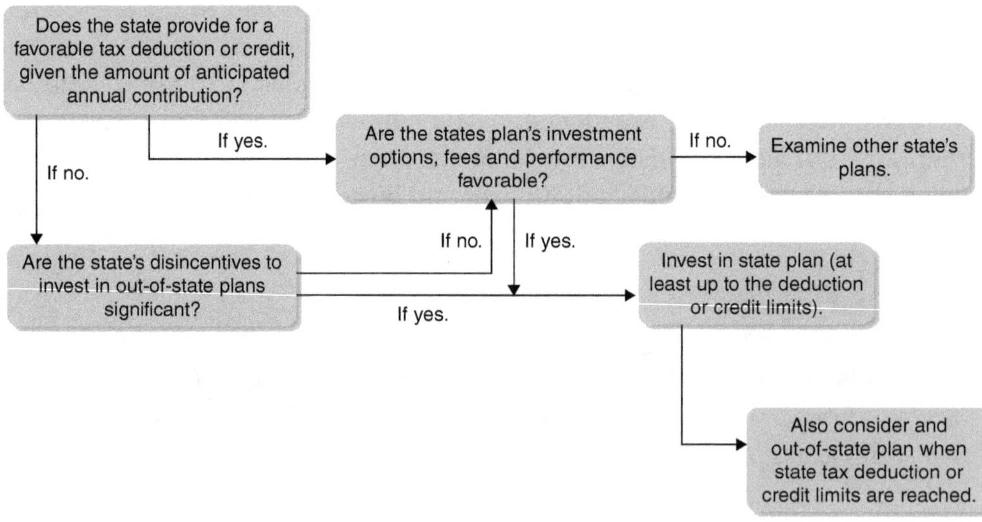

3. See **Appendix C** for this restriction in each of the 529 plans.

B. State Tax Considerations

If the taxpayer lives in a state where state tax benefits are allowed no matter where the 529 is established, then the taxpayer can focus on low fees, investment mix investment, and investment performance to pick the best overall plan. For example, Arizona, Arkansas, Minnesota, Missouri, and Pennsylvania allow tax benefits regardless of where the 529 is established. For states that allow a deduction or credit only for contributions to their own plan and that tax benefit is restricted, the taxpayer can invest in out-of-state plans once the tax benefit has been reached.

When state tax advantages are compelling, the taxpayer will most likely invest in the state plan. The first important state tax consideration is the *deduction* or *credit* for the contribution to the plan. In a few states the deduction is quite large. Examples of states that allow large tax deductions are the following: (1) Colorado, New Mexico, South Carolina, and West Virginia (unlimited); (2) Pennsylvania ($15,000 if single or $30,000 if married); (3) Illinois, Mississippi, and Oklahoma ($10,000 for single, $20,000 for married); and (4) Alabama, Arkansas, Connecticut, Michigan, New York, and North Dakota ($5,000 single or $10,000 if married).[4] Many states have deductions between $3,000 and $5,000. While some states allow deductions each year, others offer a one-time maximum.

The larger the state deduction or credit—given the amount of the contribution—the more likely the state plan is the best choice. However, when the deduction or credit is only allowed for one year, fees and investment performance become important and will reduce the benefit of the deduction the longer the fund remains invested. On the other hand, when the state allows a deduction or credit every year, it might make sense to opt for the state plan, at least up to the amount of the tax benefit—but again this would depend on the tax bracket of the taxpayer, the contribution amount and benefit, and the costs and performance of the plans.

EXAMPLE 14-1: In Year 1, Alice decides to invest $10,000 in her state plan that offers a one-time $2,000 maximum state tax deduction. Her plan's expenses average 1 percent whereas the plan in another state has expenses of .50 percent. Assuming Alice's net federal and state combined tax bracket is 20 percent (taking into account the reduced itemized deduction for state taxes due to the $2,000 deduction); assume also that the rate of return in the state plan is 3 percent but the rate of the out-of-state-plan is 5 percent. In Year 2, it would have been better to invest in the out-of-state plan. *See* **Chart 14-2**.

4. *See* **Chart 10-2** in **Chapter Ten: State Tax Planning with Section 529 Savings Plans**.

CHART 14-2 Calculating Net Benefits

State Plan Contribution	Net Tax Bracket Benefit from State Deduction or Credit	Fees (1%)	Performance (3%)	Net Values after Tax Benefit
Year 1 $ 10,000	$ 400	$ 100	$ 300	$ 10,600
Year 2 - 0 -	- 0 -	$ 100	$ 360	$ 10,860
Out-of-State Plan	**Net Tax Bracket Benefit**	**Fees** (.5%)	**Performance** (5%)	**Net Value**
Year 1 $ 10,000	- 0 -	$ 50	$ 500	$ 10,450
Year 2 - 0 -	- 0 -	$ 50	$ 523	$ 10,923

Another state tax advantage is when the state matches a percentage of the taxpayer's contribution. Michigan is an example of a state that provides for this matching grant option. Usually, this benefit is only available to low or middle-income taxpayers. When the taxpayer lives in such a state and is eligible for this matching grant, the taxpayer should stick to the state plan.

State tax disincentives must also be considered in choosing a 529 savings plan. Some states do not allow the earnings in another state's plan to be exempt from state tax. An example of such a state is Illinois.[5] Another disadvantage is that some states penalize withdrawal from the fund unless the fund has been in existence for a certain number of years. This, of course, would be a problem if the beneficiary will attend college before that time expires. Similarly, another consideration is if the beneficiary will be a resident of another state and such distributions are taxable. The last disadvantage is that most states do not allow a rollover to another state's plan without a recapture of the original deductible contribution. Again, all of these state tax rules can make the state plan of the resident donor the best choice.

Planning Pointer

Perhaps the most important reason to choose a state plan is the favorable tax deductions or credits. The state may also have unfavorable tax consequences when the taxpayer invests in out-of-state plans or changes to an out-of-state plan. These considerations and the fund's overall return are the key factors in choosing a particular state plan.

5. *See* **Chart 10-3** in **Chapter Ten: State Tax Planning with Section 529 Savings Plans**.

C. Investment Fees

When the state allows a deduction or credit for a contribution to any state plan, or when state tax considerations are not determinative, then the fees and investment performance of other state plans become important.[6] Those who charge a higher fee do not necessarily out-perform those with lower fees. For example, Wyoming's fund was below average, yet charged a .90 percent annualized program fee (on top of the cost of underlying funds) that one commentator has called "obscene."[7] Fees can reduce the overall return from the account and care must be taken to calculate all fees when choosing a plan.

Essentially, states charge four types of fees: (1) the initial origination—in other words, fees for enrolling or opening an account, (2) an annual account maintenance fee, (3) the annual investment management or mutual fund fee, and (4) a broker fee. Many of these fees are discretionary, which means they can be waived, particularly if large amounts of cash are placed in the fund. Obviously, the lower the fees, the better the choice if tax considerations, investment options, and performance are neutral.

1. The Initial Enrollment or Application Fee

Some states charge an initial cost for paperwork requirements to set up the account. This is a one-time fee and is usually very small. It can range from $10 to $90, but typically is $30 to 50. Some plans charge more for out-of-state residents.

2. Annual Account Maintenance Fees

Some states charge an annual account maintenance fee. Like the application fee, these fees are also small—usually from $10 to $50 annually. However, for a small account these fees can be significant. These fees are oftentimes waived if the donor is a resident, agrees to automatic contributions or if the original amount exceeds certain thresholds. These fees might also be waived if the donor maintains a certain minimum account balance.

3. The Annual Management or Mutual Fund Fee

Almost all states charge an annual management *mutual fund* fee. It is the annual investment management fee to monitor the investments. Some plans charge a fee to monitor the investment choice, others charge a separate fee to manage the investments inside the mutual fund. Still others combine these fees together in a "wrap fee"—one fee with no charge to handle mutual funds; TIAA-CREF plans function in this manner. These annual fees can range from as low as 0.3 percent of the

---

6. *See* **Appendix C**. Check for the "Investment Fee" and "Investment Options" on the website for the particular Section 529 plans.

7. O'Boyle, *supra* note 1.

account value to more than 2 percent of the account value. Recently, the SEC has been investigating the large fees in some state plans, cautioning that the fees can wipe out the tax advantages.[8]

4. The Broker Fee

Some 529 plans are only sold through brokers[9] and thus a "load" or sales charge is imposed. This sales charge can be paid in a single payment, in an up-front lump sum, or through regular fees charged on the value of the account—or a combination of both. These fees become significant, particularly if charged on the value of a large account. **Chart 14-3** shows the impact of a 1 percent fee over time.

EXAMPLE 14-2: If your client invests $65,000 in the state 529 plan, the load is 3 percent, and the annual sales charge is 1 percent, your client's investment is immediately reduced to $62,400 [$65,000 less $1,950, less $650], which will reduce earnings or yield from the fund.

CHART 14-3 Impact of Annual Fee over Time

Original investment		Fund value at beginning of year	Fees 1%	Account value without the fee (if return is 8%)	Account value less the fees	Difference
Year	**Amount**					
Year One	$ 10,000	$ 10,000	$ 100	$ 10,800	$ 10,700	$ 100
Year Two	$ 10,000	$ 20,700	$ 207	$ 22,464	$ 20,493	$ 1,971
Year Three	$ 10,000	$ 30,493	$ 305	$ 35,061	$ 30,188	$ 4,873
Year Four	$ 10,000	$ 40,188	$ 402	$ 48,666	$ 39,786	$ 8,880

5. Other Fees

Fees can also be charged when funds are withdrawn (exit fee), when distributions are made, when beneficiaries are changed, when the plan is rolled over into another plan, and for other services. All these fees should be considered in making the choice to invest in a particular state plan.

8. Letter from Representative Michael G. Oxley, Chairman, Comm. of Fin. Servs., U.S. House of Representatives, to the Honorable William Donaldson, Chairman, Sec. & Exch. Comm'n (July 15, 2004).

9. *See* **Appendix C**. Check for the "Exclusive Broker Sold" plans on the website for the particular Section 529 plans.

Planning Pointer

Morningstar, one of many rating services, rates the Utah Educational Savings Plan (UESP) as the best plan with the lowest fees. The plan offers a robust number of Vanguard index-fund portfolios that produce strong earnings. Its age-based fund was considered "among the top 10-age-based investment options offered by direct-sold plans." [10]

D. Account Ownership and Beneficiary Limitations

All states have different rules around account ownership, beneficiary limitations, and who can make contributions, so it is important to check the state rules before choosing what plan works best for you. In general, the account owner usually must be of legal age and a *U.S. citizen* or resident alien with a social security number or taxpayer ID. If the state imposes an age and school grade limitation, then obviously, an adult cannot be the beneficiary. Some states require the donor of the cash fund to be the account owner. Others allow third parties to contribute to the plan but consider the account owner as having made the contribution. Some states may not allow the account owner and beneficiary to be the same person. Some states may not allow the account owner to be changed. Other states do not allow the account owner to be a corporation or trust. Some states have contingencies upon the death, disability or bankruptcy of the owner, others do not. Some states require that the beneficiary be a minor. Other states allow a power of attorney only when the account owner becomes incapacitated.

E. Contribution and Withdrawal Restrictions

The advisor must examine any state restrictions on contributions to the Section 529 plan. Usually, the plans allow for small contributions but have limits at the higher ends.[11] The advisor must also beware of withdrawals that could result in penalties.

1. Minimum Initial Contributions

Some plans allow an account to be opened with as little as $25 or $50 as long as a contribution is made regularly through an automatic monthly deposit system.

10. *See Morningstar: Utah Education Savings Plan Is One of the Best in the U.S.*, MY529 (July 7, 2016), https://my529.org/morningstar-utah-educational-savings-plan-is-one-of-the-best-in-the-u-s/.

11. *See* **Chart 7-2** in **Chapter Seven: Federal Rules and Regulations for Section 529 Savings Plans**.

Other plans accept small contributions on an irregular basis. If multiple relatives are contributing to the plan, it is important that there be an option of more frequent contributions. Most plans allow for a nonowner to make a contribution to the Section 529 savings account.

2. Funding Limits/Maximum Contributions

Each state has a maximum contribution level and exceeding it could result in income tax and a penalty. Sometimes the maximum includes the earnings, sometimes it excludes the earnings. In addition, most states require a signed statement that the maximum contribution limit has not been exceeded.

EXAMPLE 14-3: Alice sets up a 529 plan in a state that has a contribution limit of $250,000. After twenty years the fund is worth $300,000. Since the fund has increased in value beyond the state limit, if Alice wants to change beneficiaries there is the possibility that the plan will not accept the full fund or Alice will have to pay a penalty on the excess.

3. Withdrawal Restrictions

Some state 529 savings plans require that money saved for a beneficiary be distributed before the beneficiary reaches a certain age. Thus, if the client wants a "dynasty" plan—one that can last for a long period of time—it is important to pick a state plan that does not impose this limitation. The effect of the *rule against perpetuities* also differs among states. Some plans limit how soon withdrawals may begin from the account. Sometimes there are expenses or penalties with withdrawals, or there can be penalties if the child does not pursue post-secondary education. Other important issues include the following: whether the plan permits withdrawals for graduate school, whether withdrawals must be paid directly to the education institution, and the purpose for which withdrawals are permitted (e.g., to pay for room and board, tuition, or for any purpose). Some plans may not allow K–12 distributions or payments on student loans.

4. Other Factors

If a client has an existing UTMA or UGMA account, it is important to know if the plan will accept those funds and arrange for their sale.[12] It may also be important if account earnings are credited daily, monthly, or quarterly. Also, some states are slow in crediting the account with the contribution.

---

12. *See* **Chapter Seven: Federal Rules and Regulations for Section 529 Savings Plans**.

F. Participation in Retail Rebate Programs

Many state plans partner with programs that give rebates to the savings plan when the customer purchases merchandise or services from various firms. This is a great way to save for college while just carrying on normal spending and consumption. There are several major programs—Upromise, Inc., Fidelity, Babymint, Edexpress and Sage Scholars—to name a few. Each works slightly differently.[13] Participants register online.

EXAMPLE 14-4: Taxpayer purchases a General Motors car and registers on the Upromise website. He/she will be given a credit of $150 in his/her 529 plan (assuming the state plan allows this).

1. Upromise Inc.

The website for *Upromise* is www.upromise.com.[14] The client can either register his/her own credit card or can receive a no fee credit card (issued by Citibank) that rebates 1.25 percent of all purchases (plus a 15 percent bonus on the total cash back). Participating merchants include a variety of well-known national chains, such as Exxon, Staples, Circuit City, Avis, and Bed, Bath and Beyond. Upromise also has a number of regional participating supermarkets, drug stores, and restaurants. It also has some realty companies, such as Century 21, ERA Real Estate, and Coldwell Banker, through which up to $3,000 could be placed in the 529 savings plan, as well as General Motors, through which a car purchase can earn up to $150. The rebates vary from 1 percent (or a flat $1) to 10 percent for some of the regional restaurants. It is best to have a partly funded 529 plan already in place rather than counting on creating one with rebates from one's purchases. Otherwise, the annual fees from the plan could easily wipe out all the savings.

2. Other Rebate Programs

Fidelity is another program which simply offers a credit card that grants a 2 percent rebate on all purchases. Thus 2 percent of all purchases will generate cash that will be deposited into the 529 plan. However, the drawback is the Fidelity credit card must be used by a Fidelity 529 plan. This is not the case with the Upromise Mastercard.

---

13. Robert Farrington, *3 Easy Ways to Save in a 529 Plan before the End of the Year*, Forbes (Nov. 29, 2018), https://www.forbes.com/sites/robertfarrington/2018/11/29/easy-ways-to-save-in-a-529-plan/?sh=4a18b9127833.

14. *See* Mark Kantrowitz, *Review: Upromise College Savings Rewards Program*, Saving for College (Nov. 26, 2019), https://www.savingforcollege.com/article/upromise-college-savings-rewards-program.

The website for *Baby Mint* is www.babymint.com and it works very much like Upromise. The credit card available is through MBNA. Like Upromise, the stores are well-known stores, such as Gap, Brooks Brothers, JC Penney, and Radio Shack. One significant difference is that there seem to be fewer big-ticket item participants, such as real estate or car companies. In addition, gift certificates qualify. Once rebates accrue, they can either go to the 529 plan or be reimbursed directly to the customer.

The website address for Edexpress is www.edexpress.com. Unlike Upromise and Babymint, there is no credit card option. There is also an annual fee. However, the rebates from some of their listed merchants tend to be slightly higher than the other programs.

G. Customer Services

Other considerations in choosing a plan are the following: availability of online account management; online account information, including regular bulletins or mailings; availability of toll-free phone numbers and reasonable service hours; wait time to talk to a customer service representative; and availability of an investment company the client prefers.

H. Rankings of the Plans

Because the variations among plans are vast, a comparison of different plans before choosing one is critical. In an effort to categorize and rank the competing plans, various rating systems are available. Three of the most popular are Morningstar,[15] savingforcollege.com,[16] and Kiplinger.[17] CNN, Money Magazine and others have also rated these plans.

Planning Pointer

Given the current fluctuation in the market, it is imperative that the client contact their investment advisor to determine the best savings plan given their level of risk and other factors.

The rating systems generally look at the fees, the investment options, and their quality. For example, Morningstar examines "investment flexibility," which is the

15. *See* www.morningstar.com.
16. *See* www.savingforcollege.com.
17. *See* Thomas M. Anderson, *Best 529 College-Savings Plans*, Kiplinger (Jan. 5, 2012), https://www.kiplinger.com/article/college/t014-c000-s001-best-529-college-savings-plans.html.

ability to allocate among funds based on risk, diversification, and rate of return.[18] The ratings provided at www.savingforcollege.com also examine state tax advantages take into consideration residency when ranking the plans. The planner must remember that investor performance may vary widely, particularly in a recession.

Before the Great Recession, some of the more aggressive investment strategies ended up being the worst plans from a performance point of view. Now, all of the best plans are open to nonresidents. The plans almost all feature respected fund managers, low annual fees, and a variety of investment options. Most also offer favorable state tax deductions or credits for contributions to the plan made by residents.

1. Morningstar[19]

Morningstar assigned ratings to 61 plans in 2020. In total these plans captured 97 percent of the more than $363 billion invested in 529 plans as of August 30, 2020. They organize their research around four key pillars: Process, People, Parent, and Price. The "Performance" factor was replaced by the four more predictive elements. Morningstar offers "medals" of Gold, Silver and Bronze, as well as Neutral and Negative ratings. Three 529 plans earned a Gold rating: (1) Michigan's Education Savings Program, (2) Bright Start Direct-Sold College Savings of Illinois, and (3) my529 from Utah. All three are directly sold. Eighteen plans earned Neutral in 2020 and eight plans received Negative ratings. Each year Morningstar does upgrades or downgrades, so for example Michigan ESP went from Silver to Gold, in large part of the "recognition of the state's long track record of first-rate investment oversight."

2. Savings for College[20]

Savings for College has a "Best Plans of 2021" ranking. When you go to the savingsforcollege website, you can click "best for my state," "best rated," "lowest fees," and "best performance." Under each of these categories, numerous plans are rated.

3. Kiplinger[21]

Each year Kiplinger ranks the various 529 state plans. His criteria are low fees, overall investment mix, best for conservative investors, best fund choices, and best advisor-sold plan. Because these rankings vary from year to year, the advisor must keep abreast of the current ratings.

---

18. It also ranks "shareholder friendliness."

19. Madeline Hume & Adam Millson, *The Top 529 College Savings Plans of 2020*, Morningstar (Oct. 27, 2020), https://www.morningstar.com/articles/1006084/the-top-529-college-savings-plans-of-2020.

20. *See Best 529 Plans of 2021*, Saving for College, https://www.savingforcollege.com/intro-to-529s/which-is-the-best-529-plan-available (last visited May 14, 2021).

21. *See* Anderson, *supra* note 17.

a. *Best for Low Fees*

Kiplinger recommends Illinois Bright Start College Savings Program if low investment costs are of primary concern. This Illinois plan has a Vanguard index-fund available in the direct-sold version where costs are "rock-bottom." The expense ratios range from 0.20 percent to 0.22 percent. The plan also levies a fee for each Vanguard portfolio selected.

b. *Best for Overall Investment Mix*

Kiplinger recommends Alaska's T. Rowe Price College Savings Plan for best overall investment mix. This plan's most expensive option costs just 0.96 percent.

c. *Best for Conservative Investors*

Kiplinger recommends Michigan Education Savings Program if you are a conservator investor who is concerned with the fluctuations of the market. Run by TIAA-CREF, this plan has a savings option that guarantees principal and a minimum annual interest rate based on a Treasury note index. That option does not even charge an annual fee. The plan also offers portfolios of TIAA-CREF mutual funds that are weighted more heavily to bond funds with very low flat fee of .045 percent.

d. *Best for Fund Choices*

Kiplinger recommends College Savings Plan of Nebraska for best fund choices. Here Nebraska offers a selection of 20 funds from American Century, Fidelity, Pimco, and Vanguard. However, this wider selection does come with higher rates. The most expensive option costs 1.64 percent and there is a $20 maintenance fee for all accounts.

e. *Best Advisor-Sold Plan*

Kiplinger recommends Virginia College America plan if the taxpayer feels most comfortable with an advisor. Of course, the taxpayer will pay more in fees. However, the "advisor can craft a portfolio with 22-top notch funds from American Funds."[22]

I. Conclusion

There are numerous factors that influence choosing the proper Section 529 savings plan. Residency requirements and ownership limitations may narrow the search. State tax deductions might be so favorable that when compared with good investment performance, the state plan is the best choice. Similarly, state tax penalties for investment in other states' plans may be so severe as to make investment in the state plan the only viable option. Time restrictions, penalties on withdrawals,

---

22. *See id.*

and state taxation of earnings should be explored. The performance of the funds over time and the fees charged are major determining factors and, if the state considerations are not compelling, will often be the determining factor in choosing the plan. The greater the variety of investment options, the more likely the advisor/investor will find a fund that suits the taxpayer's risk level and desired rate of return. Other considerations may also be important, such as contribution restrictions, asset protection, perpetuity, accessibility, and participation in retail rebate savings programs. The advisor should interview the client to determine his/her goals, level of *risk tolerance*, timetables, and other priorities. Consulting an investment or other financial advisor is also appropriate.

PART III

PREPAID TUITION PLANS

Section 529 *prepaid tuition plans* offer some of the same benefits as the Section 529 savings plan. First, they are available to all income groups. Second, they provide income, gift, estate, and generation-skipping tax advantages. Third, they can be used with other tax provisions as long as no double tax benefits result. Fourth, the same nontax benefits exist, such as financial aid compatibility, control by the owner, and asset protection. Prepaid plans are less comprehensive than Section 529 savings plans, as they do not cover all education expenses—usually just tuition. However, they can offer guaranteed tuition rates even when investment returns are low and tuition costs are high. The relatively new institutional *Private College 529 Plan* (with nearly 300 participating private school members) offers greater portability than the state prepaid plans and addresses the solvency issue of some of the state prepaid plans. However, neither of these types of prepaid plans guarantee admission to the school, and if the owner desires a refund or wishes to transfer to a Section 529 savings plan, the appreciation from the investment can be lost. **Chapter Fifteen: The State Prepaid Plan** focuses on the state prepaid plans. **Chapter Sixteen: The Prepaid Institutional Plan** discusses the *Private College 529 Plan*.

Honey, it was your idea to prepay the kids' tuition.

Chapter 15

The State Prepaid Plan

State prepaid plans were developed prior to the Section 529 savings plans and at one time were more numerous.[1] While 20 states used to offer these plans, in 2021 only 11 states offer new enrollment or have temporarily suspended enrollment while they await legislative action or the introduction of a replacement plan.[2] State prepaid plans essentially lock in future tuition rates at current prices, providing significant education cost benefits. The major problem, other than the fact that only a few states currently offer these plans, is that under most prepaid plans, the contributor must predetermine that the student's education path is to a state school.[3] By contrast, the traditional Section 529 savings plans are available in all 50 states and can be used at any state or private school. Another problem is that prepaid plans usually only cover tuition expenses while Section 529 savings plans cover room and board and other education fees.

State prepaid plans have similar requirements to savings plans. First, Section 529 requires that purchases of prepaid plans be made only in cash.[4] Second, providers must issue a separate accounting for each beneficiary.[5] Third, neither contributors to nor beneficiaries of the prepaid plans can directly or indirectly direct the earnings from the investments.[6] Fourth, interest in a prepaid plan cannot be used as a security interest.[7] Finally, the plan cannot cover more than what would be the "reasonably expected" qualified higher education expenses.[8]

---

1. *See* **Chart 6-1: Timeline for Section 529 Plans** in **Chapter Six: History of Section 529 Savings Plans**.
2. Stephanie Taylor Christensen, *The Last States with Prepaid Tuition Plans*, Investopedia (Jan. 19, 2021), https://www.investopedia.com/financial-edge/0311/the-last-states-with-prepaid-tuition-plans.aspx.
3. Two exceptions are the Washington and Florida state prepaid plans where in-state students can attend out-of-state schools.
4. I.R.C. § 529(b)(2).
5. *Id.* § 529(b)(3).
6. *Id.* § 529(b)(4).
7. *Id.* § 529(b)(5).
8. *Id.* § 529(b)(6).

State prepaid plans also have similar tax benefits to Section 529 savings plans. Anyone can contribute, no matter how high their adjusted gross income is, and no annual limit exists on contributions—other than the upper limit that can reasonably be contributed for the benefit of one individual. Although the contribution is not deductible under federal law, some states offer deductions or credits for contributions to these plans.[9] All earnings from the plan are exempt from federal income taxes when used for qualified higher education expenses (QHEE). In addition, both plans have favorable gift, generation skipping tax, and estate tax consequences. (*See* **Part II**: **Chapters Six** through **Ten** for a detailed discussion of all of these tax benefits.)

Both types of plans also offer similar nontax advantages. Not only are these accounts easy to set up and administer, but the *account owner* can also control the direction of the account. So, for example, if the beneficiary does not go to college, the account owner can change the beneficiary to another family member. The beneficiary, on the other hand has no control or access to the account. Both have the same favorable financial aid consequences. However, these plans differ in several important nontax aspects. On the negative side, account owners of prepaid plans wanting to cash out their fund will only get back their original contributions, most likely less a penalty. On the positive side, prepaids provide guaranteed payment of tuition—even when market returns are low. Thus, they are less risky than Section 529 savings plans.

A. Prepaid Plans—History and Current Status

Many states implemented state prepaid plans in the late 1990s following the enactment of Section 529 into law. Typically, these state plans allowed only state residents to purchase prepaid tuition certificates to attend a state institution of higher education. Many states also offered state income tax deductions for contributions to these plans. However, many states closed their programs to future participants or greatly increased the contract prices. Many were cancelled entirely as a result of shrinking state budgets, legislative unwillingness to increase the subsidy for higher education, and skyrocketing tuition and education costs at state institutions. In addition, investment returns for prepaid plans have not kept up with the tuition increases.[10] With the COVID-19 crisis, these plans are even more financially precarious. Currently, only 11 states have prepaid plans that have open enrollments or are only temporarily suspended. (*See* **Chart 15-1**.)

The sustainability of these plans does depend on the return on investment from the prepaid accounts to keep pace with the steady increase of tuition. Therefore,

9. *See* **Chart 10-2: State Tax Deductions or Credits** in **Chapter Ten: State Tax Planning with Section 529 Savings Plans**.

10. *See* Eileen Ambrose, *Getting Started on Saving for a Child's College Tuition Is Critical, so Make It a Habit Early*, Balt. Sun, July 31, 2005, at 1D. *See also* Sandra Block, *Prepaid College Plans Run into Financial Gaps*, USA Today, Dec. 9, 2003, at 1B.

as tuition increases drastically without accompanying increases in returns, the programs run a deficit. This is exactly what happened in many states, which led to states discontinuing the sale of contracts. For example, Colorado and Wyoming have permanently shut down their programs.[11] Kentucky, Texas, and West Virginia have closed enrollments in their plans, but still honor their obligations to past enrollees.[12] In November 2004, Virginia's state prepaid program had a deficit of $128 million, leading to substantial reforms of that program.[13] Ohio had to transfer $1,000,000 from its general fund to its plan to maintain its solvency, but now no longer offers such a plan.[14] Kentucky's prepaid plan gained notoriety when the state attorney general sued the governing board of the prepaid plan for a creative attempt to decrease the fund's deficit.[15]

State prepaid plan programs face financial difficulties when state budgets are being cut. Thus, they may not survive. When tuition increases sharply or when higher education expenses rise, then these plans are more likely to be closed or suspended. Events like pandemics and recessions may place these plans in serious jeopardy.

B. Types of State Prepaid Tuition Plans

The first thing to know about prepaid tuition plans is that they do *not* guarantee admission into the school—the child must still apply and be admitted to the school like all other students. Two main types of state prepaid plans are available: the *prepaid unit* and the *contract plan*.

Under the *prepaid unit plan*, participants purchase units that represent a fixed percentage of tuition, with one unit typically corresponding to 1 percent of a year's tuition. All participants pay the same price for the units and the price of a unit increases each year. The purchaser can buy as many units as they want each year. Then the units are redeemable in the future based on average tuition rates at a target group of schools. Under the *contract plan*, participants agree to purchase a specified number of years of tuition. The purchase price depends on the age of the child and on the type of payment (lump sum or installment). Contract plans usually offer lower prices for younger children, as the state has more time to invest the money. Typically, when inflation of tuition costs is greater than the expected return on investment under the state plan, the contract plan is a better investment

11. *See* Karin Fischer, *States Rethink Popular Aid Programs*, Chronicle of Higher Educ. 21 (Sept. 9, 2005). *See also* Christine Walton, *Colorado Shuts Down Its Prepaid Tuition Plan*, Nat'l Conference of State Legislatures 20 (May 1, 2004).

12. *See* Albert B. Crenshaw, *Prepaid Tuition: A Future Flunk-Out?*, Wash. Post, Nov. 14, 2004, at F1.

13. *Id.*

14. *Id.*

15. *See* Fischer, *supra* note 11. In Kentucky, the governing board of the prepaid plan moved $13.7 million from the state's unclaimed-property account to the prepaid plan program. The state attorney general sued the governing board, claiming that this was an unconstitutional taking of private property by the state government.

CHART 15-1 State Prepaid Plans

State Prepaid Plan	Limited to State Schools	Limited to Tuition & Required Fees	Pre-paid Units	Outsourced or State Run	Separate Plans for 2 & 4-Year Colleges	Residency Restrictions	In-state if family moves out of state	Time limit for use of credits
FLORIDA (Florida Prepaid College Plan)	No	No	No	State Run	Yes	Yes	No out-of-state fees will be charged to the beneficiary by state university or community college	Within 10 years of high school graduation
ILLINOIS (College Illinois! 529 Prepaid Tuition Program) (CLOSED to new enrollment)	No	Yes	Yes	State Run	Yes	Yes	The student will be charged out-of-state tuition	Within 10 years of projected enrollment year for original beneficiary. Once the beneficiary starts using the prepaid benefits, they have 10 years to finish using benefits

State Prepaid Plan	Limited to State Schools	Limited to Tuition & Required Fees	Pre-paid Units	Outsourced or State Run	Separate Plans for 2 & 4-Year Colleges	Residency Restrictions	In-state if family moves out of state	Time limit for use of credits
MARYLAND (Maryland Prepaid College Trust)	No	Yes	Yes	State governed investments handled by Mellon Equity Associates, LLP and Rainier Investment Management Inc.	Yes	Yes	The student will be charged out-of-state tuition	Within 10 years of high school graduation
MASSACHUSETTS (MEFA U. Plan Prepaid Tuition Program)	Yes	Yes	Yes	State Run	No	No	No residency requirement	Must use within 6 years of maturity date on tuition certificate
MICHIGAN (Michigan Education Trust)	No	Yes	Yes	State Run	Yes	Yes	The student will be charged out-of-state tuition	9 academic years from expected high school graduation date

State Prepaid Plan	Limited to State Schools	Limited to Tuition & Required Fees	Pre-paid Units	Outsourced or State Run	Separate Plans for 2 & 4-Year Colleges	Residency Restrictions	In-state if family moves out of state	Time limit for use of credits
MISSISSIPPI (Mississippi Prepaid Affordable College Savings (MPACT) Program)	No	Yes	Yes	State Run	Yes	Yes	All beneficiaries are considered residents in terms of in-state tuition	Within 10 years of projected enrollment year for original beneficiary
NEVADA (Nevada Prepaid Tuition Program)	No	Limited to only tuition	May purchase 2 or 4 years of a 4-year college	State Run	Yes	No	The student will be charged out-of-state tuition	Within 10 years of high school graduation (or up to the age of 30)
PENNSYLVANIA (PA 529 Guaranteed Savings Plan)	Yes	Yes	Yes	State Run	No	Yes	The account owner or beneficiary must be a resident to get in-state tuition	
TEXAS (Texas Tuition Promise Fund)	No	Yes	No	State Run	Yes	Yes	The student will be charged out-of-state tuition	Within 10 years of high school graduation

State Prepaid Plan	Limited to State Schools	Limited to Tuition & Required Fees	Pre-paid Units	Outsourced or State Run	Separate Plans for 2 & 4-Year Colleges	Residency Restrictions	In-state if family moves out of state	Time limit for use of credits
VIRGINIA (CLOSED on 5/1/2019 but website states developing a "new similar program.")	No	Yes	Yes	State Run	Yes	Yes	The student will be charged out-of-state tuition	Within 10 years of high school graduation
WASHINGTON (Guaranteed Education Tuition—GET)	No	No	Yes	State Run	No	Yes	The student will be charged out-of-state tuition	Within 10 years of high school graduation

than the unit plan. In other words, the contract plan works like a futures contract and the unit plan operates like a tuition index fund. Of the ten available plans (not including the Massachusetts plan, which is slightly different), seven offer the contract option while three offer the unit plan.[16]

Most prepaid tuition plans are operated by state governments, although some are outsourced to private marketing firms. Some of these plans guarantee tuition based on an enrollment-weighted average of in-state public college tuition rates. Some prepaid plans have separate plans for two and four-year colleges. A few even provide for room and board in addition to tuition and mandatory fees. Often the state's prepaid plan will pay the tuition costs of any state four-year college. In such a case, the best deal occurs when the student attends the state school with the highest tuition.

EXAMPLE 15-1: Suppose Alice purchased a prepaid plan for her son, Ben, and pays the enrollment-weighted average of the State's tuition, costing $5,000 × 4 or $20,000. If Ben attends the most expensive state school with tuition costs of $30,000, all tuition will be covered for four years, providing significant value for Alice's investment.

Some states, however, charge a premium for the tuition. So instead of paying the current tuition rate or a discounted rate, the taxpayer pays more. For example, the state of Washington charges a 20 percent premium over the current tuition charged at the priciest public university in the state. This can help keep the state plan solvent.[17] Another downside of the prepaid plan is that under many plans, if the student decides to attend an out-of-state or private college, the plan typically offers only a refund of the return of the original investment with a low interest rate. If the prepaid plan allows for payment to out-of-state or private college, the plan often will only pay the average of in-state public college tuition.

Prepaid tuition plans definitely have an advantage for certain families. For families who intend to send their child (or one of their children) to a state school, prepaid tuition plans provide a convenient and affordable tax-exempt option. These have also been recommended for families who might get a divorce, as there is less to fight over because these are no potentially sizeable liquid funds to reclaim (this is different from the 529 savings plan). For those families with little investment knowledge, these plans offer a low-risk, tax-advantaged investment vehicle, with earnings indexed to the average increase in tuition. These plans also make sense when tuition rates increase precipitously as the savings potential on the prepaid plans could be much greater than on Section 529 savings plans.

---

16. Kathryn Flynn, *Prepaid Tuition Plans*, Saving for College (Apr. 28, 2020), https://www.savingforcollege.com/article/prepaid-tuition-plans?sfc_template=article_layout_v2.

17. *See* Ron Liever, *Beating College Tuition Costs*, Wall St. J., Feb. 11, 2006.

1. Residency or Ownership Restrictions

Residency becomes important—not only as to eligibility to purchase the plan—but whether lower in-state tuition credits or more expensive out-of-state tuition credits are being purchased. Most plans require that either the account owner or the beneficiary be a state resident when the account is opened. Under most state plans, the student must be a resident at the time of application to the college to be eligible for the lower in-state tuition. Massachusetts U. Plan is the only plan available to nonresidents.

2. Limited Enrollment Periods

Some plans offer year-round enrollment opportunities. Others are only available during certain specific times of the year. For example, Florida's Prepaid Plan has an enrollment period from October through February.

3. Transferability Issues

Changing the beneficiary to another beneficiary should not be a problem if the owner of the prepaid plan remains a resident. Changing the plan to another state plan, however, could result in only a return of the original investment plus interest. Only Washington's and Florida's prepaid plans allow units to be redeemed at out-of-state schools. In most plans, when the family moves out of state, but the child attends a participating school, the family can still use the plan. They may be held responsible, however, for the difference between out-of-state and in-state tuition, depending on the plan. Some plans will treat such a student as an in-state student, allowing the plan to cover 100 percent of the cost.

4. Return on Investment and Low Risk

A key potential benefit of prepaid tuition plans is they tend to act as a hedge against economic downturns. During recessions, state governments tend to reduce support for higher education, which translates directly into increases in public college tuition rates. Thus, when other investments are dropping due to a declining stock market, the value of prepaid tuition plans will tend to increase. As many parents have a low tolerance for risks for their savings principal, these prepaid tuition plans can be very attractive under the right circumstances. On the other hand, one study showed that if you lived in Maryland and had purchased the pre-paid plan there, the return on your investment was only 4.2 percent.[18] (*See* **Chart 15-2**.)

---

18. Libby Nelson, *12 States Let You Pay College Tuition Years in Advance. But It's Not Always a Good Idea*, Vox (May 23, 2016), https://www.vox.com/2016/5/23/11714266/prepaid-tuition-529-college-savings.

CHART 15-2 Return on Investment for Prepaid Plans

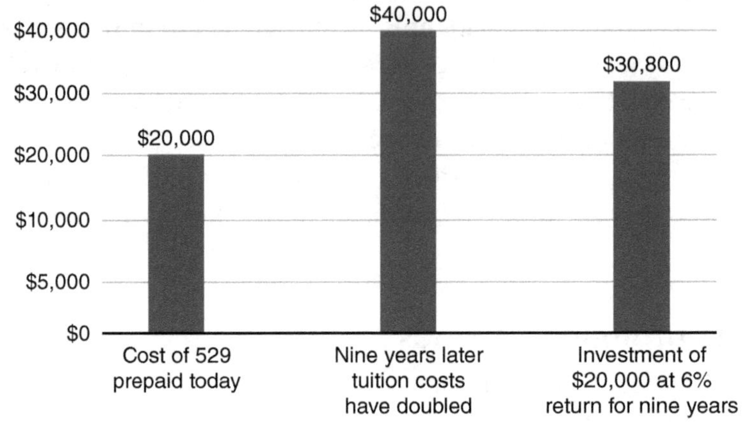

5. Security and Solvency Issues

The solvency considerations are very significant for these plans. Several prepaid plans, such as those in Alabama, Colorado, Kentucky, New Mexico, Ohio, South Carolina, West Virginia, and Wyoming, have permanently closed. Only four states' prepaid plans are guaranteed by the full faith and credit (FF&C) of the state: Florida, Massachusetts, Mississippi, and Washington.[19] Some states have no such guarantee but have a "moral obligation" provision, or like Pennsylvania, declare that their prepaid plan is "guaranteed."

6. Financial Aid

The *Deficit Reduction Omnibus Reconciliation Act of 2005*[20] grants prepaid 529s the same favorable financial aid consequences as the 529 savings plans. Previously, prepaid tuition plans were treated as a *student resource*, which meant they reduced need-based financial aid dollar for dollar. Now, under the federal methodology of FAFSA, prepaid plans are considered the asset of the parent (even if considered owned by the student). Thus, these are assessed at up to 5.64 percent of their "refund value" versus other student owned accounts, which are assessed at 20 percent. Under the institutional formula, a parent that owns the plan will be assessed from 3–5 percent, but if owned by the student, then it will be assessed at 25 percent.[21] If the prepaid plan is owned by another relative, such as a grandparent, it is not included in the financial aid formulae. However, any distribution to the student will be considered untaxed income of the student and can be assessed at 50 percent, under both the federal and institutional formulae.

19. *Are Program Benefits Backed by the Full Faith and Credit of the State?*, SAVING FOR COLLEGE, https://www.savingforcollege.com/compare_529_plans/?page=compare_plan_questions&plan_question_ids%5B%5D=112 (last visited May 14, 2021).

20. Pub. L. No. 109-171, § 8019(d)(5).

21. *See* **Chapter Nineteen: Coordinating Section 529 Plans with Financial Aid**.

Example 15-2: Suppose Ben has $10,000 saved in a prepaid 529 plan. This could potentially reduce his aid package by as much as $564 under the FAFSA. But if he had instead saved this amount in a custodianship account, his aid package could be reduced by $2,000.

7. Control, Perpetuity, and Other Nontax Considerations

Prepaid plans are the same as savings plans in terms of owner control. Unlike 529 savings plans, however, the prepaid plans, because of their terms, may not offer perpetual existence. Often the tuition credits must be used by a certain period of time, most commonly ten years after the beneficiary's date of high school graduation. Some states allow contributions to be made by charging a credit card, thus allowing contributors additional rewards for the contribution through their credit card companies.

Prepaid tuition plans also are often popular in divorce settlements because they allow each parent to pay a specified percentage of college costs by using a lump sum contribution to discharge their obligation. As with savings plans, these plans raise community property issues.[22] Thus, upon death or divorce, the non-account owner would be entitled to revoke or change half the plan.

CHART 15-3 Decision Model for Prepaid Plan

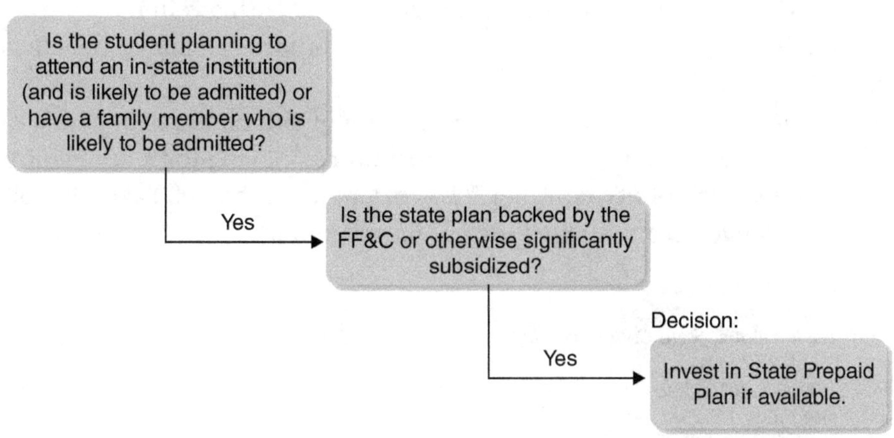

22. *See* **Chapter Seven: Federal Rules and Regulations for Section 529 Savings Plans**, B.2(a).

Planning Pointer

Most prepaid plans only cover tuition and required fees—not room and board, necessitating the coordination of the prepaid plans with other savings techniques. There is no prohibition against investing in both a prepaid plan and a Section 529 savings plan, but contributions and other rules must be coordinated. Bottom line: prepaid plans are very attractive when investment returns are low.

C. The Best State Prepaid Plans

In general, the prepaid plans are less desirable than the Section 529 plans. Perhaps the biggest problem has been the liquidity of the state funds. Nonetheless, Florida has one of the best prepaid plans. It is considered the "Cadillac of prepaid plans,"[23] and includes such features as low fees, portability, coverage of room and board, and state guarantees.[24] Washington state also has a popular prepaid plan. It features portability, good investment returns, and state guarantees.[25]

1. Florida State's Prepaid Plan

The Florida state prepaid plan is called the Florida Prepaid College Plan. Florida first opened its plan in 1986.[26] Since that time, over one million Florida residents have utilized the plan.[27] The plan's assets are worth more than $5.5 billion, with $404 million in reserves.[28] Florida does not have an income tax; therefore there are no state tax deductions or credits for contributions to the plan.[29] At the time of enrollment in the Florida Prepaid Plan, either the account owner or the beneficiary must be a Florida resident. The plan owner can cancel with a refund of the original contribution, less a penalty, or transfer the plan to another qualified beneficiary at any time.

The Florida Plan is a *contract plan*. The price of the contract depends on the age of the beneficiary and whether the contributor is paying for a community college or a four-year university contract.[30] For example, in the 2020–2021 enrollment period, prices ranged from as little as $52.65 per month ($631.80 per year) for a

23. Michael A. Olivas, *State College Savings and Prepaid Tuition Plans: A Reappraisal and Review*, 32 J.L. & Educ. 475, 482 (2003).
24. Fla. Stat. Ann. § 1009.98 (2005). *See also* Fla. Prepaid College Plan, https://www.myfloridaprepaid.com (last visited May 14, 2021).
25. Wash. Rev. Code § 28B.95.050.
26. *See* Anita Kumar, *Officials Insist That Prepaid Tuition Plan Change, but How?*, St. Petersburg Times, Apr. 23, 2004, at 5B.
27. Fla. Prepaid College Plan, *supra* note 24.
28. David Damron, *Free Tuition Almost Like Winning the Lottery*, Orlando Sentinel, Mar. 1, 2005, at B3.
29. Fla. Prepaid College Plan, *supra* note 24.
30. Fla. Stat. Ann. § 1009.98 (2005).

two-year community college plan to $47.89 per month ($574.68 per year) for a four-year university plan.[31]

EXAMPLE 15-3: University of Florida charges $6,381 in tuition for the 2020–2021 academic year. If the taxpayer prepays that amount and tuition rises 10 percent, he/she has a benefit of $638 per year.

Most of the beneficiaries of the Florida prepaid plan are elementary-school age when the plan is purchased, although a third of all beneficiaries are one year old or younger when they are enrolled.[32] Unlike many other plans, Florida allows contributors to prepay for tuition and fees as well as for room and board.[33] Florida's prepaid plans can be used at any of its 12 public universities or 28 community colleges.[34] This portability feature allows the value of the plan to be transferred to most private Florida colleges, as well as technical schools and out-of-state colleges.[35]

Florida's program is a prime example of the interplay between state higher education funding and the fate of prepaid plans. Florida's plan is incredibly popular with its citizens and, therefore, its state legislators. This popularity has helped keep Florida's state tuition rates among the lowest in the country. On the other hand, state college officials do not see the low tuition rates as a positive as they repeatedly demand that tuition be increased to improve programs, meet enrollment demands, and remain competitive with out-of-state institutions.[36]

Florida's program, in comparison to other states' prepaid tuition plans, provides a number of options for beneficiaries. Allowing beneficiaries to buy prepaid certificates for both tuition and housing is a particularly attractive feature. The plan is also extremely flexible in allowing students to transfer the funds to schools other than Florida's institutions. However, it appears the major reason for Florida's success is the state legislature's support of higher education funding and the prepaid tuition program, including its unwillingness to raise its caps on tuition increases. The consistent yearly increase of about 6 percent has allowed the returns on the prepaid plan's investment to keep pace with tuition increases and has maintained the plan's solvency. If tuition were increased by more than 7 percent, prepaid plan proponents worry that the plan would run a deficit, just like other state plans. With the COVID-19 induced recession and state budget shortfalls,

---

31. Fla. Prepaid College Plan, *supra* note 24.
32. *Id.*
33. Fla. Stat. Ann. § 1009.98(2) (2005).
34. *See Schools*, Fla. Prepaid College Plan, https://www.myfloridaprepaid.com/existing-customers/schools/ (last visited May 25, 2021).
35. Fla. Stat. Ann. § 1009.98(3) (2005).
36. Fischer, *supra* note 11.

the fear is this plan might be dropped. Legislators, worried about the diminishing credibility of Florida's diplomas, may have to make that choice.

Planning Pointer

Both the Florida and Washington plans are portable. Thus, they can be used at nearly any public or private college, university, or vocational school in the United States, as well as selected colleges in other countries. A college is eligible if it participates in federal financial aid programs through the U.S. Department of Education. To determine which schools qualify visit the Free Application for Federal Student Aid (FAFSA) website.

2. Washington State's Prepaid Plan

The Washington state prepaid plan is called the Guaranteed Education Tuition (GET) plan. GET opened in 1998 and has helped more than 57,000 students use over $1.2 billion in GET benefits.[37] Washington, like Florida, does not have an income tax, therefore no state tax deductions or credits are available for contributions to the plan. As with the Florida plan, at the time of enrollment in the GET plan, either the account owner or the beneficiary must be a Washington resident. An advantage is that it, like Florida, is guaranteed by the full faith and credit of the state.[38] And like the Florida plan, the GET is portable. Students have used GET units in all 50 states and in 15 foreign countries.

Unlike Florida, which is a contract plan, GET is a *prepaid unit plan* that includes purchasing prepaid "units" that are redeemable for future qualified higher education expenses (QHEE). The redeemable *value* of 100 units is equal to 100 percent of the cost of resident undergraduate tuition and state-mandated fees at the most expensive WA public university.[39] Individual units are valued at 1/100th of that cost and can be purchased in whole or partial amounts, from one to 800 units per student. For the 2020–2021 academic year, the most expensive Washington public university is the University of Washington-Tacoma, which charges $11,103 in tuition and state-mandated fees. That means that the current payout value for one GET unit is $111.03 or 1/100th.[40] GET units do *not* function as a prepayment of

37. *About Guaranteed Education Tuition (GET)*, WA529, https://wastate529.wa.gov/howgetworks (last visited May 14, 2021).

38. *Id.* (citing Wash. Rev. Code § 28B.95.050).

39. *Id.*

40. *2020–2021 Enrollment Guide*, WA529 (2020), https://wastate529.wa.gov/sites/default/files/2020-10/GET-Enrollment-Guide-2020-21.pdf.

tuition payments to the state of Washington; instead, GET units are redeemable for their present-day cash value to pay for QHEE at most educational institutions. QHEE includes not only tuition but room and board, books, computers, and other qualified expenses tied to the Section 529 definition.

The current GET unit price in 2020-2021 is $133, while the current payout price is $111 per unit. Thus, the cost of 100 units reflects a premium of ~20 percent. The GET governing committee sets the unit purchase price "with the input of an actuarial formula that takes into account estimated tuition, projected inflation and investment returns, and administrative costs."[41] There is a $50 enrollment fee per account, with a maximum fee of $100 per family. However, when the student enrolls in the program online, this enrollment fee is waived.

While it stings to pay a 20 percent premium on the GET investment, the future value of that investment will almost certainly provide positive returns, irrespective of market performance. Units must be held for a minimum of two calendar years before they can be redeemed, thus allowing years of growth to overcome the initial premium paid. A GET unit's redeemable value is directly tied to tuition, which is itself a product of both inflation and economic scarcity. As the redeemable value is tied to tuition costs (as opposed to investment performance), there are no management fees nor asset expenses to negatively affect the value of the investment. With no annual fees whatsoever, the account will never decrease in value from the capital originally invested. Because the GET account's value is directly tied to tuition costs, the investor is shielded from all economic risk, including temporary or long-term market instability, sub-par investment performance, and inflation rates outpacing growth. (*See* **Chart 15-4**.)

Comparatively, while other 529 plans may post similar (or greater) returns, almost all other plans are encumbered by either account-based fees, traditional investment-related fees (e.g., managerial fees, investment expense fees, etc.,), or both. Perhaps most importantly, the value of most traditional 529 accounts is directly linked to investment performance; (i.e., a beneficiary's account value would only increase in years where investment performance was positive and would actually decrease in years where investment performance was negative). In economic downturns, like the recession of 2009 and 2020, this could create a problem for parents trying to finance their child's education. If tuition costs continue to rise at faster rates than investment returns, then the value of investing in GET units will necessarily continue to rise to match those rates, yielding substantial (tax-free) returns. (*See* **Chart 15-5**.)

41. *Id.*

CHART 15-4 Washington State Plan Graphs

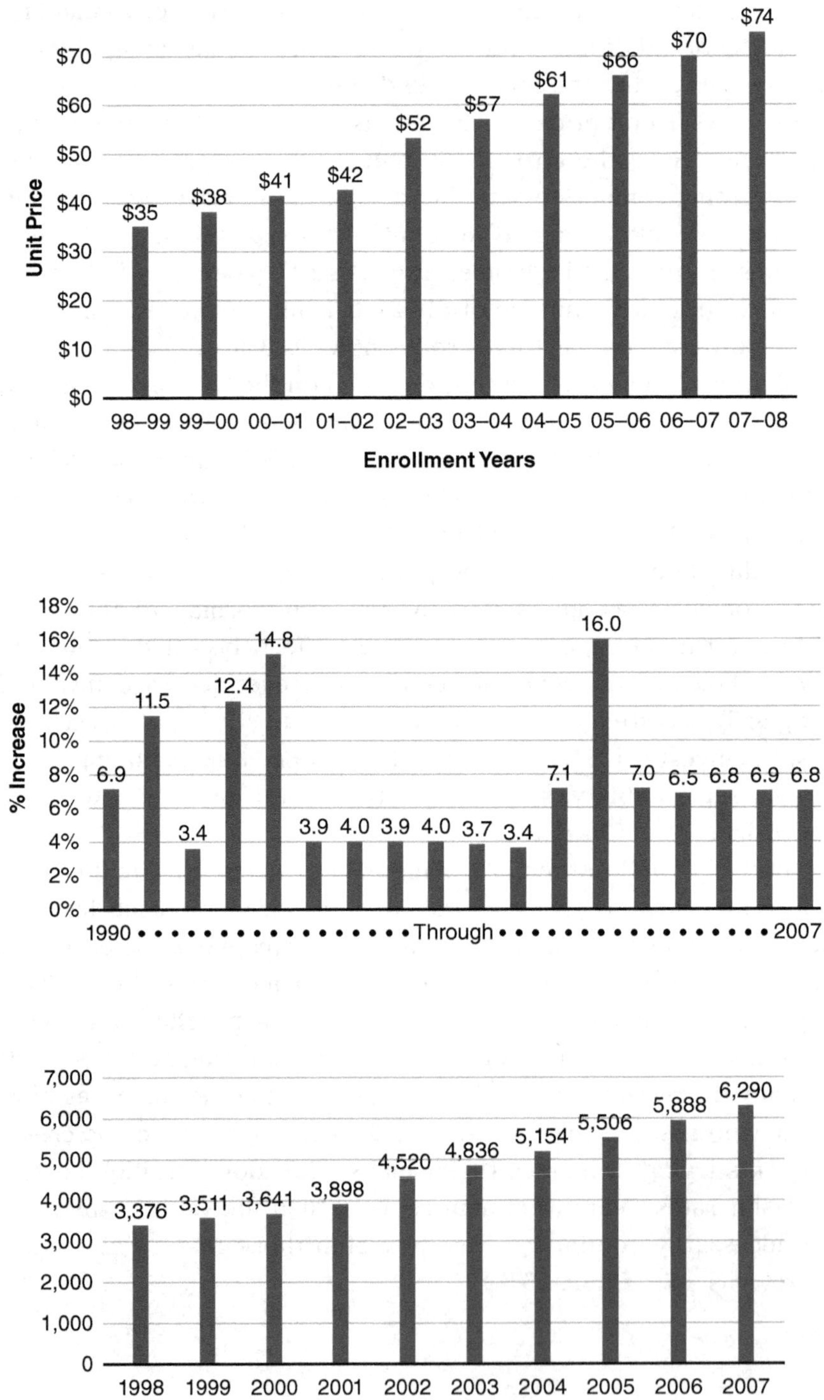

CHART 15-5 Example of GET Investment Projections

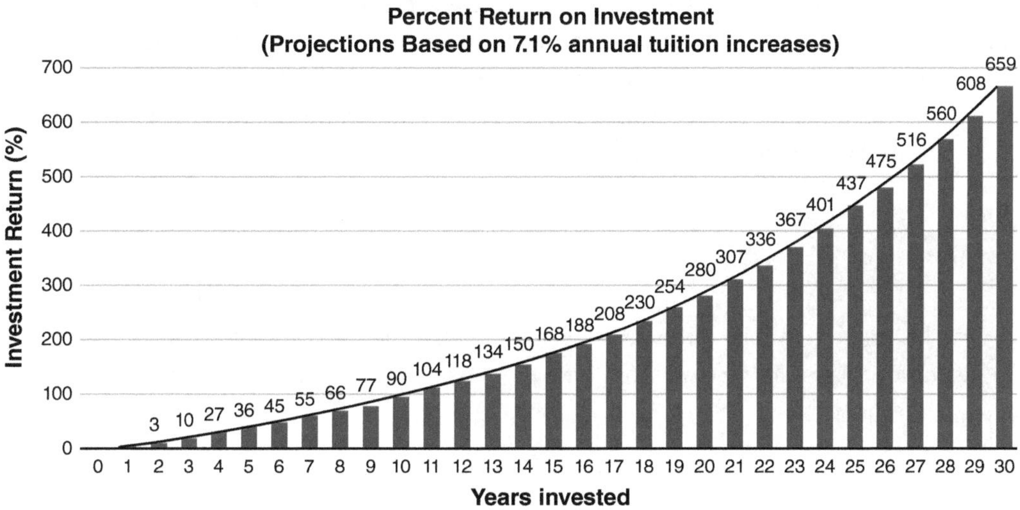

Planning Pointer

Each prepaid plan has its own participation requirements, enrollment period, contribution amounts, tuition-package options, and may differ on whether the tuition plan is guaranteed. Thus, it is imperative that the advisor discuss these variables with the client when deciding if the prepaid plan is the best education planning option and how to coordinate that plan with other savings options.

D. Which Is Better? State Prepaid Plans or the Institutional Prepaid Plan?

State prepaid plans differ from the *institutional plan* in the following respects. The institutional plan covers private colleges—and is portable among approximately 300 schools. Most state prepaid plans are not portable—although the Florida and Washington plans are the exception. The institutional plan is guaranteed by the institution, whereas some state prepaids are not guaranteed, even by the state. Again, Florida and Washington are the exception.

Although most state prepaid tuition plans limit the amount of tuition to be paid to the average cost of the schools in the state at the time the plan is set up, the institutional prepaid plans allow the payment of the entire cost of tuition. Some state prepaid plans charge a premium for tuition costs, whereas the institutional plans offer a discount from current tuition costs. An education institution seeking to offer a prepaid plan must jump through a few more hoops than the institutional plan, as Section 529 imposes two additional requirements: (1) the education institution must ensure that monies received are placed in a qualified trust and (2) it must receive a ruling or determination from the Internal Revenue Service that the program meets the requirements for a qualified tuition program.[42]

Planning Pointer

The bottom line: state prepaid plans are slowly being dismantled, whereas the institution plans are growing in the number of member schools and their popularity with the public.

E. Conclusion

The taxpayer may want to consider a state prepaid plan if there is the likelihood that at least one beneficiary in the taxpayer's family will attend an in-state school, the costs of state tuition are likely to outpace the performance in the market, and if the state offers a viable plan. The residents of Florida and Washington state have good portable prepaid plans from which to choose. Unfortunately, most taxpayers do not have this choice.

42. I.R.C. § 529(b).

Chapter 16

The Prepaid Institutional Plan

The *Private College 529 Plan* (formerly known as the Independent 529 Plan) began in 2003. This prepaid *institutional plan* was intended to eliminate some of the disadvantages of the state-run prepaid plans. It is more flexible than the state prepaid plans because it provides the student with more college options. In addition, it features national portability among its member schools. It also does not have the same liquidity issues, because many private colleges have large *endowments* and can easily bear the risk of a downturn in the market. Like the state prepaid plans, the institutional plan locks in future tuition costs at today's prices. In addition, the plan benefits can be transferred to another beneficiary or refunded if the student does not use them. However, the institutional plan offers the additional benefit of an up-front discount, which is often not provided by the state prepaid plans. (*See* **Chart 16-1** for a comparison.)

A. Features of the Institutional Plans

The *institutional plan* is called the *Private College 529 Plan* and is sponsored by a group of approximately 300 private colleges and universities.[1] These institutions, collectively called the Tuition Plan Consortium, LLC, offer prepaid tuition plans that can be used by any member or any new member that joins in the future. Included in this group are traditional liberal arts colleges, religious schools, technical training schools, historically black, and all-women's colleges. Such prestigious universities as Cornell, Princeton, Stanford, University of Chicago, and MIT, as well as many prestigious colleges, such as Amherst, Middlebury, and Pomona, are included in the list. (*See* **Chart 16-2** for a list of the member schools for 2020-2021.)

1. *How It Works*, Private College 529 Plan, https://privatecollege529.com/learn-more/plan-details/how-it-works/ (last visited May 14, 2021).

CHART 16-1 Prepaid Comparison Chart

	State Prepaid Plan	Institutional Plan
Federal Requirements	The same as Section 529 savings.	The same and: 1) must put funds in trust, and 2) must receive a ruling that program is qualified.
Tax Benefits	The same as Section 529 savings.	The same.
Liquidity Issues	A few states do not provide guarantees.	Institution bears the risk.
Covered Expenses	May limit amount of tuition to average cost. Also covers mandatory fees. Generally, no benefits for room, board, books, or supplies.	No limit on tuition. Also covers mandatory fees. No benefits for room, board, books, or supplies.
Discounts	Some states charge a premium.	All at current cost or discount.
Portability	None.	Portable among the 300 members.
Education	Undergraduate mostly, some graduate.	Undergraduate only.
Perpetual Existence	No, usually 18 years.	No, 30 years.
Financial Aid	The same as Section 529 plans.	The same.
Who can purchase	Individual, estates, corporations, partnerships, and other entities.	The same.
Refunds	Sometimes only original contribution to the plan.	Original contribution plus or minus 2%.

The *Private College 529 Plan* is administered by TIAA-CREF, which provides administrative and marketing support to the program. The plan has been approved by the Securities and Exchange Commission (SEC).[2] Under the plan, the purchaser selects up to five "sample" colleges. This designation is just a benchmark illustration of how the investment locks in tuition costs. Each quarter the purchaser receives a statement displaying the value of the account in terms of accumulated tuition benefits. The selection can be changed at any time and the purchaser can view the tuition value of any participating institution. The purchaser buys a percentage of future tuition at any one of the participating schools, but that percentage will vary for each school, depending on its current tuition rate and "certificate discount" rate.

2. *See* I.R.S. Priv. Ltr. Rul. 13024 (Dec. 17, 2002).

CHART 16-2 Participating Private Colleges (2020–2021)

Alabama

Birmingham-Southern College

Faulkner Univ.

Samford Univ.

Spring Hill College

Univ. of Mobile

Arkansas

Hendrix College

John Brown Univ.

Lyon College

California

California Institute of Technology

California Lutheran Univ.

Chapman Univ.

Claremont McKenna College

Harvey Mudd College

Mills College

Mount St. Mary's Univ.

Occidental College

Pepperdine Univ.

Pitzer College

Point Loma Nazarene Univ.

Pomona College

Saint Mary's College of California

Scripps

Stanford Univ.

Univ. of LaVerne

Univ. of Redlands

Univ. of San Diego

Univ. of S. California

Univ. of the Pacific

Westmont College

Whittier College

Colorado

Colorado College

Regis Univ.

Connecticut

Fairfield Univ.

Trinity College

Wesleyan Univ.

District of Columbia

American Univ.

Catholic Univ. of America

George Washington Univ.

Georgetown Univ.

Florida

Ave Maria Univ.

Eckard College

Jacksonville Univ.

Rollins College

Saint Leo Univ.

Stetson University

Univ. of Miami

Georgia

Agnes Scott College

Berry College

Clark Atlanta Univ.

Covenant College

Emory Univ.

LaGrange College

Mercer Univ.

Oglethorpe Univ.

Spelman College

Wesleyan College

Idaho

College of Idaho

Northwest Nazarene Univ.

Illinois

Augustana College

Bradley Univ.

Elmhurst College

Illinois Institute of Technology

Illinois Wesleyan University

Knox College

Lake Forest College

Monmouth College

North Central College

Olivet Nazarene Univ.

St. Xavier Univ.

Univ. of Chicago

Indiana

Butler Univ.

DePauw Univ.

Earlham College

Franklin College

Holy Cross College

Rose-Hulman Institute of Technology

Saint Joseph's College

Saint Mary's College

Univ. of Evansville

Univ. of Notre Dame

Valparaiso Univ.

Wabash College

(continued)

Iowa
Buena Vista Univ.
Central College
Clarke College
Coe College
Cornell College
Dordt College
Graceland Univ. Grinnell College
Loras College
Luther College
Northwestern College
Simpson College
Wartburg College

Kentucky
Centre College
Transylvania Univ.

Louisiana
Centenary College of Louisiana
Dillard Univ.
Tulane Univ.

Maryland
Goucher College
John Hopkins Univ.
Loyola College in Maryland
McDaniel College
Mount Saint Mary's Univ.
Notre Dame of Maryland

Massachusetts
Amherst College
Berklee College of Music
Boston Univ.
Brandeis Univ.
Clark Univ.
Gordon College
Hampshire College
MIT
Mt. Holyoke
Mount Holyoke College
Smith College
Springfield College
Wellesley College
Wheaton College

Michigan
Albion College
Hope College
Kalamazoo College

Minnesota
Augsburg College
Carleton College
College of St. Benedict
Concordia College
Gustavus Adolphus College
Hamline Univ.
Macalester College
Saint John's Univ.
St. Olaf College
Univ. of St. Thomas

Missouri
Culver-Stockton College
Drury Univ.
Hannibal-LaGrange College
Maryville Univ. of Saint Louis
Rockhurst Univ.
Saint Louis Univ. Stephens College
Washington Univ. in St. Louis
Webster Univ.
Westminster College

Nebraska
Concordia College
Creighton Univ.
Doane College

New Hampshire
Franklin Pierce Univ.

New Jersey
Centenary Univ.
Drew Univ.
Princeton Univ.
Rider Univ.
Stevens Institute of Technology

New York
Bard College
Canisius College
Daemen College
Elmira College
Hartwick College
Hobart & William Smith Colleges
Ithaca College
Marist College
Medaille College
Nazareth College
Niagara Univ.
Pace Univ.
Rensselaer Polytechnic Institute
Roberts Wesleyan College

Rochester Institute of Technology

Sarah Lawrence College

Skidmore College

Syracuse Univ.

Univ. of Rochester

Vassar College

Wagner College

Wells College

North Carolina

Catawba College

Duke Univ.

Greensboro College

Guilford College

Lenoir Rhyne College

Methodist College

Salem College

Wake Forest Univ.

Ohio

Ashland College

Baldwin-Wallace College

Capital Univ.

Case Western Reserve Univ.

College of Wooster

Denison Univ.

Hiram College

John Carroll Univ.

Kenyon College

Mount Vernon Nazarene Univ.

Muskingum College

Oberlin College

Ohio Wesleyan Univ.

Tiffin Univ.

Univ. of Dayton

Wittenberg Univ.

Xavier Univ.

Oklahoma

Oklahoma Christian Univ.

Southern Nazarene Univ.

Univ. of Tulsa

Oregon

Concordia Univ.

George Fox Univ.

Lewis & Clark College

Linfield College

Pacific Univ.

Reed College

Willamette Univ.

Pennsylvania

Albright College

Allegheny College

Alvernia College

Arcadia Univ.

Bucknell Univ.

Carnegie Mellon Univ.

Chatham College

Dickinson College

Drexel Univ.

Franklin & Marshall College

Gettysburg College

Grove City College

Immaculata Univ.

Juniata College

Keystone College

La Salle Univ.

Marywood Univ.

Moravian College

Muhlenberg College

Saint Francis Univ.

Susquehanna Univ.

Thiel College

Ursinus College

Washington & Jefferson College

Waynesburg Univ.

Westminster College

York College of Pennsylvania

Rhode Island

Roger Williams Univ.

South Carolina

Charleston Southern Univ.

Claflin Univ.

Columbia College

Converse College

Furman Univ.

Presbyterian College

Wofford College

South Dakota

Augustana College

Tennessee

Belmont Univ.

Carson-Newman College

Lambuth Univ.

Rhodes College

Sewanee: The Univ. Of the South

Trevecca Nazarene Univ.

Univ. of the South

Vanderbilt Univ.

(continued)

Texas	Vermont	Whitworth Univ.
Abilene Christian Univ.	Middlebury College	**West Virginia**
Austin College	Norwich Univ.	West Virginia
Baylor Univ.	Saint Michael's College	Wesleyan College
Concordia Univ. Texas	**Virginia**	Wheeling Univ.
Dallas Baptist Univ.	Bridgewater College	**Wisconsin**
Hardin-Simmons Univ.	Eastern Mennonite Univ.	Beloit College
Lubbock Christian Univ.	Hampden-Sydney College	Concordia Univ.
Rice Univ.	Hollins Univ.	Lakeland College
St. Edward's Univ.	Mary Baldwin College	Lawrence Univ.
St. Mary's Univ.	Randolph College	Ripon College
Schreiner Univ.	Shenandoah Univ.	
Southern Methodist Univ.	Sweet Briar College	
Southwestern Univ.	Univ. of Richmond	
Texas Christian Univ.	Virginia Wesleyan College	
Trinity Univ.	**Washington**	
Univ. of Dallas	Pacific Lutheran Univ.	
Univ. of Mary Hardin-Baylor	Seattle Pacific Univ.	

The *Private College 529 Plan* allows prepayment of the full cost of several years of college or allows the gradual payment of a set amount each month. As little as $25 a month is allowed as long as a minimum of $500 is accumulated within two years. The investment must stay in the plan for at least three years. The account maximum is set every year, equivalent to five years of tuition at the most expensive school in the plan. (For 2021, that amount is $305,500.) Thus, the contributions are adequate to cover all colleges or university in the plan. Currently, the fund can only be used for undergraduate education and only for mandatory fees and tuition—not books and supplies or room and board.

EXAMPLE 16-1: Five years ago, John contributed $40,000 into the *Private College 529 Plan*, the equivalent of the cost of tuition at University A at the time. This amount represents the Tuition Certificate for one year's tuition at University A. Due to inflation and other cost increases, University A is now charging $61,257 tuition. By redeeming the Tuition Certificates to cover University A's tuition this year, John would have a tax free-free savings of $21,257. *See* **Chart 16-3.**

CHART 16-3 Example of Savings Accrued over Five Years

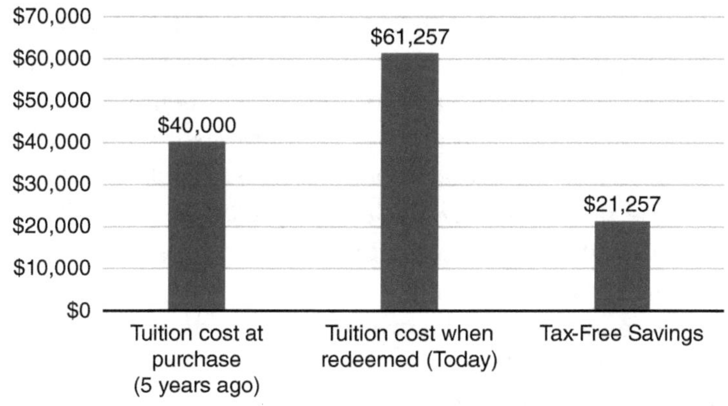

1. Residency and Transferability

One of the advantages of the institutional plan over the state prepaid plan is that there are no residency requirements and there is free transferability among member schools. As new schools join, the plan will retroactively honor the current certificate holders. If a school should withdraw from the plan, it will still honor all who became certificate holders during and prior to the time of its participation. If, however, the beneficiary does not attend any of the member schools, the institutional plan works like some prepaid plans. The beneficiary can be changed, or a refund can be obtained. The institutional plan can be rolled over at any time tax-free to a state-sponsored 529 plan. If the beneficiary does not attend college, the institutional account can be left open for up to 30 years.

Whenever a refund is sought the issue is how much, if any, of the investment is lost. Under the institutional plan, the refund is adjusted for fund performance, subject to a maximum return of 2 percent per year and a maximum loss of 2 percent per year. This may produce a better result than the refund under some prepaid state plans, where only the original contribution is returned. It may also be a better result than a 529 savings pan, if the investment loss in that account is greater than 2 percent.

EXAMPLE 16-2: Mary and John, wife and husband, purchase from the American University four years of tuition and fees for their daughter, Ann, who will graduate from high school in five years (cost $26,782/year × 4 = $107,128). In the fifth year, Ann decides to attend Harvard, a school not part of the institutional plan. The *most* Mary and John will receive as a refund will be their original contribution of $107,128 plus 2 percent return each year ($2,142.56 × 4 years or $8,570.24) (assuming no compounding of interest). However, Mary and John can leave the institutional account open to be used for other children or family members—as long as the account is not left open more than 30 years.

2. Tax Considerations

The federal tax considerations for the institutional plan are similar to state prepaid and Section 529 savings plans. The account owner is not subject to federal income tax if a tuition certificate is used to pay for tuition at a member institution. Refunds to pay for qualified higher education expenses are also free from federal income tax. Contributions qualify for the *per-donee exclusion* and, in 2021, up to $75,000 ($15,000 × 5) can be prorated over a five-year period ($150,000 if the donors are married and split the gift). State tax deductions or credits may also be allowed on contributions to the institutional plan.

The Internal Revenue Service has ruled that the redemption of tuition certificates will not constitute unrelated business income to member schools.[3] Because the school's exempt purpose is education in nature, amounts invested, earned, and then paid for education expenses are derived from that exempt purpose and are related—not unrelated business income.

3. Return on Investment and Costs

One of the benefits of the institutional plan over the savings plan is that there are no initial enrollment fees, annual fees, broker fees, or exit fees. All costs of administering and managing the assets are paid for by an annual management fee paid by the member schools. Colleges are willing to bear this expense because they can pool resources, anticipate investment gains, and spread risk. With annual tuition increases of 6 percent, a 529 savings plan would have to generate 7 percent investment return, assuming the total 529 savings plan fees equal 1 percent, to just equal the institutional prepaid plan.

In addition, the *Private College 529 Plan's* discounts make it even more valuable. The discount rates vary among schools and can be changed annually, effective July 1 of any year. Any change will only apply to new certificates.

4. Other Nontax Considerations

Although the institutional plan is not perpetual, it can last 30 years, which is much longer than most state prepaid plans. Like state prepaid plans, institutional plans no longer have an adverse impact on financial aid eligibility.[4] With the passage of the *Deficit Reduction Omnibus Reconciliation Act of 2005*, financial aid considerations are favorable for all 529 plans. Like state prepaids, institutional plans only cover tuition and mandatory fees, not room and board. Like 529 savings plans, they can be purchased by individuals, trusts, estates, corporations, partnerships, or other entities.

---

3. *Id.*
4. *See* **Chapter Nineteen: Coordinating Section 529 Plans with Financial Aid**.

B. Conclusion

The taxpayer may want to consider the prepaid institutional plan if (1) there is the likelihood that at least one beneficiary in the taxpayer's family will attend one of the 300 private institutions covered in the plan, and (2) the costs of private college tuition are likely to outpace the performance in the market. The *Private College 529 Plan* offers greater solvency and security than the state prepaid plans, as well as the advantage of no residency requirements, significant discounted tuition, and no investment fees. Like the state prepaid plan, these are an excellent way to keep up with increasing tuition costs.

Institutional plans only cover tuition and mandatory fees—not room and board, books, and supplies—thus requiring coordination with either a 529 savings plan or other tax or savings techniques. When tuition increases outpace the average rate of return on investment, the prepaid plans provide a better investment than the Section 529 savings plans. Savings plans, of course, offer the most flexibility in terms of choice of school—private or public—and in their broad coverage of graduate and professional school as well as room and board. *See* **Chart 16-4** for a comparison of the various features of these plans.

CHART 16-4 Comparison Chart

	State Prepaid	Institutional	Savings
Federal Requirements	The same	The same	The same
Tax Benefits	The same	The same	The same
Choice of Schools	State	Private	Any school
Specified Enrollment Period	Yes	Yes	No
Residency Requirements (either account owner or beneficiary)	Yes for most plans	No	No, except for a few states
Limited Duration	Yes, often 10 years after beneficiary commences college	30 years	No, can be perpetual
Financial Aid	Same as savings	Same as savings	Depends on who owns. If student owns, not considered asset under federal formula
Flexibility of Use	Undergraduate	Undergraduate only	Undergraduate and graduate

(continued)

	State Prepaid	Institutional	Savings
Types of Expenses Covered	Tuition and mandatory fees	Same as state prepaid	Tuition (up to $ 10,000 for K–12), Fees, Books, Supplies, Required Equipment, Internet, Room, Board, Principal and Interest on $ 10,000 debt for beneficiary and siblings, and Special Needs
Portability	Sometimes, but contract benefits must be valued	Yes, to other member schools	Yes
Payments Required Directly to Institution	Yes	Yes	No
Discounts	Some states charge premiums	At current cost or discount	N/A
Who Can Purchase	Individuals, trusts, estates, corporations, and other entities	The same	The same
Fees	Built in	None	Can be significant
Minimum Purchase	Sometimes one semester	One year	No
Liquidity Issues	Yes	No	No
Full Faith & Credit Safety Net	Sometimes	No, but schools guarantee solvency	No, but not relevant
Investment Risk	Risk on state	Risk on institution	Subject to market fluctuations

PART IV

COORDINATING SECTION 529 PLANS WITH OTHER EDUCATION PLANNING TECHNIQUES

For Section 529 plans to have the most beneficial impact, they must be coordinated with other savings techniques and tax benefits, as well as financial aid. We have already seen that 529s should be coordinated with Coverdell Education Savings Accounts when the client seeks to cover K–12 educational expenses.[1] Similarly, we have seen that when a client does not have cash to invest in the 529 plan, the client may want to choose custodianship accounts, trusts, or business entities to accomplish their education planning goals.[2] We have also highlighted one of the more important nontax aspects of Section 529 plans—financial aid compatibility.[3] All of these issues will be discussed more fully in **Part IV** of this book.

Part IV will explain in greater detail the coordination of the 529 with other savings planning devices, *pay-as-you-go tax benefits*, and financial aid. **Chapter Seventeen: Coordinating Section 529 Plans with Other Savings Techniques** discusses the interrelationship of the 529 plan with the various savings techniques and how these techniques, such as the Coverdell, custodianship accounts, and savings bonds, can be rolled over into the section 529 plan without adverse tax consequences. **Chapter Eighteen: Coordinating Section 529 Plans with Tax Benefits** addresses the complex issue of qualifying for tax credits or other tax benefits while owning a 529 plan. **Chapter Nineteen: Coordinating Section 529 Plans with Financial Aid** discusses the methodology for determining eligibility for financial aid and how the ownership of the 529s and other savings techniques will impact these calculations.

---

1. *See* **Chapter Four: The Best Ways to Save**, B
2. *See* **Chapter Four: The Best Ways to Save**, E.
3. *See* **Chapter Twelve: Nontax Aspects of Section 529 Savings Plans**, D.

Just think, Dear, after we pay off the PLUS loans, we both can go on a vacation.

Chapter 17

Coordinating Section 529 Plans with Other Savings Techniques

Section 529s may not be the best savings techniques in a number of circumstances. First, 529 plans require cash contributions, so taxpayers with property, or who are cash poor, might want to use other savings techniques, such as custodianship accounts or trusts. Second, the definition of "family," while quite broad under the 529 plan, may not cover expenses of cohabiting partners, friends, or distant relatives. Thus, other savings techniques will be better for coverage of nonfamily members. Third, 529 plans are limited to certain qualifying educational expenses. Thus, when the student must have funds to finance the purchase of clothes, travel, car, entertainment expenses, or other nonqualified expenses, 529 plans may need to be supplemented with other savings techniques.

When the taxpayer uses the 529 plan with another savings technique, complex coordination rules may apply. The definition of what expenditures will qualify for the particular savings technique varies considerably, from the payment of college tuition only to the expansive Section 529 QHEE definition. For example, if the taxpayer is sending their child to an expensive boarding school or their child is enrolled in both private high school and college, then *double counting* of similar expenditures from the Coverdell and the 529 must be avoided.

Because the 529 savings plan has more tax and nontax advantages then most other savings techniques, rolling those accounts over, or converting those assets, to a 529 savings plan might make education planning sense. Assets in custodianship, accounts Coverdell accounts, and in savings bonds can be easily converted into a Section 529 plan. All of these conversions can occur with minimal tax consequences.

A. The Cash Contribution Restriction

Section 529 requires the contribution of cash. Some taxpayers might only have property, or limited cash, and thus the Section 529 plan will not be the proper savings vehicle for them—at least initially. Later, they may convert these noncash assets into a 529 plan. The savings mechanisms that allow for noncash contributions include: (1) the custodianship account, (2) the *trust*, and (3) the *family limited partnership* or *limited liability company*.

1. The Custodianship Account

Custodianship accounts were initially established under the *Uniform Gifts to Minors Act* (1956, revised, 1966) (UGMA).[1] Now, 48 states and the District of Columbia have adopted the *Uniform Transfers to Minors Act* (1983) (UTMA).[2] Only Vermont and South Carolina are still UGMA states.

In contrast to Section 529 plans, UTMA transfers to custodian accounts are not restricted to cash contributions. Under the UTMA, *any* type of property can be transferred: interests in real property, tangible property, business interests, annuity contracts, irrevocable powers of appointment, and rights under contracts.[3] Thus, under the UTMA, a minor could conceivably be a shareholder in a C corporation, a member of a limited liability corporation, or a member of a limited partnership[4]—although the account custodian controls the benefits of the membership until the minor reaches the age of majority. For example, the account custodian serves as the minor's proxy with respect to voting the minor's shares in a C corporation and would have a fiduciary duty to vote the minor's shares for the minor's benefit. Thus, UTMA accounts are appealing as any type of property may be contributed, and the account custodian still maintains some control over the benefits of a minor's membership.

While more limited in scope, UGMA accounts can also contain contributions other than cash. The 1966 revision of the UGMA, however, only broadened the Act's scope to include contributions in the form of securities, bank deposits, and insurance. Because UGMA/UTMA accounts are not limited to cash contributions, the donor has more options for funding a custodianship account than are allowed for Section 529 plans. This greater flexibility, however, comes at the cost of the donor's control over the account assets and also is accompanied by potential unfavorable tax consequences.

Perhaps the biggest drawback of custodianship accounts is that the account can terminate before the child attains his/her education goals. Depending on state

1. Uniform Gifts to Minors Act, 8A U.L.A. 375 (1956, rev. 1966) [hereinafter UGMA]. (South Carolina and Vermont are the only states that follow UGMA, and Vermont currently has a bill pending to change to UTMA.)

2. Uniform Transfers to Minors Act, 8B U.L.A. 497 (1983, amended 1986) [hereinafter UTMA].

3. UTMA § 1(6).

4. Some states limit the type of property in which a custodian can invest.

law,[5] the account must be distributed to the beneficiary between the ages of 18 and 25—regardless of whether the beneficiary is a spendthrift, uses illegal substances, or otherwise cannot manage the property. In reality, therefore, the custodian has less control over UGMA or UTMA funds than an account owner has over a Section 529 plan. In addition to the requirement of distribution at the age of majority, on "petition of an interested party[6] or by the minor (if the minor has attained the age of 14 years) the court may order the custodian to deliver or pay to the minor or expend for the minor's benefit so much of the custodial property as the court considers advisable for the use or benefit of the minor."[7]

Like Section 529 plans, UTMA/UGMA accounts can be established by anyone. In other words, the donor's annual income does not restrict his/her ability to establish a UTMA/UGMA account. Furthermore, annual contributions to UTMA/UGMA accounts are not limited to set dollar amounts. UTMA accounts can be set up through a trust instrument or guardianship. Therefore, contribution or creation of the account is not restricted to gifts made during the donor's lifetime; the accounts can be set up or additional contributions made after the donor's death. This can be accomplished, for example, through a life insurance designation or under a will or trust provision. The personal representative, trustee or conservator may decide that a transfer to a minor through a custodianship is not inconsistent with the will or trust that directs the transfer of property to the minor, and may create the custodianship,[8] even if the transferor did not authorize the creation of such an account. Lastly, distributions from such an account can be used for any educational expenditures.[9]

Negative income tax results may arise if the beneficiary is a full-time dependent student and under the age of 24, in which case, the *kiddie tax* might apply.[10] In this case, the child will be taxed on the income earned from the custodianship account assets at the high trust and estate tax rates. However, if the income from the account is used to support the minor then the parent custodian will be subject to income tax under the grantor tax rules.[11] But the donor could also be liable for

---

5. UTMA § 20(1) requires that the assets be distributed when the beneficiary reaches the age of 21. However, state laws vary. Note also that Illinois allows a custodian to transfer the assets into a § 2503(c) trust. *See* 760 Ill. Comp. Stat. 20/15(a-5).

6. "Interested party" includes the transferor, a parent, a conservator, a guardian, a public agency, or a creditor. UTMA § 14 cmt.

7. UTMA § 14(b).

8. Even when the will or trust does not authorize the personal representative or trustee to make such a transfer, the UTMA allows such a transfer if (1) the personal representative or trustee considers the transfer to be in the best interests of the minor, (2) the transfer is not prohibited or inconsistent with the provisions of the will or trust, and (3) the transfer is authorized by the court if it exceeds $10,000. UTMA § 6.

9. The custodianship account is likely to count against the child for financial aid purposes. *See* **Chapter Nineteen: Coordinating Section 529 Plans with Financial Aid**.

10. *See* **Chapter Eight: Federal Income Tax Planning with Section 529 Savings Plans**.

11. I.R.C. § 677. *See also* Rev. Rul. 56-484, 1966-2 C.B. 23; Rev. Rul. 59-357, 1959-2 C.B. 212; Rev. Rul. 70-348, 1970-2 C.B. 193.

those taxes if they do not relinquish control, use the assets, or do not make a completed gift transaction.

The gift and *generation-skipping* transfer (GST) taxes are straightforward for these accounts, whereas the estate tax consequences are more complicated. Generally, the transfer to the custodianship account will qualify for the *per-donee annual gift tax exclusion* and thus not be subject to a GST tax. The estate tax consequences will depend on who is the custodian, how the property is used, and whether the minor dies during the custodianship. Generally, if the beneficiary dies before the age of majority, the account assets will be includable in his/her estate. If, on the other hand, the donor dies before the beneficiary attains the age of majority and the donor is the custodian of the account, the property in the account will be includable in the donor's gross estate.[12] If the spouse of the donor is the custodian, some courts have used the reciprocal trust doctrine to reconstrue the transaction and include the UGMA/UTMA assets in the donor's estate.[13] Generally, if the custodian is not the grantor, the asset will not be part of the grantor's or custodian's gross estate so long as the custodian has not used the custodial account assets for the minor's support.

2. The Trust

Trusts, like custodianship accounts, are not subject to any cash contribution limitations. In addition, they have no restrictions on distributions, unless, of course, the trust specifies such restrictions. Trusts offer the client a high degree of control. They do not have the disadvantage of UGMA/UTMAs that distribution must occur when the minor attains a certain age. Trusts can delay distributions indefinitely if desired.

Trusts are always important upon the death of the grantor if education goals have yet to be met. Trusts are also an excellent inter vivos income and asset-splitting technique for wealthy taxpayers. In any case, the terms of the trust can be used to provide education incentives. The disadvantages of trusts are that they are costly to set up and administer and can have onerous income tax consequences. For a detailed discussion of the *Section 2503(c) trust*, the *Section 2503(b) trust*, the *Crummey* trust, and the *incentive trust*, see **Chapter Seventeen: Comparing 529s with Trusts** in Nancy E. Shurtz's *Education Planning: Taxes Trusts, and Techniques* (ABA 2009). *See* **Chart 17-1** that compares three of those trusts.

12. Also note that the account may be included in the donor's estate under I.R.C. § 2035 even if the donor/custodian resigns if the donor/custodian dies within three years of resignation.
13. Exch. Bank & Trust Co. of Fla. v. United States, 694 F.2d 1261, 1263 (Fed. Cir. 1982).

CHART 17-1 Comparison of Irrevocable Trusts

	§ 2503(b) Trust	§ 2503(c) Trust	*Crummey* Trust
Required Dispositive Provisions	Yes, for the "benefit" of beneficiary	Yes, for the "benefit" of beneficiary	None, and trustee can consider other resources of beneficiary
Accumulation of Income	No	Yes	Yes
Delayed Distribution of Principal	No	Yes	Yes
Required Termination Date	No	Yes	No
Multiple Beneficiaries	No	No	Yes
Income Tax	Taxed to the beneficiary to the extent of trusts' DNI except if to discharge legal obligation to support a grantor trust	Taxed to the beneficiary to the extent of trusts' DNI except if to discharge legal obligation to support a grantor trust	Could be a grantor trust or taxed to beneficiary if right to withdraw lasts whole year
Gift Tax	Income must be paid to the beneficiary annually	Property and income must be expended for benefit of beneficiary before age 21 and if not so expended must be distributed to beneficiary outright at 21 and if beneficiary dies before distribution the property must be taxed in beneficiary's estate	A lapse of a power is treated as a taxable gift except if one beneficiary trust or no more than $5,000
Estate Tax	If property could be used to satisfy parent's support obligation could be taxed in parent's estate, otherwise depends on interests and powers under §§ 2036, 2038 & 2041	If property could be used to satisfy parent's support obligation could be taxed in parent's estate, otherwise depends on interests and powers under §§ 2036, 2038 & 2041.	Property subject to power of withdrawal or general power if appointment included in power holder's estate; otherwise depends on donor's interests and powers under §§ 2036, 2038 & 2041
GST Tax	If transfer to a "skip person" will qualify for GST annual exclusion	If transfer to a "skip person" will qualify for GST annual exclusion	Does not qualify for GST annual exclusion unless § 2642(c) conditions met

3. The Limited Partnership or Limited Liability Corporation

Using *family limited partnerships* (FLPs) and *limited liability companies* (LLCs), like custodianships and trusts, do not require cash contributions. The contribution to the entity is usually business, rather than personal property—although investment property could be transferred as well. The advantage of these techniques is that the gift of the interest or shares to the student can be discounted so a greater amount can be given within the limited $15,000 per-donee exclusion. With liberal estate tax exemptions, however, this may not be a major consideration.[14]

The typical FLP consists of one or more general partners (usually the parents or grandparents) and one or more limited partners (usually the child or children). The partner manages the assets in the FLP and makes investment choices. Similarly, the LLC can be managed by the parents who can exert substantial control over distributions and investments.

Both of these entities are quite flexible and provide income, estate, and gift tax advantages, as well as nontax advantage like control and asset protection. They can be used for active businesses, for investment property, and as a borrowing tool. They can be amended and adapted to meet the changing needs of the family. *See* **Chart 4-10: Comparing FLP/LLCs with 529 Plans** in **Chapter Four: The Best Ways to Save**.

B. Qualified Family Member

Both a Section 529 plan and a Coverdell can be established for any designated beneficiary—even if that beneficiary is unrelated to the contributor. However, once the individual is named in the document in the account, that beneficiary can only be changed to a family member of that beneficiary. Although quite expansive, the definition does not include significant others, friends, and distant relatives. For these individuals, other savings techniques would have to be utilized to provide for the needed education expenditures. (*See* **Chart 17-2**.)

CHART 17-2 Qualified Beneficiaries upon Rollover to New Beneficiary

- A spouse of the original beneficiary
- A lineal descendent, such as child, grandchild, or great grandchild
- A stepchild, stepmother, or stepfather (but no step grandchildren)
- A brother, sister, stepbrother, or stepsister
- A lineal ancestor, such as father, mother, or grandparent
- A niece or nephew
- A mother or sister of the original beneficiary's mother or father
- A first cousin
- An in-law, either mother, father, sister, brother, son, or daughter
- Husband or wife of anyone on this list

14. **Chart 9-4** in **Chapter Nine: Estate Planning with Section 529 Savings Plans.**

C. Different Qualifying Expenses

Section 529 plans are restricted to qualified education expenses (QHHE), so expenses for basics like clothing, transportation, travel, and entertainment are not covered. However, many of the savings strategies are much more limited in their definition of qualified expenditures than the Section 529 plan. Some only apply for the payment of college tuition. Others include tuition and related academic fees. Others, like the 529 savings and Coverdell, are broader and include room, board, equipment, and books. Some have no limitations and thus can be used for all education-related expenses. Thus, eligible taxpayers need to plan for a combination of these tax benefits to adequately cover *all* education expenses. *See* **Chart 17-3**.

The narrowest definition of qualified education expenses arises for the gift tax exclusion for direct gifts of tuition to the institution (the *Section 2503(e) transfer*), and for most state prepaid plans, and the *Private College 529* plans. These tax provisions cover only *tuition*. Section 2503(e) covers tuition payment to state-approved private or parochial K–12 institutions, as well as to qualified higher education institutions. Most prepaid 529 plans (both state and institutional) only cover tuition, although there are exceptions, like Florida, that cover room and board.[15]

The Traditional and Roth IRAs cover tuition plus required fees, which include any fee required as part of the student's degree program as well as non-academic fees that are required.[16]

The savings bond interest exclusion covers tuition and required fees as long as those fees are academic fees—nonacademic fees are not covered, even if required.[17] Fees associated with sports, games, or hobbies are not academic fees unless they are associated with courses that are part of the individual's degree program. Similarly, expenses unrelated to an individual's academic course of instruction are generally not qualified under any of the preceding savings' provisions. Section 529s and Coverdells have broader definitions but their definitions of qualified expenditures do not exactly overlap. These differences are discussed in the next section.

As discussed earlier, trusts, custodianships, and traditional investments can be used for any expenses. Proceeds from a loan or from an IRA after the taxpayer reaches 59½ can be used for any expense. Gifts from relatives that are not paid directly to the institution can also be used for any expense, as can current earnings and traditional investments. Thus, health insurance, medical care, transportation, clothes, entertainment, and other costs of attending college can be financed through these devices.

---

15. *See* **Chapter Fifteen: The State Prepaid Plan**.

16. Student activity fees if required can be qualified expenses under Treas. Reg. § 1.25 A-2.

17. I.R.C. § 135(c)(2). Prop. Reg. § 1.241-2 seems to suggest that only student activity fees not required to be paid are not classified as academic fees. This seems to contradict Section 25(f)(1)(C), which indicates that only fees required to be paid by all students would be qualified.

CHART 17-3 Qualifying Expenses under Education Savings Techniques[18]

(X—Means Expense Is Covered)

Code Provision	Tuition	Academic Fees	Supplies, and Equipment	Books	Room & Board	Travel and other personal expenses	K–12	Other
Gift Tax Exclusion (§ 2503(e))	X As long as tuition paid directly to the educational institution							
Gifts from Relatives Not Paid Directly to the Educational Institution	X	X	X	X	X	X	X	X
Traditional IRA	X	X						Non-academic fees if required
Roth IRA	X	X						
Savings Bond Interest Exclusion (§ 135)	X	X						Non-academic fees if required
Exclusion for Distributions from a Coverdell (§ 530)	X	X	X	X	X		X	Special needs covered for special beneficiaries
Exclusions for Distributions from Section 529 Prepaid	X	X			Most prepaids do not cover			Special needs covered for special beneficiaries
Exclusions for Distributions from Section 529 Savings Plan	X	X	X	X	X		Up to $10,000 of tuition for K–12	Special needs covered for special beneficiaries. Up to $10,000 of qualified student debt.
Trusts	X	X	X	X	X	X	X	X
Traditional Investments	X	X	X	X	X	X	X	X
Custodianship Accounts	X	X	X	X	X	X	X	X
Loans	X	X	X	X	X	X	X	X
IRA Distribution after 59½	X	X	X	X	X	X	X	X

18. *Preset Law and Analysis Relating to Tax Benefits for Higher Education*, Staff of the Joint Comm. on Taxation (July 21, 2004) (adapted from Table 3, at 46).

Planning Pointer

The taxpayer's ultimate objective is to maximize the coverage of college expenses with tax advantaged savings techniques. Section 529 savings plans provide expansive coverage of college expenses: tuition (including K–12 tuition of up to $10,000), required fees, books, supplies, equipment, room and board, and even payment of $10,000 of qualified student debt. The 529 savings plan can be supplemented with loans or gifts or other savings to cover additional expenses.

D. Coordination of Savings Techniques

Although there is quite a bit of overlap in the definitions of qualified expenses under the various savings techniques, these definitions are not identical. Planning is often needed to fully use all tax benefits. And when different accounts are used for the same expenses, coordination is required to avoid double tax benefits, as these are not permitted.

1. Maximizing Qualifying Expenses

Many of the tax techniques need very little coordination and work well together. For example, the donor can make a *Section 2503(e) transfer* of tuition directly to the educational institution and avoid gift tax on the transfer while at the same time using the 529 plan to pay for this tuition. In addition, use of traditional investments, custodianship accounts, trusts, and IRA distributions after 59½ can all be used for any expense, so the payment of qualified expenditures should be reserved for the tax savings techniques. However, when IRA distributions before age 59½, Roth distributions, or interest on savings bonds are used for tuition and academic fees, then other savings techniques should not be used for those expenses.

Perhaps one of the more difficult savings techniques to coordinate are the Coverdell and the 529 plan. Both of these savings mechanisms cover higher education tuition, required fees, books, supplies, and equipment as well as room and board.[19] They also have the same definition of *special needs* services in the case of certain beneficiaries.[20] The *American Recovery and Reinvestment Act of 2009* expanded the QHEE definition for Section 529 plans to include "computer technology and equipment," including Internet access. The Coverdell covers these when purchased

19. I.R.C. § 529(e)(3)(B)(ii). Section 530 uses the same definition as Section 529. An exception is that the Coverdell defines eligible room and board by reference to the 1998 amendments to 20 U.S.C. 1087 Section 472 of the Higher Education Act, whereas Section 529 uses the 1996 definition of eligible room and board. This difference results in the Section 529 plan having a dollar limitation for purposes of determining whether a student's room and board qualify for QHEE when the student lives off campus, whereas Section 530 does not. For both, the room and board are frozen at historical 2001 levels unless the student lives in university housing, for which the actual cost of housing is allowed.

20. I.R.C. § 529(e)(3)(A).

and used in K–12. *Tax Cuts and Jobs Act of 2017* expanded the definition of QHEE for 529s to include up to $10,000 of K–12 tuition. Coverdells can cover more than $10,000 of K–12 tuition and also cover other *"qualified elementary and secondary school expenses"* (QESSE) not covered by Section 529. QESSE include: (1) expenses for tuition, fees, academic tutoring, books, supplies, and equipment for K–12 education—similar to those for higher education as provided in Section 529(e)(3);[21] (2) expenses for room and board, uniforms, transportation, and supplementary items and services, such as extended day programs, as required or provided by the K–12 school;[22] and (3) expenses for the purchase of any computer technology or equipment or Internet access or related services.[23] Transportation expenses required by the school, such as the cost of a mandatory school bus, could be covered. Fees for after-school or extended-day programs are also allowed if payment must be made to the school.

Computer technology and equipment is defined in Section 170(e)(6)(F)(i) as computer software (as defined by Section 197(e)(3)(B)), computer or peripheral equipment (as defined by Section 168(i)(2)(B)), and fiber optic cable related to computer use. The computer technology, equipment, or services must be used by the beneficiary and the beneficiary's family during any of the years the beneficiary is in elementary or secondary school. Expenses will not be qualified if they are for computer software designed for sports, games, or hobbies, unless predominately educational in nature.[24] Because of these differences in qualifying expenditures, if the taxpayer has both accounts, they will need to use the appropriate account for the qualified expenditure to assure tax-free treatment of the distribution.

EXAMPLE 17-1: Alice has decided to send her son Ben to private high school. Ben's expenses include tuition, mandatory fees, books, supplies, uniforms, a computer, special tutoring for an Advanced Placement course, and costs of a mandatory school bus. All of these expenses are qualified under the Coverdell provisions. In addition, if Ben were sent off to boarding school, all room and board expenses would also be covered under the Coverdell plan. In comparison, under the 529 plan, only $10,000 of Ben's private high school tuition would be covered.

21. *Id.* § 530(b)(4)(A)(i).
22. *Id.* § 530(b)(4)(A)(ii).
23. *Id.* § 530(b)(4)(A)(iii).
24. *Id.*

Planning Pointer

One of the advantages of the Coverdell over the 529 plan is the ability to use the account funds to pay for *unlimited* private or parochial high school expenses, including room and board. Coverdell funds can also be used for SAT/ACT review courses and tutoring—expenses that could help the student get into college. Before college begins, the Coverdell funds can be used to purchase a computer and can be used for uniforms and transportation associated with K–12 education.

2. Avoiding Double Counting

Obviously, if the taxpayer has enough qualified higher education expenses to cover all of these tax benefits, the taxpayer will not be taxed.

EXAMPLE 17-2: Ben has $4,000 of college tuition. He receives a $2,000 distribution from a Coverdell and a $2,000 distribution from a Section 529 plan to pay for this tuition. The distribution exactly covers the qualified higher education expenses, so no tax applies on the distributions.

However, when the taxpayer has both a Coverdell and a 529 savings plan, a somewhat complicated allocation problem may arise when Section 529 savings plans and the Coverdell cover the same expenses.[25] As we just mentioned, a similarity in definitions could result in a duplication and thus a double tax benefit. When distributions from the Section 529 plans and Coverdell exceed qualified expenditures, any excess will be taxed at ordinary rates to the beneficiary and be subject to the *ten percent penalty* or additional tax. In these circumstances a pro rata allocation of these excess expenditures must be made. Then, the earnings ratio for each of these two accounts is applied to that excess.

25. The student loan interest provision also allows for room and board, but since this is usually a deduction after college, the same coordination issue may not arise.

EXAMPLE 17-3: Ben has $12,000 of tuition expenses (either from college or K–12). Assume Ben receives a distribution from a Coverdell in the amount of $10,000 and from a Section 529 Savings plan in the amount of $15,000.

Total QHEE	$12,000
529 Distribution	$15,000
Coverdell Distribution	$10,000
Total Distributions	$25,000

Allocated to Section 529: Qualified = $7,200; Nonqualified = $7,800

Nonqualified distribution multiplied by earnings ratio 30% = $2,340

Allocated to Coverdell: Qualified = $4,800; Nonqualified = $5,200

Nonqualified distribution multiplied by earnings ratio 50% = $2,600

Total income subject to tax = $4,940

Plus additional tax of 10% on nonqualified distributions = $494

The taxpayer, alternatively, should be able to allocate all of the distribution from either the Coverdell or the 529 plan, whichever could cover the QHEE, thus reducing overall taxes. This same process applies when other savings techniques are used for the same expenses. A decision can be made as to which savings technique should bear the tax—and that may depend on the earnings ratio of that account.

EXAMPLE 17-4: Same as **Example 17-3** but taxpayer allocates all of the QHHE to the Coverdell distribution of $10,000. None of the earnings from the Coverdell (here 50%) will be triggered. A portion ($2,000) of the QHHE could be allocated to the 529 plan, but the earning (here 30%) on the nonqualified $13,000 distribution ($3,900) will be taxed—as it is not used for (QHHE). In addition, a penalty tax on these earnings ($390 × 10%) will be imposed.

The taxpayer must always avoid using more than one tax-advantaged savings technique for the *same* qualifying education expense. When this occurs, then the distribution or payment will no longer receive a tax benefit. In addition, the ten percent *penalty tax* may be imposed.

E. Conversions into Section 529 Savings Plans

Most of the savings techniques, such as custodianship accounts, Coverdell accounts, or savings bonds can be converted into a Section 529 plan. All of these conversions can occur with minimal tax consequences. Because the 529 plan has more tax and nontax advantages than these other savings techniques, such a rollover might make education planning sense.

1. Custodianship Accounts

Some states and custodianship law might allow custodianship accounts under Uniform Gifts to Minors Act (UGMA)/Uniform Transfers to Minors Act (UTMA) or trusts to be transferred to a Section 529 plan.[26] As is the case with other noncash assets, the UGMA/UTMA or trust assets are deemed sold, as Section 529 Plans can only take cash contributions. The taxes due on this deemed sale will be paid by the beneficiary (minor) because when the assets were held in the UGMA/UTMA account or trust, they were legally owned by the minor, despite the fact that a custodian or trustee had control of the account or trust until the minor reached the age of majority. As in the case of noncash assets, any income or capital gain will be taxed to the full-time dependent student under age 24 at the trust and estate tax rates—and any loss could be limited by the loss limitation rules. After such a conversion, any earnings on the Section 529 fund are not taxed when used for "qualified education expenditures."

If the UGMA/UTMA is rolled into a Section 529 plan, the beneficiary of the Section 529 plan must remain the beneficiary of the custodianship account and cannot be changed without the beneficiary's consent. The rationale for the control passing to the beneficiary in these instances is that the UGMA/UTMA were owned by the beneficiary prior to the transfer into the Section 529 plan. When such conversions occur, the financial aid implications can be complex. At the time the UGMA/UTMA account assets are sold for cash and placed in the 529 account, any income or gain will be assessed as the student's income under both the federal and institutional methodology.[27] After such a conversion, the UGMA/UTMA/529 plan is owned by the student, but under the changes made by the *Deficit Reduction Omnibus Reconciliation Act (DRORA) of 2005*, should be assessed as the parent's assets under the federal formula. Under the institutional formula, these assets are still considered the student's and assessed at 25 percent.

---

26. Uniform Gifts to Minors Act, 8C U.L.A. 25 (2000); Uniform Transfers to Minors Act, 8A U.L.A. 297 (2000).

27. For tax purposes, the income from this sale will be taxed under the "kiddie tax" at the marginal rates of trusts and estates.

Planning Pointer

When an UGMA/UTMA account is funded, an irrevocable transfer of the asset to the beneficiary occurs. Thus, once the beneficiary reaches the age of majority, the donor cannot be assured that the funds will be used for higher education expenses because the beneficiary will have complete control over the account funds. When the 529 plan permits, transferring UGMA/UTMA assets into a Section 529 savings plan should be considered. Such a transfer may later deter the previous UGMA/UTMA beneficiary from taking the funds and using them for reckless and/or non-education purposes. Once contributed by the custodian to a Section 529 savings plan, the assets cannot be withdrawn for non-qualified expenses without incurring the imposition of an income tax and an additional ten percent penalty tax. The only drawback of such a strategy is the immediate imposition of a capital gains tax (at the trust rate when the "kiddie tax" applies) upon conversion of the custodianship assets to cash.

2. Coverdell Accounts

As with the custodianship account, if the Coverdell is rolled into a Section 529 plan,[28] the beneficiary of the Section 529 plan must remain the beneficiary and cannot be changed without the beneficiary's consent. Again, the rationale is that the beneficiary of the Coverdell is entitled to that account prior to the transfer into the Section 529 plan. Once converted, distributions from a Coverdell account for qualified education expenses are tax free, just as in the case of Section 529 plans.[29] Like the 529, the Coverdell is favored under financial aid formulae.

When the contributions to the Section 529 plan are made with tax-free earnings from a Coverdell, these amounts are not included in the investment in the contract under Section 72. Thus, when applying the annuity rules, earnings from a Coverdell can be taxed unless used for qualified education purposes.

EXAMPLE 17-5: Alice has contributed $34,000 ($2,000 × 17 years) to a Coverdell account for her son, Ben. The Coverdell account has accumulated $25,811 of interest ($59,811 – $34,000). If in the year before Ben turns 18, Alice transfers this account to a Section 529 savings plan, the original $34,000 investment will be excluded from tax even if the distribution is nonqualified. If the distribution is qualified, all earnings ($25,811) will be tax free. On the other hand, the income earned up to that point and distributed for a nonqualified purpose can be taxed and subjected to a 10 percent penalty.

28. I.R.C. § 530(b)(2)(B).
29. *Id.* § 530(b)(2)(A)(i).

Planning Pointer

Because of the favorable rules under the federal financial aid formula for Section 529 plans, it may make sense to roll UGMA/UTMA assets and Coverdell assets into them, if the family would otherwise qualify for financial aid and the student intends to attend a state college or university.

3. Savings Bonds

Like the UTMA/UGMA and Coverdell ESA, savings bonds can be converted into 529 plans. In fact, under Section 135, a qualified expense can actually be a contribution to a Section 529 savings plan.[30] The conversion of the bond and transfer of the proceeds into a Section 529 plan provides several benefits. First, if parents anticipate having adjusted gross income above the relatively low phase-out Section 135 limits by the time the child goes to school, they can cash in the bonds and roll them into a 529 plan. Another advantage of transferring the bond proceeds into a Section 529 plan is that the definition of qualified expenses will be broadened to include room, board, student fees, books, K–12 tuition, etc. Qualified higher education expenses (QHEE) for Section 135 purposes only includes tuition and fees required for enrollment at an eligible education institution.[31]

One disadvantage is that when a savings bond is transferred to a Section 529 plan, there can be no increase in the investment in the contract for purposes of applying the Section 72 annuity rules for any portion of such contribution that is not includible in gross income.[32] Thus, when applying the annuity rules, interest from the bonds can be taxed—unless used for qualified education purposes.[33]

Planning Pointer

Some advisors believe that a relative can purchase the bond and dump the proceeds into a Section 529 plan naming himself as owner and beneficiary.[34] This would allow tax-free treatment of the interest. Then later, the owner would be able to change the beneficiary to another relative. This strategy would only work, however, if the owner met the age and income restrictions of Section 135.

30. *Id.* § 135(c)(2)(C).
31. *Id.* (Also allows transfer into a Coverdell ESA.)
32. *Id.*
33. See **Example 17-7** for application of a similar rule in a Coverdell conversion.
34. *See* David J. Braverman, The Standard & Poor's Guide to Saving and Investing for College 41 (McGraw-Hill 2004).

F. Conclusion

Sometimes because of the restricted rules of the 529 plan—such as the requirement of cash contributions, definition of family member, and qualified education expenses—other savings mechanisms are used to supplement the Section 529 plan. When this happens, coordination is necessary between the 529 savings plan and other savings techniques. In particular, when the same education expenses are paid from two or more saving mechanisms, then complex coordination rules may apply. It must be remembered, however, that the Coverdell, the custodianships, and saving bonds can all be easily converted to a 529 plan without adverse tax consequences. When that happens all the benefits of a 529 plan, such as financial aid, tax benefits, and expanded qualified expenses, will apply to the converted account.

Chapter 18

Coordinating Section 529 Plans with Tax Benefits

In addition to coordinating Section 529 plans with other savings techniques, it is important to coordinate the 529 savings plan with the *pay-as-you-go tax benefits.*[1] The code usually allows the taxpayer to benefit from more than one tax provision but sets forth rules that prevent a taxpayer from realizing duplicate benefits from the same expenditures.[2] What is important for this chapter is that 529s cannot be *double counted* when the taxpayer uses any of the following tax benefits for the same qualifying benefits: (1) the AOTC and Lifetime Learning Credit, (2) scholarships, (3) grants (including Pell Grants), (4) veteran's benefits, (5) early withdrawals from IRAs, (6) employer-provided educational assistance programs, (7) educational savings bonds, (8) ordinary and necessary business educational expense deductions, and (9) the student loan interest deduction.[3] Complex coordination rules can apply when qualifying expenses, qualifying taxpayers, eligible institutions, and amounts of the benefit differ among the provisions. Often it is very difficult to determine whether to use the 529 plan or which tax benefit to choose.

A. General Coordination Rules

As we discussed in the last chapter, the definitions of qualifying education expenses may vary among the provisions. In addition, the qualifying taxpayers may differ, as well as the eligible institution and tax benefit. As in the savings area, considerable variation exists in the tax rules. However, in this chapter we discuss coordinating the various savings techniques with the pay-as-you-go tax provisions.

1. *See* **Chapter Five: When Savings Are Not Enough**, A.

2. For example, the taxpayer cannot take the AOTC and the Lifetime Learning Credit for the same beneficiary.

3. The student loan interest deduction does not allow a deduction for "which a deduction is allowed the taxpayer under any other provision." *See* I.R.C. § 221(e)(1).

1. Different Definitions of Qualified Expenditures

As we discussed in the previous chapter, the qualifying education definitions vary among the savings provisions, but they also vary among the tax provisions. The narrowest definition of qualified education expenses arises for employer-provided tuition reduction programs under Section 117(d), as that tax benefit *only* applies to tuition. The American Opportunity Credit and the Lifetime Learning Credit, as well as the Traditional and Roth IRAs, cover tuition plus required fee; this includes any fee required as part of the student's degree program as well as nonacademic fees that are required.[4] The American Opportunity Tax Credit for post-2008 years covers "required course materials" in addition to tuition and related fees. Employer-provided educational assistance (Section 127) has a broader definition and applies to tuition, required fees, supplies, and equipment "incurred by or on behalf of an employee for education." Supplies would include such things as art supplies, calculators, notebooks, etc. "Supplies which may be retained" by the taxpayer do not qualify.[5] Equipment could include computers. Section 127, however, does not cover books. No requirement exists that these expenditures must be required by the course of study. As you can see just from these brief descriptions, the definitions for qualifying education expenses can vary; thus, it is extremely important for the advisor to closely check the definitions of any and all saving and tax techniques used in the education plan.

Scholarship exclusions cover tuition and required fees, supplies, and equipment, as well as books, but these all must be *required* for the course of study.[6] The scholarship exclusion does not cover room and board. If the taxpayer is an employee and either obtains reimbursement from his/her employer for educational expenses as a working condition fringe under Section 132 or pays for the expenses him/herself and seeks and obtains a reimbursement from the employer, the expenses will include not only tuition and related fees but travel to and from the school as well as lodging and 50 percent of meals if the taxpayer is "away from home."[7] Although the definition of qualified expense and these business-type provisions is quite expansive, it is not easy to plan to benefit from them. First, most employers are not willing to pay for these expenses. When these expenses are unreimbursed then they are denied under the *TCJA* of 2017 as a *miscellaneous itemized deduction*—at least until 2026. Second, to qualify, the expenses must be legitimate business expenses that either maintain and improve the employee's work skills or are required by his/her employer.[8] Third, no benefit is allowed if the expenses qualify the taxpayer for a new job or meet the minimum requirements of the job.[9]

The broader definitions of qualifying education expenses apply to the Coverdell and the 529 savings plan. As we discussed in the prior chapter, the Coverdell

---

4. Student activity fees if required can be qualified expenses under Treas. Reg. § 1.25 A-2.
5. I.R.C. § 127(c)(1).
6. *Id.* § 117(b)(2)(B).
7. *Id.* § 162(a)(2).
8. See discussion in **Chapter Five: When Savings Are Not Enough**, A(c).
9. *Id.*

covers more K–12 related expenditures than the Section 529 plan, including uniforms, transportation, and tuition greater than $10,000. Section 529 savings plans are broader when it comes to college expenditures and even cover up to $10,000 for the payment of principal or interest on qualified student loans.[10] Both techniques cover qualified special needs expenditures. *See* **Chart 18-1** for a comparison of the education expenses covered by the various tax benefit provisions.

CHART 18-1 Treatment of Expenses under Education Tax Benefit Rules[11]

(X—Means Expense Is Covered)

Code Provision	Tuition	Academic Fees	Supplies, and Equipment	Books	Room & Board	Travel and other personal expenses	K–12	Other
Exclusion for qualified tuition reduction (§ 117(d))	X						As long as tuition paid directly to the educational institution	
American Opportunity Tax Credit (§ 25A)	X	X	If required "course material"	If required "course material"				Nonacademic fees if required
Lifetime Learning Credit (§ 25A)	X	X						Nonacademic fees if required
Employer Assistance Programs (§ 127)	X	X	X					
Exclusion for Scholarship (§ 117)	X	X	X	X				
Exclusions for Distributions from Section 529 Prepaid	X	X			Most prepaids do not cover			Special needs covered for special beneficiaries
Exclusions for Distributions from Section 529 Savings Plan	X	X	X	X	X		Up to $ 10,000 tuition	Special needs, computer or peripheral equipment, Internet, registered apprenticeship programs, and qualified education loan repayments (up to $ 10,000)

(continued)

10. *See* **Chapter Seventeen: Coordinating Section 529 Plans with Other Savings Techniques**, D.

11. *Preset Law and Analysis Relating to Tax Benefits for Higher Education*, Staff of the Joint Comm. on Taxation (July 21, 2004) (adapted from Table 3, at 46).

Code Provision	Tuition	Academic Fees	Supplies, and Equipment	Books	Room & Board	Travel and other personal expenses	K–12	Other
Exclusions for Distributions from a Coverdell (§ 530)	X	X	X	X	X		X	Special needs, academic tutoring, computer or peripheral equipment, and Internet
ATL Deduction for Interest on Loans for Qualified Education Expenses (§ 221)	X	X	X	X	X	Covered to extent included in cost of attendance for financial aid purposes		Covered to extent included in cost of attendance for financial aid purposes
Working Condition Fringe or Business Deduction (§ 132 or 162)	X	X		X	X	Can get travel and lodging if away from home in pursuit of business—but only 50% of meals		
Home Equity Loan Interest (§ 163(h) after 2025)	X	X	X	X	X	X	X	X

2. No Double Counting of Qualified Expenses

When a taxpayer qualifies for more than one tax benefit, the taxpayer must reduce the qualified expenditures by the amount of similar expenses that are used for another provision. If the only expense is tuition (unrealistically) then it is easy to calculate qualifying expenses and the remaining qualifying expenses.

EXAMPLE 18-1: Ben has $12,000 of tuition expense for his first year of college. Ben pays the tuition expenses from the following sources:

Grants	$ 3,000
Scholarship	$ 1,000
Employer educational assistance	$ 5,250
Expenses taken into account for figuring the AOTC Credit	$ 2,000
Qualified Tuition Expenses	$11,250
Remaining Qualified Tuition Expenses	$ 750

Ben was able to benefit from four education tax benefits and has qualified tuition expenses remaining, which could be paid for by a Coverdell or Section 529 plan.

The problem, however, is that the typical student will have expenses other than tuition. Thus, an order for reduction of expenses is essential. Since taxpayers can elect out of the educational credits, the exclusions should apply *first* to reduce qualified expenses before credits apply, unless the taxpayer elects to take the credits. According to Section 25A(g)(2)(A), the expenses used in excluding scholarships or grants under Section 117 must be determined prior to applying the AOTC and Lifetime Learning Credit. Section 117 covers tuition and academic fees just like the AOTC and Lifetime Learning Credit but also covers supplies, equipment, and books. After deducting for Section 117 exclusions, taxability of distributions from Section 529s and Coverdells are determined. Since Section 529s and Coverdells are more expansive in their coverage, they can cover everything a scholarship covers *plus* room and board.

EXAMPLE 18-2: Assume Ben has the following expenses for college: tuition ($15,000); academic fees ($2,000); nonacademic fees ($1,000); books ($800); supplies/equipment ($200); room/board ($20,000); computer ($2,000) (assume not qualified). Assume further that Ben is not a dependent of another and has earnings of $15,000. If Ben receives a scholarship of $6,000, and otherwise qualifies for the Lifetime Learning Credit, he must *first* reduce the qualified educational expenses allowed under the Section 117 scholarship provision by $6,000 *before* any credits can be taken. Scholarships cover tuition, required fees, books, and supplies but not nonacademic fees.

Section 117 Qualified Expenses (QE):

Tuition	$15,000
Academic Fees	$2,000
Books	$800
Supplies/equipment	$200
Total	**$18,000**
Less Scholarship	$6,000
Remainder	**$12,000**

The remainder of the expenses not covered by the scholarship is $12,000. However, not all of this remainder can be covered by qualified expenses for the purposes of Lifetime Learning Credit. Books, supplies, and equipment do not qualify for that credit. Thus, a proportional allocation must be made because only the tuition and academic fees can be used for purposes of calculating the credit.

Tuition ($15,000/$18,000 × 12,000)	= $10,000
Academic Fees ($2,000/$18,000 × 12,000)	= $ 1,334
Books, supplies/equipment ($1,000/$18,000 × 12,000)	= $ 666
	$12,000

The tuition and academic fees remaining after the allocation ($11,334) exceed the $10,000 allowed under the Lifetime Learning Credit, so Ben will receive a credit of $2,000. The uncovered tuition and fees ($1,334) plus the uncovered books and supplies ($666) plus room and board ($20,000) could be covered by either a Section 529 or a Coverdell distribution.

A taxpayer is able to claim a tax-free distribution from a 529 plan and, in the same year, have a tax-free distribution from a Coverdell ESA *and* use either the *American Opportunity Credit (AOTC)* or the *Lifetime Learning Credit.* Thus, a taxpayer can use those three planning techniques in the same year to increase tax benefits and minimize out-of-pocket expenses for education. The only restriction is that the distribution from the Section 529 plan cannot be used to pay the same expenses for which either a credit is claimed or the Coverdell distribution is used. Since the Section 529 (and the Coverdell) cover room and board but the credits do not, the total higher education expenses can be allocated to maximize the greatest tax benefit.

EXAMPLE 18-3: Assume that Ben is a full-time student with the following expenses: $15,000 tuition; $7,000 room and board; $2,000 books, equipment, and supplies. Ben may claim the Lifetime Learning Credit using up $10,000 of the tuition, claim a $5,000 Coverdell distribution for the remaining tuition, and still use $9,000 from the 529 plan to pay for books, equipment, and supplies.

If a distribution from a Section 529 plan and the Coverdell is used to pay for the same higher education expenses, the expenses must be allocated between the distributions in each account and a tax paid based on the respective *earnings ratios* of each account. On the other hand, if any of the distribution from the Section 529 plan is used to pay expenses used for either the AOTC or Lifetime Learning Credit, then an allocation can be made based on the best overall tax results. A comparison between the tax savings realized from taking an excludable withdrawal from the Section 529 plan must be compared with the tax benefits realized from claiming the credit.

EXAMPLE 18-4: Ben receives a $20,000 distribution from his 529 plan to cover $20,000 of tuition expenses. If Ben elects to use $10,000 of the tuition expense for the Lifetime Learning Credit, he will have to pay income tax on the earnings (and a penalty) on $10,000 of his 529 plan. If the earnings ratio of the 529 is 5 percent then $10,000 × 5% = $500 is taxed, plus a $50 penalty. Assuming Ben is a taxpayer, the $2,000 credit against his taxes is a better choice. Thus, Ben will elect to pay taxes on the earnings on the nonqualified $10,000 529 distribution (plus the penalty on those earnings).

3. Double Counting Is Sometimes Allowed

In some circumstances, however, the code allows for *double counting*.[12] For example, payment of educational expenses by gift or inheritance (such as direct payments of tuition under the *Section 2503(e) transfer* rule) by the grandparent will not disqualify the education credits to the parent or student. Payment for services, such as wages, withdrawals from student's personal savings, and amounts received from taxable scholarships, also will not reduce QEE.[13] Payments made from an IRA after the taxpayer reaches 59½ are also not considered, so this distribution can be used along with the tax credits or tuition or other deductions. Finally, loans usually do not prevent the tax benefits. Thus, the taxpayer can take out a loan and pay for education expenses currently—thus receiving the credits. However, the student loan interest deduction provision does not allow that deduction for any expense "for which a deduction is allowed the taxpayer under any other provision."[14]

4. Different Qualifying Taxpayers

Eligible qualifying taxpayer beneficiaries vary considerably under the tax provisions. The most restrictive is the Section 127 employer-provided education assistance for the exclusive benefit of the employee. This would be true for the working condition exclusion under Section 132 and the employer reimbursed trade or business education expense. Other employer-provided benefits, such as the tuition reduction under Section 117(d), apply to the employee's spouse and dependent children—as well as the employee (but was intended to cover long-term employees of the educational institution).

Similarly, provisions for the Section 135 savings bonds proceeds exclusion and the AOTC and the Lifetime Learning Credit apply to the taxpayer, the taxpayer's spouse, and any dependent children. Any individual can qualify for the Traditional and Roth IRAs. However, under the IRAs, the qualified educational expenses must be for a member of the *family* of the IRA owner. The Traditional and Roth IRAs expand the definition of family to include grandchildren in addition to spouse and

12. In general, when proceeds come from the following, they can be double counted: wages, loans, gifts, inheritances, and withdrawals from the student's personal saving or taxable scholarships. I.R.C. § 25A(g)(2)(C) (lists "gifts," bequests, and inheritances).

13. *See* IRS Pub. 970: Tax Benefits for Education (2019).

14. I.R.C. § 222(c).

dependent children. Any taxpayer can qualify to set up the Section 529 and 530 accounts—even corporate employers and charitable organizations—and the beneficiary need not be related to the owner or donor. However, once a beneficiary is established, a rollover can occur to only a member of the family, but this would include first cousins, nieces, and nephews, as well as the immediate family. For the after-college *above-the-line* student loan interest deduction, the eligible taxpayer is the taxpayer responsible for paying the qualified loan obligation. However, only one such deduction is allowed per return, even if both husband and wife have qualified loans. (*See* **Chart 18-2**.)

CHART 18-2 Eligible Taxpayer Beneficiaries under Education Tax Provisions

(X—Means Expense Is Covered)

	Taxpayer	Taxpayer's Spouse and Dependents	Member of Family Defined to Include Grandchildren	Member of Family Defined to Include Nieces, Nephews, and First Cousins
Employer Provided Educational Assistance (§ 127)	If employee			
Exclusion for qualified tuition reduction (§ 117(d))	If employee	X		
Working Condition Fringe or Business Deduction (§ 132 or 162)	If employee			
Saving Bond Interest (§ 135)	X	X		
American Opportunity Tax Credit (§ 25A)	X	X		
Lifetime Learning Credit (§ 25A)	X	X		
Traditional IRA	X	X	X	
Roth IRA	X	X	X	
Section 529	X	X	X	X
Coverdell	X	X	X	X
ATL Deduction for Interest on Loans for Qualified Education Expenses (§ 221)	X Student with loan Parent with loan or parent with dependent student with loan			

5. Eligible Educational Institution

In order to qualify for the tax benefit, the educational institution *must* be eligible under the specific plan; all plans require this. The American Opportunity and Lifetime Learning credits, the Traditional/Roth IRAs, the Coverdell, and the 529 provisions all have similar definitions. Section 529 defines eligible educational institutions by reference to Section 481 of the Higher Education Act. This definition generally includes "accredited post-secondary educational institutions offering credit towards a bachelor's degree, an associate's degree, or another recognized post-secondary credential."[15] Certain for-profit institutions and post-secondary vocational institutions would also be eligible institutions. The institution must be eligible to participate in the Department of Education student aid programs.[16] The *Tax Cuts and Jobs Act of 2017* extended this definition of educational institution under Section 529 Plans to include any school providing elementary or secondary education as determined under state law.[17] This definition conforms now to the Coverdell definition of educational institution for payment of qualified K–12 expenses.

Under Section 221, the student loan interest deduction has a broader definition of "qualified institution." It includes the Section 481 definition of the Higher Education Act but also includes "an institution conducting an internship or residency program leading to a degree or certificate awarded by an institution of higher education, a hospital, or a health care facility which offers postgraduate training."[18] The broadest definition of qualified education institution occurs with the Section 117 scholarship and the *Section 2503(e) direct tuition payment* provisions. Here, the regulations define "educational organization" as one "which normally maintains a regular faculty and curriculum and normally has a regularly organized body of students in attendance at the place where its educational activities are carried on."[19] This broad definition allows students to exclude scholarships from those qualified institutions but does not allow expenses paid to these same institutions to qualify for any other educational benefit.[20]

15. 20 U.S.C. § 1088 (LexisNexis, Lexis Advance through Public Law 116-259, approved Dec. 23, 2020. Some sections may be more current.).

16. Joint Comm. on Taxation, 105th Cong., General Explanation of Tax Legislation Enacted in 1997, at 7 (Comm. Print 1997).

17. I.R.C. § 530(b)(4)(B).

18. *Id.* § 221(d)(2) (last sentence).

19. Treas. Regs. §§ 1.117-3(b), 25.2503-6(b)(2) (which has the same language except uses "regularly enrolled," not "organization").

20. I.R.C. § 221(e)(2)(B).

6. Per Student vs. Per Return

Most of the education tax provisions apply on a per-student basis. However, there are two exceptions. We just mentioned that student loan interest applies per return.[21] The other exception is the Lifetime Learning Credit, which is also calculated on a per-return basis. Thus, in one year a parent with two students could take the American Opportunity Tax Credit in their first four years for each child but would be entitled to only one Lifetime Learning Credit.[22] This also would preclude a parent from taking this credit at the same time for more than one child.

EXAMPLE 18-5: John and Sue are thinking of getting married. They both have graduated from college with loans that would qualify for the Section 221 student interest deduction. They both expect to earn around $50,000. If they do not get married, they each can receive the $2,500 deduction for a total of $5,000. On the other hand, if they get married, they will only be entitled to one $2,500 deduction.

7. Amount of Benefit Varies

The *amount* of the college expenses that are covered by a tax benefit—even when the qualified expenses are defined similarly—are different among the provisions. The American Opportunity Tax Credit (AOTC) is limited to $4,000 of qualified expenses. The Lifetime Learning Credit is limited to $10,000 of qualified expenses. When the tax credits (or other tax benefits) are not adjusted for inflation, they cannot keep pace with the rise in tuition (or student loan interest) rates. Thus, most of the tax provisions are inadequate to keep pace with the increasing costs of education. The Coverdell has no education expenses limit for QEESE, but because the contribution limit is $2,000 and cannot be made after the beneficiary turns 18, it is of limited benefit for the higher-priced colleges. The Section 529 savings plan is the most liberal of the tax provisions, allowing savings of substantial amounts with coverage of tuition and related fees plus room, board, and other expenses. However, the Section 529 plan only allows up to $10,000 of K–12 tuition, whereas the QEESE under the Coverdell is much more expansive. Similarly, the 529 allows the payment of student loan interest *and* principal of up to $10,000, but the above-the-line student loan interest deduction is limited to $2,500 of interest. Thus, coordination among the tax provisions is recommended when the amount of the benefit varies among those provisions.

---

21. *Id.* § 221(a), (e)(2).
22. *Id.* § 25A(c)(1).

B. Choosing the Best Tax Benefit

Because double benefits are usually not allowed, planning for the right benefit or combination of benefits can be complex. Choosing the *best* tax benefit will depend on the following factors: (1) the taxpayer's adjusted gross income, (2) who the taxpayer is—the parent or student, (3) the total *amount* of college expenses, (4) the *type* of expenses covered, (5) the taxpayer's marginal income tax bracket, and (6) in the case of Section 529s and Coverdells, the earnings percentages on the accounts.[23]

1. No Double Benefits for the Pay-as-You-Go Benefits

For simplicity, let us assume the taxpayer has no savings plan and must choose between the pay-as-you-go tax benefits: the AOTC or the Lifetime Learning Credit. The taxpayer is allowed to claim the same eligible student in the same year for only one of these benefits. The qualifying expenses are slightly different. The AOTC covers "required course materials" in addition to tuition and related fees and also is refundable. After the *Coronavirus Aid, Relief, and Economic Security Act of 2021,* the adjusted gross income limitations for both credits will be the same. Thus, when qualified expenses are greater than $10,000, the $2,500 AOTC will most likely trump the $2,000 Lifetime Learning Credit.

Obviously, the AOTC can be claimed only if the student is in their first four years of college. Assuming the taxpayer can qualify for both the AOTC and the Lifetime Learning credits, the taxpayer cannot claim both for the same eligible student in the same taxable year. Therefore, the taxpayer must decide which credit is better. The AOTC is slightly larger ($2,500 compared to $2,000) and covers more expenses (required course materials). Therefore it is the better choice. Furthermore, when the taxpayer is in a lower tax bracket, the AOTC is partially refundable. Lastly, the AOTC is per student and works well with the Lifetime Learning Credit, which is per return.

EXAMPLE 18-6: In 2021, Alice pays $5,000 in qualified tuition, related expenses, and course materials for her dependent son, Ben. Ben is in his first year of college. In the same year, Alice pays $500 in qualified tuition and related expenses for a computer course that will improve her job skills. Assuming all other relevant requirements are met, Alice may claim an American Opportunity Tax Credit for $4,000 of the $5,000 qualified expenses attributable to Ben. Alice may not, however, add Ben's $1,000 excess expenses to her $500 of qualified tuition and related expenses in computing the amount of the Lifetime Credit. Furthermore, the Lifetime Credit is only allowed per return, so the maximum allowed would be $800 (20% × $4,000) for Ben's expenses. Thus, Alice would take a $2,500 AOTC for Ben's expenses and a $100 (20% of $500) Lifetime Credit for her expenses in tax year 2021.

23. *See* **Chart 17-3** in **Chapter Seventeen: Coordinating Section 529 Plans with Other Savings Techniques**.

2. Which Taxpayer Is Better? Parent or Student?

Oftentimes it is even more difficult to plan who should be the taxpayer.[24] If the parent is in a high bracket, not only will the *dependent tax credit* be denied, but the parent will be unable to use the education credits. For 2021, the phase-out for the dependent tax credit is $240,000 for the single taxpayer, whereas for the education credits, the phase-out is $80,000 to $90,000 for a single taxpayer. Since the dependency tax credit is only a meager $500, it might make sense for the student to be the taxpayer. On the other hand, when the student does not earn the threshold of taxable amounts, the credits are not going to be of much benefit. However, the AOTC is partially refundable, so it will appeal to the low-income student with no tax liability.

3. When Taxpayer Is Eligible for Pay-as-You-Go and Savings Benefits

Since the educational credits can only be used for tuition and related expenses (course materials for the AOTC) and not room and board, the eligible taxpayers may use either this credit *and* also the Section 529 or the Coverdell. In other words, the taxpayer will not have to choose between the pay-as-you-go tax benefits and the 529 or Coverdell. Rather, the taxpayer, if they plan well and are diligent, can use both a pay-as-you-go tax benefit plan *and either* the 529 *or* the Coverdell plan.

Taxpayers that can take both a Section 529 and Coverdell can allocate all the distribution to one or the other account depending on the earnings ratios. In the alternative, the taxpayer could choose not to fund expenses with the Section 529 plan—deferring these until graduate school—and otherwise use the Coverdell and qualify for the credits. This might make sense when the student lives at home (or has large amounts saved in the Coverdell or Section 529 plan), or the taxpayer may opt not to take the credits and just opt to take the Section 529 plan and Coverdell. If college expenses are paid from a 529 plan or Coverdell and the taxpayer claims either the AOTC or Lifetime Credit for the same expenses, then some of the Section 529 or Coverdell distribution will be subject to tax, plus an additional *ten percent penalty tax*. Deciding on what to do depends on tax benefits. The credits may be better when earning rates in 529 and Coverdells are low. On the other hand, the credits should not be elected when earnings ratios and taxpayer's AGI are high. When the taxpayer clearly has income within the range allowed for the credits, it is almost always going to be better to elect the credit, particularly if the earnings ratios for the Section 529 plan and Coverdells are low. Those high-income taxpayers who cannot take the credit can still benefit from Section 529.

---

24. *See* **Chapter Eight: Federal Income Tax Planning with Section 529 Savings Plans**, F.5.

If the taxpayer is in the phase-out income levels, the calculations become a bit more complicated. The amount of the allowable credit would be compared to the taxes paid on the earnings on the Section 529 or Coverdell plus the *ten percent additional tax* to be paid.

EXAMPLE 18-7: Assume that the single parent has an AGI of $90,000 and the qualified tuition expenses are $8,000. (Assume there are no other expenses because the taxpayer student lives at home). Only part of the normal 20 percent Lifetime Learning Credit would be available as the single parent is in the phase-out level (20% × $8,000 = $1,600). This tax benefit would be compared to the tax on the earnings portion of the $8,000 (let's say $2,400 × 30% tax rate of taxpayer) plus the 10 percent additional tax on the 2,400 or $960 ($720 + $240). Thus, it may be better to take the $1,600 Lifetime Learning Credit.

Prior to *EGTRRA*, a Hope/Lifetime Learning Credit had to be elected by filing Form 8863. Now, Section 25A automatically applies unless the taxpayer elects out of it. One instance in which electing not to take the credits might be advisable is when the earnings percentage for the 529 and Coverdell accounts are high, and the tax bracket of the taxpayer is at the top of the phase-out level for the credits. The credit might produce a less favorable result since the income from the Section 529 and Coverdell accounts will be taxed and will carry a *ten percent additional tax* when not used for qualified educational purposes. However, double benefits are allowed where educational expenses are paid with return of capital, so a careful analysis of the various factors—taxpayer's AGI, etc.—are important. Furthermore, the AOTC is refundable, so that refund would have to be compared with the penalty.

If the qualified expenses exceed the total distribution (principal plus earnings), then none of the earning is included in income. However, if the expenses do not exceed this distribution, then a portion of the excess will be taxed. If the distribution is received in part from the Coverdell and in part from the 529, the adjusted qualifying expenses must be allocated between the two distributions in order to determine how much the earnings is taxed. The earnings ratio might be higher for one account than the other, so the taxpayer should check to use the higher earnings account for the qualified expenses.[25]

4. When Exclusions or Deductions Are Added into the Mix

Although scholarships and grants will be the most common exclusion the student is likely to receive, it may be possible the student could qualify for the Section 127

25. *See* **Chart 17-3** in **Chapter Seventeen: Coordinating Section 529 Plans with Other Savings Techniques**.

employer educational assistance, the Section 117(d) qualified tuition reduction, or the Section 132 education working condition fringe benefit. All of these exclusions would reduce qualified expenses, but an allocation might have to be made so that the qualifying expenses are not double counted.

When the taxpayer is eligible for the Section 162 ordinary and necessary business expense deduction and also eligible for the credits, it is better for the taxpayer to claim the credit in the portion of the qualifying expense and then use the remaining amounts for the Section 162 deduction. Under Section 162, transportation, lodging, and a portion of meals are allowed as a deduction if the taxpayer is "away from home" in pursuit of qualified education. Under the *Consolidated Appropriations Act of 2021,* 100 percent of the meals are allowed if used at restaurants, otherwise 50 percent of meals are allowed.[26] When lodging could be covered by a Coverdell or a Section 529 plan, the taxpayer must determine whether the tax benefit under Section 162 will be greater and if it is better to pay tax on the earnings from the Coverdell or Section 529 account with an additional tax. Most likely it would be better to forego the Section 162 deduction.

5. Student Loan Interest

As with other tax benefits, no double benefits are allowed under Section 221, the student loan interest deduction. Qualified expenses under this provision are quite broad, including everything that would be included in the student's cost of attendance. Any loan interest under Section 221 attributable to expenses that were used for an educational exclusion, savings, deduction, or credit provision would be denied.

EXAMPLE 18-8: Alice took out a PLUS loan of $10,000 to pay for Ben's first-year college expenses. If $4,000 of the tuition expenses were allocated to the AOTC, then only interest on the $6,000 remaining loan could be deducted under Section 221. Presumably, that $6,000 was used for qualifying educational expenses or for personal expenses of the students, such as transportation, health, and entertainment.

The *SECURE Act* now allows a distribution from a 529 savings plan to be used for the payment of not only interest but principal on a qualified student loan of the designated beneficiary and any sibling. If the distribution from the 529 is used for interest on a loan, the taxpayer would not also be allowed to take the above-the-line student loan interest deduction under Section 221.

26. I.R.C. § 274(n).

EXAMPLE 18-9: Assume that the 529 plan has a balance of $25,000 and Ben has QHEE for tuition, room, and board of $21,000. If Ben borrows $4,000 of qualifying education loans and takes a distribution of $21,000 from the 529 plan to pay for QHEE, the entire distribution would not be taxed. Ben could subsequently use the remaining $4,000 in the 529 plan to repay the education loan. However, Ben should not receive any tax deduction for any interest paid on that loan.

C. Conclusion

This chapter illustrates some of the complexity of planning for educational tax benefits while owning a 529 plan. Not only are the qualifying expenses, qualifying taxpayers, eligible institutions, and amounts of the benefit different, but many of the tax provisions have their own unique rules. Coordinating the rules and planning is difficult because choosing the best combination of benefits depends on a multitude of factors, such as the taxpayer's AGI and marginal tax rate, the amount and type of college expenses, and whether the taxpayer is the parent or student. Section 529 savings plans cover any school, cover most college expenses (plus $10,000 for K–12 tuition and $10,000 for student loan debt), and have no contribution or taxpayer eligibility rules. The advisor should be careful, however, not only when planning for the future but when undertaking current planning options.

Chapter 19

Coordinating Section 529 Plans with Financial Aid

This chapter will describe the methodology for determining financial aid and how the taxpayer's ownership of a 529 plan can optimize the *financial aid award*. This chapter will also compare the ownership of 529 plans with other savings techniques in the financial aid calculations. The following example of a *financial aid award* is a useful introduction to the terminology, all of which will be explained in this chapter.[1]

EXAMPLE 19-1: The *Cost of Attendance* (COA) for one *award year* at Faber University is $10,000, and the *dependent* student's *Expected Family Contribution* (EFC), which is derived from the *Free Application for Federal Student Aid* (FAFSA) or from the *College Scholarship Service* (CSS)/*Financial Aid PROFILE®*, is $2,000. The student's *Financial Need* (FN) is thus $8,000 ($10,000 – $2,000). The *Financial Aid Administrator* (FAA) or *Financial Aid Officer* (FAO) at Faber University conducts a *needs-based analysis* and offers the student a $4,000 *financial aid package*, resulting in an unmet need, or gap, of $4,000 ($8,000 – $4,000). The family is thus responsible for paying both the EFC of $2,000 and the gap of $4,000.

A. Methodology: In General

Two major formulae are used to determine a financial aid award—the *Federal Methodology Formula* (FMF) and the *Institution Methodology Formula* (IMF). The FMF is primarily used for state colleges and universities, whereas the IMF is primarily used for private colleges and universities. Unfortunately, under both formulae the cost of attendance for college may be underestimated, and the *Expected Family*

1. And every term that is *italicized* in this book is defined in the **Glossary**.

Contribution (EFC) may be overestimated. Therefore, the *real* financial need of the student may be much greater than the school's *actual* financial aid award. This is important information that could influence the final decision of which school to attend.

In general, the school estimates an average student's *Cost of Attendance* (COA); the COA includes tuition, fees, room and board, books, supplies, travel expenses, and personal expenses such as clothing, entertainment, and transportation.[2] Many schools also include the cost of a personal computer. A particular student's *actual* cost of attending school can vary dramatically from the COA estimated by the higher education institution. How can the actual cost of attending school vary dramatically from the COA? Some examples include supplemental study materials that are not required for classes, but the student needs to understand the course; a broader wardrobe than a school might determine necessary, etc. This difference highlights what financial aid professionals call *perceived need* versus *demonstrated need. Perceived need* is what a student believes he/she needs to pay the bills. *Demonstrated need,* on the other hand, is what the financial aid calculations are designed to cover. Financial aid professionals will only attempt to meet a student's *demonstrated* need.[3]

Planning Pointer

The applicant must be aware that not only may the *Expected Family Contribution* (EFC) be grossly overstated, but the *Cost of Attendance* (COA) may be grossly understated. Consequently, the applicant may need to take out additional government or private loans or otherwise try to meet the needs of the student.

Subtracting *Expected Family Contribution* from *Cost of Attendance* will determine financial need and how much *need-based aid* the student may receive. This type of aid includes: (1) *Federal Pell Grants*, (2) *Federal Supplemental Educational Opportunity Grant (FSEOG),* (3) *Direct Subsidized Loan*, and (4) *Federal-Work Study*.[4]

EXAMPLE 19-2: If Ben's COA (determined by the institution) is $16,000 and his EFC is $12,000, then Ben's financial need is $4,000. Thus, Ben is not eligible for more than $4,000 in need-based-aid.

2. 20 U.S.C. § 1087 ll.
3. For further discussion of demonstrated need versus perceived financial need, see DR. HERM DAVIS & JOYCE KENNEDY, COLLEGE FINANCIAL AID FOR DUMMIES (IDG Books Worldwide 1997).
4. *See* **Chart 5-4** in **Chapter Five: When Savings Are Not Enough**.

Non–need-based aid is financial aid that is not based on *Expected Family Contribution*. What matters here is the *Cost of Attendance*. Here COA is subtracted from the financial aid awarded so far (including scholarships), and that will equal eligibility for non–need-based aid.

EXAMPLE 19-3: If Ben's COA is $16,000 and Ben receives $4,000 of need-based aid, Ben will be eligible for $12,000 of non–need-based aid.

1. Determine Who Will Apply for Aid

The person who applies for financial aid will be subject to a detailed financial analysis. Therefore, sorting out who will be the applicant is of paramount importance to the financial aid process. The system assumes that parents will pay for or contribute toward their children's higher education and that, therefore, a parent will be the applicant. In fact, that is the basic rule unless a student is *independent*, in which case the student applies for and receives the award without any involvement or commitment from their parents.

Students are *independent*—and therefore required to file a financial aid application instead of their parents—when they are:

- 24 years of age by December 31 of the award year.
- An orphan or a ward of the court, or were a ward of the court until age 18.
- Married or have legal dependents other than a spouse.
- A graduate or professional student.
- A veteran of the U.S. armed services.
- An active member of the armed forces.
- Deemed independent in the *professional judgment* of the FAO based upon documented unusual circumstances.

If the student is dependent, the *custodial parent* or parents must submit income and asset data. If the student is living with parents who are married, FAFSA and the PROFILE require both parents *and* the student to submit data. In the case of a student of divorced parents, only the income and assets of the student and the parent with whom the student lived more than half of the year is included in FMF. This parent might not be the parent that claims the dependent credit for the student for tax purposes because dependency can be bargained away at divorce and given to the parent without custody who has higher income.[5] In the case of a dependent student of divorced parents, any contribution to the *cost of attendance* by the noncustodial parent whose assets and income are not counted in the financial aid

5. I.R.C. § 152(e). Head of household status is the more valuable tax advantage. The dependent tax credit is a meager $500.

formula is considered a *student resource*, which will reduce aid dollar for dollar. If the *custodial parent* has remarried, the assets and income of the new spouse must also be included in the calculation. The student could also be part of the "household" of the *noncustodial parent* for purposes of determining need for that parent's other children's financial need.

If the parent is widowed or never married, then FAFSA and the PROFILE require data from the student and the parent. If a widowed parent has remarried, then the parent and the parent's new spouse must apply.

EXAMPLE 19-4: Ben lives with his mother Alice more than half the year. Alice is divorced from John, who claims the dependency tax credit for Ben. For FMF purposes, only Alice's income and assets are examined, but any contribution John makes to Ben's education would be a *student resource*. If John has another child, Susan, from a marriage to Mary, Ben would be included in that "household" for purposes of determining the financial need of Susan. In addition, both John and Mary's income and assets would be examined to determine Susan's financial aid.

The school *Financial Aid Officers* (FAOs) have flexibility to use *professional judgment* (PJ) in many critical areas, including when determining whether a student is truly *independent.* Many schools will go beyond the basic federal guidelines described above to impose a harsher standard, while others will consider additional factors that make it easier for students to be classified as independent. If a student has special circumstances that render them constructively independent (e.g., the student's only parent is in prison), they should contact the school's financial aid office before proceeding any further in the application process.

2. Fill Out an Application for Student Aid (FAFSA or PROFILE)

After a student's status is determined, the financial aid applicant must file a *Free Application for Federal Student Aid* (FAFSA) and/or a *College Scholarship Service (CSS)/Financial Aid PROFILE®* application. The FAFSA uses the *Federal Methodology Formula* (FMF), as opposed to the PROFILE application, which uses the *Institutional Methodology Formula* (IMF). Both are filed each academic year, and both provide a detailed financial statement upon which FAOs rely in order to determine a family's ability to pay for college and the size and type of the award. In general, a student's *Basic Financial Need* (BFN) will equal his/her *Cost of Attendance* (COA) less his/her *Expected Family Contribution* (EFC).[6] When EFC equals or exceeds the COA, no *need-based* financial aid is given; but when COA exceeds EFC, the student will be deemed eligible for need-based financial aid. The particular education institution calculates the student's cost of attendance (COA). Thus, any particular student

6. 20 U.S.C. § 1087 kk (2000).

will have as many COA figures as the institutions to which he/she applies. The Department of Education calculates the EFC based on the FAFSA, thus there is only one EFC number a student is given. The school's FAO then uses the EFC to calculate the student's financial aid award package. A student could apply to ten schools and receive ten different COAs; thus, the COA each school determines will likely play a large role in the decision-making process for the student.

The FAFSA can be filed in any of the following four ways: (1) manually completing the form and mailing it to the regional processor listed on the form; (2) filing electronically through the college, where possible; (3) filing electronically using the U.S. Department of Education's FAFSA Express software (downloaded from www.ed.gov); or by (4) filing online by contacting www.fafsa.ed.gov. Paper FAFSAs take four to six weeks to process, while electronic ones take only one week. This difference in timing is something to keep in mind.

Students must fill out the *College Scholarship Service (CSS)/Financial Aid PROFILE®* in addition to the FAFSA if the student intends to attend a private college or university. The CSS/Financial Aid PROFILE® can be completed and filed online at https://profileonline.collegeboard.com/index.jsp. Unlike FAFSA, completion of the CSS/Financial Aid PROFILE® is not free. A fee is charged based on the number of schools to which the student submits the information. Some private schools have their own formula, which is usually a modification of the IMF. These private school formulas generally ask additional questions that are unique to that particular higher education institution.

Planning Pointer

FAFSA applications can be submitted between January 1 and June 30. The information is only current up to December 31 of the year in which the aid application was submitted. For this reason, a student may have to file two FAFSAs in order to get through an academic year. For example, if a student files a timely FAFSA, receives aid, and begins classes in September, the student will need to file a new FAFSA in order to commence a new semester in January unless the school's financial aid department completed the January award prior to December 31, which is permitted. Students or families who anticipate a substantial change in income should use this schedule to their advantage. Submitting a FAFSA promptly is also advantageous because many financial aid departments award aid on a first-come, first-served basis. To hedge against the prospect of a school running out of financial aid, a student's FAFSA should ideally be completed and filed online in early January. This is particularly important for work-study applicants as this type of award tends to run out quickly. Though the FAFSA requires information from the prior year's tax return, applicants are permitted to merely estimate their adjusted gross income and other tax information for purposes of the FAFSA and then update their FAFSA after the tax return is complete. A good piece of advice is to complete and file the FASFA early in order to best maximize the potential financial aid package.

B. The Federal Methodology Formula

The *Federal Methodology Formula* (FMF) is the first of two formulae that determine eligibility for financial aid. The FMF is used by most public colleges and universities in the U.S. to determine eligibility for federal aid, such as *Pell Grants* and *Direct Subsidized Loans*. The calculation for the *Expected Family Contribution* (EFC) examines the income and assets of the parents and student—unless the student is independent, then the formula just examines the student's income and assets. Special rules apply if the family has low income.[7]

From 22 percent–47 percent of the parent's *discretionary income* is considered available to pay the dependent student's higher education costs—the COA—as well as up to 5.64 percent of the parents' *discretionary assets*. The income percentage is based on income level. The FMF also requires that 50 percent of the student's *discretionary income* (less an exemption amount and an allowance for taxes) and 20 percent of the student's *discretionary assets* are also available to cover the COA. (*See* **Chart 19-1**.)

CHART 19-1 Federal Methodology EFC Formula

Parent's Discretionary Assets	Up to 5.64%
Parent's Discretionary Income	22–47%
Student's Discretionary Assets	20%
Student's Discretionary Income	50%

The formula for calculating the income and assets under the FMF is very complicated. **Chart 19-2** gives an overview of how difficult this calculation can be. The following sections will discuss each step in this process.

7. 20 U.S.C. § 1087 oo–qq. *See* B(3)(b) later in this chapter.

CHART 19-2 Computation of Expected Family Contribution—General Formula

Parent's Discretionary Income **[Step One]**	**Assessment** **[Step Three]**
Equals	
Adjusted Gross Income	Parent's percentage contribution from income (22–47%) depending on income.
Plus	
Untaxed Income or Benefits	
Less	
Allowances Income Protection State Taxes Employment Expense College Savings Child Support Taxes	
Plus	
Parent's Discretionary Net Worth [Step Two]	Parent's contribution from assets up to 5.64%.
Equals	
Assets	
Less	
Nonassessable Assets (Annuities, life insurance, retirement accounts, personal items, personal residence, family farm or business, sibling's assets, financial aid)	
Less	
Education Savings and Asset Protection Allowance	
Plus	
Student's Discretionary Income **[Step One]**	Student's contribution from income is 50%. Scholarships/grants; VA benefits; payments from tuition plans, payment from employer-provided education assistance plan.
Less Income Protection Allowance	There is no asset protection allowance for the student.
Plus	
Student's Net Worth **[Step Two]**	Student's percentage contribution from assets is 20%.
Equals Expected Family Contribution (EFC)	

1. STEP ONE: Calculate Discretionary Income of Parent and Student

The computation of *Expected Family Contribution* (EFC) begins with the *discretionary income* of the parents and student—unless the student is independent; if the student is independent, then the formula just examines the student's income and assets. *Discretionary income* is calculated by starting with the *gross income* from the 1040 Tax Form. Then, certain deductions for expenses are subtracted. Then, income is adjusted upward for *untaxed income and benefits* and downward for certain allowances.

a. *Gross Income Less Deductions*

Discretionary income for financial aid purposes begins with the taxpayer's *gross income* from Form 1040 and includes wages, taxable interest, dividends (whether ordinary or qualified), any state and local income tax refund, net business income, net capital gains, and net rental income. It includes unemployment compensation, taxable social security benefits, pensions, annuity income, and "other income" such as gambling winnings, jury duty compensation or prizes, etc.

After calculating gross income, certain deductions are allowed while others are not allowed. Most of the *above-the-line deductions*, that is, those used in arriving at *adjusted gross income* under Section 62, are allowed. The business-related deductions from Schedule C are allowed. The rental expenses (including depreciation) from Schedule E are allowed, as is the $3,000 capital loss on sales of capital assets from Schedule D. In addition, the educator expense (Section 62(a)(2)(D)), certain business expenses of reservists, performing artists and fee-basis government officials (Section 62(a)), the self-employment health insurance deduction (Section 162), and half of the self-employment tax are allowed. Personal above-the-line deductions, such as payments to health savings accounts and the above-the-line student interest deduction (Section 221) on loans, are also allowed.

Interestingly, the retirement-related deductions are not allowed. These include payments to tax-deferred pension and savings plans, IRA deductions, payments to SEP, SIMPLE, and Keogh plans. These are considered untaxed income and increase *discretionary income*, as do untaxed pensions or IRA distributions. Also, when a Traditional IRA is converted to a Roth, income is increased by any amount reported on the return. On the other hand, the contributions to a 401(k) plan as well as the penalty on early withdrawal are allowed as a deduction for both tax and financial aid purposes. No deduction is allowed for the *standard deduction* (Section 63) or most of the *itemized deductions* or *below-the-line* deductions (*See* Tax Form: Schedule A). Instead of these deductions, certain *allowances* are used to calculate discretionary income.

b. *Untaxed Income and Benefits*

The FMF adjusts income upwards by adding back certain *untaxed income or benefits* that represent economic income or the ability to pay for financial aid purposes. Therefore, tax-exempt interest income (Section 103), child support received, certain untaxed social security benefits (Section 86), worker's compensation, veterans' benefits, living allowances paid to members of the military or clergy, and insurance settlements (Section 104) are all added back, but not the earned income credit (Section 24), the additional child credits (Section 22), the dependent tax credit (Section 24), and welfare benefits. Proceeds from the sale of a principal residence (Section 121) can be excluded up to $250,000 for a single or head of household taxpayer and $500,000 if married. However, for purposes of financial aid—*all* of these proceeds must be counted *unless* reinvested in another property at the time the financial aid application is due. The American Opportunity Tax Credit, to the extent it is refundable, should probably not be considered untaxed income for financial aid purposes.

Most fringe benefit exclusions are not added back. For example, meals and lodging provided for the convenience of the employer (Section 119), discounts and other fringe benefits (Section 132), and medical benefits provided by the employer (Section 105–106), including employer contributions toward medical insurance and contributions to pensions or retirement plans (Section 401), are not added back. However, the FMF does add back contributions to or payments from a flexible spending arrangement. Therefore, up to $5,000 must be included under the dependent care plan (Section 129) and any applicable amounts under the medical savings plan (Section 220).

Planning Pointer

When the grandparents set up a 529 plan, it will not be an asset of the parent or the student. However, any distribution from that plan for college will constitute *untaxed income* of the *student* and be assessed at 50 percent for financial aid purposes.[8] Similarly, a distribution from a Roth IRA owned by the student is treated like grandparent-owned 529s. Any money withdrawn for college will constitute untaxed income of the student and be taxed at 50 percent.

Certain *nonassessable income* will not constitute discretionary income. These include loan amounts, financial aid grants, scholarships, and employer-provided education assistance benefits. *See* **Chart 19-3**. However, scholarships (Section 117), up to $5,250 of employer assistance (Section 127), and VA benefits will be considered a *resource* and will reduce the financial aid dollar for dollar. Certain accessions to wealth, such as damage awards for physical injury (Section 104), federal and state disaster funds, food stamps, subsidized housing, childcare welfare benefits, Native American payments, life insurance proceeds (Section 101), and gifts and inheritances (Section 102)—all of which are excluded for income tax purposes—are also not considered income for financial aid purposes. However, gifts

8. This will be true under both formulae.

may be considered a *resource*, such as direct tuition payments to an educational institution. (*Section 2503(e) transfer*).

CHART 19-3 Financial Aid Income Calculation: Items Included as Untaxed Income and Benefits, or Nonassessable Income, or Resources

Untaxed income and benefits	Nonassessable income	Resource
• Tax exempt interest • Child Support • Deductible IRA, SIMPLE IRA, SEP, or Keogh contributions • Untaxed portions of retirement, pension, or life insurance withdrawals or benefits including distributions from Coverdells and Roth IRAs • Certain Roth withdrawals • Distributions from 529 plans owned by the grandparents • Payments to tax-deferred pension and savings plans • Worker's compensation benefits • Veteran's benefits • Living allowance paid to members of military, clergy, and others • Insurance settlements • Tuition Deduction[9] • Unreinvested proceeds from sale of principal residence • Contributions to or payments from flexible spending accounts • Any other untaxed income and benefits or income exclusions	• Welfare benefits • TANF • Foreign income exclusion • Untaxed portion of Social Security benefits • Earned income tax credit • Refund from additional per child tax credit • Credit for federal tax on special fuels • Loan proceeds • Financial aid grants • Scholarships • IRA Rollovers • Employer provided education assistance benefits • VA benefits • Federal and state disaster funds • Some types of insurance proceeds • Food stamps • Subsidized Housing • State payments for foster care and adoption assistance • Childcare benefits provided by the Child Care Program and Social Services Block Grant Programs • Per capital payments to Native Americans from the Per Capita Act or the Distribution of Judgment Funds Act unless they exceed $2,000	• Scholarships • Employer-provided education assistance benefits • Gifts paid directly to the college for tuition • VA education benefits

9. This tax benefit expired at the end of 2020. See discussion in **Chapter Five: When Savings Are Not Enough**.

c. *Allowances and Other Adjustments*

The following allowances reduce the applicant's discretionary income: (1) *The Income Protection Allowance*, (2) *Annual Education Savings and Asset Protection Allowance*, (3) *Employment Expense Allowance*, and (4) *Allowance for Federal, State, and Other Taxes*. Another thing to remember is that income is assessed based on the number of students in college.

i. Income Protection Allowance

Instead of deductions, the *income protection allowance*[10] is supposed to be large enough to cover these expenses. The *income protection allowance* considers the number of dependent people in the "household" and the number of students in college at one time. This allowance is intended to cover personal living expenses, such as rent (or mortgage interest and real estate taxes), utilities, clothes, food, and childcare expenses for dependent children, entertainment, travel, etc. However, in most cases, this allowance is unreflective of the true costs of one's living expenses. Thus, for example, for the 2019–2020 *academic year*, the student income protection allowance was only $6,600, whereas the parents were actually spending between $18,580 and $39,430, depending on the size of the household and the number of students enrolled in college.[11]

ii. Annual Education Savings Allowance

The *Annual Education Savings and Asset Protection Allowance* protects a portion of net worth (assets less debts) from being considered available for postsecondary educational expenses. There are three asset protection allowance tables—one for parents of dependent students, one for independent students without dependents other than a spouse, and one for independent students with dependents other than a spouse.

EXAMPLE 19-5: A trust in the amount of $100,000 is set up, income for ten years to the beneficiary and then reversion to the settler parent. The present value of the parent's right to the trust principal will be a parent's asset, and the income from the trust will be the student's income.

10. For updated information on the Income Protection Allowance and the other allowances, look in the Federal Register or contact Ms. Marya Dennis, Management and Program Analyst, U.S. Department of Education, Union Center Plaza, 830 First Street, NE., Washington, DC 20202. Telephone: (202) 377-3385.

11. Allie Grace Garnett, *How Is Income Treated on the FAFSA?*, Edmit, https://www.edmit.me/blog/how-is-income-treated-on-the-fafsa/ (last visited May 14, 2021).

iii. Employment Expense Allowance

The *employment expense allowance*, which is used for parents of dependent students and for married, independent students, recognizes additional expenses incurred by working spouses and single-parent households. The allowance is based upon the marginal differences in costs for a two-worker family compared to a one-worker family for food away from home, apparel, transportation, and household furnishings and operations.

iv. Allowance for Federal, State, and Other Taxes

The federal financial aid formula provides an *allowance for federal income tax paid.* Federal income tax paid includes any alternative minimum tax liability (Section 56–58). The formula also deducts Medicare and Social Security taxes paid. In addition, the financial aid formula provides an allowance for state taxes providing a certain percentage of income as a deduction depending on the state. Unfortunately, the state tax table does not accurately reflect the particular taxpayer's situation since the option now exists for taking *either* a state income tax *or* a state sales tax. The tables also do not account for issues that arise when a taxpayer lives and works in different states and pays taxes in more than one jurisdiction. Consequently, both the *income protection allowance* and the *allowance for state taxes* are often unrepresentative (except for the poorest taxpayer) of actual expenses incurred.

Planning Pointer

The calculation of *expected family contribution* (EFC) can be quite complicated. Starting from gross income, the taxpayer adjusts upward for untaxed income and benefits, downward for certain expenses, and adjusts downward again for the following:

- the income protection allowance
- the allowance for state taxes
- the employment expense allowance
- the annual education savings allowance
- federal income and social security taxes actually paid
- child support actually paid
- any reduction by the FAO.

The remaining income is then assessed at up to 47 percent for the parent and 50 percent for the student. The resulting number frequently shocks the taxpayer because it often is unreflective of the actual ability of the family to contribute to the costs of college, as the EFC tends to be much higher than what the family can actually afford to contribute.

2. STEP TWO: Calculate Assets and Liabilities of Parent and Student

After the income is calculated, then the parents' and student's *discretionary assets* at the date of the application are valued at market value. Again, only the assets of the student are examined if they are independent. Certain liabilities and allowances are subtracted to determine the *discretionary net worth*. This step begins with certain assets, which are measured at their fair market value at the time the financial aid application is signed. Assets include real estate (fair market value less mortgages), trust funds, money market funds, mutual funds, stocks, bonds, other securities, CDs, saving accounts, and land sale contracts.

Under the FMF there are certain *nonassessable assets*—assets that are not included in either parent or child's assets. Annuities, life insurance policies, retirement accounts (including 401(k), 403(b), IRA, SEP, Keogh, and Roth IRA), unexpended financial aid, restricted bank accounts, and personal items such as clothing and household goods are non-assessable. The family's personal residence is not assessable—as opposed to the IMF in which home equity is assessed as an asset—but a second or vacation home is assessed under the FMF if mortgage interest is deducted on that home. Assets held in the sibling's name are not counted.

The value of the assets of a small family business with 100 or fewer full-time or full-time equivalent employees is not reported, as long as the family owns and controls more than 50 percent of the business. "Family" here is defined as (1) persons directly related to the applicant (parents, siblings, or cousins) and (2) persons who are related by marriage (spouses, stepparent, or sister/brother-in-law).[12] Also, the value of the family farm is not included in the formula if (1) the farm constitutes the family's principal place of resident and (2) the family materially participates in the farm operations. If the farm is held in a partnership form and otherwise qualifies, then nothing is included in the formula. However, if the farm is held in corporate form, the family must own 100 percent of the stock to have the farm value excluded.

A small business, 50 percent owned and controlled by the family and employing 100 full-time employees, is also excluded. However, if the business or farm does not qualify, then a portion of the net value of a farm or business is included in the calculation of an expected contribution. Business or farm value includes the current market value of the land, buildings, cash, machinery, equipment, inventory, receivables, etc. Business or investment farm debts are subtracted but only debts in which the business or farm was used as collateral. Accounts payables, mortgages, and other debt are also subtracted. (*See* **Chart 19-4**.)

12. *See Small Business Exclusion*, FINAID, https://finaid.org/fafsa/smallbusiness/ (last visited May 25, 2021).

CHART 19-4 Nonassessable Assets

Nonassessable assets
• Annuities
• Life insurance
• Retirement accounts including 401(k), 403(b), IRA, SEP, Keogh, Roth IRA
• Unexpended financial aid
• Personal items such as clothes and household items (note that debt corresponding to personal items cannot be listed on the financial aid application forms)
• Restricted bank accounts
• Personal residence (FM), although the second or vacation residences are assessed if interest is deducted on second home
• Family farm or family farm corporations (if family owns all stock, materially participates in farm operation, and has corporation as principal place of residency) and partnerships are not assessed
• Small family business (if family owns and controls more than 50 percent of a business that has 100 or fewer-full time or full-time equivalent employees)
• Siblings' assets

All other assets are counted. Rentals, real estate investments, stocks, bonds, money market funds, mutual funds, bank accounts, CDs, savings,[13] trust assets, and other similar assets are also counted. All of these investment assets are assessed at fair market value—unless assets are assessed at zero because the taxpayer falls under the low-income exception.[14] Rental property is assessed at fair market value less mortgages.

Liabilities or debts are generally not considered subtractions. The exception is secured debt, such as mortgages. Credit card debt, car loans, and other unsecured and personal loans (including federal and Plus loans) are not subtracted from assets. Certain debt is favored and will result in a subtraction: margin loans and passbook loans are examples. Lastly, a percentage is considered available for the parent's contribution.

3. STEP THREE: Assessment

The FMF calculates student's income and assets the same way as parent's income and assets, but a different percentage is applied to calculate the EFC. In general, the parent's income is assessed on a sliding scale based on income and from 22–47 percent. The student's income is similarly assessed. However, the asset assessment is quite different depending on if the parents' or students' assets are being calculated. The parent's assets are only assessed up to 5.6 percent, whereas

13. *See* D, The Potential Impact of Various Forms of Savings on Financial Aid, later in this chapter.
14. *See* B.3, STEP THREE: Assessment, later in this chapter.

student assets are assessed at 20 percent. Special rules apply to independent students, when more than one dependent in the family is attending college, and for low-income families.

a. *Independent Students*

If a student is considered *independent*, parental income (and assets) are ignored, and only the student's discretionary income and available assets are assessed in the formula.[15] Independent students are entitled to an asset protection allowance that will vary depending on age and marital status. An independent student with no dependents will be treated differently than an independent student with non-spouse dependents. In addition, independent students with non-spousal dependents receive additional allowances. Their income is assessed at 50 percent and their assets at 20 percent, the same as if they were dependent.

b. *Assessment Schedules Based on Number of Students in College*

The EFC is divided by the number of students in college in the household. Two schedules, one for parents of dependent students and one for independent students with dependents other than a spouse, are used to determine the EFC toward educational expenses from family financial resources. For dependent students, the EFC is derived from an assessment of the parents' *Adjusted Available Income* (AAI). For independent students with dependents other than a spouse, the EFC is derived from an assessment of the family's AAI. The AAI represents a measure of a family's financial strength, which considers both income and assets.

c. *Special Rules for Low-Income Applicants*

When the student, or family of the student, has low income, the EFC will automatically be zero when the applicant (or family, if applicant is dependent) earns less than a certain amount and are eligible to file Form 1040A or 1040EZ, or when they are not required to file any income tax return. The *Automatic Zero EFC* is not available to an independent student with dependents (other than spouse). After 2008, the income threshold amount increases based on changes in the Consumer Price Index. As an example, for the 2019–2020 *academic year,* families with annual incomes below $27,000 who filed a 1040A or 1040 EZ will not have any of their income counted in the FAFSA.[16]

Another special rule applies to families at low-income levels, those with adjusted gross incomes of less than $50,000 for 2019. Under the *Simplified Needs Test,* the student (and parent if the student is dependent) must have received benefits under a means-tested Federal benefit program, such as food stamps, SSI, TANF, certain school lunch programs, or certain supplemental nutrition programs for women and children (WIC). Under the *Simplified Needs Test,* only the income is

---

15. 20 U.S.C. § 1087oo–qq.
16. Garnett, *supra* note 11.

assessed. It applies if one of the student's parents is a dislocated worker as defined in Section 101 of the Workforce Investment Act of 1998.[17] Independent students are eligible if the student is a dislocated worker. Also, the time frame during which both dependent and independent students may have received means-tested federal benefits to establish eligibility for the simplified needs test will be extended from 12 to 24 months.

Planning Pointer

Care must be taken not to file the regular Form 1040 when the taxpayer is eligible to file form 1040A or 1040 EZ. Otherwise, the taxpayer risks losing the special financial aid benefits for low-income applicants. Only those taxpayers that are not self-employed, not partners or shareholders in an S Corporation or LLC, not beneficiaries of trust, who do not have rent or royalty income, and have no capital gains, are eligible to file Form 1040A or 1040EZ.

C. The Institutional Methodology Formula

The *Institutional Methodology Formula* (IMF) is used by some 3,000 private colleges and scholarship programs to dispense institutional aid. A college may use the FMF to distribute any federal financial aid at its disposal and may also use the IMF to distribute its own private funds. In general, the IMF digs deeper into a family's financial situation than the FMF because colleges want to ensure that their own funds go to the neediest students. Differences arise not only in the definition of income and assets but also in the allowances that are subtracted. The portion of the assets and income assessed are also different. *See* **Chart 19-5.**

CHART 19-5 Comparison of Percentage Difference

	Federal (FMF)	Institutional (IMF)
Parent Assets	Up to 5.64%	From 3–5%
Student Assets	20%	25%
Parent Income	22–47%	22–46%
Student Income	50%	50%

17. Dislocated worker status may arise from one of the following factors: losing one's job, being laid off, receiving unemployment compensation, being self-employed but unemployed due to economic conditions, being a "displaced homemaker," or having trouble finding employment.

The IMF uses *adjusted gross income* from the tax return, and like the FMF, adds untaxed income, such as child support and other income. Some subtractions are similar to the FMF, such as those for federal income and FICA tax. However, instead of a state tax table, the IMF allows a subtraction for *actual* state, local, sales, and property taxes paid. In addition, the IMF provides the following allowances: (1) a medical and dental expense allowance to account for exceptional medical and dental expenses, (2) an employment expense allowance to account for expenses related to working outside the home (those for single earners and two-earner couples), (3) an Annual Education Savings Allowance (AESA) for the education expenses of younger children, (4) an Income Protection Allowance (IPA), a standard defined by the U.S. Department of Commerce, representing an amount below which a family has no ability to contribute to the child's educational costs, and (5) an elementary/secondary tuition allowance to account for expenses paid by the family for private elementary or secondary school tuition (this allowance is at the discretion of the institution). The IMF expects a minimum contribution from each student and assumes all students work full-time during the summer.

The IMF, like the FMF, includes all categories of assets and is intended to be comprehensive. Like the IMF, pension assets are not counted, due in large part to the difficulty of valuation. The PROFILE, however, includes many of the assets not included in the FAFSA, such things as the value of the family home, farm, and business, as well as parents' assets held in the names of the student's siblings. Again, this is because the IMF is more comprehensive, and digs deeper into the family assets, than the FMF.

Three allowances are then subtracted from the net value of these assets: (1) an *Emergency Reserve Allowance* (ERA) which protects for unanticipated expenses and is based on family size and average expenses as reported by the federal Consumer Expenditure Survey, (2) a *Cumulative Education Savings Allowance* (CESA) of an amount a family needs to save to finance their children's education, and (3) a *Low Income Asset Allowance* that recognizes that a family with very low income needs additional asset protection.

Like the FMF, the IMF varies depending on whether or not the student is independent. A student is automatically considered independent if he/she is 24 years old, a veteran of the armed forces, a master's or doctoral candidate, married, has legal dependents other than a spouse, or is declared independent by a court. Like the FMF, the custodial parent (and their spouse if married) is assessed, and some colleges require financial information from both biological parents when parents are divorced or separated. Like the FMF, the number of people in the household is relevant, although the assessment is slightly different. Under the IMF, if two children are in college then 60 percent of the parent's contribution is to be used, and if three children are in college, then 45 percent is required.

CHART 19-6 Summary of Asset and Income Difference between the FMF and the IMF

	Federal Methodology Formula	**Institutional Methodology Formula**
Automatic Zero EPC when income below $30,000. Simplified Needs Test for parents if applicant receives means-tested Federal benefits or is a dislocated worker	Recognizes	Does not recognize
Home Equity, Family Farm assets, and Qualified Small Business	Not Included No assessment of farm if families living on farm and "materially participates" No assessment of business if 50% owned and controlled and less than 100 full-time employees	Included
Minimum student contribution from summer job	Not Required	Required even if student does not work
Savings accounts in names of student's siblings	Not Required	Parents must report these
Student's assets Parent's assets	Assessed at 20% Assessed up to 5.64%	Assessed at 25% Assessed between 3–5%
Flexible spending accounts for childcare and medical care	Not required	Must be reported
Estimate of how much money parents expect to earn in the coming year	Not required	Required
Anticipated outside scholarships and relatives' contributions	Not required	Students must provide an estimate
Members of household enrolled in college	Parents and dependent children counted. EFC divided equally among all in college	Only dependent children counted (at college's discretion) If two children in college then 60% counted and if three then 45%
Income Protection Allowance	Based on poverty figures from the 1960s (adjusted for inflation)	Based on current Consumer Expenditure Survey data

	Federal Methodology Formula	Institutional Methodology Formula
Employment Expense Allowance	Allowed	Allowed
Emergency Reserve Allowance	Not Allowed	Allowed
Education Savings Allowance	Allowed	Allowed
Losses from Tax Schedules C, D, E, and F	Allowed	May not be allowed (at college's discretion)
Unreimbursed Medical Expenses	Deductible minus 7.5% of AGI	Allowance for extraordinary medical and dental expenses
Private School Tuition of other household members	Not considered	May have an allowance against income (at college's discretion)
Divorced Parents	Assets of custodial parent (including spouse of that parent) and transfers from other parent constitute resources	Considers assets of both parents
Siblings' Assets	Not considered unless owned by parent (such as a 529 plan)	Are considered
Siblings' Income	If file own return (even if subject to "kiddie tax") will not be considered	Same
Student's Income	Assessed at 50%	Same
All assets	Excluded if meet the simplified needs test	All assets assessed even if file simple tax return
Prepaid tuition plan	Considered an asset of parent at "refund value" (usually capital contributed)	Considered an asset
Coverdell ESA	Asset of parent	Asset of student
Retirement Assets	Not assessed	Usually not assessed
Section 529 Plans	Asset of owner or parent if student is owner	Asset of owner
Custodial Accounts	Asset of beneficiary	Asset of beneficiary
Trusts	Asset of beneficiary	Asset of beneficiary
Parent's Income	Assessed between 22–47%	Assessed between 22–46%
FLP or LLC	Asset of owner of shares	Asset of owner of shares
Employer Assistance	Nonassessable Income	Nonassessable income
AOTC & Lifetime Learning	Not Income or asset	Not Income or asset

CHART 19-7 Financial Need as a Variable of Cost

Calculation	Public College	Private College
COA	$15,000	$40,000
less		
EFC	$10,000	$10,000
= BFN*	$ 5,000	$30,000

*The BFN or Basic Financial Need, can be met through grants, scholarships, loans, or work-study. Different schools will offer different *financial aid awards.*

Some private colleges collect information that is different from the traditional institutional formula and may even have an entirely unique financial aid formula. For example, the 568 Group[18] admits students on a need-blind basis; this group is comprised of about 25 elite colleges, including Amherst, Columbia, Duke, MIT, Rice, Yale, and Williams. These schools use the PROFILE information but make it fairer, for example, by adding a standard cost-of-living allowance for expensive cities like New York and Boston.

Other private schools have their own unique formula. Some schools may require make and model of car, year in which home was purchased and cost, current value of IRA and other pension plans, and income and assets of the noncustodial parent. Some colleges count Section 529 savings plans heavily, expecting the student to spend 25 percent of the balance each year regardless of the owner. Some of the wealthiest Ivy League schools increase the asset protection allowance for parents that rent to equalize the equity in a typical home. They often lower the expected contribution from student assets. Furthermore, wealthy schools with huge endowments provide aid mostly in the form of grants.[19]

Whichever formula is used, a student or family may have special circumstances that are not taken into account in the formulae. In such circumstances, the student/family should be advised to schedule a meeting with the institution's FAO. It is within the FAO's discretion to increase the student's COA for extraordinary needs. Examples might include exceptional medical needs, illness or death in the family, a parent out-of-work, educational transportation, etc. However, requests to increase COA for some *perceived* needs will most likely be refused. For example, financial aid professionals are likely to frown on a student's perceived need because of expensive car payments, shopping habits, or travel plans. To successfully negotiate a better financial aid package, the advisor should assist the student/family in preparing reasonable arguments for an increase and often document the underlying rationales.

18. 568 Presidents Grp., http://www.568group.org/home/ (last visited May 14, 2021).
19. *See* **Chart 5-5** in **Chapter Five: When Savings Are Not Enough**.

CHART 19-8 Calculation of Adjusted Need (AN)

Cost of Attendance (COA)	Tuition, fees, room and board, books and supplies, travel to and from the university, personal expenses such as clothing and entertainment, and cost of computer.
less Expected Family Contribution (EFC)	Parents' contribution from income and assets plus student's contribution from income and assets.
= Basic Financial Need (BFN)	
less Student Resources (SR)	Scholarships, gifts paid directly to the college for tuition, payments from employer-provided education assistance plan, VA education benefits.
= Adjusted Need (AN)	

Planning Pointer

It is very difficult to plan whether or not a family will be eligible for financial aid in the future. However, all families regardless of their income should apply for financial aid even if they believe they will not qualify; annual changes to the requirements make it very difficult to predict award availability without actually filing a FAFSA.

D. The Potential Impact of Various Forms of Savings on Financial Aid

Various forms of savings are counted in both financial aid formulae. It is logical to assess these savings under the presumption that they can be used for the cost of the student's college attendance. However, the type of savings and how the savings are titled will make a big difference under the two financial aid formulae. Savings constitute assets and are assessed between 3–5.64 percent if owned by the parent versus 20–25 percent if owned by the student. Therefore, it may be better to have assets held by parents or even grandparents. However, distributions from the savings account could be considered income and taxed at a higher rate than if considered assets. These distributions may even constitute a *resource* and reduce financial aid dollar for dollar. This section of the chapter will examine the 529 savings plan, the 529 prepaid plan, the Coverdell, and other savings techniques. It will compare them under each of the two different federal aid formulae.

1. 529 Savings Plans

The 529 savings plans are often owned by the parent. If the parent owns the plan, the asset is considered the parent's asset. The *Deficit Reduction Omnibus Reconciliation Act (DRORA) of 2005* changed the federal formula for financial aid purposes.

DRORA held that Section 529s should be considered the parent's assets even when owned by the student. Thus, this act favorably treats these assets as an assessment to the parent, and the assessment is much lower than if owned by the student or if distributed and considered student income or resource. Assets held in the student's name will be depleted 20 percent under the FMF. On the other hand, assets held by parents will only be assessed up to 5.64 percent under FMF. However, under DRORA and the FMF, the assets in a Section 529 plan are not considered the assets of the student but of the parent and will be assessed accordingly.

Likewise, when there has been a rollover into a Section 529 from a UGMA/UTMA account or a Coverdell, the owner should remain the student but be assessed to the parent under DRORA. However, under the IMF, these assets are still considered owned by the student and are assessed at 25 percent.

EXAMPLE 19-6: Alice, Ben's mother, rolls over a custodianship account and a Coverdell into a Section 529 plan. The assets in the UGMA must be sold, and any gain is income to Ben, assessed at 50 percent under both the FMF and the IMF. The value of the total account should also be considered Ben's asset under the IMF and will be assessed at 25 percent, but under the FMF will be considered an asset of Alice and be assessed up to 5.6 percent.

The federal law seems clear that for purposes of the FMF, any distribution from the 529 savings plan, once counted as an asset to the parent, will not constitute income or a *resource.* Under the IMF, it is much less clear.

EXAMPLE 19-7: Alice is the owner of a 529 savings plan for her son Ben. The account value is $250,000 and represents principal of $150,000 and earnings of $50,000. The total value of the account ($250,000) would constitute Alice's asset under both the FMF and the IMF.

If the grandparents or other relatives own the Section 529 plan, the plan is not considered an asset in either financial aid formula. However, any distribution from the 529 to the student account to pay for college will most likely be treated as untaxed income to the student and assessed at 50 percent under both formulae. Starting in the 2023–24 academic year, a new simplified FASA will no longer consider distributions from grandparent's 529s as assessed as student income.[20]

Under the *College Cost Reduction Act (CCRA) of 2007,* distributions from 529 plans that are counted as the parent's assets are not subject to federal income

20. Kathryn Flynn, *New FAFSA Removes Roadblocks for Grandparent 529 Plans*, Saving for College (Feb. 18, 2021), https://wordpress.savingforcollege.com/article/new-fafsa-removes-roadblocks-for-grandparent-529-plans.

tax and are excluded from "total income" under the federal financial aid formula. Furthermore, under CCRA such distributions are not considered "other financial assistance" that reduce aid.

EXAMPLE 19-8: Assume Ben has a Section 529 savings account of $10,000 as a high school senior. Under the institutional formula, Ben will be expected to use $2,500 for the freshman year (leaving $7,500) $1,875 for the sophomore year (leaving $5,625), $1,406 for the junior year (leaving $4,219), and $1,055 for the senior year. All that remains of the $10,000 is $3,164. When the same account is held by his parents, they would be expected to tap $2,059 of the $10,000, leaving $7,941. If the assets were in the grandparents' name, then nothing would be included in the financial aid formula.

If the grandparent owns the account and the advisor wants to get around this problem, the account owner could be changed to the parent (although some plans do not allow this unless the original owner has died). In addition, if the grandparent decided to transfer ownership of a 529 account to his/her own child, this might be considered a gift at the time of the change of ownership.[21] The law is uncertain here. Another approach is to wait until the FAFSA has been filed, then roll over a year's worth of distributions from the grandparent-owned 529 into a parent-owned one in the same state's plan.

Otherwise, a risk exists of adverse state tax consequences. Waiting until after the FAFSA is filed and using the money before the next FASA will have no impact on the financial aid eligibility. One can also withdraw money for a qualified expense after January 1 of the student's sophomore year (if the student plans to finish in four years). Otherwise, make this withdrawal two years before the student intends to graduate. The FAFSA looks back two years, so this will mean that the grandparent-owned plan will not affect financial aid for college at all; however, if the student plans to attain professional or postgraduate education, it will affect financial aid for future education within two years. It is always allowable to take the money out of the grandparent's 529 after college is finished and use it to pay off student loans. However, that is a qualified expense only up to $10,000. Any earnings on the payment of unqualified loan amounts will result in an income tax, as well as a *ten percent penalty*.

---

21. See discussion in **Chapter Nine: Estate Planning with Section 529 Savings Plans** on the Advance Notice of proposed rulemaking. Under those rules, a gift could occur only at the time property is received by the grandparent.

Planning Pointer

In general, it is better to have the parents own the 529 plan. If the grandparents own the plan, then it is not an asset of the parent or student, but any distribution from the plan will most likely be assessed as student income at 50 percent. Care must be taken to change the ownership from the grandparent to the parent as this may trigger tax consequences. A better approach is to withdraw a distribution from the grandparent plan after January 1 and either pay for a qualified expense before the next FAFSA application or transfer this to the parent's 529 plan. After the *SECURE Act*, $10,000 of loan principal and interest of a qualified beneficiary can be paid for with 529 funds after the student has finished college.

2. Section 529 Prepaid Tuition Plan

Before the *Deficit Reduction Omnibus Reconciliation Act (DRORA) of 2005*, prepaid plans were considered a *resource* of the student and reduced financial aid dollar for dollar. After the DRORA, these plans (along with Section 529 savings plans and Coverdells) are not considered "an *asset* of the student" but rather an asset of the parent.[22] Of course, prepaid tuition plans were never considered the student's "*asset*" under the federal formula. They were always considered a *resource.* This also makes sense to the extent that the prepaid was used for tuition. It would seem to reduce the need for financial aid—similar to a scholarship. The intent of the DRORA, however, is to treat prepaid plans (and Coverdells as well as rollovers of Coverdells and custodianships into 529 savings plans) the same as 529 savings plans for purposes of the federal aid formula. Therefore, these are assessed as the asset of the parent under the FMF. However, the FAFSA application only assesses these prepaid plans at their "refund value." This would usually be the amount that could be withdrawn or transferred and would usually be equivalent to the amount of the original capital contribution. This "refund value" would thus be much lower than the value of a 529 savings plan.

Any prepaid plan of a sibling owned by the parent will be treated similarly. When owned by a grandparent, none of the assets are considered in the federal financial aid formula. After CCRR, the principal and earnings from these accounts that are used to pay for college expenses are not considered income of the student or a resource. Prepaid plans originally funded by the parent are considered parental assets under the IMF. Of course, private colleges may decide to assess these differently. Any prepaid plan owned by the sibling is also treated as an asset of the parent and assessed under the IMF.

---

22. Pub. L. No. 109-171, § 8019(d)(5), 120 Stat. 4 (2006).

3. The Coverdell ESA

Before DRORA, the value of the Coverdell account was considered an asset of the student under the federal methodology formula (FMF). After enactment of the DRORA, these assets will be considered an asset of the parent and assessed up to 5.6 percent.[23] DRORA changed the *federal* formula by stating that a Coverdell would "not be considered a student asset" when "owned by the student." In addition, Coverdells that have been transferred into the 529 savings plan will be assessed to the parent, even though technically owned by the student. CCRA also makes clear that distributions from the Coverdell are not considered income or resources.[24]

EXAMPLE 19-9: Ben, a dependent of Alice, has a Coverdell established in his name, and Alice is the responsible party. In the first year of college (when the value of the account is $20,000), Ben takes a $10,000 distribution from the account. The $20,000 value of the account will not constitute an asset to Ben nor will the distribution of $10,000 be considered his income or a resource. Instead, the $20,000 will be assessed up to 5.6 percent as Alice's asset.

Under the institutional methodology formula (IMF) used by private schools, the Coverdell is considered a parent asset if the account is in the parent's name or the parent is custodian. As such, this asset would reduce aid by 3–5 percent of the balance each year. The account is considered the student's asset if anyone other than the parent is custodian. Unlike the FMF, any distributions of principal and earnings are treated as the student's income under the IMF and assessed at 50 percent. *See* **Chart 19-5.**

CHART 19-9 Impact of DRORA for 529 Plans and Coverdells

Asset Owned by Parent	• Assessed at up to 5.64% as parent asset
Asset Owned by Student	• Assessed at up to 5.64% as parent asset
Asset Owned by Grandparent	• 0 assessed
Distribution for qualified education expenses	• Not income • Not a resource • Or, at the discretion of the FAO, could be either of the above

23. Pub. L. No. 109-171, § 8019(d)(5).

24. Since these accounts are considered owned by the student, it is clear from the intent of this act that the Coverdell account is not to be considered a resource. U.S. Dep't of Educ., Federal Student Aid Handbook: 2020–2021, Award, Application and Verification Guide.

Planning Pointer

DRORA and CCRA *only apply to the federal formula*; the institutional formula remains the same as before the act. Under DRORA, the Section 529 plans and Coverdell when owned by the student will be assessed as an asset of the parent under the federal formula. Under CCRA, distributions from 529 savings plans, prepaid plans, and Coverdells are not includible as gross income in the federal financial aid, and distributions are not considered financial assistance or a resource. However, the advisor should be aware that the financial aid officer has considerable discretion and could consider these when they are used to pay for tuition and other higher education expenses.

4. Other Savings Techniques

The assessment of savings under the two formulae (other than 529s and Coverdells) will generally depend on who owns the asset. When financial aid is a probability, savings in the parent's name are better than savings in the student's name because the assessment percentage is much lower. Direct ownership of savings assets by the student will be assessed at 20 percent under the federal formula and 25 percent under the institutional formula. Any interest or income from these assets will be assessed at 50 percent. Additionally, assets considered the student's, such as custodianships and trusts, may preclude the student from being eligible for financial aid. Thus, savings accounts solely in the name of the student should be avoided if the student wishes to be eligible for financial aid.

Generally, sibling's assets are not considered in the federal methodology but are considered in the institutional formula. The IMF will also assess the sibling's assets in a Coverdell account and in the sibling's Section 529 plan to the parent (if the parent is the owner) as an asset. The younger sibling's income, however, will not be included in either formula if that income does not appear on the parent's tax return.

The financial aid assessment of 529s and Coverdells under the FMF are treated favorably when owned by the parent or student beneficiary. However, other savings mechanisms may be quite differently treated. *See* **Chart 19-11**. This section will discuss two of the savings mechanisms typically used for educational purposes: (1) joint savings accounts and (2) custodianship accounts.

a. *Joint Savings Account*

Joint savings accounts between parent and student will be considered a parental asset when the parent's social security number appears on the account. Therefore, when the student saves, these funds should be placed in this account. The student can draw from the account and have significant control. Of course, the income interest from the account will be considered the income of the parent for tax purposes and thus their income for financial aid purposes and is assessed at up to 47 percent or 50 percent. Any student earnings, of course, would be assessed at 50 percent.

b. Custodian Accounts (UGMA/UTMA)

Custodian accounts are one of the worst places to put savings for any student, regardless of whether he/she attends public or private college. The present value of the custodial account is considered a student asset and assessed at 20 percent under the FMF and 25 percent under the IMF. Any income or capital gains from the account are considered the student's income and assessed at 50 percent, even when there has been no distribution from the account. In addition, under recent legislation,[25] the cut-off age for the kiddie tax is raised to 24 if the child is a full-time dependent student, and the student will be taxed on any income or gain at the top trust and estate tax rates until he/she reaches age 24.

EXAMPLE 19-10: Same as **Example 19-9**, but Ben has a custodianship account. In the first year of college, when there is no distribution from the account, the $20,000 value will be assessed at 20 percent under FMF and 25 percent under the IMF ($4,000 and $5,000 respectively). In addition, any income from the account or capital gains from the sale of assets in the account that would be needed for a cash distribution in Ben's second year of college would be Ben's income and assessed at 50 percent (even though taxed at the top trust and estate tax rates). Then when $10,000 is distributed, 50 percent of $10,000 or $5,000 is assessed plus 20 percent or 25 percent of the remaining value [$20,000 – $10,000 – (either $4,000 or $5,000) is assessed].

5. Family Home, Farm, or Business

The net value of the family home, farm, or small business is not counted as an asset under the FMF. The family home must be the principal place of residence, not a vacation home. In addition to being the principal residence, the family must "materially participate" in the farm's operations. The small business must be 50 percent owned and controlled by the family and must employ no more than 100 full-time employees. From a planning point of view, if the student plans on attending a state school, the mortgages on the home, farm, or business can be paid off with other assets, thus reducing those assets and increasing aid. Under the IMF, the value of the home, farm, and business are considered assets.

25. Tax Increase Prevention and Reconciliation Act of 2005, § 511, 26 U.S.C. § 1(g) (2005).

EXAMPLE 19-11: Alice has a home (value $250,000, mortgage $100,000). If Alice sells all her investment assets (value $100,000) in the year *before* the financial aid base year and uses the proceeds to pay off the $100,000 mortgage, she has not only reduced her income (the income on the investment assets) but also her assets (the value of both the home and the investments) under FMF.

6. Family Limited Partnership (FLP) or Limited Liability Corporation (LLC)

FLPs and LLCs are considered assets of the partner, limited partner, or shareholder and will be fully counted as an asset under both the FMF and the IMF. If the assets in these entities are investment properties, they are assessed at their fair market value. Under the financial aid formulae there is no marketability or control discount like there is under the gift tax rules.

Because FLPs and LLCs are taxed as conduits, any income earned by the FLP or LLC attributable to the parent's ownership interest will be assessed up to 47 percent under the FMF and up to 46 percent under the IMF, even when no actual distribution is made. If the student owns the interest, any income attributable to it will be assessed at 50 percent under both formulae. Again, no distribution is required for the 50 percent assessment to be made.

EXAMPLE 19-12: The family has dumped stocks into a FLP. The husband and wife each have a 49 percent interest and their college-age child, Ben, has a 2 percent interest. If the stocks are valued at $100,000 on the financial aid application date, then Ben's 2 percent interest will be assessed as an asset at 2 percent under the FMF (or $2,000). No discounts arise here if this is not a business. If Ben is a dependent, his parents' 98 percent interest will be assessed at 5 percent to 6 percent. In addition, any income attributable to Ben and his parents by virtue of the conduit tax rules will result in a 50 percent assessment for Ben and up to a 47 percent (FMF) or up to 46 percent (IMF) assessment for his parents (even when no distribution is made).

7. Gifts

Parents who transfer income as gifts to dependent students for payment of college expenses do not include this income in the financial aid formulae. The source of this gift has already been counted, either as income (such as earnings) or an asset (such as savings). If the student is independent, the parent's assets and income are not counted in the formulae, however, any gifts from parents or other relatives will be considered either untaxed income or a *resource* and will reduce aid dollar for dollar. This is true under both the FMF and the IMF. Grandparents or other relatives' assets and income are not calculated in any financial aid formulae, but gifts from them can have a negative financial aid impact. If the grandparent or other relative makes a gift to the student prior to the base year and the gift is deposited in a savings, checking, or investment account, or otherwise invested in an asset, the value of the asset will count as the student's asset and will be assessed at either 20 percent under the FMF or 25 percent under the IMF. If the grandparent or other relative makes a gift to the parent, this will be an asset of the parent and assessed to them. If the grandparent or other relative makes a direct tuition payment under the *Section 2503(e) transfer* rules to the educational institution in order to obtain the benefit of the annual gift-tax present interest exclusion, the payment will be considered a *resource* and will reduce the student's financial aid dollar for dollar. *See* **Chart 19-10: Timing of Gift Transfer**.

EXAMPLE 19-13: Ben has been receiving a $10,000 gift from his grandmother for the last two years. He now has $24,000 in that gift account. For financial aid purposes, 20 percent of that account ($4,800) under the FMF or 25 percent of that account ($6,000) under the IMF will be assessed. In addition, the income from the account will be assessed as student income (50% under both formulae). If, instead, his grandparents give Ben $24,000 this year to pay for his college expenses, all 100 percent or $24,000 will reduce his financial aid.

8. Insurance

The cash surrender value of life insurance is not considered an asset under the FMF.[26] Therefore, insurance is a great place for investing assets if (1) the student plans to attend a public school and (2) purchasing insurance makes sense from a financial planning perspective. Private colleges might ask about insurance, in which case the cash surrender value could be assessed as a parent asset under the IMF.

EXAMPLE 19-14: Alice, Ben's mom, has a $1,000,000 insurance policy on her life. She has built up cash surrender value of $100,000. Alice can borrow against her policy to pay for Ben's college education, and neither the value of the policy nor the loan amount will be considered in the FMF. The $100,000, however, could be considered an asset of the parent under the IMF and assessed at 5 percent.

26. U.S. Dep't of Educ., *supra* note 23.

CHART 19-10 Timing of Gift Transfers

				Financial Aid Consequences	
Gift	**From**	**To**	**When**	**FMF**	**IMF**
$ 15,000	Non-Parent	Student	Before College	If student saves, then student asset reduces aid 20%	If student saves, then student asset reduces aid 25%
$ 15,000	Non-Parent	Student	During College	Resource so reduces aid 100%	Resource so reduces aid 100%
$ 15,000	Non-Parent	Student	After College	No effect	No effect
$ 15,000	Non-Parent	Parent	Before College, During College, After College	If parent saves, then parent asset. Reduces aid up to 5.6%	Same. Asset of parent. Reduces aid from 3–5%
$ 15,000	Parent	Dependent student	During College	No effect. Already counted	Already counted
$ 15,000	Parent	Independent student	During College	Resource so reduces aid 100%	Resource so reduces aid 100%
$ 15,000	Parent	Dependent student	After College	No effect	No effect
$ 15,000	Parent	Dependent student	Before College	If student saves in traditional savings, then student asset and reduces aid 20%. If student saves in Coverdell or 529 plans, then a parent asset and reduces aid up to 5.6%.	If student saves in traditional savings, then student asset and reduces aid 25%. If student saves in Coverdell or 529 plans, then a student asset and reduces aid 25%.

9. Retirement Assets

Retirement assets, like equity in a home and cash surrender value life insurance, are not considered assets under the FMF. However, a tax-deductible contribution to a retirement fund during the base income year will be assessed as income.[27] Any contribution made before the base year of the financial aid application will be shielded as an asset. In a year of a rollover—when a Traditional IRA is converted to a Roth IRA, income is increased by an amount reported on the return.

Under the IMF, increasing numbers of schools are asking about Roth IRAs and other retirement assets. These schools most likely are considering these as potential assets that could be tapped for college. Under the worst-case scenario, these would be assessed as the parent's asset contribution.

EXAMPLE 19-15: Each year for ten years, Bill and Mary make contributions to a Traditional IRA and a Roth IRA. Their contributions total $150,000, and the accounts are valued at $250,000. The couple can increase their aid eligibility under the FMF because $250,000 is not included. Their $100,000 savings will not be assessed. Under the IMF, all $250,000 could be assessed from 3–5 percent.

If retirement assets are used to pay for college, however, 100 percent of the distribution—both income and principal—is counted as part of the parent's asset contribution.

10. Savings Bonds

Savings bonds that qualify for tax-advantaged treatment cannot be owned by anyone younger than 24 years old. Thus, the bonds are usually considered the parent's asset and reduce aid by 3–5.64 percent, depending on the formulae. If redeemed, the interest is tax exempt (Section 135), but this is *income* for financial aid purposes and thus will be assessed as income to the owner. Cashing in bonds is recommended in the student's last year of college to avoid adverse financial aid consequences. Thus, they can be used to pay off any college debt.

EXAMPLE 19-16: Savings bonds that cost $50,000 and are held by Alice, the parent of Ben, are cashed in at the end of Ben's junior year in high school. The interest consists of $40,000 and is excluded from Alice's taxes because she has low AGI and otherwise qualifies under Section 135. For purposes of determining financial aid, the $50,000 value of the bonds is an asset and assessed at from 3 to 5.6 percent, depending on the formulae. The tax-exempt interest of $40,000 is added back to Alice's income and assessed at up to 47 percent or 50 percent, depending on the formulae.

27. *See Completing the FAFSA 2020–2021*, *supra* note 12.

Once the bonds are cashed, however, they no longer are considered assets. For unqualified bonds, the treatment for financial aid purposes will depend on who owns the bond. If the parent owns the bond, they count as the parent's asset; if owned by the student, they count as the student's asset. Any income from a non-qualified bond is also assessed to the owner as *income*.

11. Trusts

Assets in a trust will be assessed according to the ownership, powers, and interests in the trust. Assets in a revocable trust of the parent are considered the parent's asset. For an irrevocable trust, the assets are attributable to the person who owns the beneficial interest in the trust.[28] The present value of that interest—whether an income interest or an interest in principal or in both—must be determined. Even if the trust instrument restricts the beneficiary's access to the trust, it is still an asset.

For example, if the terms of the trust require that the income accumulate, as might be the case in a Section 2503(c) trust, the beneficiary must report the value of the right to future income as an asset. If the terms of the trust give the trustee discretion to apply the principal for education purposes, as would be the case in a Section 2503(b) trust, the beneficiary must report this value. If it is a multiple beneficiary *Crummy* trust, the interest of the student beneficiary must be determined. The trust officer can usually calculate this, but if not, the financial aid officer will do so. Both the federal and institutional formula apply this rule. There is one exception to the rule, and that is that a restricted trust is not an asset of the beneficiary; this occurs when the court has established a trust for the benefit of the beneficiary. For example, when the beneficiary has had a car accident and the trust fund is established by court order to pay future medical benefits, this trust will not be treated as an asset.

EXAMPLE 19-17: Ben is the beneficiary of a *Crummy* trust set up for him by his grandparents. The value of his beneficial interest is $50,000. Under the FMF 20 percent ($10,000) will be assessed, and under the IMF 25 percent ($12,500) will be assessed.

When the beneficiary receives income from the trust, the income must be reported in the year in which it is received and is treated as the student's income under both the FMF and the IMF—reducing aid by 50 percent.

---

28. U.S. Dep't of Educ., *supra* note 23.

Planning Pointer

Trusts, like custodianship accounts, are one of the worst places for saving for college. Perhaps the harsh treatment may be a result of the belief that only wealthy kids have trust funds. This, of course, is not always true as trusts can be established by the death of a parent, and these testamentary trusts are treated under the same formulae as inter vivos trusts.

EXAMPLE 19-18: Mary's mom died while she was in college, and Mary was the sole beneficiary of her mom's trust—which Mary can invade for education purposes. The full value of the trust would be considered an asset for Mary and be assessed at either 20 percent under the FMF or 25 percent under the IMF. Every year the remaining "balance" will be assessed as well.

CHART 19-11 Impact of Tax Savings Plan Ownership on Financial Aid

	Owned by the Parent		**Owned by Dependent Student**	
	FMF	**IMF**	**FMF**	**IMF**
All Assets Unless Exception	Excluded if meets the simplified means test, otherwise assessed at up to 5.64%	Asset of Parent assessed at 3%–5%	Asset of Student assessed at 20% after HERA	Asset of Student assessed at 25%
Coverdells	Considered Parent asset	Considered Parent asset	Considered Parent asset	Considered Student asset
Custodial Account	N/A (Considered owned by student)	N/A (Considered owned by student)	Considered Student Asset. Earnings from account considered Student's income	Considered Student Asset. Earnings from account considered Student's income
Family Home	No Assessment	May assess to Parent if parents have equity	N/A	N/A
Family Farm	No assessment if family is living on farm and "materially participates"	Assessment even if family lives there and "materially participates"	N/A (not considered owned by student)	N/A (not considered owned by student)

(continued)

	Owned by the Parent		Owned by Dependent Student	
	FMF	**IMF**	**FMF**	**IMF**
FLPs & LLCs	Value of share/ interest of parent is Parent's assessment	Value of share/ interest of parent is Parent's assessment	Value of students shares/ interest Student asset Income from entity considered Student income on shares/ interest student owns	Value of students shares/ interest Student asset Income from entity considered Student income on shares/ interest student owns
Gifts	If parent receives gifts then treated as asset	If parent receives gifts then treated as asset	Gifts from relatives other than parents treated as resource	Gifts from relatives other than parents treated as resource
Insurance	Not assessed	Usually not considered	Not assessed	Usually not considered
Retirement	Not assessed Distribution will trigger all 100% considered parent's asset	Sometimes considered	Not assessed but distribution trigger assessment	Sometimes considered
Savings Bonds	Assessed as Parent's asset	Assessed as Parent's asset	N/A (must be 24 to own)	N/A (must be 24 to own)
Section 529 Savings & Prepaids	Assessed as Parent's asset The earnings portion of a distribution should be in student's income for next year	Assessed as Parent's asset The earnings portion of a distribution should be in student's income for next year	Not considered Student asset but Parent asset No assessment from distribution	Considered Student asset Unclear if distribution will be considered

	Owned by the Parent		Owned by Dependent Student	
	FMF	**IMF**	**FMF**	**IMF**
Trusts	N/A	N/A	If principal in the name of the student, then Student's asset unless a restricted trust If student receives income from trust then this is Student's income If income accumulates for benefit of student and is not distributed, the present value of that interest is Student asset	If principal in the name of the student, then Student's asset unless a restricted trust If student receives income from trust then this is Student's income If income accumulates for benefit of student and is not distributed, the present value of that interest is Student asset

E. Conclusion

In order to obtain financial aid, the student will need to fill out annually either the FAFSA or PROFILE or both. The federal methodology formula (used in the FAFSA) is quite different from the institutional methodology formula (used in the PROFILE), but both are quite complex. *See* **Chart 19-12**. Both formulae attempt to determine the family's financial need based on complex income and asset calculations. Unfortunately, both formulae tend to overestimate family contributions and underestimate costs—thus compelling the family to take out more loans or come up with a way to meet this gap. Sometimes even wealthy taxpayers who have saved can qualify for financial aid. Type of assets, titling of assets, timing of the liquidation of assets, and timing of distributions are all important considerations in determining financial aid. In general, 529s are favorable assets to have for purposes of qualifying for financial aid when owned by the student or the parent. Lower and middle-income families, who are more likely to qualify for financial aid than the wealthy family, may receive significant tax benefits as well as scholarships, grants, fellowships, and loans, all of which can have an impact on financial aid.

CHART 19-12 Federal (FMF) and Institutional (IMF)— Similarities and Differences

Similarities	Differences
• Both IMF and FMF consider the income and assets of the stepparent if the custodial parent is remarried.	• IMF considers more family assets, such as home equity on principal place of residence. • IMF does not ignore family assets for families with income under $50,000. • IMF considers assets of siblings under 19 and not enrolled in higher education. • IMF assumes a minimum student contribution from summer employment. • IMF considers dental/medical expenses not covered by insurance and expenses of private. • IMF has a smaller reduction in the parent contribution when more than one child is enrolled in in college at the same time. • IMF removes paper losses such as depreciation. • IMF considers finances of non-custodial parent. • NOL carryovers, etc. that artificially reduce adjusted gross income. • IMF subtracts allowances for cumulative education saving and emergency reserves. • IMF considers regional differences in cost of living. • IMF yields a higher expected family contribution.

Conclusion

Because of the significant advantages of the Section 529 plan, including several modifications made by recent tax legislation, this book focuses on those plans. **Part I** of the book focuses on developing an education plan that includes savings and discusses the strategies when savings are inadequate to pay for the high cost of education. **Part II** discusses the tax and nontax advantages of the 529 plan. **Part III** explores the state prepaid plan and the Private College 529 institutional plan. Finally, **Part IV** examines coordination of 529 plans with other savings techniques, tax benefits, and financial aid.

Section 529 savings plans offer excellent federal tax benefits to taxpayers at all income levels. Substantial amounts can be contributed to these accounts to meet the reasonably expected education needs of the beneficiary. Although contributions are not deductible on the federal return, the earnings grow tax-free, and the appreciation, including earnings, are not taxed as long as the funds are distributed for qualified higher education purposes. In addition, the plan can be rolled over to a different plan or a different qualified beneficiary without tax consequences. Section 529 can be coordinated with other tax benefits (such as the American Opportunity Tax Credit and the Lifetime Learning Credit), other savings techniques (such as the Coverdell), as well as with financial aid. The 529 plan also offers state income tax advantages as many states allow an unlimited or limited deduction or credit to contributions to these plans.

In addition to income tax benefits, Section 529 savings plans offer significant gift, generation-skipping (GST), and estate tax advantages. The donor can accelerate the per-donee annual exclusion by contributing five times that amount to the 529 plan—with no adverse gift tax consequences. Married couples can contribute twice that amount if they split the gift. In addition, the portion excludable from gift tax is also excludable from GST consequences—even if the beneficiary is a grandchild. Furthermore, the donor or owner is not subject to estate tax consequences on the fund value, even though the owner can change the beneficiary of the plan, switch state investment strategies or plans, or reclaim the fund for his/her personal benefit. Thus, the 529 savings plan is a great estate planning tool for parents and grandparents who want to help their children or grandchildren pay for their education.

In addition to the tax benefits of a Section 529 savings plan, there are a number of nontax advantages as well. First, the owner of a Section 529 savings plan retains significant control, including the right to revoke the fund. Second, unlike most tax-advantaged gifts, a minor will not gain control of the Section 529 fund at the age of 18. Third, some states allow Section 529 plans to last forever. Fourth, under federal bankruptcy law, as well as in many states, Section 529 plans are not subject to creditor's claims. Fifth, Section 529 plan assets may not count as assets of the student beneficiary for financial aid purposes but instead be assessed at the lower rates of the parent. Lastly, the taxpayer can set up this plan with minimal expense with the assurance of a secure investment and good returns. Overall, a Section 529 savings plan allows the owner to maintain significant control over the funds while simultaneously keeping the funds away from the children and creditors.

Section 529 prepaid tuition plans offer some of the same benefits as the Section 529 savings plan. First, they are available to all income groups. Second, they provide income, gift, estate, and generation-skipping tax advantages. Third, they can be used with other tax provisions so long as no double tax benefits result. Fourth, the same nontax benefits exist, such as financial aid compatibility, control by the owner, and asset protection. Prepaid plans are less comprehensive than Section 529 savings plans, as they do not cover all education expenses—usually just tuition. However, they can offer guaranteed tuition rates even when investment returns are low and tuition costs are high. The relatively new Private College 529 institutional plan (with nearly 300 participating private school members) offers greater portability than the state prepaid plans and addresses some of the solvency issues of the state prepaid plans as well. However, neither of these plans guarantee admission to the school, and if the owner desires a refund or wishes to transfer to a Section 529 savings plan, the appreciation from the investment can be lost.

When the taxpayer has cash to invest, the Section 529 Savings Plan mechanism provides many more advantages than do the Coverdells, the savings bonds, and the custodianship accounts. Fortunately, all three of these mechanisms can be converted into the Section 529 plan with minimal tax disadvantages. Additionally, all the various savings techniques can be effectively coordinated with the Section 529 plans to pay for both qualified and nonqualified education expenses.

Section 529 plans can be coordinated with other education tax benefits, although these coordination rules can be extremely complicated. First, too many of the tax provisions overlap and have inconsistent definitions for qualifying educational expenditures. Second, several of the tax provisions provide either marriage penalties or marriage bonuses. Third, the tax provisions are not always compatible with the financial aid provisions. Lastly, the tax benefits are not adequate to help the low- and middle-income taxpayers fund their children's college costs.

The 529 plan has come a long way since the *Michigan Education Trust* was first set up in 1986. The *Small Business Job Protection Act of 1996* gave birth to Section 529, and it has been expanded since then, particularly as it relates to the definition of what qualifies for higher education expenses. The *American Recovery and Reinvestment Act of 2009* expanded the definition of QHEE to include "certain computer technology and equipment" and "special needs" equipment. The *Tax Cuts and Jobs Act of 2017* expanded the definition of QHHE to include payments of up to $10,000 in tuition for parochial and private K–12 education. The *Stephen Beck Jr., Achieving a Better Life Experience Act of 2014* enacted the Section 529A and the ABLE account. Subsequently, the *Tax Cuts and Jobs Act of 2017* allowed the ABLE accounts to be rolled over into the Section 529 plan. Lastly, the *Setting Every Community Up for Retirement Enhancement Act of 2019* broadened the definition of QHEE further by supporting apprenticeships and the payment of principal and interest on a qualified student loan up to $10,000 for not only the beneficiary of the 529 plan but his/her siblings.

The counselor must always advise the client about the possibility of change in the law. It is very likely that the 529 plan will change again. The next modification to the law might include homeschooling expenses as QHEEs; these proposals are already being suggested in light of the COVID-19 pandemic and the likelihood of another virus. There is also little doubt that the tax and financial aid systems are in need of simplification. The tax rules should be coordinated with financial aid accurately to reflect ability to pay. The tax benefits should be equitable and provide significant incentives for education-related activities. Continued subsidies in this area are essential for our national economic goals and continued "enlightened" democracy. With the importance of higher education in obtaining high-paying and long-lasting jobs, it is no surprise that educational planning is a common goal among most families. Despite our ever-changing society, one thing remains certain—educational planning will continue to be an important family goal.

APPENDICES

Appendix A

Acronyms and Abbreviations

ABLE	Achieving a Better Life Experience
AOTC	American Opportunity Tax Credit
529 Plan	Internal Revenue Code Section 529 Savings Account
2001 Act	Economic Growth and Tax Relief Reconciliation Act of 2001
AGI	Adjusted Gross Income
BAPCP	The Bankruptcy Abuse Prevention and Consumer Property Act of 2005
COA	Cost of Attendance
DB	Designated Beneficiary
DNI	Distributable Net Income
ESA	Coverdell Education Savings Account
NI	Distributed Net Income
EFC	Expected Family Contribution
EGTRRA	Economic Growth and Tax Relief Reconciliation Act of 2001
FAFSA	Free Application for Federal Student Aid
FLP	Family Limited Partnership
FMF	Federal Methodology Formula
GST	Generation-Skipping Tax
HERA	Higher Education Reconciliation Act of 2006
IMF	Institutional Methodology Formula

IRA	Individual Retirement Account
IRS	Internal Revenue Service
LLC	Lifetime Learning Credit
MAGI	Modified Adjusted Gross Income
MID	Miscellaneous Itemized Deduction
QESEE	Qualified Elementary and Secondary Education Expenses
QHEE	Qualified Higher Education Expenses
QSTP	Qualified State Tuition Program
QTP	Qualified Tuition Program
QTRE	Qualified Tuition and Related Expenses
SECURE	The Setting Every Community Up for Retirement Enhancement Act of 2009
SNT	Simplified Needs Test
SSI	Social Security Income
BJPA	The Small Business Job Protection Act of 1996
TRA	The Taxpayer Relief Act of 1997
TCJA	The Tax Cuts and Jobs Act of 2017
TIPRA	Tax Increase Prevention and Reconciliation Act of 2006
UGMA	Uniform Gifts to Minors Act
UTMA	Uniform Transfers to Minors Act
WCFB	Working Condition Fringe Benefits

Appendix B

Chart of Helpful Websites

Financial Aid Calculations	www.finaid.org www.collegeboard.org https://fsapartners.ed.gov/sites/default/files/attachments/2020-08/2122EFCFormulaGuide.pdf
Scholarship Information	opportunity.collegeboard.org
Information on 529 Plans	Lists each state and what the 529 deduction is: http://www.finaid.org/savings/state529deductions.phtml Compares each state's 529 plans: https://www.savingforcollege.com/college-savings-201 Other: www.savingforcollege.com
Student Aid and Free Application for Federal Student Aid	www.studentaid.gov www.studentaid.gov/h/apply-for-aid/fafsa
College Savings Plans Network (links to each plan)	www.collegesavings.org
Ratings of the Best and Worst 529 Plans	ww.morningstar.com. www.savingforcollege.com. www.kiplinger.com/article/college/t014-c000-s001-best-529-college-savings-plans.html

Appendix C

Summary of State-by-State 529 Plans

State	Program	Prepaid (P)/ Direct (D) or Advisor (A)	Website	State Statute Section
Alabama	CollegeCounts 529 Advisor Fund	A	www.CollegeCounts529advisor.com/	ALA. CODE § 16-33C-6
Alabama	CollegeCounts 529 Fund	D	www.CollegeCounts529.com	
Alaska	Alaska 529	D	Alaska529plan.com	ALASKA STAT. § 14.40.802–.817
Alaska	T. Rowe Price College Savings Plan	D	www3.troweprice.com/usis/personal-investing/products-and-services/college-savings-plans/t-rowe-price-college-savings-plan.html	
Alaska	John Hancock Freedom 529	A	www.jhinvestments.com/529	
Arizona	College Savings Bank (CSB)	D	collegesavings.com/Arizona/	ARIZ. REV. STAT. § 15-1871 to -1879
Arizona	The Fidelity Arizona College Savings Plan	D	www.fidelity.com/arizona	
Arizona	InvestEd	A	www.waddell.com	
Arkansas	iShares 529 plan	A	www.ishares529.com/content/homelogon.html	ARK. CODE ANN. § 6-84-101 to -113
Arkansas	The Gift College Investing Plan	D	www.arkansas529.org/home.html	
California	ScholarSave 529	D	www.scholarshare.com	CAL. ED. CODE §§ 69980–69994

State	Program	Prepaid (P)/ Direct (D) or Advisor (A)	Website	State Statute Section
Colorado	Collegeinvest Direct Portfolio College Savings Plan	D	www.collegeinvest.org/	COLO. REV. STAT. § 23-3.1-206.7, -214 (2003)
Colorado	Collegeinvest Smart Choice College Savings Plan	D	www.collegeinvest.org/	COLO. REV. STAT. § 23-3.1-301 to -309 (2003)
Colorado	Collegeinvest Stable Value Plus College Savings Plan	D	www.collegeinvest.org/	
Colorado	Scholars Choice College Savings Program	A	www.scholars-choice.com	
Connecticut	The Connecticut Higher Education Trust (CHET)	D	www.aboutchet.com	CONN. GEN. STAT. § 3-22a to -22o (2003)
Connecticut	CHET Advisor	A	www.hartfordfunds.com/products /college-saving...	
Delaware	Delaware College Investment Plan	D	www.fidelity.com/delaware	DEL. CODE §§ 3483–3491 (2004)
District of Columbia	DC College Savings Plan	D & A	www.DCCollegeSavings.com	D.C. CODE § 47-4501 to -4512
Florida	Florida Prepaid College Plans	P	www.myfloridaprepaid.com	FLA. STAT. § 1009.97, .971–.976
Florida	Florida 529 Savings Plan	D	www.florida529plans.com	FLA. STAT. § 1009.98, .981–.984
Georgia	Path2College 529 Plan	D	www.Path2College529.com	GA. CODE ANN. § 20-3-630 to -642 (2002)
Hawaii	HI529	D	www.hi529.com	HAW. REV. STAT. § 256-1 to -7 (2003)
Idaho	Idaho College Savings Program (IDeal)	D	www.idsaves.org	IDAHO CODE § 33-5401 to -5408 (2004)
Illinois	College Illinois! (On hold pending legislation)	P	www.collegeillinois.com	110 ILL. COMP. STAT. 979/1–/99 (2004)
Illinois	Bright Start College Savings Program	D	www.brightstartsavings.com	110 ILL. COMP. STAT. 947/75 (2004)
Illinois	Bright Start College Savings Program	A	www.brightstartadvisor.com	

State	Program	Prepaid (P)/ Direct (D) or Advisor (A)	Website	State Statute Section
Illinois	Bright Directions College Savings Program	A	www.brightdirections.com	
Indiana	CollegeChoice 529 Direct Savings Plan	D	www.collegechoicedirect.com	Burns Ind. Code Ann. § 21-9-8-1 to -9-8-2 (2004)
Indiana	CollegeChoice CD 529 Savings Plan	D & A	www.collegechoicecd.com	
Indiana	CollegeChoice Advisor 529 Savings Plan	A	www.collegechoiceadvisor529.com/	
Iowa	College Savings Iowa	D	www.collegesavingsiowa.com	Iowa Code § 12D.1–.11
Iowa	1Advisor 529 Plan	A	www.iowaadvisor529.com	
Kansas	Learning Quest	D	www.learningquest.com	Kan. Stat. Ann. § 75-640 to -648 (2003)
Kansas	Learning Quest Advisor	A	www.learningquest.com	
Kansas	Schwab 529 College Savings Plan	D	www.schwab.com/529	
Kentucky	KY Saves 529	D	www.kysaves.com	Ky. Rev. Stat. § 164A.300–.380 (2004)
Kentucky	Kentucky's Affordable Prepaid Tuition (KAPT) (closed since 2004)	P	www.getkapt.com	Ky. Rev. Stat. § 164A.700–.709
Louisiana	Student Tuition Assistance and Revenue Trust (START) Savings Program	D	www.startsaving.la.gov	La. Rev. Stat. § 17:3048.1–.4 (2004)
Maine	NextGen 529 – Direct Series	D	www.nextgenforme.com	Me. Rev. Stat. tit. 20-A, §§ 11471–11486 (2003)
Maine	NextGen 529 – Select Series	A	www.nextgenforme.com	
Maryland	Maryland College Investment Plan	D	maryland529.com/college-savings-plans-of-mary...	Md. Educ. Code Ann. § 18-19A-01 to -07 (2003)

State	Program	Prepaid (P)/ Direct (D) or Advisor (A)	Website	State Statute Section
Maryland	Maryland Prepaid College Trust (not enrolling)	P	maryland529.com/college-savings-plans-of-mary...	MD. EDUC. CODE ANN. § 18-1901 to 1916 (2003)
Massachusetts	U.Fund College Investing Plan	D	www.fidelity.com/ufund	MASS. GEN. LAWS ANN. ch. 15C, §§ 5A, 16, 14B; MASS. GEN. LAWS ANN. ch. 29, § 49C (2004)
Massachusetts	The U.Plan Prepaid Tuition Program	P	www.mefa.org/uplan	MASS. GEN. LAWS ANN. ch. 180, § 17L (2004)
Michigan	Michigan Education Trust	P	www.setwithmet.com	MICH. COMP. LAWS SERV. § 390.1421–.1444 (2004)
Michigan	Michigan Education Savings Program	D	www.misaves.com	MICH. COMP. LAWS SERV. § 390.1471–.1486 (2004)
Michigan	MI 529 Advisor Plan	A	www.mi529advisor.com	
Minnesota	Minnesota College Savings Plan	D	www.mnsaves.org/	MINN. STAT. § 136G.01–.14 (2003)
Mississippi	Mississippi Prepaid Affordable College Tuition (MPACT) Program	P	www.treasurerlynnfitch.ms.gov/collegesavingsm...	MISS. CODE ANN. § 37-155-1 to -27 (2004)
Mississippi	Mississippi Affordable College Savings (MACS)	D	www.ms529.com/home.shtml	MISS. CODE ANN. § 37-155-101 to -125 (2004)
Missouri	Missouri 529 College Savings Plan	D	www.missourimost.org	MO. REV. STAT. § 360.010–.140 (2004)
Montana	Achieve Montana	D	achievemontana.com/	MONT. CODE ANN. § 15-30-111(8); § 15-62-101 to -104; § 15-62-201 to -209 (2003)
Nebraska	Nebraska Educational Savings Trust "NEST" Direct Plan	D	www.nest529.com	NEB. REV. STAT. § 85-1801 to -1814 (2003)
Nebraska	Nebraska Educational Savings Trust "NEST" Advisor Plan	A	www.nest529advisor.com/	
Nebraska	TD Ameritrade 529 College Savings Plan	D	collegesavings.tdameritrade.com/index.asp	

State	Program	Prepaid (P)/ Direct (D) or Advisor (A)	Website	State Statute Section
Nebraska	The State Farm 529 Savings Plan	A	www.statefarm.com/finances /education-savings-...	
Nevada	Nevada Prepaid Tuition Program	P	NVPrepaid.gov	NEV. REV. STAT. § 353B.001–.009; § 353B.010–.190 (2004)
Nevada	SSGA Upromise 529 Plan	D	www.ssga.upromise529.com	NEV. REV. STAT. § 353B.001–.009; § 353B.300–.370; § 353B.800–.810
Nevada	The Vanguard 529 College Savings Plan	D	personal.vanguard.com/us /whatweoffer/college /vanguard529	
Nevada	Wealthfront 529 Plan	A	Wealthfront.com/529	
New Hampshire	UNIAUE College Investing Plan	D	www.fidelity.com/unique	N.H. REV. STAT. ANN. 195-H:1–:10 (2003)
New Hampshire	Fidelity Advisor 529 Plan	A	advisor.fidelity.com	
New Jersey	NJBEST 529 College Savings Plan	D	www.hesaa.org/students/njbest	N.J. STAT. § 18A:71B-35 to -46 (2004)
New Jersey	Franklin Templeton 529 College Savings Plan	A	www.franklintempleton.com /retail/pages/generi...	
New Mexico	The Education Plan's Prepaid Tuition Program (no longer offered)	P	www.tepnm.com	N.M. STAT. ANN. § 7-2-32 to -33; § 21-1-40 (2004)
New Mexico	The Education Plan	D	www.theeducationplan.com	N.M. STAT. ANN. § 7-2-32 to -33; § 21-21K-1 to -7 (2004)
New Mexico	Scholar'sEdge	A	www.scholarsedge529.com	
New York	New York's 529 Advisor-Guided College Savings Program	A	www.ny529advisor.com/home	N.Y. EDUC. LAW § 695 to 695-g (2004)
New York	New York's 529 College Savings Program Direct Plan	D	www.nysaves.org	

State	Program	Prepaid (P)/ Direct (D) or Advisor (A)	Website	State Statute Section
North Carolina	North Carolina's National College Savings Program	D	CFNC.org/NC529	N.C. GEN. STAT. § 116D-1 to -49 (2004)
North Dakota	College SAVE	D & A	www.collegesave4u.com	N.D. CENT. CODE § 6-09-38 (2003)
Ohio	CollegeAdvantage Direct 529 Savings Plan	D	www.CollegeAdvantage.com	OHIO REV. CODE ANN. 3334.01–.17 (2004)
Ohio	CollegeAdvantage Advisor 529, offered by BlackRock	A	www.blackrock.com /collegeadvantage	
Oklahoma	Oklahoma College Savings Plan	D	www.ok4saving.org	OKLA. STAT. tit. 31, § 1.A.26; OKLA. STAT. tit. 70, § 3970.1–.12 (2004)
Oklahoma	OklahomaDream 529 Plan	A	www.okdream529.com	
Oregon	Oregon College Savings Plan	D	www.oregoncollegesavings.com	OR. REV. STAT. § 316.680(1)(l), (2)(J); § 316.699; § 348.841–.873 (2003)
Oregon	Oregon College Savings Plan	A	www.mfs.com/en-us/individual -investor/planning-for-the-future .html	
Pennsylvania	Pennsylvania 529 Guaranteed Savings Plan	P	www.pa529.com	24 PA. STAT. § 6901.301–.317 (2004)
Pennsylvania	Pennsylvania 529 Investment Plan	D	www.pa529.com	
Rhode Island	CollegeBound Saver	A	www.collegebound529.com	R.I. GEN. LAWS § 16-57-6.1 to -6.7 (2004)
South Carolina	SC Tuition Prepayment Program (SCTPP)	P	www.scgrad.org	S.C. CODE ANN. § 12-6-1120, -1140; § 59-2-10 to -160 (2003)
South Carolina	Future Scholar 529 College Savings Plan – Direct Investment Program	D	www.futurescholar.com/	S.C. CODE ANN. § 12-6-1120, -1140; § 59-2-10 to -160 (2003)
South Carolina	Future Scholar 529 College Savings Plan – Advisor Program	A	www.futurescholar.com/	

State	Program	Prepaid (P)/ Direct (D) or Advisor (A)	Website	State Statute Section
South Dakota	CollegeAccess 529	D & A	www.collegeaccess529.com	S.D. CODIFIED LAWS § 13-63-1 to -32 (2003)
Tennessee	TNStars College Savings 529 Program	D	www.tnstars.com	TENN. CODE ANN. § 49-7-801 to -826; § 49-7-901 to -907 (2004)
Tennessee	Tennessee's Baccalaureate Education System Trust Prepaid Plan	P	www.tnbest.com	
Texas	Texas Tuition Promise Fund	P	www.texastuitionpromisefund .com	TEX. EDUC. CODE § 54.6001–.644 (2004)
Texas	Texas Guaranteed Tuition Plan (Newborn enrollments only)	P	www.tgtp.org	
Texas	LoneStar 529 Plan	A	www.lonestar529.com	TEX. EDUC. CODE § 54.701–.716 (2004)
Texas	Texas College Savings Plan	D	www.texascollegesavings.com	
Utah	my529	D	www.my529.org	UTAH CODE ANN. § 53B-8a-101 to -114 (2004)
Vermont	Vermont Higher Education Investment Plan	D	www.vheip.org/	16 V.S.A. § 2875–2879f (2003)
Virginia	Prepaid529 (permanently closed for new enrollments)	P	www.virginia529.com	VT. STAT. ANN. tit. 16, §§ 2875–2879f (2003)
Virginia	Invest529	D	www.virginia529.com	
Virginia	CollegeAmerica	A	www.americanfunds.com	
Washington	Guaranteed Education Tuition (GET)	P	www.get.wa.gov	WASH. REV. CODE § 28B.95.010–.900 (2004)
Washington	DreamAhead College Investment Plan	D	wastate529.wa.gov/	

State	Program	Prepaid (P)/ Direct (D) or Advisor (A)	Website	State Statute Section
West Virginia	SMART529 Prepaid Tuition Plan	P	Terminated 9/30/2021	W. VA. CODE § 11-21-12a; § 18-30-1 to -13 (2003)
West Virginia	SMART 529 WV Direct	D	www.SMART529.com	W. VA. CODE § 11-21-12a; § 18-30-1 to -13 (2003)
West Virginia	SMART 529 Select	D	www.SMART529Select.com	
West Virginia	The Hartford SMART 529	A	www.hartfordfunds.com/college-saving/overview...	
Wisconsin	Edvest College Savings Program	D	www.Edvest.com	WIS. STAT. § 14.63–.65 (2003)
Wisconsin	Tomorrow's Scholar College Savings Plan	A	www.tomorrowsscholar.com	
Wyoming	College Achievement Plan		Closed in 2006	WYO. STAT. § 21-16-801 to -818 (2003)

Appendix D

Qualified Tuition Programs [26 U.S.C.S. § 529]

§ 529. QUALIFIED TUITION PROGRAMS

(a) General rule. A qualified tuition program shall be exempt from taxation under this subtitle. Notwithstanding the preceding sentence, such program shall be subject to the taxes imposed by section 511 (relating to imposition of tax on unrelated business income of charitable organizations).

(b) Qualified tuition program. For purposes of this section—(1) In general. The term "qualified tuition program" means a program established and maintained by a State or agency or instrumentality thereof or by 1 or more eligible educational institutions—

(A) under which a person—

(i) may purchase tuition credits or certificates on behalf of a designated beneficiary which entitle the beneficiary to the waiver or payment of qualified higher education expenses of the beneficiary, or

(ii) in the case of a program established and maintained by a State or agency or instrumentality thereof, may make contributions to an account which is established for the purpose of meeting the qualified higher education expenses of the designated beneficiary of the account, and

(B) which meets the other requirements of this subsection.

Except to the extent provided in regulations, a program established and maintained by 1 or more eligible educational institutions shall not be treated as a qualified tuition program unless such program provides that amounts are held in a qualified trust and such program has received a ruling or determination that such program meets the applicable requirements for a qualified tuition program. For purposes of the preceding sentence, the term "qualified trust" means a trust which is created or organized in the United States for the exclusive benefit of designated beneficiaries and with respect to which the requirements of paragraphs (2) and (5) of section 408(a) are met.

(2) Cash contributions. A program shall not be treated as a qualified tuition program unless it provides that purchases or contributions may only be made in cash.

(3) Separate accounting. A program shall not be treated as a qualified tuition program unless it provides separate accounting for each designated beneficiary.

(4) Limited investment direction. A program shall not be treated as a qualified tuition program unless it provides that any contributor to, or designated beneficiary under, such program may, directly or indirectly, direct the investment of any contributions to the program (or any earnings thereon) no more than 2 times during a calendar year.

(5) No pledging of interest as security. A program shall not be treated as a qualified tuition program if it allows any interest in the program or any portion thereof to be used as security for a loan.

(6) Prohibition on excess contributions. A program shall not be treated as a qualified tuition program unless it provides adequate safeguards to prevent contributions on behalf of a designated beneficiary in excess of those necessary to provide for the qualified higher education expenses of the beneficiary.

(c) Tax treatment of designated beneficiaries and contributors.

(1) In general. Except as otherwise provided in this subsection, no amount shall be includible in gross income of—

(A) a designated beneficiary under a qualified tuition program, or

(B) a contributor to such program on behalf of a designated beneficiary, with respect to any distribution or earnings under such program.

(2) Gift tax treatment of contributions. For purposes of chapters 12 and 13—

(A) In general. Any contribution to a qualified tuition program on behalf of any designated beneficiary—

(i) shall be treated as a completed gift to such beneficiary which is not a future interest in property, and

(ii) shall not be treated as a qualified transfer under section 2503(e).

(B) Treatment of excess contributions. If the aggregate amount of contributions described in subparagraph (A) during the calendar year by a donor exceeds the limitation for such year under section 2503(b) [26 USCS § 2503(b)], such aggregate amount shall, at the election of the donor, be taken into account for purposes of such section ratably over the 5-year period beginning with such calendar year.

(3) Distributions.

(A) In general. Any distribution under a qualified tuition program shall be includible in the gross income of the distributee in the manner as provided under section 72 to the extent not excluded from gross income under any other provision of this chapter.

(B) Distributions for qualified higher education expenses. For purposes of this paragraph—

(i) In-kind distributions. No amount shall be includible in gross income under subparagraph (A) by reason of a distribution which consists of providing a benefit to the distributee which, if paid for by the distributee, would constitute payment of a qualified higher education expense.

(ii) Cash distributions. In the case of distributions not described in clause (i), if—

(I) such distributions do not exceed the qualified higher education expenses (reduced by expenses described in clause (i)), no amount shall be includible in gross income, and

(II) in any other case, the amount otherwise includible in gross income shall be reduced by an amount which bears the same ratio to such amount as such expenses bear to such distributions.

(iii) Exception for institutional programs. In the case of any taxable year beginning before January 1, 2004, clauses (i) and (ii) shall not apply with respect to any distribution during such taxable year under a qualified tuition program established and maintained by 1 or more eligible educational institutions.

(iv) Treatment as distributions. Any benefit furnished to a designated beneficiary under a qualified tuition program shall be treated as a distribution to the beneficiary for purposes of this paragraph.

(v) Coordination with American Opportunity and Lifetime learning credits. The total amount of qualified higher education expenses with respect to an individual for the taxable year shall be reduced—

(I) as provided in section 25A(g)(2), and

(II) by the amount of such expenses which were taken into account in determining the credit allowed to the taxpayer or any other person under section 25A.

(vi) Coordination with Coverdell education savings accounts. If, with respect to an individual for any taxable year—

(I) the aggregate distributions to which clauses (i) and (ii) and section 530(d)(2)(A) apply, exceed

(II) the total amount of qualified higher education expenses otherwise taken into account under clauses (i) and (ii) (after the application of clause (v)) for such year, the taxpayer shall allocate such expenses among such distributions for purposes of determining the amount of the exclusion under clauses (i) and (ii) and section 530(d)(2)(A).

(C) Change in beneficiaries or programs.

(i) Rollovers. Subparagraph (A) shall not apply to that portion of any distribution which, within 60 days of such distribution, is transferred—

(I) to another qualified tuition program for the benefit of the designated beneficiary,

(II) to the credit of another designated beneficiary under a qualified tuition program who is a member of the family of the designated beneficiary with respect to which the distribution was made, or

(III) before January 1, 2026, to an ABLE account (as defined in section 529A(e)(6)) of the designated beneficiary or a member of the family of the designated beneficiary.

Subclause (III) shall not apply to so much of a distribution which, when added to all other contributions made to the ABLE account for the taxable year, exceeds the limitation under section 529A(b)(2)(B)(i).

(ii) Change in designated beneficiaries. Any change in the designated beneficiary of an interest in a qualified tuition program shall not be treated as a distribution for purposes of subparagraph (A) if the new beneficiary is a member of the family of the old beneficiary.

(iii) Limitation on certain rollovers. Clause (i)(I) shall not apply to any transfer if such transfer occurs within 12 months from the date of a previous transfer to any qualified tuition program for the benefit of the designated beneficiary.

(D) Special rule for contributions of refunded amounts

In the case of a beneficiary who receives a refund of anyqualified higher education expensesfrom aneligible educational institution,subparagraph (A) shall not apply to that portion of any distribution for the taxable year which is recontributed to a qualified tuition program of which such individual is a beneficiary, but only to the extent such recontribution is made not later than 60 days after the date of such refund and does not exceed the refunded amount.

(4) Estate tax treatment.

(A) In general. No amount shall be includible in the gross estate of any individual for purposes of chapter 11 by reason of an interest in a qualified tuition program.

(B) Amounts includible in estate of designated beneficiary in certain cases. Subparagraph (A) shall not apply to amounts distributed on account of the death of a beneficiary.
(C) Amounts includible in estate of donor making excess contributions. In the case of a donor who makes the election described in paragraph (2)(B) and who dies before the close of the 5-year period referred to in such paragraph, notwithstanding subparagraph (A), the gross estate of the donor shall include the portion of such contributions properly allocable to periods after the date of death of the donor.

(5) Other gift tax rules. For purposes of chapters 12 and 13 —
(A) Treatment of distributions. Except as provided in subparagraph (B), in no event shall a distribution from a qualified tuition program be treated as a taxable gift.
(B) Treatment of designation of new beneficiary. The taxes imposed by chapters 12 and 13 [26 USCS §§ 2501 et seq. and 2601 et seq.] shall apply to a transfer by reason of a change in the designated beneficiary under the program (or a rollover to the account of a new beneficiary) unless the new beneficiary is—
(i) assigned to the same generation as (or a higher generation than) the old beneficiary (determined in accordance with section 2651), and
(ii) a member of the family of the old beneficiary.

(6) Additional tax. The tax imposed by section 530(d)(4) shall apply to any payment or distribution from a qualified tuition program in the same manner as such tax applies to a payment or distribution from an[a] Coverdell education savings account. This paragraph shall not apply to any payment or distribution in any taxable year beginning before January 1, 2004, which is includible in gross income but used for qualified higher education expenses of the designated beneficiary.

(7) Treatment of elementary and secondary tuition

Any reference in this subsection to the term "qualified higher education expense" shall include a reference to expenses for tuition in connection with enrollment or attendance at an elementary or secondary public, private, or religious school.

(8) Treatment of certain expenses associated with registered apprenticeship programs

Any reference in this subsection to the term "qualified higher education expense" shall include a reference to expenses for fees, books, supplies, and equipment required for the participation of adesignated beneficiaryin an apprenticeship program registered and certified with the Secretary of Labor under section 1 of the National Apprenticeship Act (29 U.S.C. 50).

(9) Treatment of qualified education loan repayments

(A) In general

Any reference in this subsection to the term "qualified higher education expense" shall include a reference to amounts paid as principal or interest on any qualified education loan (as defined in section 221(d)) of the designated beneficiary or a sibling of the designated beneficiary.

(B) Limitation

The amount of distributions treated as a qualified higher education expense under this paragraph with respect to the loans of any individual shall not exceed $10,000 (reduced by the amount of distributions so treated for all prior taxable years).

(C) Special rules for siblings of the designated beneficiary

(i) Separate accounting

For purposes of subparagraph (B) and subsection (d), amounts treated as a qualified higher education expense with respect to the loans of a sibling of the designated beneficiary shall be taken into account with respect to such sibling and not with respect to such designated beneficiary.

(ii) Sibling defined

For purposes of this paragraph, the term "sibling" means an individual who bears a relationship to the designated beneficiary which is described in section 152(d)(2)(B).

(d) Reports. Each officer or employee having control of the qualified tuition program or their designee shall make such reports regarding such program to the Secretary and to designated beneficiaries with respect to contributions, distributions, and such other matters as the Secretary may require. The reports required by this subsection shall be filed at such time and in such manner and furnished to such individuals at such time and in such manner as may be required by the Secretary.

(e) Other definitions and special rules. For purposes of this section—

(1) Designated beneficiary. The term "designated beneficiary" means—

(A) the individual designated at the commencement of participation in the qualified tuition program as the beneficiary of amounts paid (or to be paid) to the program,

(B) in the case of a change in beneficiaries described in subsection (c)(3)(C), the individual who is the new beneficiary, and

(C) in the case of an interest in a qualified tuition program purchased by a State or local government (or agency or instrumentality thereof) or an organization described in section 501(c)(3) [26 USCS § 501(c)(3)] and exempt from taxation under section 501(a) [26 USCS § 501(a)] as part of a scholarship program operated by such government or organization, the individual receiving such interest as a scholarship.

(2) Member of family. The term "member of the family" means, with respect to any designated beneficiary—

(A) the spouse of such beneficiary;

(B) an individual who bears a relationship to such beneficiary which is described in subparagraphs (A) through (G) of section 152(d)(2);
(C) the spouse of any individual described in subparagraph (B); and
(D) any first cousin of such beneficiary.

(3) Qualified higher education expenses.

(A) In general. The term "qualified higher education expenses" means—

(i) tuition, fees, books, supplies, and equipment required for the enrollment or attendance of a designated beneficiary at an eligible educational institution; and

(ii) expenses for special needs services in the case of a special needs beneficiary which are incurred in connection with such enrollment or attendance.

(iii) expenses for the purchase of computer or peripheral equipment (as defined in section 168(i)(2)(B)), computer software (as defined in section 197(e)(3)(B)), or Internet access and related services, if such equipment, software, or services are to be used primarily by the beneficiary during any of the years the beneficiary is enrolled at an eligible educational institution.

Clause (iii) shall not include expenses for computer software designed for sports, games, or hobbies unless the software is predominantly educational in nature. The amount of cash distributions from allqualified tuition programs described in subsection (b)(1)(A)(ii) with respect to a beneficiary during any taxable year shall, in the aggregate, include not more than $10,000 in expenses described in subsection (c)(7) incurred during the taxable year.

(B) Room and board included for students who are at least half-time.

(i) In general. In the case of an individual who is an eligible student (as defined in section 25A(b)(3)) for any academic period, such term shall also include reasonable costs for such period (as determined under the qualified tuition program) incurred by the designated beneficiary for room and board while attending such institution. For purposes of subsection (b)(6), a designated beneficiary shall be treated as meeting the requirements of this clause.

(ii) Limitation. The amount treated as qualified higher education expenses by reason of clause (i) shall not exceed—

(I) the allowance (applicable to the student) for room and board included in the cost of attendance (as defined in section 472 of the Higher Education Act of 1965 (20 U.S.C. 1087ll), as in effect on the date of the enactment of the Economic Growth and Tax Relief Reconciliation Act of 2001) as determined by the eligible educational institution for such period, or

(II) if greater, the actual invoice amount the student residing in housing owned or operated by the eligible educational institution is charged by such institution for room and board costs for such period.

(4) Application of section 514. An interest in a qualified tuition program shall not be treated as debt for purposes of section 514.

(5) Eligible educational institution. The term "eligible educational institution" means an institution—

(A) which is described in section 481 of the Higher Education Act of 1965, as in effect on the date of the enactment of this paragraph, and

(B) which is eligible to participate in a program under title IV of such Act.

(f) Notwithstanding any other provision of this section, the Secretary shall prescribe such regulations as may be necessary or appropriate to carry out the purposes of this section and to prevent abuse of such purposes, including regulations under chapters 11, 12, and 13 of this title.

Appendix E

Proposed Regulations to Section 529

SEC. 1.529-1 QUALIFIED STATE TUITION PROGRAM, UNRELATED BUSINESS INCOME TAX AND DEFINITIONS.

(a) *In general.* A qualified State tuition program (QSTP) described in section 529 is exempt from income tax, except for the tax imposed under section 511 on the QSTP's unrelated business taxable income. A QSTP is not required to file Form 990, Return of Organization Exempt From Income Tax, Form 1041, U.S. Income Tax Return for Estates and Trusts, or Form 1120, U.S. Corporation Income Tax Return. A QSTP may be required to file Form 990-T, Exempt Organization Business Income Tax Return. See Secs. 1.6012-2(e) and 1.6012-3(a)(5) for requirements for filing Form 990-T.

(b) *Unrelated business income tax rules.* For purposes of section 529, this section and Secs. 1.529-2 through 1.529-6:

(1) *Application of section 514.* An interest in a QSTP shall not be treated as debt for purposes of section 514. Consequently, a QSTP's investment income will not constitute debt-financed income subject to the unrelated business income tax merely because the program accepts contributions and is obligated to pay out or refund such contributions and certain earnings attributable thereto to designated beneficiaries or to account owners. However, investment income of a QSTP shall be subject to the unrelated business income tax as debt-financed income to the extent the program incurs indebtedness when acquiring or improving income-producing property.

(2) *Penalties and forfeitures.* Earnings forfeited on prepaid educational arrangements or contracts and educational savings accounts and retained by a QSTP, or amounts collected by a QSTP as penalties on

refunds or excess contributions are not unrelated business income to the QSTP.

(3) *Administrative and other fees.* Amounts paid, in order to open or maintain prepaid educational arrangements or contracts and educational savings accounts, as administrative or maintenance fees, and other similar fees including late fees, service charges, and finance charges, are not unrelated business income to the QSTP.

(c) *Definitions.* For purposes of section 529, this section and Secs. 1.529-2 through 1.529-6:

Account means the formal record of transactions relating to a particular designated beneficiary when it is used alone without further modification in these regulations. The term includes prepaid educational arrangements or contracts described in section 529(b)(1)(A)(i) and educational savings accounts described in section 529(b)(1)(A)(ii).

Account owner means the person who, under the terms of the QSTP or any contract setting forth the terms under which contributions may be made to an account for the benefit of a designated beneficiary, is entitled to select or change the designated beneficiary of an account, to designate any person other than the designated beneficiary to whom funds may be paid from the account, or to receive distributions from the account if no such other person is designated.

Contribution means any payment directly allocated to an account for the benefit of a designated beneficiary or used to pay late fees or administrative fees associated with the account. In the case of a tax-free rollover, within the meaning of this paragraph (c), into a QSTP account, only the portion of the rollover amount that constituted investment in the account, within the meaning of this paragraph (c), is treated as a contribution to the account as required by Sec. 1.529-3(a)(2).

Designated beneficiary means—

(1) The individual designated as the beneficiary of the account at the time an account is established with the QSTP;

(2) The individual who is designated as the new beneficiary when beneficiaries are changed; and

(3) The individual receiving the benefits accumulated in the account as a scholarship in the case of a QSTP account established by a State or local government or an organization described in section 501(c)(3) and exempt from taxation under section 501(a) as part of a scholarship program operated by such government or organization.

Distributee means the designated beneficiary or the account owner who receives or is treated as receiving a distribution from a QSTP. For example, if a QSTP makes a distribution directly to an eligible educational institution to pay tuition and fees for a designated beneficiary or a QSTP makes a distribution in the form of a check payable to both a designated beneficiary and an eligible educational institution, the distribution shall be treated as having been made in full to the designated beneficiary.

Distribution means any disbursement, whether in cash or in-kind, from a QSTP. Distributions include, but are not limited to, tuition credits or certificates, payment vouchers, tuition waivers or other similar items. Distributions also include, but are not limited to, a refund to the account owner, the designated beneficiary or the designated beneficiary's estate.

Earnings attributable to an account are the total account balance on a particular date minus the investment in the account as of that date.

Earnings ratio means the amount of earnings allocable to the account on the last day of the calendar year divided by the total account balance on the last day of that calendar year. The earnings ratio is applied to any distribution made during the calendar year. For purposes of computing the earnings ratio, the earnings allocable to the account on the last day of the calendar year and the total account balance on the last day of the calendar year include all distributions made during the calendar year and any amounts that have been forfeited from the account during the calendar year.

Eligible educational institution means an institution which is described in section 481 of the Higher Education Act of 1965 (20 U.S.C 1088) as in effect on August 5, 1997, and which is eligible to participate in a program under title IV of such Act. Such institutions generally are accredited post-secondary educational institutions offering credit toward a bachelor's degree, an associate degree, a graduate level or professional degree, or another recognized post-secondary credential. Certain proprietary institutions and post-secondary vocational institutions also are eligible institutions. The institution must be eligible to participate in Department of Education student aid programs.

Final distribution means the distribution from a QSTP account that reduces the total account balance to zero.

Forfeit means that earnings and contributions allocable to a QSTP account are withdrawn by the QSTP from the account or deducted by the QSTP from a distribution to pay a penalty as required by Sec. 1.529-2(e).

Investment in the account means the sum of all contributions made to the account on or before a particular date less the aggregate amount of contributions included in distributions, if any, made from the account on or before that date.

Member of the family means an individual who is related to the designated beneficiary as described in paragraphs (1) through (9) of this definition. For purposes of determining who is a member of the family, a legally adopted child of an individual shall be treated as the child of such individual by blood. The terms brother and sister include a brother or sister by the halfblood.

Member of the family means—

(1) A son or daughter, or a descendant of either;
(2) A stepson or stepdaughter;
(3) A brother, sister, stepbrother, or stepsister;
(4) The father or mother, or an ancestor of either;
(5) A stepfather or stepmother;
(6) A son or daughter of a brother or sister;
(7) A brother or sister of the father or mother;
(8) A son-in-law, daughter-in-law, father-in-law, mother-in-law, brother-in-law, or sister-in-law; or
(9) The spouse of the designated beneficiary or the spouse of any individual described in paragraphs (1) through (8) of this definition.

Person has the same meaning as under section 7701(a)(1).
Qualified higher education expenses means—

(1) Tuition, fees, and the costs of books, supplies, and equipment required for the enrollment or attendance of a designated beneficiary at an eligible educational institution; and
(2) The costs of room and board (as limited by paragraph (2)(i) of this definition) of a designated beneficiary (who meets requirements of paragraph (2)(ii) of this definition) incurred while attending an eligible educational institution:
    (i) The amount of room and board treated as qualified higher education expenses shall not exceed the minimum room and board allowance determined in calculating costs of attendance for Federal financial aid programs under section 472 of the Higher Education Act of 1965 (20 U.S.C. 108711) as in effect on August 5, 1997. For purposes of these regulations, room and board costs shall not exceed $1,500 per academic year for a designated beneficiary residing at home with parents or guardians. For a designated beneficiary residing in institutionally owned or operated housing, room and board costs shall not exceed the amount normally assessed most residents for room and board at the institution. For all other designated beneficiaries the amount shall not exceed $2,500 per academic year. For this purpose the term academic year has the same meaning as that term is given in 20 U.S.C. 1088(d) as in effect on August 5, 1997.
    (ii) Room and board shall be treated as qualified higher education expenses for a designated beneficiary if they are incurred during any academic period during which the designated beneficiary is enrolled or accepted for enrollment in a degree, certificate, or other program (including a program of study abroad approved for credit by the

eligible educational institution) that leads to a recognized educational credential awarded by an eligible educational institution.

In addition, the designated beneficiary must be enrolled at least half-time. A student will be considered to be enrolled at least half-time if the student is enrolled for at least half the full-time academic workload for the course of study the student is pursuing as determined under the standards of the institution where the student is enrolled. The institution's standard for a full-time workload must equal or exceed the standard established by the Department of Education under the Higher Education Act and set forth in 34 CFR 674.2(b).

Rollover distribution means a distribution or transfer from an account of a designated beneficiary that is transferred to or deposited within 60 days of the distribution into an account of another individual who is a member of the family of the designated beneficiary. A distribution is not a rollover distribution unless there is a change in beneficiary. The new designated beneficiary's account may be in a QSTP in either the same State or a QSTP in another State.

Total account balance means the total amount or the total fair market value of tuition credits or certificates or similar benefits allocable to the account on a particular date. For purposes of computing the earnings ratio, the total account balance is adjusted as described in this paragraph (c).

SEC. 1.529-2 QUALIFIED STATE TUITION PROGRAM DESCRIBED.

(a) *In general.* To be a QSTP, a program must satisfy the requirements described in paragraphs (a) through (i) of this section. A QSTP is a program established and maintained by a State or an agency or instrumentality of a State under which a person
   (1) May purchase tuition credits or certificates on behalf of a designated beneficiary that entitle the beneficiary to the waiver or payment of qualified higher education expenses of the beneficiary; or
   (2) May make contributions to an account that is established for the purpose of meeting the qualified higher education expenses of the designated beneficiary of the account.

(b) Established and maintained by a State or agency or instrumentality of a State—
   (1) Established. A program is established by a State or an agency or instrumentality of a State if the program is initiated by State statute or regulation, or by an act of a State official or agency with the authority to act on behalf of the State.
   (2) Maintained. A program is maintained by a State or an agency or instrumentality of a State if—

(i) The State or agency or instrumentality sets all of the terms and conditions of the program, including but not limited to who may contribute to the program, who may be a designated beneficiary of the program, what benefits the program may provide, when penalties will apply to refunds and what those penalties will be; and

(ii) The State or agency or instrumentality is actively involved on an ongoing basis in the administration of the program, including supervising all decisions relating to the investment of assets contributed to the program.

(3) *Actively involved.* Factors that are relevant in determining whether a State, agency or instrumentality is actively involved include, but are not limited to: whether the State provides services or benefits (such as tax, student aid or other financial benefits) to account owners or designated beneficiaries that are not provided to persons who are not account owners or designated beneficiaries; whether the State or agency or instrumentality establishes detailed operating rules for administering the program; whether officials of the State or agency or instrumentality play a substantial role in the operation of the program, including selecting, supervising, monitoring, auditing, and terminating any private contractors that provide services under the program; whether the State or agency or instrumentality holds the private contractors that provide services under the program to the same standards and requirements that apply when private contractors handle funds that belong to the State or provide services to the State;

whether the State provides funding for the program; and, whether the State or agency or instrumentality acts as trustee or holds program assets directly or for the benefit of the account owners or designated beneficiaries. If the State or an agency or instrumentality thereof exercises the same authority over the funds invested in the program as it does over the investments in or pool of funds of a State employees' defined benefit pension plan, then the State or agency or

instrumentality will be considered actively involved on an ongoing basis in the administration of the program.

(c) *Permissible uses of contributions.* Contributions to a QSTP can be placed into either a prepaid educational arrangement or contract described in section 529(b)(1)(A)(i) or an educational savings account described in section 529(b)(1)(A)(ii), or both, but cannot be placed into any other type of account.

(1) A prepaid educational services arrangement or contract is an account through which tuition credits or certificates or other rights are acquired that entitle the designated beneficiary of the account to the waiver or payment of qualified higher education expenses.

(2) An educational savings account is an account that is established exclusively for the purpose of meeting the qualified higher education expenses of a designated beneficiary.

(d) *Cash contributions.* A program shall not be treated as a QSTP unless it provides that contributions may be made only in cash and not in property. A QSTP may accept payment, however, in cash, or by check, money order, credit card, or similar methods.

(e) *Penalties on refunds*—(1) General rule. A program shall not be treated as a QSTP unless it imposes a more than de minimis penalty on the earnings portion of any distribution from the program that is not—

(i) Used exclusively for qualified higher education expenses of the designated beneficiary;

(ii) Made on account of the death or disability of the designated beneficiary;

(iii) Made on account of the receipt of a scholarship (or allowance or payment described in section 135(d)(1) (B) or (C)) by the designated beneficiary to the extent the amount of the distribution does not exceed the amount of the scholarship, allowance, or payment; or

(iv) A rollover distribution.

(2) *More than de minimis penalty*— (i) In general. A penalty is more than de minimis if it is consistent with a program intended to assist individuals in saving exclusively for qualified higher education expenses. Except as provided in paragraph (e)(2)(ii) of this section, whether any particular penalty is more than de minimis depends on the facts and circumstances of the particular program, including the extent to which the penalty offsets the federal income tax benefit from having deferred income tax liability on the earnings portion of any distribution.

(ii) *Safe harbor.* A penalty imposed on the earnings portion of a distribution is more than de minimis if it is equal to or greater than 10 percent of the earnings.

(3) *Separate distributions.* For purposes of applying the penalty, any single distribution described in paragraph (e)(1) of this section will be treated as a separate distribution and not part of a single aggregated annual distribution by the program, notwithstanding the rules under Sec. 1.529-3 and Sec. 1.529-4.

(4) *Procedures for verifying use of distributions and imposing and collecting penalties*—(i) In general. To be treated as imposing a more than de minimis penalty as required in paragraph (e)(1) of this section, a program must implement practices and procedures to identify whether a distribution is subject to a penalty and collect any penalty that is due.

(ii) *Safe harbor.* A program that falls within the safe harbor described in paragraphs (e)(4)(ii) (A) through (E) of this section will be treated as implementing practices and procedures to identify whether a more than de minimis penalty must be imposed as required in paragraph (e)(1) of this section.

(A) *Distributions treated as payments of qualified higher education expenses.* The program treats distributions as being used to pay for qualified higher education expenses only if—

(1) The distribution is made directly to an eligible educational institution;
(2) The distribution is made in the form of a check payable to both the designated beneficiary and the eligible educational institution;
(3) The distribution is made after the designated beneficiary submits substantiation to show that the distribution is a reimbursement for qualified higher education expenses that the designated beneficiary has already paid and the program has a process for reviewing the validity of the substantiation prior to the distribution; or
(4) The designated beneficiary certifies prior to the distribution that the distribution will be expended for his or her qualified higher education expenses within a reasonable time after the distribution; the program requires the designated beneficiary to provide substantiation of payment of qualified higher education expenses within 30 days after making the distribution and has a process for reviewing the substantiation; and the program retains an account balance that is large enough to collect any penalty owed on the distribution if valid substantiation is not produced.

(B) *Treatment of all other distributions.* The program collects a penalty on all distributions not treated as made to pay qualified higher education expenses except where—

(1) Prior to the distribution the program receives written third party confirmation that the designated beneficiary has died or become disabled or has received a scholarship (or allowance or payment described in section 135(d)(1) (B) or (C)) in an amount equal to the distribution; or
(2) Prior to the distribution the program receives a certification from the account owner that the distribution is being made because the designated beneficiary has died or become disabled or has received a scholarship (or allowance or payment described in section 135(d)(1) (B) or (C)) received by the designated beneficiary (and the distribution is equal to the amount of the scholarship, allowance, or payment) and the program withholds and reserves a portion of the distribution as a penalty. Any penalty withheld by the program may be refunded after the program receives third party confirmation that the designated beneficiary has died or become disabled or

has received a scholarship or allowance (or payment described in section 135(d)(1) (B) or (C)).

(C) *Refunds of penalties.* The program will refund a penalty collected on a distribution only after the designated beneficiary substantiates that he or she had qualified higher education expenses greater than or equal to the distribution, and the program has reviewed the substantiation.

(D) *Documentation of amounts refunded and not used for qualified higher education expenses.* The program requires the distributee, defined in Sec. 1.529-1(c), to provide a signed statement identifying the amount of any refunds received from eligible educational institutions at the end of each year in which distributions for qualified higher education expenses were made and of the next year.

(E) *Procedures to collect penalty.* The program collects required penalties by retaining a sufficient balance in the account to pay the amount of penalty, withholding an amount equal to the penalty from a distribution, or collecting the penalty on a State income tax return.

(f) *Separate accounting.* A program shall not be treated as a QSTP unless it provides separate accounting for each designated beneficiary. Separate accounting requires that contributions for the benefit of a designated beneficiary and any earnings attributable thereto must be allocated to the appropriate account. If a program does not ordinarily provide each account owner an annual account statement showing the total account balance, the investment in the account, earnings, and distributions from the account, the program must give this information to the account owner or designated beneficiary upon request. In the case of a prepaid educational arrangement or contract described in section 529(b)(1)(A)(i) the total account balance may be shown as credits or units of benefits instead of fair market value.

(g) *No investment direction.* A program shall not be treated as a QSTP unless it provides that any account owner in, or contributor to, or designated beneficiary under, such program may not directly or indirectly direct the investment of any contribution to the program or directly or indirectly direct the investment of any earnings attributable to contributions. A program does not violate this requirement if a person who establishes an account with the program is permitted to select among different investment strategies designed exclusively by the program, only at the time the initial contribution is made establishing the account. A program will not violate the requirement of this paragraph (g) if it permits a person who establishes an account to select between a prepaid educational services account and an educational savings account. A program also will not violate the requirement of this paragraph (g) merely because it permits its board members, its employees, or the board members or employees of a contractor it hires to perform administrative services to purchase tuition credits or certificates or make contributions as described in paragraph (c) of this section.

(h) *No pledging of interest as security.* A program shall not be treated as a QSTP unless the terms of the program or a state statute or regulation that governs the program prohibit any interest in the program or any portion thereof from being used as security for a loan. This restriction includes, but is not limited to, a prohibition on the use of any interest in the program as security for a loan used to purchase such interest in the program.

(i) *Prohibition on excess contributions*—(1) In general. A program shall not be treated as a QSTP unless it provides adequate safeguards to prevent contributions for the benefit of a designated beneficiary in excess of those necessary to provide for the qualified higher education expenses of the designated beneficiary.

(2) *Safe harbor.* A program satisfies this requirement if it will bar any additional contributions to an account as soon as the account reaches a specified account balance limit applicable to all accounts of designated beneficiaries with the same expected year of enrollment. The total contributions may not exceed the amount determined by actuarial estimates that is necessary to pay tuition, required fees, and room and board expenses of the designated beneficiary for five years of undergraduate enrollment at the highest cost institution allowed by the program.

SEC. 1.529-3 INCOME TAX TREATMENT OF DISTRIBUTEES.

(a) *Taxation of distributions*—(1) In general. Any distribution, other than a rollover distribution, from a QSTP account must be included in the gross income of the distributee to the extent of the earnings portion of the distribution and to the extent not excluded from gross income under any other provision of chapter 1 of the Internal Revenue Code. If any amount of a distribution is forfeited under a QSTP as required by Sec. 1.529-2(e), this amount is neither included in the gross income of the distributee nor deductible by the distributee.

(2) *Rollover distributions.* No part of a rollover distribution is included in the income of the distributee. Following the rollover distribution, that portion of the rollover amount that constituted investment in the account, defined in Sec. 1.529-1(c), of the account from which the distribution was made is added to the investment in the account of the account that received the distribution. That portion of the rollover amount that constituted earnings of the account that made the distribution is added to the earnings of the account that received the distribution.

(b) *Computing taxable earnings*— (1) Amount of taxable earnings in a distribution—(i) Educational savings account. In the case of an educational savings account, the earnings portion of a distribution is equal to the product of the amount of the distribution and the earnings ratio, defined in Sec. 1.529-1(c). The return of investment portion of the distribution is equal to the amount of the distribution minus the earnings portion of the distribution.

(ii) *Prepaid educational services account.* In the case of a prepaid educational services account, the earnings portion of a distribution is equal to the value of the credits, hours, or other units of education distributed at the time of distribution minus the return of investment portion of the distribution. The value of the credits, hours, or other units of education may be based on the tuition waived or the cash distributed. The return of investment portion of the distribution is determined by dividing the investment in the account at the end of the year in which the distribution is made by the number of credits, hours, or other units of education in the account at the end of the calendar year (including all credits, hours, or other units of education distributed during the calendar year), and multiplying that amount by the number of credits, hours, or other units of education distributed during the current calendar year.

(2) Adjustment for programs that treated distributions and earnings in a different manner for years beginning before January 1, 1999. For calendar years beginning after December 31, 1998, a QSTP must treat taxpayers as recovering investment in the account and earnings ratably with each distribution. Prior to January 1, 1999, a program may have treated distributions in a different manner and reported them to taxpayers accordingly. In order to adjust to the method described in this section, if distributions were treated as coming first from the investment in the account, the QSTP must adjust the investment in the account by subtracting the amount of the investment in the account previously treated as distributed. If distributions were treated as coming first from earnings, the QSTP must adjust the earnings portion of the account by subtracting the amount of earnings previously treated as distributed. After the adjustment is made, the investment in the account is recovered ratably in accordance with this section. If no previous distribution was made but earnings were treated as taxable to the taxpayer in the year they were allocated to the account, the earnings treated as already taxable are treated as additional contributions and added to the investment in the account.

(3) *Examples.* The application of this paragraph (b) is illustrated by the following examples. The rounding convention used (rounding to three decimal places) in these examples is for purposes of illustration only. A QSTP may use another rounding convention as long as it consistently applies the convention. The examples are as follows:

Example 1. (i) In 1998, an individual, A, opens a prepaid educational services account with a QSTP on behalf of a designated beneficiary. Through the account A purchases units of education equivalent to eight semesters of tuition for full-time attendance at a public four-year university covered by the QSTP. A contributes $16,000 that includes payment of processing fees to the QSTP. In 2011 the designated beneficiary enrolls at a public four-year university. The QSTP makes distributions on behalf of the designated beneficiary to the university in August for the fall semester and in December for the spring semester. Tuition for full-time attendance at the university is $7,500 per academic year in 2011 and 2012, $7,875 for the academic year in 2013, and $8,200 for the academic year in 2014. The only expense covered by the QSTP distribution is tuition for four academic years. The calculations are as follows:

2011

Investment in the account as of 12/31/2011	=	$16,000
Units in account	=	8
Per unit investment	=	$2,000
Units distributed in 2011	=	2
Investment portion of distribution in 2011 ($2,000 per unit × 2 units)	=	$4,000
Current value of two units distributed in 2011	=	$7,500
Earnings portion of distribution in 2011 ($7,500 – $4,000)	=	$3,500

2012

Investment in the account as of 12/31/2012 ($16,000 – $4,000)	=	$12,000
Units in account	=	6
Per unit investment	=	$2,000
Units distributed in 2012	=	2
Investment portion of distribution in 2012 ($2,000 per unit × 2 units)	=	$4,000
Current value of two units distributed in 2012	=	$7,500
Earnings portion of distribution in 2012 ($7,500 – $4,000)	=	$3,500

2013

Investment in the account as of 12/31/2013 ($12,000 – $4000)	=	$8,000
Units in account	=	4
Per unit investment	=	$2,000
Units distributed in 2013	=	2
Investment portion of distribution in 2013 ($2,000 per unit × 2 units)	=	$4,000
Current value of two units distributed in 2013	=	$7,875
Earnings portion of distribution in 2013 ($7,875 – $4,000)	=	$3,875

2014

Investment in the account as of 12/31/2014 ($8,000 - $4000)	=	$4,000
Units in account	=	2
Per unit investment	=	$2,000
Units distributed in 2014	=	2
Investment portion of distribution in 2014 ($4,000 per unit × 2 units)	=	$4,000
Current value of two units distributed in 2014	=	$8,200
Earnings portion of distribution in 2014 ($8,200 - $4,000)	=	$4,200

12/31/2014 (after distributions)

Investment in the account as of 12/31/2014 ($4,000 - $4000)	=	0

(ii) In each year the designated beneficiary includes in his or her gross income the earnings portion of the distribution for tuition.

Example 2. (i) In 1998, an individual, B, opens a college savings account with a QSTP on behalf of a designated beneficiary. B contributes $18,000 to the account that includes payment of processing fees to the QSTP. On December 31, 2011, the total balance in the account for the benefit of the designated beneficiary is $30,000 (including distributions made during the year 2011). In 2011 the designated beneficiary enrolls at a four-year university. The QSTP makes distributions on behalf of the designated beneficiary to the university in August for the fall semester and in December for the spring semester. Tuition for full-time attendance at the university is $7,500 per academic year in 2011 and 2012, $7,875 for the academic year in 2013, and $8,200 for the academic year in 2014. The only expense covered by the QSTP distributions is tuition for four academic years. On the last day of the calendar year the account is allocated earnings of 5% on the total account balance on that day. Under the terms of the QSTP, a penalty of 15% is applied to the earnings not used to pay tuition. The calculations are as follows:

2011

Investment in the account	=	$18,000
Total account balance as of 12/31/2011	=	$30,000
Earnings as of 12/31/2011	=	$12,000
Distributions in 2011	=	$7,500
Earnings ratio for 2011 ($12,000 ÷ $30,000)	=	40%
Earnings portion of distributions in 2011 ($7,500 × .4)	=	$3,000
Return of investment portion of distributions in 2011 ($7,500 - $3,000)	=	$4,500

2012

Investment in the account as of 12/31/2012 ($18,000 - $4,500)	= $13,500
Total account balance as of 12/31/12 [($30,000 - $7,500) × 105%]	= $23,625
Earnings as of 12/31/2012	= $10,125
Distributions in 2012	= $7,500
Earnings ratio for 2012 ($10,125 ÷ $23,625)	= 42.9%
Earnings portion of distributions in 2012 ($7,500 × .429)	= $3,217.50
Return of investment portion of distributions in 2012 ($7,500 - $3,217.50)	= $4,282.50

2013

Investment in the account as of 12/31/2013 ($13,500 - $4,282.50)	= $9,217.50
Total account balance as of 12/31/13 [($23,625 - $7,500) × 105%]	= $16,931.25
Earnings as of 12/31/2013	= $7,713.75
Distributions in 2013	= $7,875
Earnings ratio for 2013 ($7,713.75 ÷ $16,931.25)	= 45.6%
Earnings portion of distributions in 2013 ($7,875 × .456)	= $3,591
Return of investment portion of distributions in 2013 ($7,875 –$3,591)	= $4,284

2014

Investment in the account as of 12/31/2014 ($9,217.50 - $4,284)	= $4,933.50
Total account balance as of 12/31/14 [($16,931.25 - $7,875) × 105%]	= $9,509.06
Earnings as of 12/31/2014	= $4,575.56
Distributions in 2014 for qualified higher education expenses (QHEE)	= $8,200
Distributions in 2014 not for qualified higher education expenses (Non-QHEE)	= $1,309.06
Total distributions	= $9,509.06
Earnings portion of QHEE distribution in 2014 [($8,200 ÷ $9,509.06) x $4,575.56]	= $3,945.68
Return of investment portion of QHEE distribution in 2014	= $4,254.32
Earnings portion of Non-QHEE distribution subject to penalty [($1,309.06 ÷ $9,509.06) × $4,575.56)]	= $629.89
Return of investment portion of non-QHEE distribution in 2014	= $679.17

(ii) In years 2011 through 2013 the designated beneficiary includes in gross income the earnings portion of the distributions for tuition. In year 2014 the designated beneficiary includes in gross income the earnings portion of the distribution for tuition, $3,945.68, plus the earnings portion of the distribution that was not used for tuition after reduction for the penalty, i.e. $535.41 ($629.89 minus a 15% penalty of $94.48).

(c) *Change in designated beneficiaries*—(1) General rule. A change in the designated beneficiary of a QSTP account is not treated as a distribution if the new designated beneficiary is a member of the family of the transferor designated beneficiary. However, any change of designated beneficiary not described in the preceding sentence is treated as a distribution to the account owner, provided the account owner has the authority to change the designated beneficiary. For rules related to a change in the designated beneficiary pursuant to a rollover distribution see Secs. 1.529-1(c) and 1.529-3(a)(2).

(2) *Scholarship program.* Notwithstanding paragraph (c)(1) of this section, the requirement that the new beneficiary be a member of the family of the transferor beneficiary shall not apply to a change in designated beneficiary of an interest in a QSTP account purchased by a State or local government or an organization described in section 501(c)(3) as part of a scholarship program.

(d) *Aggregation of accounts.* If an individual is a designated beneficiary of more than one account under a QSTP, the QSTP shall treat all contributions and earnings as allocable to a single account for purposes of calculating the earnings portion of any distribution from that QSTP. For purposes of determining the effect of the distribution on each account, the earnings portion and return of investment in the account portion of the distribution shall be allocated pro rata among the accounts based on total account value as of the close of the current calendar year.

SEC. 1.529-4 TIME, FORM, AND MANNER OF REPORTING DISTRIBUTIONS FROM QSTPS AND BACKUP WITHHOLDING.

(a) *Taxable distributions.* The portion of any distribution made during the calendar year by a QSTP that represents earnings shall be reported by the payor as described in this section.

(b) *Requirement to file return*—(1) Form of return. A payor must file a return required by this section on Form 1099-G. A payor may use forms containing provisions similar to Form 1099-G if it complies with applicable revenue procedures relating to substitute Forms 1099. A payor must file a separate return for each distributee who receives a taxable distribution.

(2) *Payor.* For purposes of this section, the term ``payor'' means the officer or employee having control of the program, or their designee.

(3) *Information included on return.* A payor must include on Form 1099-G—

(i) The name, address, and taxpayer identifying number (TIN) (as defined in section 7701(a)(41)) of the payor;

(ii) The name, address, and TIN of the distributee;

(iii) The amount of earnings distributed to the distributee in the calendar year; and

(iv) Any other information required by Form 1099-G or its instructions.

(4) *Time and place for filing return.* A payor must file any return required by this paragraph (b) on or before February 28 of the year following the calendar year in which the distribution is made. A payor must file the return with the IRS office designated in the instructions for Form 1099-G.

(5) *Returns required on magnetic media.* If a payor is required to file at least 250 returns during the calendar year, the returns must be filed on magnetic media. If a payor is required to file fewer than 250 returns, the prescribed paper form may be used.

(6) *Extension of time to file return.* For good cause, the Commissioner may grant an extension of time in which to file Form 1099-G for reporting taxable earnings under section 529. The application for extension of time must be submitted in the manner prescribed by the Commissioner.

(c) Requirement to furnish statement to the distributee—(1) In general. A payor that must file a return under paragraph (b) of this section must furnish a statement to the distributee. The requirement to furnish a statement to the distributee will be satisfied if the payor provides the distributee with a copy of the Form 1099-G (or a substitute statement that complies with applicable revenue procedures) containing all the information filed with the Internal Revenue Service and all the legends required by paragraph (c)(2) of this section by the time required by paragraph (c)(3) of this section.

(2) *Information included on statement.* A payor must include on the statement that it must furnish to the distributee—

(i) The information required under paragraph (b)(3) of this section;

(ii) The telephone number of a person to contact about questions pertaining to the statement; and

(iii) A legend as required on the official Internal Revenue Service Form 1099-G.

(3) *Time for furnishing statement.* A payor must furnish the statement required by paragraph (c)(1) of this section to the distributee on or before January 31 of the year following the calendar year in which the distribution was made. The statement will be considered furnished to the distributee if it is mailed to the distributee's last known address.

(4) *Extension of time to furnish statement.* For good cause, the Commissioner may grant an extension of time to furnish statements to distributees of taxable earnings under section 529. The application for extension of time must be submitted in the manner prescribed by the Commissioner.

(d) *Backup withholding.* Distributions from a QSTP are not subject to backup withholding.

(e) *Effective date.* The reporting requirements set forth in this section apply to distributions made after December 31, 1998.

SEC. 1.529-5 ESTATE, GIFT, AND GENERATION-SKIPPING TRANSFER TAX RULES RELATING TO QUALIFIED STATE TUITION PROGRAMS.

(a) *Gift and generation-skipping transfer tax treatment of contributions after August 20, 1996, and before August 6, 1997.* A contribution on behalf of a designated beneficiary to a QSTP (or to a program that meets the transitional rule requirements under Sec. 1.529-6(b)) after August 20, 1996, and before August 6, 1997, is not treated as a taxable gift. The subsequent waiver of qualified higher education expenses of a designated beneficiary by an educational institution (or the subsequent payment of higher education expenses of a designated beneficiary to an educational institution) under a QSTP is treated as a qualified transfer under section 2503(e) and is not treated as a transfer of property by gift for purposes of section 2501. As such, the contribution is not subject to the generation-skipping transfer tax imposed by section 2601.

(b) Gift and generation-skipping transfer tax treatment of contributions after August 5, 1997—(1) In general. A contribution on behalf of a designated beneficiary to a QSTP (or to a program that meets the transitional rule requirements under Sec. 1.529-6(b)) after August 5, 1997, is a completed gift of a present interest in property under section 2503(b) from the person making the contribution to the designated beneficiary. As such, the contribution is eligible for the annual gift tax exclusion provided under section 2503(b). The portion of a contribution excludible from taxable gifts under section 2503(b) also satisfies the requirements of section 2642(c)(2) and, therefore, is also excludible for purposes of the generation-skipping transfer tax imposed under section 2601. A contribution to a QSTP after August 5, 1997, is not treated as a qualified transfer within the meaning of section 2503(e).

(2) *Contributions that exceed the annual exclusion amount.*

(i) Under section 529(c)(2)(B) a donor may elect to take certain contributions to a QSTP into account ratably over a five year period in determining the amount of gifts made during the calendar year. The provision is applicable only with respect to contributions not in excess of five times the section 2503(b) exclusion amount available in the calendar year of the contribution. Any excess may not be taken into account ratably and is treated as a taxable gift in the calendar year of the contribution.

(ii) The election under section 529(c)(2)(B) may be made by a donor and his or her spouse with respect to a gift considered to be made one-half by each spouse under section 2513.

(iii) The election is made on Form 709, Federal Gift Tax Return, for the calendar year in which the contribution is made.

(iv) If in any year after the first year of the five year period described in section 529(c)(2)(B), the amount excludible under section 2503(b) is increased as provided in section 2503(b)(2), the donor may make an additional contribution in any one or more of the four remaining years up to the difference between the exclusion amount as increased and the original exclusion amount for the year or years in which the original contribution was made.

(v) *Example*. The application of this paragraph (b)(2) is illustrated by the following example:

Example. In Year 1, when the annual exclusion under section 2503(b) is $10,000, P makes a contribution of $60,000 to a QSTP for the benefit of P's child, C. P elects under section 529(c)(2)(B) to account for the gift ratably over a five year period beginning with the calendar year of contribution. P is treated as making an excludible gift of $10,000 in each of Years 1 through 5 and a taxable gift of $10,000 in Year 1. In Year 3, when the annual exclusion is increased to $12,000, P makes an additional contribution for the benefit of C in the amount of $8,000. P is treated as making an excludible gift of $2,000 under section 2503(b); the remaining $6,000 is a taxable gift in Year 3.

(3) *Change of designated beneficiary or rollover*. (i) A transfer which occurs by reason of a change in the designated beneficiary, or a rollover of credits or account balances from the account of one beneficiary to the account of another beneficiary, is not a taxable gift and is not subject to the generation-skipping transfer tax if the new beneficiary is a member of the family of the old beneficiary, as defined in Sec. 1.529-1(c), and is assigned to the same generation as the old beneficiary, as defined in section 2651.

(ii) A transfer which occurs by reason of a change in the designated beneficiary, or a rollover of credits or account balances from the account of one beneficiary to the account of another beneficiary, will be treated as a taxable gift by the old beneficiary to the new beneficiary if the new beneficiary is assigned to a lower generation than the old beneficiary, as defined in section 2651, regardless of whether the new beneficiary is a member of the family of the old beneficiary. The transfer will be subject to the generation-skipping transfer tax if the new beneficiary is assigned to a generation which is two or more levels lower than the generation assignment of the old beneficiary. The five year averaging rule described in paragraph (b)(2) of this section may be applied to the transfer.

(iii) *Example*. The application of this paragraph (b)(3) is illustrated by the following example:

Example. In Year 1, P makes a contribution to a QSTP on behalf of P's child, C. In Year 4, P directs that a distribution from the account for the benefit of C be made to an account for the benefit of P's grandchild, G. The rollover distribution is treated as a taxable gift by C to G, because, under section 2651, G is assigned to a generation below the generation assignment of C.

(c) *Estate tax treatment for estates of decedents dying after August 20, 1996, and before June 9, 1997.* The gross estate of a decedent dying after August 20, 1996, and before June 9, 1997, includes the value of any interest in any QSTP which is attributable to contributions made by the decedent to such program on behalf of a designated beneficiary.

(d) Estate tax treatment for estates of decedents dying after June 8, 1997—

(1) In general. Except as provided in paragraph (d)(2) of this section, the gross estate of a decedent dying after June 8, 1997, does not include the value of any interest in a QSTP which is attributable to contributions made by the decedent to such program on behalf of any designated beneficiary.

(2) *Excess contributions.* In the case of a decedent who made the election under section 529(c)(2)(B) and paragraph (b)(3)(i) of this section who dies before the close of the five year period, that portion of the contribution allocable to calendar years beginning after the date of death of the decedent is includible in the decedent's gross estate.

(3) *Designated beneficiary decedents.* The gross estate of a designated beneficiary of a QSTP includes the value of any interest in the QSTP.

SEC. 1.529-6 TRANSITION RULES.

(a) *Effective date.* Section 529 is effective for taxable years ending after August 20, 1996, and applies to all contracts entered into or accounts opened on August 20, 1996, or later.

(b) *Programs maintained on August 20, 1996.* Transition relief is available to a program maintained by a State under which persons could purchase tuition credits, certification or similar rights on behalf of, or make contributions for educational expenses of, a designated beneficiary if the program was in existence on August 20, 1996. Such program must meet the requirements of a QSTP before the later of August 20, 1997, or the first day of the first calendar quarter after the close of the first regular session of the State legislature that begins after August 20, 1996. If a State has a two-year legislative session, each year of such session shall be deemed to be a separate regular session of the State legislature. The program, as in effect on August 20, 1996, shall be treated as a QSTP with respect to contributions (and earnings allocable thereto) pursuant to contracts entered into under the program. This relief is available for contributions (and earnings allocable thereto) made before, and the contracts entered into before, the first date on which the program becomes a QSTP. The provisions of the program, as in effect on August 20, 1996, shall apply in lieu of section 529(b) with respect to such contributions and earnings. A program shall be treated as meeting the transition rule if it conforms to the requirements of section 529, Secs. 1.529-1 through 1.529-5 and this section by the date this document is published as final regulations in the Federal Register.

(c) *Retroactive effect.* No income tax liability will be asserted against a QSTP for any period before the program meets the requirements of section 529, Secs. 1.529-1 through 1.529-5 and this section if the program qualifies for the transition relief described in paragraph (b) of this section.

(d) *Contracts entered into and accounts opened before August 20, 1996*—(1) In general. A QSTP may continue to maintain agreements in connection with contracts entered into and accounts opened before August 20, 1996, without jeopardizing its tax exempt status even if maintaining the agreements is contrary to section 529(b) provided that the QSTP operates in accordance with the restrictions contained in this paragraph (d). However, distributions made by the QSTP, regardless of the terms of any agreement executed before August 20, 1996, are subject to tax according to the rules of Sec. 1.529-3 and subject to the reporting requirements of Sec. 1.529-4.

(2) *Interest in program pledged as security for a loan.* An interest in the program, or a portion of an interest in the program, may be used as security for a loan if the contract giving rise to the interest was entered into or account was opened prior to August 20, 1996 and the agreement permitted such a pledge.

(3) *Member of the family.* In the case of an account opened or a contract entered into before August 20, 1996, the rules regarding a change in beneficiary, including the rollover rule in Sec. 1.529-3(a) and the gift tax rule in Sec. 1.529-5(b)(3), shall be applied by treating any transferee beneficiary permitted under the terms of the account or contract as a member of the family of the transferor beneficiary.

(4) *Eligible educational institution.* In the case of an account opened or contract entered into before August 20, 1996, an eligible educational institution is an educational institution in which the beneficiary may enroll under the terms of the account or contract.

Appendix F

Advance Notice of Proposed Regulation: NOTICE 2018-58

GUIDANCE ON RECONTRIBUTIONS, ROLLOVERS AND QUALIFIED HIGHER EDUCATION EXPENSES UNDER SECTION 529

I. Purpose and Overview

This notice announces that the Department of the Treasury (the Treasury Department) and the Internal Revenue Service (the IRS) intend to issue regulations providing clarification regarding (1) the special rules for contributions of refunded qualified higher education expenses to a qualified tuition program under § 529(c)(3)(D) of the Internal Revenue Code (Code); (2) the new rules under § 529(c)(3)(C)(i)(III) permitting a rollover from a qualified tuition program to an ABLE account under § 529A; and (3) the new rules under § 529(c)(7) treating certain elementary or secondary school expenses as qualified higher education expenses.

II. Background

Under § 529, a State or its agency or instrumentality may establish or maintain a program that permits a person to prepay or contribute to an account for a designated beneficiary's qualified higher education expenses (QHEEs). In addition, an eligible educational institution may establish or maintain a program that permits a person to prepay a designated beneficiary's QHEEs. These programs are collectively referred to as section 529 qualified tuition programs (QTPs). Section 529(c)(3) provides that distributions (including any attributable earnings) from a QTP are not included in gross income if such distributions do not exceed the designated beneficiary's QHEEs. To the extent distributions exceed the designated beneficiary's QHEEs, a portion of the distribution is included in gross income.

Prior to its amendment by "An Act to provide for reconciliation pursuant to titles II and V of the concurrent resolution on the budget for fiscal year 2018", Pub.L. 115-97 (the "2017 Act"), signed into law on December 22, 2017, § 529(e)(3)(A) defined QHEEs to include tuition, fees, books, supplies, and equipment required for the enrollment or attendance of a designated

eligible educational institution. In the case of a special needs beneficiary, QHEEs include expenses for special needs services that are incurred in connection with such enrollment or attendance. QHEEs also include reasonable costs for room and board for eligible students as defined in § 25A(b)(3) (generally, those who are enrolled at least half-time).

Sections 529(c)(3)(C)(i)(I) and (II) permit a tax-free rollover of a distribution from a QTP, made within 60 days of the distribution, to another QTP for the benefit of either the same designated beneficiary or another designated beneficiary who is a member of the family of the original designated beneficiary. However, Notice 2001-81, 2001-52 I.R.B. 617, provides that the distributing QTP must provide a breakdown of the earnings portion of the rollover amount to the recipient QTP and, until the recipient QTP receives appropriate documentation showing the earnings portion, the entire rollover amount is treated as earnings. Notice 2001-81 applies the same rule to a direct transfer (i.e., a trustee-to-trustee transfer) from a QTP to another QTP.

Section 529(c)(3)(D), added to the Code by the Protecting Americans from Tax Hikes Act of 2015 (PATH Act), part of the Consolidated Appropriations Act, 2016 (Pub. L. 114-113), addresses situations in which QTP funds are distributed for a beneficiary's QHEEs, but some portion of those expenses is refunded to the beneficiary by the eligible educational institution. This could occur, for example, if the beneficiary were to drop a class mid-semester. Section 529(c)(3)(D) provides that the portion of such a distribution refunded to an individual who is the beneficiary of a QTP by an eligible educational institution is not subject to income tax to the extent that the refund is recontributed to a QTP of which that individual is the beneficiary not later than 60 days after the date of such refund and does not exceed the refunded amount. Section 529(c)(3)(D) applies to refunds received after December 31, 2014. The PATH Act also included a transition rule with regard to the deadline for recontributing a refund received after 2014 but before the date of enactment (December 18, 2015). Specifically, those refunded distributions are exempt from income tax if they were recontributed to the beneficiary's QTP not later than February 16, 2016 (60 days after the date of enactment of the PATH Act).

The 2017 Act added § 529(c)(3)(C)(i)(III) which provides that a distribution from a QTP made after December 22, 2017, and before January 1, 2026, is not subject to income tax if, within 60 days of the distribution, it is transferred to an ABLE account (as defined in § 529A(e)(6))2 of the designated beneficiary or a member of the family of the designated beneficiary. Under § 529(c)(3)(C)(i), the amount of any rollover to an ABLE account is limited to the amount that, when added to all other contributions made to the ABLE account for the taxable year, does not exceed the contribution limit for the ABLE account under § 529A(b)(2)(B)(i), i.e., the annual gift tax exclusion amount under § 2503(b).

In addition, the 2017 Act expanded the definition of QHEEs to include tuition in connection with the designated beneficiary's enrollment or attendance at an elementary or secondary public, private, or religious school. See § 529(c)(7). The 2017 Act also amended § 529(e)(3)(A) to limit the total amount of these tuition distributions for each designated beneficiary to $10,000 per year from all QTPs of the designated beneficiary. Both amendments apply to distributions made after December 31, 2017.

III. Recontribution of Refunded QHEEs

The Treasury Department and the IRS are aware of concerns expressed by QTP administrators regarding the administrative burdens that would arise if a recontribution of a refunded QHEE is treated in the same manner as a rollover under Notice 2001-81 requiring a breakdown of the earnings portion of the recontribution. Because the amount is refunded by the eligible educational institution, which will have no information regarding the income portion of each tuition payment (whether made from a single or multiple QTPs), QTP administrators generally would be unable to determine the earnings portion of the recontribution. Accordingly, the Treasury Department and the IRS intend to issue regulations providing that the entire recontributed amount will be treated as principal. This rule of administrative convenience will eliminate the burdens associated with determining the earnings portion. Furthermore, because the recontributed amount previously was taken into account in applying the overall contribution limit under § 529(b)(6), the Treasury Department and the IRS anticipate that the regulations will provide that the recontributed amount does not count against the limit on contributions on behalf of the designated beneficiary under § 529(b)(6). In addition, consistent with § 529(c)(3)(D), the Treasury Department and the IRS anticipate that the regulations will confirm that the recontribution must be to a QTP for the benefit of the designated beneficiary who received the refund of QHEEs, although the recontribution need not be to the QTP from which the distributions for the QHEEs were made.

IV. Rollover From a QTP to an Able Account

In accordance with new § 529(c)(3)(C)(i)(III), the Treasury Department and the IRS intend to issue regulations providing that a distribution from a QTP made after December 22, 2017, and before January 1, 2026, to the ABLE account of the designated beneficiary of that QTP, or of a member of the family of that designated beneficiary, is not subject to income tax if two requirements are satisfied. First, the distributed funds must be contributed to the ABLE account within 60 days after their withdrawal from the QTP. Second, the distribution, when added to all other contributions made to the ABLE account for the taxable year that are subject to the limitation under § 529A(b)(2)(B)(i) (the annual gift tax exclusion under § 2503(b)), must not exceed that limitation. Specifically, the regulations are expected to provide that the sum of the distribution and all other contributions to the ABLE account for the taxable year, other than contributions of the designated beneficiary's compensation as described in § 529A(b)(2)(B)(ii), must not exceed the annual gift tax exclusion for that taxable year. Consistent with the longstanding approach of treating direct transfers similarly to rollovers in Notice 2001-81, the Treasury Department and the IRS also anticipate that the regulations will provide that the same rules will apply regardless of whether such a QTP distribution is rolled over to an ABLE account or instead is transferred by a direct transfer from a QTP to an ABLE account.

To the extent that a direct transfer (or, in the case of a rollover, a contribution of the distributed amount) would cause the contribution limit under § 529A(b)(2)(B)(i) to be exceeded, it would be subject to income tax and a 10% additional tax under § 529(c)(6), if applicable. Therefore, the Treasury Department and the IRS anticipate that the regulations will require a QTP to prohibit the direct transfer of any amount that would cause the limit under § 529A(b)(2)(B)(i) to be exceeded. Furthermore, a qualified ABLE program is prohibited from accepting certain contributions in excess of the limitations applicable to ABLE accounts, and any violation of those rules could cause the designated beneficiary to incur tax, and could impact adversely the ABLE beneficiary's eligibility for certain public benefits.

The Treasury Department and the IRS encourage the QTP designated beneficiary, in the case of a rollover, or the QTP, in the case of a direct transfer, to contact the qualified ABLE program before contributing any funds to the ABLE account to ensure that the § 529A(b)(2)(B)(i) limit will not be exceeded. However, the Treasury Department and the IRS anticipate that the regulations will provide that, in the case of a direct transfer, any excess contribution that is rejected by the qualified ABLE program and returned to the QTP will not be deemed to be a new contribution to the QTP for purposes of the § 529(b)(6) contribution limit.

Further, the Treasury Department and the IRS anticipate that the regulations will specify that, for purposes of identifying the ABLE accounts permitted to receive such a rollover from a designated beneficiary's QTP, a member of the family of the designated beneficiary means a member of the family as defined in § 529(e)(2), rather than the more limited definition in § 529A(e)(4) that applies for purposes of qualified ABLE programs.

V. Section 529 Expansion of QHEEs to Include Elementary and Secondary Education Tuition Expenses

Consistent with new § 529(c)(7) and (e)(3)(A), respectively, the Treasury Department and the IRS anticipate that the regulations will provide that QHEEs include tuition in connection with the designated beneficiary's enrollment or attendance at an elementary or secondary public, private, or religious school, but that such QHEEs are limited to a total of $10,000 per year per designated beneficiary, regardless of the number of QTPs making such distributions for that same designated beneficiary. The Treasury Department and IRS intend to issue regulations defining the term "elementary or secondary" to mean kindergarten through grade 12 as determined under State law, consistent with the definition applicable for Coverdell education savings accounts in § 530(b)(3)(B). Coverdell education savings accounts are another type of tax-favored savings account governed under § 530 and also may be established to pay for tuition and other expenses in connection with enrollment or attendance at an elementary or secondary public, private, or religious school. Applying the same definition to both a QTP and a Coverdell education savings account will facilitate the allocation of expenses between those two accounts as is required by § 530(d)(2)(C)(ii) if a designated beneficiary receives distributions from both a QTP and a Coverdell education savings account and those total distributions exceed the designated beneficiary's qualified expenses.

VI. Reliance

Before the issuance of the proposed regulations described in this notice, taxpayers, beneficiaries, and administrators of 529 and ABLE programs may rely on the rules described in sections III, IV, and V of this notice.

VII. Drafting Information

The principal author of this notice is Peter A. Holiat of the Office of the Associate Chief Counsel (TEGE). For further information regarding this notice contact Mr. Holiat at 202-317- 4541 (not a toll-free number).

Appendix G

IRS Notice 2001-81 (Section 529 Programs)

This notice provides guidance regarding certain recordkeeping, reporting, and other requirements applicable to qualified tuition programs described in 529 of the Internal Revenue Code, in light of certain amendments made to § 529 by the Economic Growth and Tax Relief Reconciliation Act of 2001 (Pub. L. No. 107-16, 115 Stat. 38) (EGTRRA).

Among other changes to 529, EGTRRA: (1) expands the definition of qualified tuition program to include certain prepaid tuition programs established and maintained by one or more eligible educational institutions; (2) provides an exclusion from gross income for distributions from a State 529 program (and, beginning in 2004, a prepaid tuition program established and maintained by one or more eligible educational institutions) which are used to pay for qualified higher education expenses of the designated beneficiary; (3) repeals the requirement that a 529 program impose a more than de minimis penalty on any refund of earnings not used for qualified higher education expenses of the beneficiary; and (4) replaces that penalty with an additional 10-percent tax on the amount of a distribution from a 529 program that is includible in gross income (with certain exceptions). In general, these amendments are effective for taxable years beginning after December 31, 2001.[1]

In light of these changes, and to give 529 programs adequate time to implement appropriate recordkeeping and reporting procedures, the Internal Revenue Service and the Treasury Department are issuing this guidance, which they intend to incorporate in final regulations under 529. Section 529 programs and their participants may rely on this notice pending the issuance of final regulations under § 529.

---

1. Unless otherwise indicated, references herein are to Section 529 of the Internal Revenue Code, as amended by EGTRRA.

A. IMPOSITION OF A PENALTY AND VERIFICATION OF PURPOSE OF A DISTRIBUTION.

As currently in effect (prior to the effective date of EGIRRA), § 529(b)(3) provides that a program is not treated as a qualified § 529 program unless it imposes a more than de minimis penalty on any refund of earnings that is not: (a) used for qualified higher education expenses of the designated beneficiary; (b) made on account of the death or disability of the designated beneficiary; or (c) made on account of certain scholarships or other educational assistance received by the beneficiary. Prop. Treas. Reg. § 1.529-2(e) provides rules on de minimis penalties and procedures for verifying the use of distributions and imposing and collecting penalties.

EGTRRA repeals § 529(b)(3), effective for taxable years beginning after December 31, 2001. Therefore, the final regulations under § 529 will provide that, with respect to any distributions made after December 31, 2001, a § 529 program will no longer be required to verify how distributions are used or to collect any penalty. However, with respect to any distributions made on or before December 31, 2001, a § 529 program must continue to verify whether the distribution is used for qualified higher education expenses of the beneficiary and to collect a more than de minimis penalty on nonqualified distributions.

B. REPORTING OF DISTRIBUTIONS.

Section 529(d) provides that a § 529 program shall make reports regarding the program to the Internal Revenue Service and to designated beneficiaries regarding contributions, distributions, and such other matters as the Internal Revenue Service may require. Prop. Treas. Reg. § 1.529-4 requires a State tuition program to report on Form 1099-G, Certain Government Payments, the earnings portion of any distribution made during the year, together with other information such as the name, address and TIN of the distributee. A § 529 program must furnish a statement to the distributee on or before January 31st of the year following the calendar year in which the distribution is made. In addition, a § 529 program must file Form 1099-G on or before February 28th of the year following the calendar year in which the distribution is made.

These reporting requirements continue in effect for distributions made in 2001. Thus, with respect to any distributions made in 2001, a § 529 program must furnish statements to the distributees on or before January 31, 2002, and file returns on Form 1099-G on or before February 28, 2002.

In light of the expansion of § 529 to include prepaid tuition programs established and maintained by one or more eligible educational institutions (which may be private institutions), the Internal Revenue Service will issue a new form, Form 1099-Q, for taxable years beginning after December 31, 2001. A copy of Form 1099-Q is available on the IRS website at www.irs.gov.

C. CALCULATION OF EARNINGS.

1. In general.

Section 529(c)(3)(A) provides that a distribution from a § 529 program is includible in the gross income of the distributee in the manner as provided under § 72, to the extent not excluded from gross income under any other provision of Chapter 1 of the Code. Section 529(c)(3)(D)(iii) provides that, except to the extent provided by the Secretary, the value of the contract, income on the contract, and the investment in the contract are to be computed as of the close of the calendar year.

2. Recordkeeping requirements with respect to rollover contributions.

Section 529(b)(3)[2] states that a program must provide a separate accounting for each designated beneficiary. Prop. Treas. Reg. § 1.529-2(f) requires a § 529 program to maintain records with respect to the designated beneficiary of each account showing the total investment in the account and any earnings attributable thereto.

In the case of a contribution to a § 529 account that represents a transfer from a Coverdell education savings account described in § 530(b)(2)(B), a transfer of proceeds of a qualified U.S. Savings Bond described in § 135(c)(2)(C), or a "rollover" of amounts from another § 529 program account (each, a "rollover contribution"), the recipient § 529 program must determine the basis and earnings portions of the amounts contributed. (*See* Prop. Treas. Reg. § 1.529-3(a)(2), which provides that the earnings portion of the rollover amount must be added to the earnings of the account that received the contribution.)

Although this requirement was not changed by EGTRRA, § 529 programs have indicated that there is some confusion about the requirement that a § 529 program determine and maintain records that reflect the basis and earnings portions of any rollover contribution. Accordingly, it is expected that final regulations will clarify that, when accepting a contribution, a § 529 program must ask whether the contribution is a rollover contribution from a Coverdell education savings account, a qualified U.S. Savings Bond, or another § 529 program. If the contribution is a rollover contribution, the § 529 program must determine the earnings portion of the contribution, and add that amount to the earnings recorded in the account to which the rollover contribution is made. Until the § 529 program receives appropriate documentation showing the earnings portion of the contribution, the program must treat the entire amount of the contribution as earnings in the § 529 account receiving the distribution. For this purpose, "appropriate documentation" means: (1) in the case of a rollover contribution from a Coverdell education savings account, an account statement issued by the financial institution that acted as trustee or custodian of the education savings account that shows basis and earnings in the account; (2) in the case of a rollover contribution from the

2. Section 529(b)(4) was renumbered as 529(b)(3) by EGTRRA.

redemption of qualified U.S. Savings Bonds, an account statement or Form 1099-INT issued by the financial institution that redeemed the bonds showing interest from the redemption of the bonds; and (3) in the case of a rollover contribution from another § 529 program, a statement issued by the distributing § 529 program that shows the earnings portion of the distribution.

3. Rollover statement between § 529 programs.

In the case of any direct transfer (*i.e.*, trustee-to-trustee rollover) between § 529 programs, the distributing program must provide to the receiving program a statement setting forth the earnings portion of the rollover distribution within 30 days after the distribution or by January 10th of the year following the calendar year in which the rollover occurred, whichever is earlier. This rule is effective for direct transfers between § 529 programs that occur on or after January 1, 2002.

4. Timing of earnings calculation.

Consistent with § 529(c)(3)(D), the proposed regulations provide that the earnings portion of any distribution is determined by applying an earnings ratio, generally the earnings allocable to an account as of the close of the year divided by the total account balance as of the close of the calendar year, determined by adding back the amount of all distributions made during the year. *See* Prop. Treas. Reg. § 1.529-1(c).

In response to comments received on the proposed regulations, and consistent with the Secretary's authority under § 529(c)(3)(D)(iii) to adopt a different rule, the Treasury Department and the Internal Revenue Service expect that final regulations will revise the time for determining the earnings portion of any distribution from a § 529 account. It is expected that final regulations will provide that, effective for distributions made after December 31, 2002, programs will be required to determine the earnings portion of each distribution as of the date of distribution. In the case of direct transfers between § 529 programs, this requirement is effective for distributions made after December 31, 2001. In the case of any State program for which this change would require legislation and whose State legislature has a biennial legislative session, the program will have until January 1, 2004, to conform to this method of calculating earnings.

5. Aggregation of Accounts.

Section 529 (c)(3)(D)(i) provides that to the extent provided by the Secretary, all § 529 programs of which an individual is a designated beneficiary shall be treated as one program. Prop. Treas. Reg. § 1.529-3(d) provides that all accounts maintained by a § 529 program for the benefit of a designated beneficiary shall be treated as a single account for purposes of calculating the earnings portion of any distribution. Based on comments received on the proposed regulations, it is expected that the final regulations will provide that only accounts maintained by a

§ 529 program and having the same account owner and the same designated beneficiary must be aggregated for purposes of computing the earnings portion of any distribution. For this purpose, a State that has both a prepaid § 529 program and a § 529 savings program should consider each program separately for purposes of calculating the earnings portion of any distribution from either the prepaid or the savings program. These changes will apply for purposes of the earnings calculation only, and will not affect the application of § 529(b)(6) (prohibition on excess contributions).[3] The § 529(b)(6) limit will continue to be applied based upon all accounts, both savings and prepaid, in programs established and maintained by the State for the benefit of the same designated beneficiary.

Comments on Future Guidance Invited

The Internal Revenue Service invites comments on the matters described in this notice and any other matters relating to § 529 and the regulations thereunder. Please send written comments by March 25, 2002, to: CC:ITA:RU (Notice 2001-81), room 5226, Internal Revenue Service, POB 7604, Ben Franklin Station, Washington DC 20044. Submission may be hand-delivered Monday through Friday between the hours of 8 a.m. and 5 p.m. to CC:ITA:RU (Notice 2001-81), Courier's Desk, Internal Revenue Service, 1111 Constitution Avenue, NW, Washington DC. Alternatively, taxpayers may submit comments electronically via the Internet by selecting the "Tax Regs" option on the IRS Home Page, or by submitting comments directly to the IRS Internet site at http://www.irs.gov/prod/tax_regs/regslist.html. Comments will be available for public inspection.

DRAFTING INFORMATION

The principal author of this notice is Monice Rosenbaum of the Office of Division Counsel/Associate Chief Counsel (Tax Exempt and Government Entities). For further information regarding this notice contact Ms. Rosenbaum at (202) 622-6070 (not a toll-free number).

3. Section 529(b)(7) was renumbered as 529(b)(6) by EGTRRA.

GLOSSARY

ACTS

Achieving a Better Life Experience (ABLE) Act of 2014 [Also known as the Stephen Beck Jr., Achieving a Better Life Experience Act]; Pub. L. No. 113-295, 128 Stat. 4010 (2014).

The American Recovery and Reinvestment Act (ARRA) of 2009; Pub. L. No. 111-5; H.R. 1 (2009).

The American Rescue Plan Act (ARP) of 2021; H.R. 1319, 117th Cong. (2021).

Bankruptcy Abuse Prevention and Consumer Protection Act (BAPCPA) of 2005; Pub. L. No. 109-8, 119 Stat. 23 (2005).

College Cost Reduction and Access Act (CCRAA) of 2007; Pub. L. No. 110-84, 121 Stat. 784 (2007).

College Scholarship Fraud Prevention Act (CSFPA) of 2000; Pub. L. No. 106-420, 114 Stat. 1867 (2000).

The Consolidated Appropriations Act (CAA) of 2021; Pub. L. No. 116-260, H.R. 133 (2021).

The Coronavirus Aid, Relief, and Economic Security (CARES) Act of 2020; Pub. L. No. 116-123, H.R. 748 (2019–20).

Deficit Reduction Act (DRA) of 2005; Pub. L. No. 109-171, 120 Stat. 4 (2005).

Economic Growth and Tax Relief Reconciliation Act (EGTRRA) of 2001; Pub. L. No. 107-16, 115 Stat. 38 (2001).

Emergency Economic Stabilization (EESA) Act of 2008; Pub. L. No. 110-343, H.R. 1424 (2008).

Higher Education Act (HEA) of 1965; Pub. L. No. 89-329, 79 Stat. 1219 (1965).

Higher Education Act (HEA) of 2008; Pub. L. No. 110-315, H.R. 4137 (2008).

Higher Education Reconciliation Act (HERA) of 2005 (Title VIII of the Deficit Reduction Act); Pub. L. No. 109-171, 120 Stat. 4, 155 (2006).

Housing Assistant Tax (HAA) Act of 2008; Pub. L. No. 110-289, H.R. 5720 (2008).

Job Creation and Worker Assistance Act (JCWA) of 2002; Pub. L. No. 107-147, 116 Stat. 21 (2002).

Make College Affordable Act (MCAA) of 2007; H.R. 193, 110th Cong. (introduced in House Jan. 1, 2007).

Pension Protection Act (PPA) of 2006; Pub. L. No. 109-280, 120 Stat. 780 (2006).

Setting Every Community Up for Retirement Enhancement (SECURE) Act of 2019; Pub. L. No. 116-94, H.R. 1994, 116th Cong. (2019–20).

Small Business and Work Opportunity Act (SBWCA) of 2007; Pub. L. No. 110-28, 121 Stat. 189 (2007).

Small Business Job Protection Act (SBJP) of 1996; Pub. L. No. 104-188, 110 Stat. 1755 (1996).

Tax Cuts and Jobs Act (TCJA) of 2017; Pub. L. No. 115-97, 94 Stat. 2390 (2017).

Tax Increase Prevention and Reconciliation Act (TIPRA) of 2005; Pub. L. No. 109-222, 120 Stat. 345 (2006).

Taxpayer Relief Act (TRA) of 1997; Pub. L. No. 105-34, 111 Stat. 788 (1997).

Tax Relief and Health Care Act (TRHCA) of 2006; Pub. L. No. 109-432, 120 Stat. 2922 (2006).

Working Families Tax Relief (WFTRA) Act of 2004; Pub. L. No. 108-311, 118 Stat. 1166 (2004).

TERMS

-A-

ABLE Account: A savings account for those with an eligible disability who want to prepare for a more independent and secure future.

Above-the-Line (or above-the-line deduction): These are the deductions that are claimed by individuals under Section 62. They are taken from gross income in reaching adjusted gross income.

Academic Credit: The unit of measurement given by an educational institution when a student fulfills course requirements.

Academic Year: A term of enrollment, usually running from the fall through the spring and measured by quarters, semesters, or trimesters or by clock or credit hours.

Acceptance Form: The written acknowledgement issued by the college to the student who receives an offer of acceptance to the college (usually comes with an Award Letter).

Account: A formal record of transactions relating to a particular designated beneficiary. It includes prepaid and saving accounts described in Section 529 and also the Coverdell account described in Section 530.

Account Owner: The person who, under the terms of the prepaid or savings plan, is entitled to select or change the designated beneficiary of an account, to designate any person other than the designated beneficiary to whom funds may be paid from the account, or to receive distributions from the account if no such other person is designated.

Accrued Interest (or accrual): The cost of the loan represented by an interest rate that is totaled prior to payment.

Acknowledgement Report: Report given to PROFILE applicants disclosing their Expected Family Contribution.

Acquisition Indebtedness: Debt secured by a qualified residence which incurs to taxpayer in acquiring, construction, or substantially improving the residence.

Actual Cost of Attendance: Includes tuition and related expenses, supplies, books, room, and board plus personal expenses, such as transportation, medical costs, etc.

Additional Tax: (*See* Penalty Tax)

Adjusted Available Income: The actual amount of family income used to determine financial need.

Adjusted Gross Income (AGI): All gross income under Section 61 of the Internal Revenue Code less allowable adjustments under Section 62.

Adjusted Need (for financial aid purposes): Cost of Attendance less Expected Family Contribution less Resources.

Adjusted Qualified Education Expenses (AQEE): To prevent double benefits, qualified education expenses must be reduced or adjusted if those expenses have been used in other exclusions, deductions, or credit provisions.

Advanced Placement (AP): These courses, offered by high schools, help students earn college credits while in high school, thus lowering overall costs of college.

Advisor (or broker-sold) Plans: Section 529 savings plans that can be obtained through a professional advisor.

Age-based Investment or Portfolio Options: Investment option providing a mix of stocks and bonds based on the beneficiary's AGI. The younger the beneficiary, the riskier and more aggressive the investments.

Allowances: Deductions from the income that is assessed under both the federal and institutional methodology financial aid formulae.

Allowance for Federal Income Tax Paid: An allowance for federal, state, and social security taxes paid that is subtracted from income assessed under the federal financial aid formula.

Alternative Minimum Tax (AMT): A complicated calculation of income tax that is owed by the taxpayer if higher than the regular tax.

American Opportunity Tax Credit (AOTC): A partially refundable credit that was added by the American Recovery and Reinvestment Act of 2009.

Amortization: The specific period of time over which a payment (such as a loan) is made.

Annual Education Savings and Asset Protection Allowance: One of the allowances under the federal financial aid formula that is intended to protect a portion of the applicant's net worth.

Annual Exclusion Amount: (*See* Per-Donee Annual Exclusion)

Annuities: A contractual arrangement between an obligor (insurance company) and a contract holder, in which a payee or annuitant is entitled to periodic payments.

Appropriate Documentation: Requirement of documentation by a financial aid officer to justify financial need.

Assets: Property that parent or student owns. In this book they refer to savings accounts, traditional investments, real estate, etc. used in calculating the Expected Family Contribution (EFC) for financial aid purposes.

Automatic-Zero EFC: When financial aid applicant earns less than a certain amount ($27,000 in 2020) and either files no return or Form 1040A or 1040EZ, then applicant has a zero Expected Family Contribution.

Award Letter: An official document issued by financial aid office listing aid awarded and terms and conditions, along with an admission offer.

Award Year: The period of time during which a student's financial aid award is based. For example, the 2021–22 award year is between July 1, 2021 and June 30, 2022.

-B-

BabyMint: A program that designates an amount (or rebate) to a Section 529 plan when the consumer purchases a particular corporation's product.

Base Year or Base Income Year: The calendar year (January 1–December 31) prior to the year for which Financial Aid is requested. Information in this year is used to determine eligibility for financial aid.

Basic Financial Need (BFA): The Cost of Attendance less Expected Family Contribution.

Below-the-Line: A nontechnical term used to indicate that a deduction is an itemized deduction rather than an above-the-line deduction.

Beneficiary or Designated Beneficiary: The individual designated as the beneficiary of the 529 plan, the Coverdell account, the trust, etc., at the time an account or trust is established.

Budget: An estimate of the total cost of attending college, including tuition, fees, books, supplies, computers, room and board, travel, loan fees, medical, clothes, entertainment, and other expenses.

-C-

Campus-based Aid: Financial aid administered by the university, such as Perkins Loans, FSEOG, and work-study.

Campus-based Programs: Financial Aid programs (Perkins Loan, FSEOGs, and Federal Work Study) that are funded by the federal government but administered by the college or university.

Cancellation (of debt): When the student loan is forgiven and the student need not repay the loan. Medical persons can get these loans cancelled in exchange for working in rural and low-income areas. These are tax free under Section 108(f).

Capitalized Interest: When interest accrues on the loan while the student is in college, the interest is added to the principal balance of the loan, which is the amount that then needs to be repaid.

Cash Surrender Value: The cash surrender value is the sum of money an insurance company pays to a policyholder or an annuity contract owner in the event that their policy is voluntarily terminated before its maturity or an insured event occurs.

Collateral: Money or property promised in order to obtain or secure a loan and, if the debtor defaults, can be used to pay back the loan.

College Savings Plan: (*See* Section 529 plans)

College Scholarship Service (CSS)/Financial Aid PROFILE: (*See* PROFILE Form)

College Sure CDs: Certificate of Deposits that help parents finance college because their rates are based on college inflation.

Consolidation or Consolidated Loans: Combining loans from multiple lenders into a single loan to reduce monthly payment amount and/or increase the repayment period.

Contract Plan: Type of state prepaid tuition Section 529 plan where participant agrees to purchase a specified or number of years of tuition.

Contribution Donor: Person who initially transfers cash to a Section 529 plan.

Contributor: (*See* Contribution Donor)

COA: (*See* Cost of Attendance)

Corporate Debt Securities: Securities issued by a corporation that typically mature in one to ten years. These investments are less secure than Treasury securities but more secure than corporate equity, like preferred and common stock.

Cost of Attendance (COA): The total cost (tuition, fees, room, board, supplies, transportation, personal expenses) of attending college for one year.

Coverdell Educational Savings Accounts (Coverdell or ESA): A savings account created to entice parents and students to save for education expenses. A Coverdell is set up to pay for qualified higher education and qualified elementary and secondary expenses of a designated beneficiary.

Creditworthy: An individual with no negative credit history.

***Crummey* Trust:** A trust that may avoid the early distribution to a minor through powers that give the beneficiary (usually a minor) the right to demand a withdrawal of funds from the trust for some reasonable period of time.

Cumulative Savings Allowance: Allowances or subtractions used to value assets under the IMF or institutional methodology formula.

Custodial Parent: The parent with whom the dependent student lives and whose financial information is used under the federal methodology when parents are divorced or separated.

Custodian: Someone who has been lawfully appointed to take custody of a thing or person. UGMA and UTMA, for example, call for putting property for the benefit of a minor into the hands of a custodian.

Custodian Account: An account established with a bank or other IRS-approved custodian and set up through the UGMA or the UTMA where the custodian holds money or investments for the benefit of a minor beneficiary until they reach the age of majority.

-D-

Deemed Completed Gifts: Transfers to a Section 529 account even when the donor/account owners can "undo" the gift by taking back the funds.

Default: Failure to repay a loan according to the terms of the lender.

Deferment (or deferred interest): A period during which borrower may suspend loan payments.

Demand Loan: A loan payable on demand by the lender.

Demonstrated Need (or demonstrated financial need): The difference between the student's cost of attendance and the expected family contribution.

Dependency Exemption: A deduction for dependents that was suspended for tax years 2018 through 2025.

Dependent Credit (or dependent tax credit): A $500 nonrefundable credit for qualifying dependents other than children.

Dependent Student: For tax purposes, a student under the age of 24 whose parents provide more than half of his/her financial support. For financial aid purposes, a student who is not married; has not reached age 24; has no legal dependents; is not a veteran, or an orphan, or ward of the court; and who must submit income and asset information along with parent.

Designated Beneficiary: (*See* Beneficiary)

Direct Consolidation Loans: (*See* Consolidation)

Direct Gifts (or gifts): A lifetime transfer of property by a donor to a donee (or educational institution) for less than full and adequate consideration in money or money's worth.

Direct PLUS Loans: Long-term loans made available to the parents and graduate students up to the cost of attendance amounts minus other financial assistance.

Direct Skip: A generation-skipping transfer consisting of direct transfers of an interest in property from a transferor to a "skip" person or a person two or more generations below the transferor, *See* I.R.C. § 2612(e).

Direct Subsidized Loan: (*See* Subsidized Federal Loan)

Direct Unsubsidized Loan: (*See* Unsubsidized Federal Loan)

Disability: (*See* Special Needs)

Discretionary Assets: (*See* Assets)

Discretionary Income: (*See* Income)

Discretionary Net Worth: For purposes of financial aid, assets less liabilities.

Disqualifying Distribution: Distribution from a 529 plan that is not used for qualified higher education expenses, or otherwise flunks the Section 529 rules.

Distributee: The designated beneficiary or the account owner who receives or is treated as receiving a distribution.

Distribution: Any disbursement, whether in cash or in-kind.

Donor: (*See* Contribution Donor)

Double Counting: Rules that prohibit the taxpayer from claiming two or more educational tax benefits for the same educational expense.

-E-

Early Decision: An admission program whereby a college admits students earlier in the year and requires the student to sign a pledge to commit to attending that institution.

Earnings: The total account balance on a particular date minus the investment in the account as of that date.

Earnings ratio: The amount of earnings allocable to the account on the last day of the calendar year divided by the total account balance on the first day of that calendar year.

Education: For purposes of this book, secondary schools (including private and parochial K–12), college, university, or apprenticeships (including undergraduate, graduate, and professional schooling).

Education Planning: The identification, development, and implementation of strategies designed to attain, efficiently and effectively, the educational goals of the student.

Education Assistance: (*See* Employer-Provided Education Assistance Program)

Education IRA: (*See* Coverdell Education Savings Account)

Education Tuition Deduction: (*See* Tuition Deduction)

EFC: (*See* Expected Family Contribution)

Eligible Educational Institution: Any accredited college, university, vocational school, or other postsecondary educational institution eligible to participate in any of the student aid programs administered by the Department of Education. This includes private, public, and religious institutions.

Eligible Program: A program of education that complies with Title IV, allowing the student to be eligible for financial aid.

Eligible Student: Student that is carrying at least half the normal full-time workload for the course of study that the student is pursuing at an eligible educational institution. An eligible student may not be eligible if they have been convicted of a felony drug charge or is not a U.S. citizen or resident alien.

Emergency Reserve Allowance: Allowances or subtractions used to value assets under the IMF or institutional methodology formula.

Employer-Provided Education Assistance Program: Section 127 of the code allows an employer to provide a fringe benefit exclusion of up to $5,250 toward an employee's qualified tuition and expenses for attending a graduate or undergraduate program.

Employment Expense Allowance: A deduction against income in the federal and institutional methodology for a working parent.

Employment-Related Education Exclusions: Benefits to an employee that an employer can provide Can include employer-provided Education Assistance Programs under Section 127 and working condition fringe benefits under Section 132. The benefit is excludable by the employee and deductible by the employer.

Endowments: Funds raised by colleges and universities or property owned and managed by them providing a permanent source of income. A large endowment means a greater ability of the school to support scholarships and financial aid.

Enrolled: The completion of registration requirements at the educational institution.

Exceptional Financial Need: An eligibility criterion for FSEOG and Perkins loans.

Excess Contribution: Contribution to a retirement IRA or a Coverdell account in excess of that which is permitted statutorily. Such contributions usually result in an excise tax.

Expected Family Contribution (EFC): The amount a family is expected to contribute to a student's education, based on family earnings, assets, savings, and number of children in college.

-F-

FAFSA (Federal Application for Student Aid or Free Application for Federal Student Aid): The form that must be filled out by parents and student to apply for aid at public colleges and universities.

Family Incentive Trust: Intervivos or testamentary trusts which encourage the beneficiary to engage in certain behavior, such as attending college.

Family Limited Partnership: A form of partnership with one general partner (with unlimited liability) and one or more limited partners (with liability only up to their contributions) that is taxed as a conduit for federal income tax purposes.

Family or Member of the Family: An individual who is related to the designated beneficiary.

Federal Direct Student Loan Program (FDSLP): The program named for loans that are both guaranteed and funded by the federal government. Also known as Direct Lending.

Federal Methodology (or Federal Need Analysis Methodology): The needs analysis formula maintained by the federal law to determine expected family contribution.

Federal Parent Loans for Undergraduate Schools: (*See* PLUS Loans)

Federal Pell Grant: (*See* Grants)

Federal Perkins Loan Program: (*See* Perkins Loan)

Federal PLUS Loans: (*See* PLUS Loans)

Federal Supplemental Education Opportunity Grant (FSEOG): A federal grant for undergraduate students with exceptional financial need.

Federal Work Study (FWS): A federal program that provides part-time jobs for college students with financial aid.

Fees: Education expenses imposed by an educational institution that can arise from academic or nonacademic reasons. Also charges under 529 plans for enrollment fees, annual maintenance fees, and asset management fees.

Fellowships: Usually given to graduate students to cover tuition and fees and in addition a stipend to teach or perform research. Like scholarships, they need not be repaid.

Final Distribution: The distribution from the account that reduces the account to zero.

Financial Aid: Financial assistance in the form of grants, loans, scholarships, and work study.

Financial Aid Award: (*See* Award Letter)

Financial Aid Letter: (*See* Aid Letter)

Financial Aid Offer: The total amount of federal aid offered by the college or university.

Financial Aid Officer (FAO) (or counselor): Also known as Federal Aid Administrator (FAA) or Financial Aid Advisor (FAA) or Financial Aid Coordinator. A college or university employee responsible for interpreting and implementing administration of financial aid.

Financial Aid Package: (*See* Award Letter)

Financial Need: The difference between the cost of attendance (COA) and the expected family contribution (EFC).

Fixed Interest Loan: This is a loan for which the interest rate remains constant for the duration of the loan.

FMF: (*See* Federal Methodology Formula)

FPLUS: (*See* Federal Parent Loan for Undergraduate Students or PLUS loans)

Free Application for Federal Student Aid (FAFSA): (*See* FAFSA)

Front End Loading: Allowing more than the annual per-donee annual exclusion.

FSEOG: (*See* Federal Supplemental Education Opportunity Grant)

Full-time Undergraduate School: A student who is taking a minimum of 12 semester or quarter hours per academic term; 24 semester or 36 quarter hours per academic year; or 24 clock hours per week.

FWS: (*See* Federal Work Study)

401(k), 403(b): The names of two of the more popular deferred compensation plans in which employees elect to defer part of their earnings until a later date, usually retirement.

-G-

Generation-Skipping Tax (GST Tax): The generation-skipping tax is a tax that may be due on a transfer that skips a generation or where the beneficiary of the transfer is 37.5 years younger than the donor. The GST exemption amount is the same as the estate tax exemption amount.

Generation-Skipping Transfer: (*See* Generation-Skipping Tax)

Gift (or deemed to operate as gift): A direct or indirect lifetime transfer of property by a donor for less than full and adequate consideration in money or money's worth. *See* Reg. § 25.2511.

Gift Aid: Aid, other than grants or scholarships, based on need that need not be paid back.

Grace Period: Period during which loan payments need not be made. The time when student graduates or enrollment status drops below half-time.

Grants: Financial aid available from the federal government, state agencies, and colleges, that does not have to be repaid.

Gross Income: Income from whatever source derived taxed under Section 61 of the Internal Revenue Code. Includes wages, profit from business, rental, financial instruments, capital, and other sources, such as alimony, pensions, etc.

Gross Income Test: Test used by the Code to determine if someone can be claimed as a dependent or if the taxpayer may claim head of household status.

-H-

Half-time: At least six semester or quarter hours per term or 12 semester or 18 quarter hours per year—at least 12 hours per week. A student must attend school at least halftime to receive aid from the Federal Pell Grants, FSEOG, Federal Work Study, and Federal Perkins Loans.

High-Income Families: In general, families making over $200,000 who do not benefit from the tax credits, but who can benefit from the savings incentives, the Parent PLUS loans, and scholarships.

Home Equity: The portion of a home's value that represents the difference between the fair-market value of the home and the balances remaining on any mortgage loans secured on the home.

Home Equity Line of Credit (HELOC): A variable rate loan that is similar to revolving credit. Minimum monthly payments do not amortize the loan; however, once an amount is paid off the taxpayer can borrow the amount again without needing a new loan.

Home Equity Loan (or home equity indebtedness): A debt against a homeowner's equity in their principal house, or vacation house which supports an itemized deduction for qualified residence interest under Section 163(h).

Hope Scholarship Credit (Hope Credit): A nonrefundable tax credit (prior to 2009) against federal income tax of up to $1,500 per year per student (adjusted for inflation) calculated on student qualified education expenses of $2,000 for the first two years of post-secondary education. After 2009, *see* American Opportunity Tax Credit.

-I-

IMF: (*See* Institutional Methodology Formula)

Incentive Trust: A trust that has provisions that provide incentives for the beneficiary to accomplish certain things, like education.

Income: In this book, parent and student income used in calculating Expected Family Contribution for financial aid purposes.

Income Protection Allowance: A deduction against income in both the federal and institutional methodologies.

Independent 529 Plan: A type of institutional plan that was changed to the Private College 529 Plan.

Independent Student: For financial aid purposes, a student who is either married, 24 years old or older, enrolled in graduate education, has legal dependents other than spouse, is an orphan or ward of the court, or a veteran of the armed forces. Financial aid will be determined without reference to parental income or assets.

Institutional Costs: Costs for tuition, fees, institutionally owned or operated room and board and other fees charged by the educational institution.

Institutional Methodology Formula (IMF): The formula used to determine financial need by private colleges and universities.

Institutional Plan: (*See* Private College 529 Plan)

Insurance: (*See* Universal Life and Term Insurance) An agreement whereby for a consideration, one promises to pay money or its equivalent to another for the destruction, death, loss, or injury of someone or something.

Internal Revenue Service (IRS): U.S. government agency responsible for federal tax collection and federal tax law enforcement.

Intervivos Transfer or Trust: A transfer or trust created during the life of the transferor or trustor.

Investment in the account: The sum of all contributions made to the account on or before a particular date less the aggregate amount of contributions included in distributions, if any, made from the account on or before that date.

IRA (or Individual Retirement Account): Any of several tax-deferred savings/investment accounts including the Traditional IRA, the Nontraditional IRA, and the Roth IRA.

Irrevocable intervivos trusts (or irrevocable trusts): A trust that can never be changed once it is created.

Itemized Deductions: (*See* Below-the-line Deductions)

-K-

Kiddie Tax: Tax imposed on the child at the marginal rates of trusts and estates on unearned income from accounts and trusts for a child under the age of 24 who is a dependent student, or under the age of 18 if not a dependent student.

-L-

Lifetime Gift Tax Exemption: (*See* Unified Credit Exemption Amount)

Lifetime Learning Credit: A nonrefundable tax credit against federal income taxes of up to $2,000 per year per return calculated on qualified higher education expenses of $10,000.

Limited Liability Company (LLC): A hybrid entity similar to a corporation (with limited personal liability of its owners for the debts and action of the LLC) and similar to a partnership (providing the benefit of pass-through taxation).

Loan: An advance of funds requiring the recipient to repay the specified amount under prescribed conditions.

Loan Forgiveness or Loan Forgiveness Program: All or a part of the student loan may be released or forgiven when student works in the public service, the military, or in certain medical practice.

Loan Repayment Program: A special program available to qualified students who have attended college on federally funded student loans and work in certain areas.

Low Income Asset Allowance: Allowances or subtractions used to value assets under the IMF or institutional methodology formula.

Low-income Families: Families that have difficulty saving enough money for college costs and thus can benefit from many pay-as-you-go tax incentives as well as financial aid.

-M-

Manager: (*See* Plan Manager)

Marital Deduction: An unlimited deduction for interspousal transfers when determining taxable gifts or the taxable estate.

Maximum Contribution: The total amount that may be put aside in a college savings plan for one beneficiary.

Member of the Family: (*See* Family)

Merit-Based (or non-need-based): A means of determining eligibility for certain types of financial aid based on academic, athletic, musical, artistic, or other talents—not need.

Michigan Education Trust (MET): A program created by the Michigan legislature in 1986 in order to allow Michigan residents to save for future college expenses arising from a student attending any Michigan public college or university. Under the program, residents paid a stipulated amount into the fund or trust to cover future tuition.

Middle-Income Taxpayer: In general, taxpayers who can benefit from the various savings techniques, most tax credits, financial aid, and scholarships.

Miscellaneous Itemized Deduction (MID): A term defined in Section 67 to describe itemized deductions other than those specifically set forth, such as medical, taxes, charitable, and casualty expenses. Typical miscellaneous itemized expenses include unreimbursed business expenses, production of income expense (other than business, rent and royalties), and tax preparation fees. These deductions have been suspended for tax years 2018 through 2025.

Mutual Funds: A professionally managed investment product that sells shares to investors and pools the capital it raises to purchase investments. The shares are redeemable at net asset value. Such funds qualify for the special dividends paid deduction.

-N-

National Science and Mathematics Access to Retain Talent (or SMART) Grants: Grants given to high school students who have taken a "rigorous academic curriculum" in math and science.

Need-based: A means of determining eligibility for certain types of financial aid based on financial need.

Net Investment Income Tax: A 3.8 percent surtax on the lesser of the taxpayer's investment income or the amount by which the taxpayer's modified adjusted gross income exceeds certain threshold amounts.

Nonassessable Assets: Assets not included in the financial aid calculations.

Nonassessable Income: Income not included in the financial aid calculations.

Noncustodial Parent: A parent whose children do not live with them for the majority of the time. This parent does not have custody of the student, but their income can be assessed under the institutional financial aid formula (IMF).

Nondeductible Traditional IRA: An IRA where contributions are not deductible, but earnings grow tax-free.

Noninstitutional Costs: Costs of the post-secondary institution that are not assessed by the institution, such as off-campus housing, books, supplies, transportation, and personal expenses.

Non-Need-Based: A means of determining eligibility for certain types of financial aid that is not based on financial need.

Nonqualified Distributions: Distributions which are not qualified, either because they are not used for qualified educational purposes or for some other reason.

Nonqualified Educational Expenses: Depending on the tax provisions, nonqualified educational expenses could be books, equipment, room and board, and other related education expenses, such as transportation, medical, etc.

Nonresident Alien: An individual whose residence is not within the U.S. and who is not a citizen of the U.S.

-O-

Original issue discount: The shortfall between the issue price of a debt instrument and its stated redemption price at maturity *See* I.R.C. §§ 1272(a)(1) & 1273(a)(1).

Origination Fees (or loan origination fee): Fees (usually a percentage of the loan amount) paid by borrowers to the originator of the loan to offset various costs with maintaining the student or parent loan.

Out-of-State Student: A student who is not a legal resident of the state or local district that supervises the educational institution.

Owner (or account owner): The person who has the rights to change the beneficiary, change the investment strategy or demand the Section 529 funds account.

-P-

Parent Loans for Undergraduate Students: (*See* PLUS Loans)

Parent's Contribution (PC): Amount parent can be expected to contribute to cost of student's education each year under the federal or institutional formulae for calculating aid.

Parity Issue: Where state provides special tax benefits to its own residents for contribution to its own 529 plans, but not to out-of-state plans.

Participants: The term often refers to the owner of a Section 529 plan.

Part-Time Student: A student who attends an educational institution less than full time.

Pay-as-You-Go Techniques or Pay-as-You-Go Tax Benefits: A term that describes several tax benefits that can help the student *while* they attend school. Such things as direct gifts from relatives, the American Opportunity Tax Credit, the Lifetime Learning Credit, and Employment-Related Education Benefits.

Pell Grants: The largest federal grant program in which the college determines the amount of the need-based grant, based on federal guidelines as to eligibility and award amounts.

Penalty Tax (*See* Additional Tax or Ten Percent Penalty): Another name for the ten percent additional tax paid for nonqualified distributions from a Section 529 plan or the ten percent penalty tax for early withdrawal from a Coverdell. A penalty is paid in addition to any regular income taxes on that withdrawal.

Perceived Need: Not actual need as calculated in the financial aid formula but need based on the student's perspective.

Per-Donee Annual Gift Tax Exclusion Amount (or per-donee annual exclusion): A code provision (§ 2503) allowing a donor to exclude the first $15,000 (in 2021) of total gifts made during each calendar year to each donee. Allowed only for present interests.

Perkins Loans: Federally insured loans funded by the federal government and awarded to the school. These loans have fixed interest rate and extended payment periods.

Person: Includes an individual, trust, estate, partnership, association, or corporation.

Personal Disability Insurance: Insurance that covers a portion or all of one's income upon one becoming disabled.

Per Stirpes: A method of dividing an estate where the descendants of the deceased share as a group in the portion to which the deceased would have been entitled.

Plan Manager: The financial services company retained by a state to manage the state's 529 savings plan.

PLUS Loans: A federally subsidized educational loan program in which parents (or graduate students after HERA of 2005) borrow up to the total cost of attendance. Eligibility is not based on need and after HERA of 2005 the interest is fixed.

Portability: A reference to the power of the owner of a Section 529 plan to shift rights from one plan to another.

Post-Secondary Institution: Referred to as colleges, universities, and vocational schools.

Prepaid Plan (or prepaid tuition plan or prepaid institutional plan): Either a state-sponsored plan or an institutional plan that allows for the purchase of future college costs at today's prices.

Prepaid Unit Plan: Type of state prepaid tuition plan where participants purchase units that represent a fixed percentage of tuition.

Present Interest: An unrestricted noncontingent right to the immediate use, possession, or enjoyment of property, or the income from such property.

Principal Residence: The home lived in most of the year by the taxpayer. It can be a house, houseboat, house trailer, cooperative apartment, condominium, or other type of residence.

Private College 529 Plan: A type of 529 prepaid tuition plan that is sponsored by a group of 300 private colleges and universities.

Professional Judgment (PJ): The discretion of the FAO or FAA to recalculate the aid formulae.

PROFILE Form: A need analysis document written and produced by the College Board in Princeton, New Jersey, and used by many private colleges and universities.

Prudent Investor Rule: The standard for trustees and custodians as to investments under their control. The standard gives fiduciaries flexibility in permitting investing on a total-return basis rather than requiring that the prudence of investments be considered in an asset-by-asset basis.

-Q-

Qualified Course Materials: A new term added to § 25A by the American Recovery and Reinvestment Act of 2009. *See* I.R.C. § 25A(i)(3). Not defined in the Code or regulations, but would probably cover books, supplies, and equipment required for the first four years of post-secondary education.

Qualified Elementary and Secondary School Expenses (QESSE): As defined in the Code, this term means (i) expenses for tuition, fees, academic tutoring, special needs services in the case of a special needs beneficiary, books, supplies, and other equipment which are incurred in connection with the enrollment or attendance of the designated beneficiary of the trust as an elementary or secondary school student at a public, private, or religious school, (ii) expenses for room and board, uniforms, transportation, and supplementary items and services (including extended day programs) which are required or provided by a public, private, or religious school in connection with such enrollment or attendance, and (iii) expenses for the purchase of any computer technology or equipment (as defined in Section 170(e)(6)(F)(i)) or Internet access and related services, if such technology, equipment, or services are to be used by the beneficiary and the beneficiary's family during any of the years the beneficiary is in school. This last clause does not include expenses for computer software designed for sports, games, or hobbies unless the software is predominately educational in nature. *See* I.R.C. § 530(b)(4).

Qualified Higher Education Expense (QHEE): As defined in the Code, the term means (i) tuition, fees, books, supplies, and equipment required for the enrollment or attendance of a designated beneficiary at an eligible education institution and (ii) expenses for special needs services in the case of a special needs beneficiary which are incurred in connection with such enrollment or attendance. It also includes payment of up to $10,000 of K–12 tuition and up to $10,000 student loan interest and debt of a qualified beneficiary and sibling. It also includes supplies and equipment required for the participation in an apprenticeship program registered and certified by the Secretary of Labor. *See* I.R.C. § 529(e)(3).

Qualified Residential Interest: An itemized deduction allowed under Section 163(h)(3) for interest which is paid or incurred on "acquisition indebtedness" with respect to a qualified residence. The interest deduction for "home equity indebtedness" has been suspended for tax years 2018 through 2025.

Qualified Retirement Plan (QRP): A qualified plan that is a retirement plan.

Qualified State Tuition Plan (QSTP): An investment account for college savings first established by the Small Business Job Protection Act of 1996. Now more commonly referred to as a Section 529 plan or a QTP.

Qualified Tuition Program (QTP): Formerly referred to as a QSTPs. QTPs are established and maintained in order to allow either prepayment of an eligible student's qualified higher education expenses at an eligible institution or contribution to an account established for future payment of an eligible student's qualified higher education expenses at an eligible institution. QTPs can be established and maintained by a state (or an agency/instrumentality of the state) or by one or more eligible educational institutions. See above for definition of an eligible educational institution and eligible student.

-R-

Real Estate Investment Trusts (REIT): A security that is sold on major exchanges in a similar manner to stocks. It is a way for an investor to participate in the real estate market in an easily liquidating form. The REIT itself will invest in real estate (either directly, through properties, or mortgages).

Reasonably Expected Qualified Education Expenses: The standard under the Section 529 savings plan that allows contributions to be adequate to meet the reasonable expected education expenses.

Recipient: The individual or entity who receives the Form 1099 from the 529 plan administrator.

Refinancing or Refinanced Loans: The practice of borrowing against encumbered property. Refinancing can increase the interest-to-principal ratio of loan payments or allow for a cash payment with no taxable gain.

Relationship Test: Test used by the Code to determine if someone can be claimed as a dependent or if the taxpayer may claim head of household status.

Resource: (*See* Student Resource)

Responsible Individual or Party: Under the Coverdell, the person who will administer the account consistent with the requirements of Section 530.

Retail Plans: 529 Plans that you can obtain without advice from a professional advisor.

Revocable Living Trust (or Revocable Trust): A trust that is subject to a power to revest title of the trust to the grantor. This is a trust whose income is taxed to the grantor.

Risk tolerance: The degree of security the investor wants in making various investments.

Rollover or Roll Over: A tax-deferred transaction in which the account is reinvested in comparable accounts.

Rollover Distribution: One or more distributions from a qualified account to another similar account.

Room and Board: Rent and food.

Roth IRA: An IRA formed under Section 408A in which the taxpayer may not deduct contributions but will receive tax free distributions if they were made more than five years after the IRA was established.

Rule Against Perpetuities: A rule that prevents people from using legal instruments to exert control over the ownership of private property for a time long beyond the lives of people living at the time the instrument was written.

-S-

Savings Bond: (*See* Series EE Bond and Series I Bond)

Savings Plan: (*See* Section 529 Savings Plan)

Scholarships: Funds used to pay for higher education that do not have to be repaid. Scholarships can be merit or need based.

Section 401(k) Plan: Retirement plan available to common law employees from all nongovernmental employers.

Section 403(b) Plan: A nonprofit employer's equivalent to a Section 401(k) plan.

Section 457 Plan: Deferred compensation plan available to certain state and local government and nongovernmental entities that are tax exempt under Section 501.

Section 529 Plans: There are either tax-advantaged Section 529 Savings Plans or Section 529 prepaid plans.

Section 529 Prepaid Plan: Either a state-sponsored plan or an institutional plan that allows for the purchase of future colleges costs at today's prices.

Section 529 Savings Plan (or Section 529 College Savings Plan): One of many investment vehicles for college savings. Name arises from internal revenue code section that created this investment tool. Also known as a qualified state tuition plan (although the more accurate term post-EGTRRA is Section 529 plan because private institutions may now create these plans).

Section 2503(b) Trusts: A type of trust created by law, allowing for the saving of assets in an irrevocable trust, with all income earned being distributed to the child. Under the "kiddie tax" the child would pay income tax on the income from the trust at the marginal tax rates of the trust and estate. When the child reaches 25, the trustee must distribute the remaining trust assets outright to the child.

Section 2503(c) Trusts: A trust specifically created by tax law, allowing for the saving of assets in an irrevocable trust, with all income earned being kept in trust. The trust pays all income tax on the earnings at the trust's income tax rate.

Section 2503(e) Transfer: When tuition is paid *directly* to the educational institution, then none of the transfer is counted in the gift tax calculations.

Self-Help Aid: When student takes out a loan or works as a part of the financial aid award.

Series EE Bond: A Treasury savings bond that is issued at 50 percent of the face value of the bond. These bonds mature in 20 years but have a lifespan of 30 if the investor chooses. For bonds purchased May 2005 or after, there is a fixed interest rate. Interest is paid when the bond is redeemed. The bond can be redeemed any time after 12 months. A three-month interest penalty applies to bonds redeemed during the first five years. Financial institution reports interest earnings (difference between redemption value and purchasing price) on IRS Form 1099-INT. Interest earned on the bond is exempt from state and local income taxes and eligible for tax benefits if redeemed and used for qualified education expenses.

Series I Bond: A Treasury savings bond that is issued at face value. It is a nonmarketable bond that earns a combined fixed rate and variable inflation rate (adjusted semi-annually). Interest earned on this bond is exempt from state and local income taxes and is eligible for federal tax benefits if the funds are used for qualified education expenses.

Simple Retirement Accounts (SIMPLE IRA): An IRA–based plan that allows small employers to make contributions to their own or their employee's retirement.

Simplified Employee Pension IRA (SEP IRA): A less complicated means for an employer to establish an IRA plan for him/herself and his/her employees.

Simplified Needs Test: An alternative method used to calculate the family's expected contribution to college costs for federal aid purposes. Assets are not counted if parent's AGI is below a certain amount.

Single-fund Options: Investment options offering one specific investment, such as a Real Estate Investment Trust, global bonds, small caps, etc.

Skip Person: A person two generations below a transfer of property.

Special Needs: Those with physical, mental, or emotional disability, including learning disabilities.

Special Needs Trust (SNT): A legal arrangement and fiduciary relationship that allows a physically or mentally disabled person to receive income without reducing their eligibility for public assistance disability benefits.

Spendthrift Clause: A provision that keeps a trust from being liable for the debts of its beneficiaries, and/or prohibits transfer of the interest in trust.

Split Gift: An election by one spouse to split (or double) the gift and thus qualify twice the amount per-donee exclusion.

Standard Deduction: An allowance granted to most individuals. § 63(c).

State and Municipal Bonds (or state and local bonds): A bond issued by a State or a political subdivision of the State. Interest on this bond is tax-exempt but is included in the alternative minimum tax calculation.

Statement of Educational Purpose: Statement signed by the financial aid recipient indicating agreement to use all financial aid funds awarded for educational or educationally related purposes only.

State-Sponsored Prepaid Tuition Plan: A state-sponsored plan that allows for the purchase of future colleges costs at today's prices.

Student: (*See* Eligible Student)

Student Aid Report (SAR): A report that summarizes the student's data inputs as recorded by the FAFSA, lists the student's EFC, and may provide fundamental information about the student. Student Asset: The total amount of funds owned by the student and available under the financial aid formulae for contributions to the student's education. This includes cash savings and checking accounts as well as other assets.

Student Contribution: The amount of money the student is expected to contribute towards cost of attendance under the federal and institutional formulae.

Student Deduction: An allowance under the FAFSA in the calculation of Expected Family Contribution.

Student Loan Interest Deduction (on qualified education loan): An above-the-line deduction under Section 221 of up to $2,500 for interest on qualified indebtedness incurred for qualified higher education expenses.

Student Resource: A source of income, like a gift or scholarship, that reduces financial aid dollar for dollar.

Subsidized Loans: Administered by the Direct Loans or Federal Family Education Loan (FFEL) program and awarded to students who demonstrate financial need. Borrowers are not charged interest when considered half-time students.

Successor Owner (or custodian): The next owner of the account.

Sunset: Legislation coming to an end unless new legislation is passed to keep it alive.

Support: Amounts provided in cash or in kind to provide necessities to another.

Support Test: Test used by the Code to determine if someone can be claimed as a dependent or if the taxpayer may claim head of household status.

-T-

Taxable Income: Income earned from wages, salaries, and tips, as well as interest income, dividend income, business income, and rent income. Calculated by subtracting from gross income all allowable deductions and exemptions. *See* I.R.C. § 63.

Ten Percent Penalty: (*See* Additional Tax or Penalty Tax)

Term Insurance: A form of life insurance which purchaser acquires for a limited period of time, without any renewal rights.

Term Loan: Any loan that is not a demand loan.

Testamentary Trust: A trust established pursuant to a decedent's will.

Tolerance for Risk or Risk Tolerance: An investor's ability to psychologically endure the potential of losing money on an investment.

Total Account Balance: The total amount of the total fair market value of the account on a particular date.

Traditional IRA: A type of individual retirement arrangement allowing a maximum deductible contribution of $6,000 (2021 amount for taxpayer under 50) or $7,000 (2021 amount for taxpayer age 50 and older) when employee is not covered by a pension plan at work. *See* I.R.C. § 408.

Treasury Securities (or T-bills): These are debts of the U.S. offered with different maturity dates and backed by the U.S. government.

Trustee: A person who holds legal title to property for the purpose of protecting or conserving it for the benefit of others.

Trusts: (*See* Section 2503(b) Trust, Section 2503(c) Trust, *Crummey* Trust, Testamentary Trusts)

Tuition (or Tuition and Fees): The amount the college charges for instruction, educational programs, and learning facilities.

Tuition and Fees Deduction: This was an above-the-line deduction under Section 222 for qualified higher education expenses and fees that expired at the end of 2020.

Tuition Payment Plan: A strategy by which payments for present costs of post-secondary education is extended into a future period of time.

Tuition Reduction: (*See* Education-Tuition Deduction)

Tuition Reduction Program: Program offered by colleges and universities to their employees that subsidize all or part of the tuition costs of that school or another school under a reciprocal agreement.

-U-

Unified Credit Exemption Amount (or Lifetime Gift Tax Exemption): A limited amount of assets that a person is allowed to gift to other parties without having to pay gift, estate, or generation skipping transfer taxes.

Uniform Gifts to Minors Act (UGMA): An act adopted by most states to allow minors to hold property in the form of a custodial account. When an account is created under this act, legal title is held by the minor. However, a custodian (adult) is named to control the account until the minor reaches the age of majority. When a state adopts the act, the state establishes the age of majority (typically an age between 18 and 21).

Uniform Transfers to Minors Act (UTMA): The successor act to the UGMA.

Unmet Need: The difference between the total cost of attendance at college and the Estimated Family Contribution (EFC) and other assets.

Unsubsidized Federal Loan: Federal loans available to students regardless of financial need. Interest and principal payments may be deferred while the student is in school.

Untaxed Income and Benefits: Amount of income earned by a student or parent that does not appear on the Federal tax return but still must be reported on the FAFSA.

Upromise: A program that designates an amount to a Section 529 plan when the consumer purchases a particular corporate product.

U.S. Citizen: A native or naturalized member of the United States.

U.S. Department of Education (ED): Government agency that administers several federal student financial aid programs, including the Pell Grant, work study, Perkins loans, the FELP and the FDIP.

-V-

Variable Interest Rate: The interest rate is not fixed and is adjusted at regular intervals, usually once a year.

Variable Life Insurance: A form of life insurance under which the consumer gets flexible premiums, a flexible death benefit and control over a segregated asset account of the life insurance company.

Veterans Educational Benefits: Assistance programs for veterans and service persons for education or training.

-W-

Ward of the Court: A person under the care of the court.

Wash Sale: A transaction in stock where the loss is deferred under Section 1911. Purpose is to defer individuals from selling stock and promptly repurchasing identical property.

Wealthy Families: (*See* High-Income Families)

Whole Life Insurance: A form of life insurance coverage that provides for insurance payments during the lifetime of the insured in one lump sum or in periodic payments.

Working Condition Fringe Benefit (WCFB): A type of fringe benefit which may be deductible by the employer and nontaxable to the employee under Section 132(a)(3). The benefit is excludable to the extent that the cost of the property or service provided would be deductible as an ordinary and necessary business expense or as depreciation.

Work Study: (*See* Federal Work Study)

Index

A

B

C

F

G

H

J

K

L

M

U

V

W